A Devil and Her Love Song

Story & Art by
Miyoshi Tomori

Volume 10

A Devil and Her Love Song

Volume 10
CONTENTS

The devil makes me LOVELY!!!

STORY THUS FAR

Shintaro Kurosu is not exactly shy about being touchy-feely with Maria. Shin Meguro, on the other hand, distances himself from Maria because he fears that being physically close will remind her of her painful past. As he struggles with this decision, he pours his feelings for her into his piano playing and opts to perform in a concert to let her hear what's really in his heart.

But when the day of the concert comes, Maria is attacked and winds up listening to Shin's performance from outside the concert hall. Afterwards, Yusuke finds her and hugs her—and Shin, who'd gone looking for her, sees the two of them embracing. The misunderstanding is only made worse when he calls her later that night...

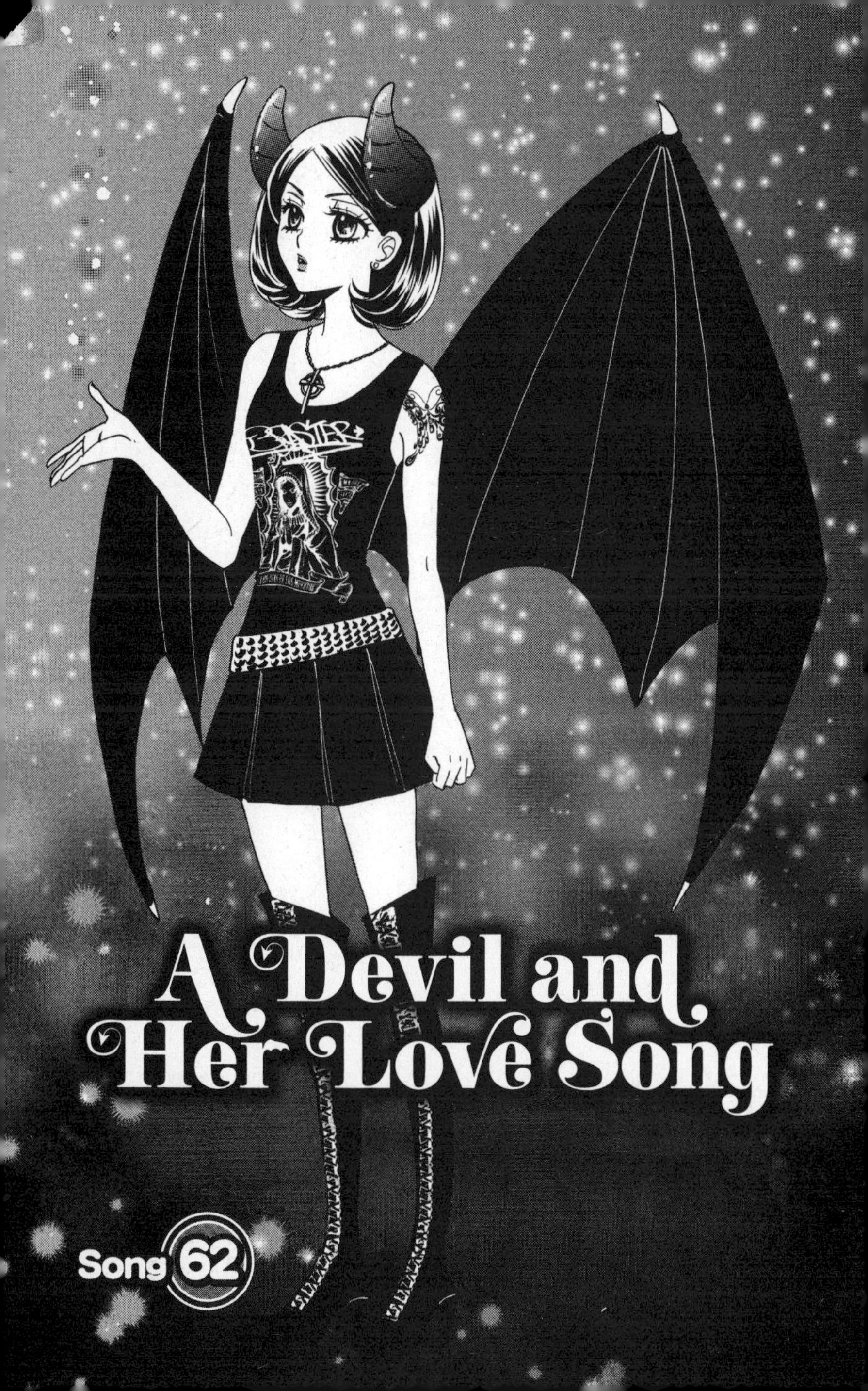
A Devil and Her Love Song
Song 62

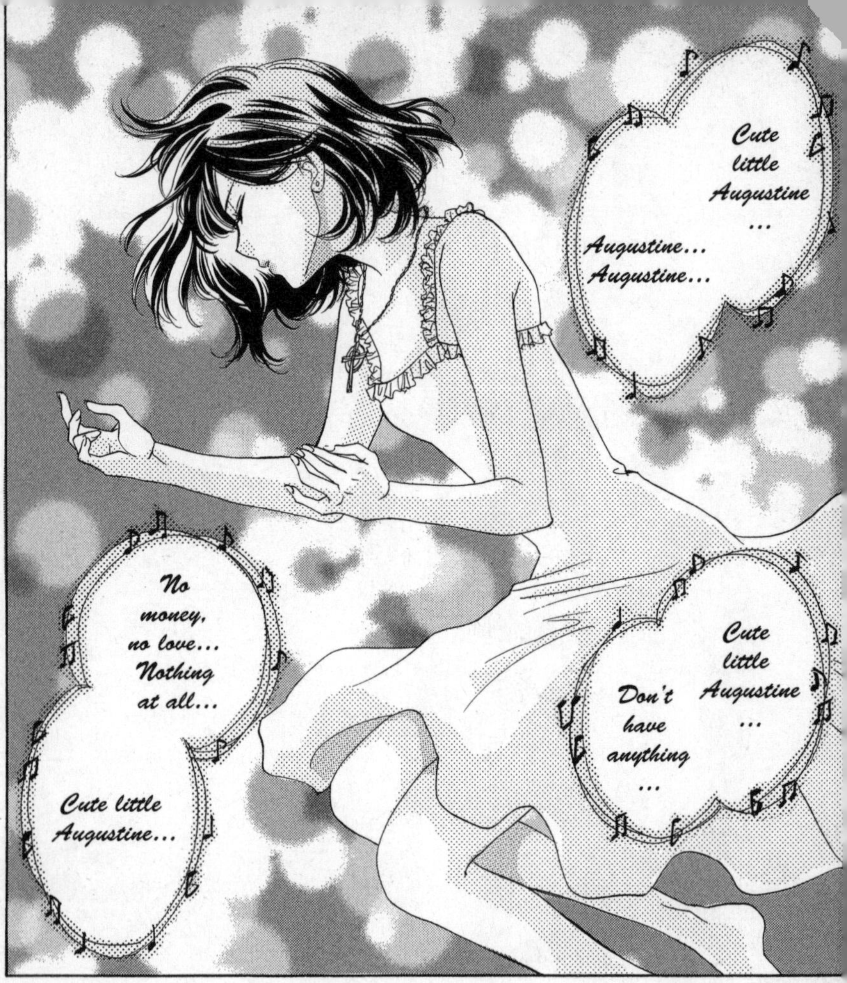
Cute little Augustine ...
Augustine... Augustine...
Cute little Augustine ...
Don't have anything ...
No money, no love... Nothing at all...
Cute little Augustine...

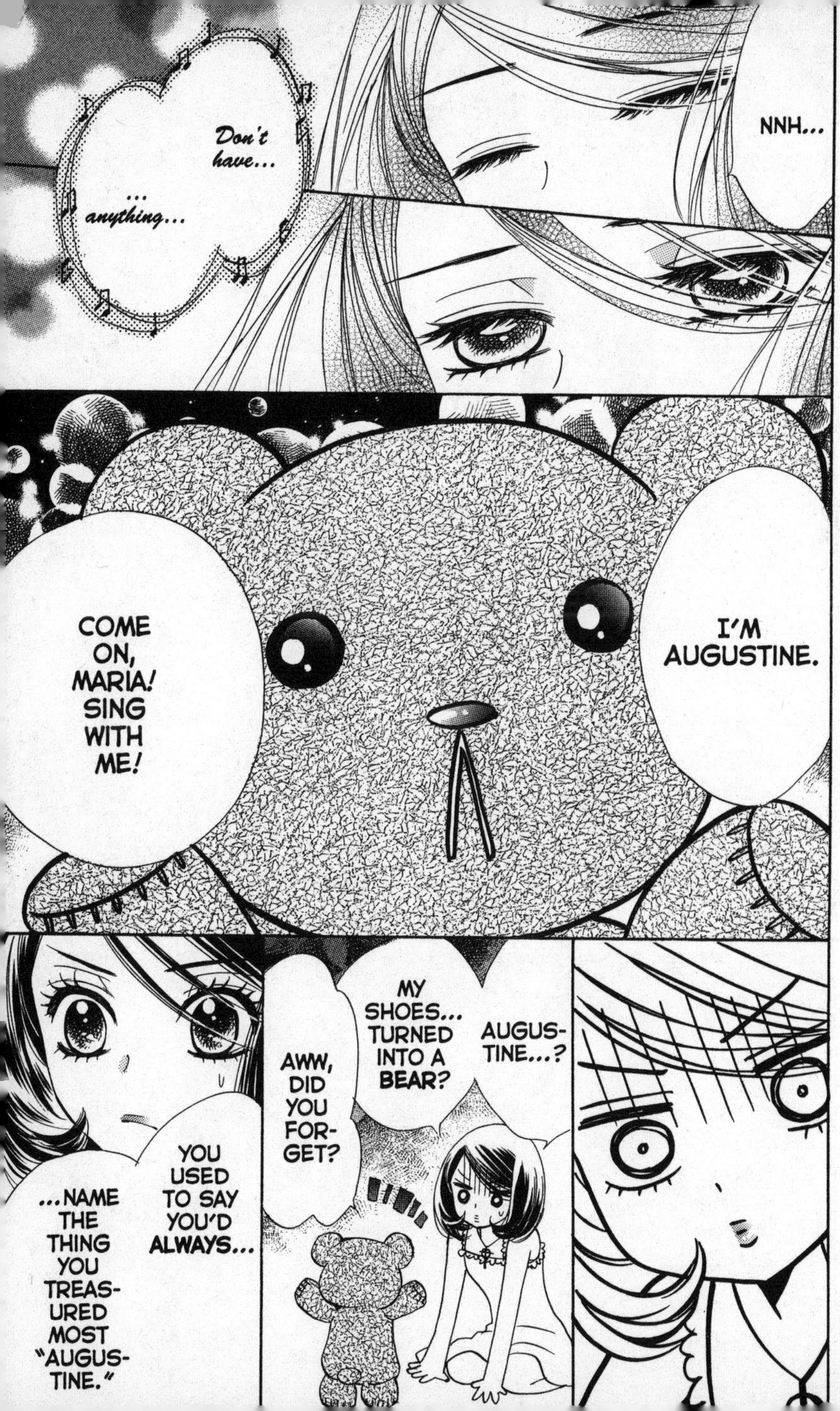
NNH...
Don't have... ...anything...
I'M AUGUSTINE.
COME ON, MARIA! SING WITH ME!
AUGUS-TINE...?
MY SHOES... TURNED INTO A BEAR?
AWW, DID YOU FOR-GET?
YOU USED TO SAY YOU'D ALWAYS...
...NAME THE THING YOU TREAS-URED MOST "AUGUS-TINE."

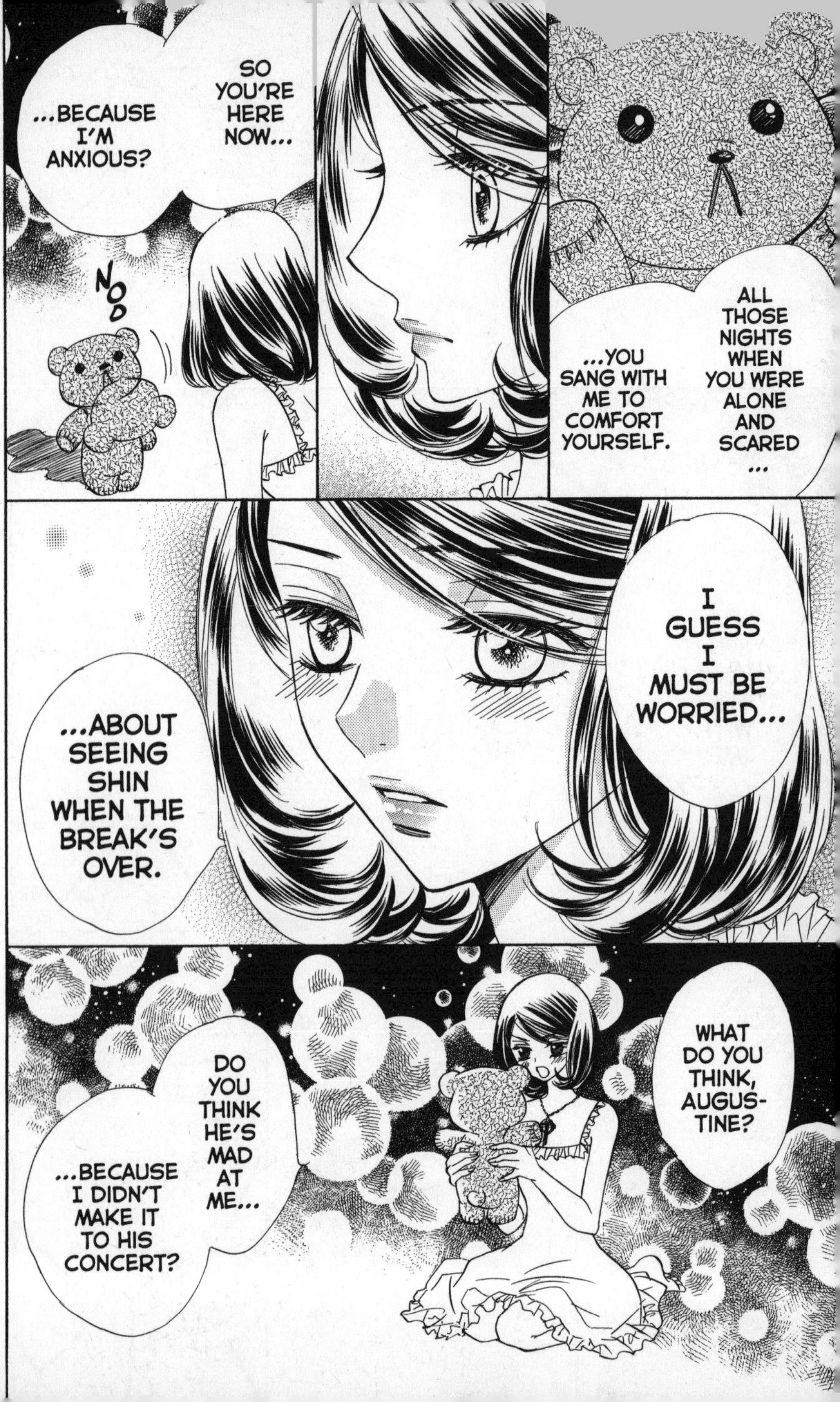
ALL THOSE NIGHTS WHEN YOU WERE ALONE AND SCARED...
...YOU SANG WITH ME TO COMFORT YOURSELF.
SO YOU'RE HERE NOW...
...BECAUSE I'M ANXIOUS?
NOD
I GUESS I MUST BE WORRIED...
...ABOUT SEEING SHIN WHEN THE BREAK'S OVER.
WHAT DO YOU THINK, AUGUS-TINE?
DO YOU THINK HE'S MAD AT ME...
...BECAUSE I DIDN'T MAKE IT TO HIS CONCERT?

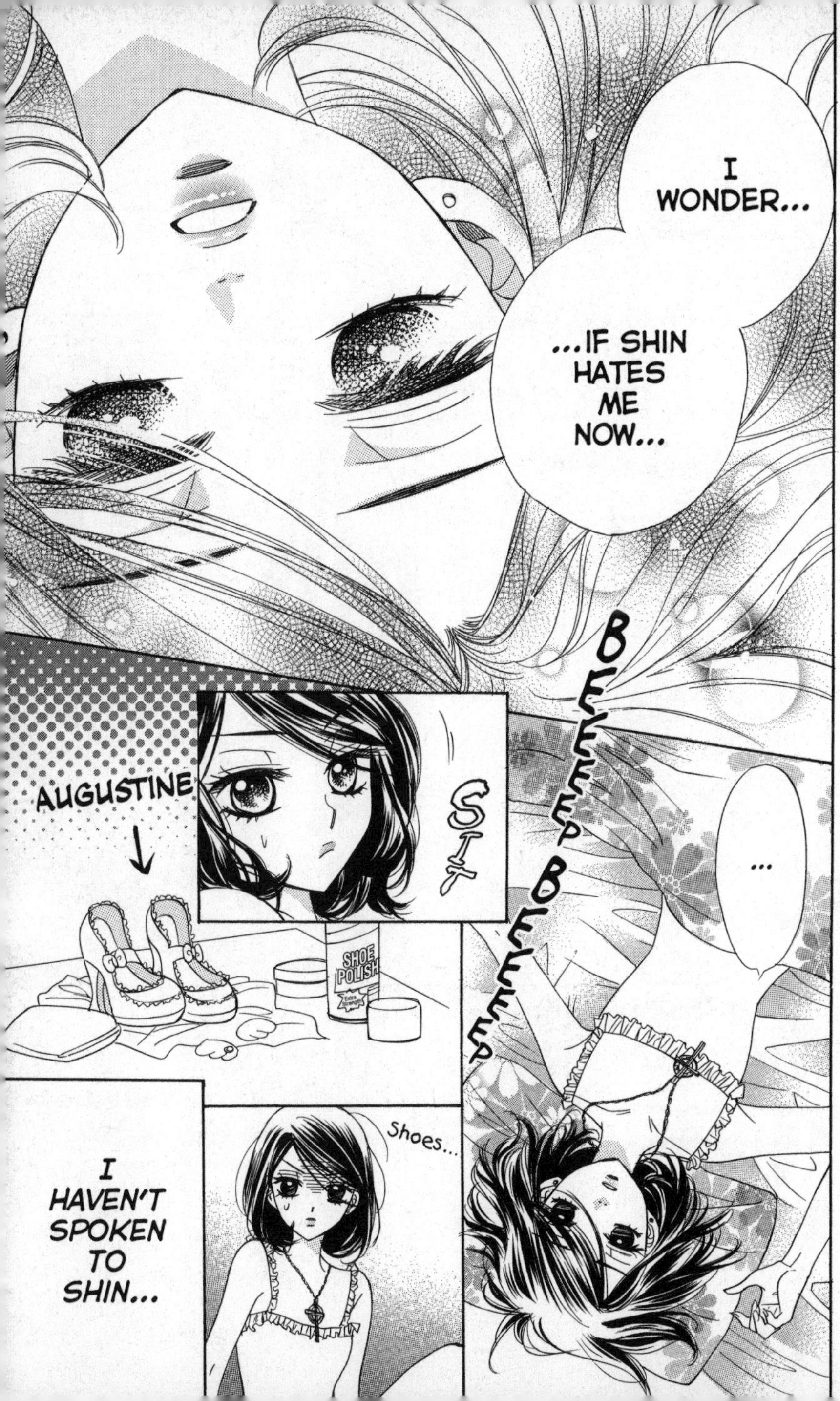
I WONDER...
...IF SHIN HATES ME NOW...
BEEEEP BEEEEP
...
SIT
AUGUSTINE
SHOE POLISH
Extra Strength
Shoes...
I HAVEN'T SPOKEN TO SHIN...

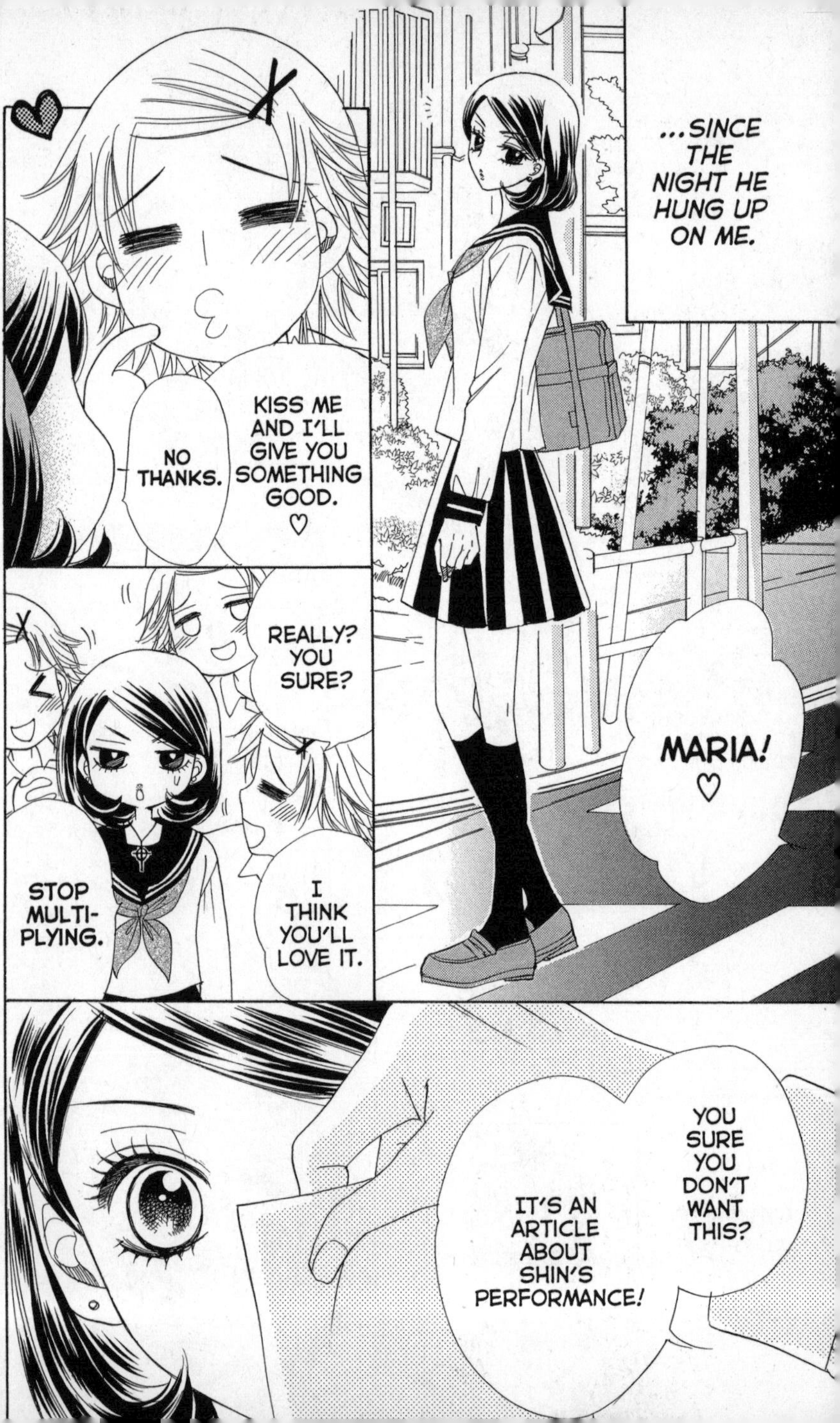
...SINCE THE NIGHT HE HUNG UP ON ME.
MARIA! ♡
KISS ME AND I'LL GIVE YOU SOMETHING GOOD. ♡
NO THANKS.
REALLY? YOU SURE?
I THINK YOU'LL LOVE IT.
STOP MULTI-PLYING.
YOU SURE YOU DON'T WANT THIS?
IT'S AN ARTICLE ABOUT SHIN'S PERFORMANCE!

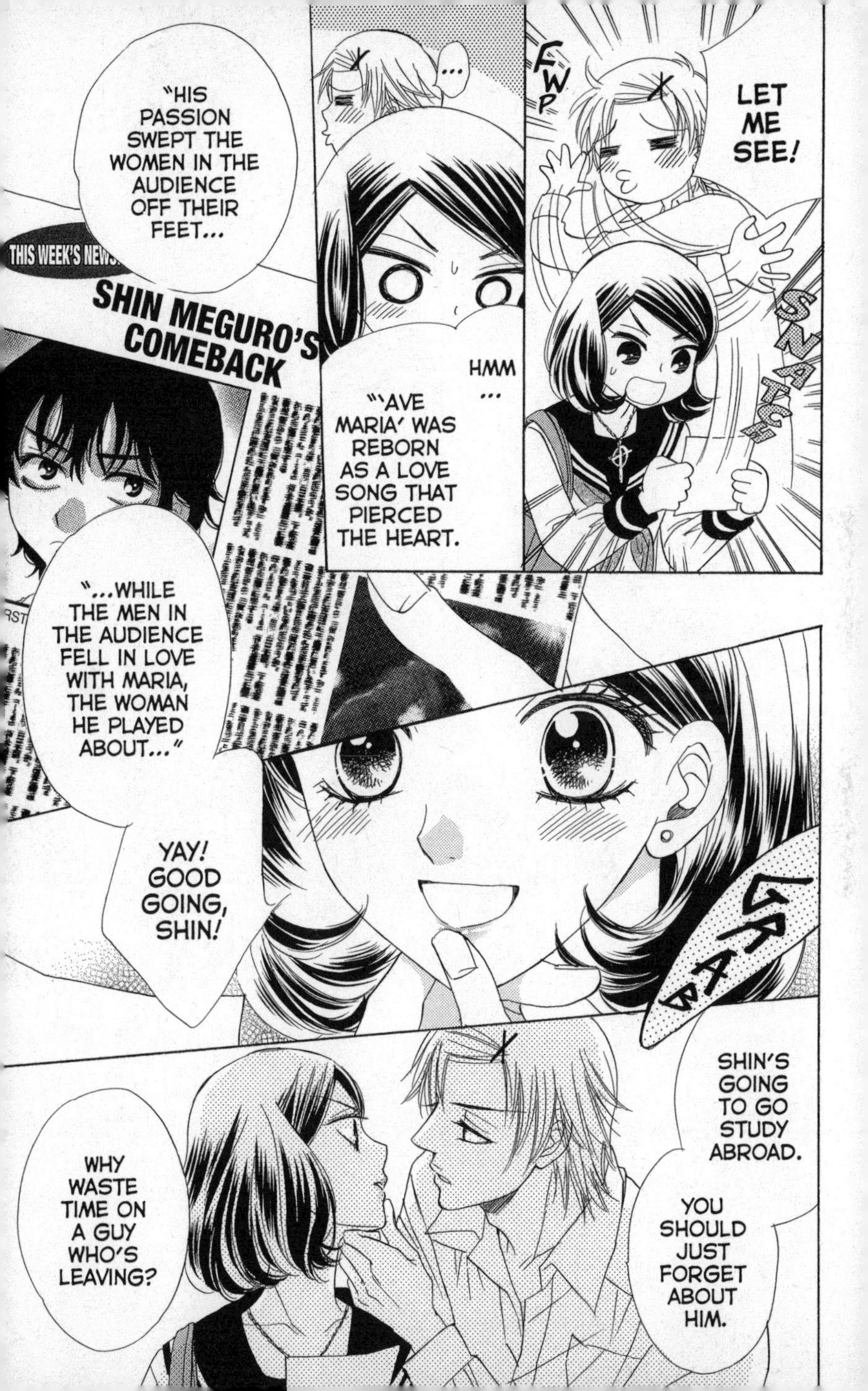
FWP
LET ME SEE!
SNATCH
...
HMM...
"'AVE MARIA' WAS REBORN AS A LOVE SONG THAT PIERCED THE HEART.
"HIS PASSION SWEPT THE WOMEN IN THE AUDIENCE OFF THEIR FEET...
THIS WEEK'S NEWS
SHIN MEGURO'S COMEBACK
"...WHILE THE MEN IN THE AUDIENCE FELL IN LOVE WITH MARIA, THE WOMAN HE PLAYED ABOUT..."
GRAB
YAY! GOOD GOING, SHIN!
SHIN'S GOING TO GO STUDY ABROAD.
YOU SHOULD JUST FORGET ABOUT HIM.
WHY WASTE TIME ON A GUY WHO'S LEAVING?

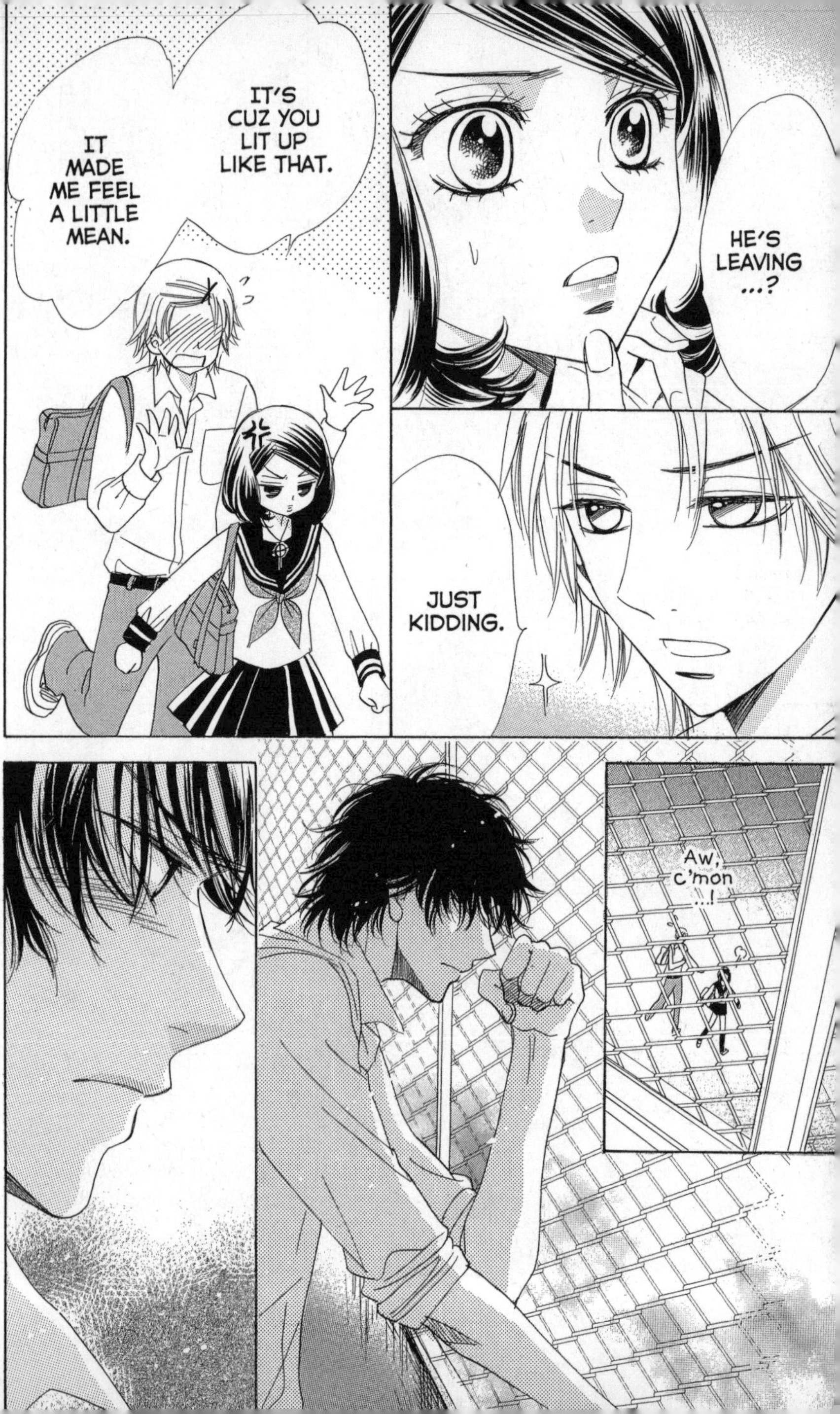
HE'S LEAVING ...?
JUST KIDDING.
IT'S CUZ YOU LIT UP LIKE THAT.
IT MADE ME FEEL A LITTLE MEAN.
Aw, c'mon ...!

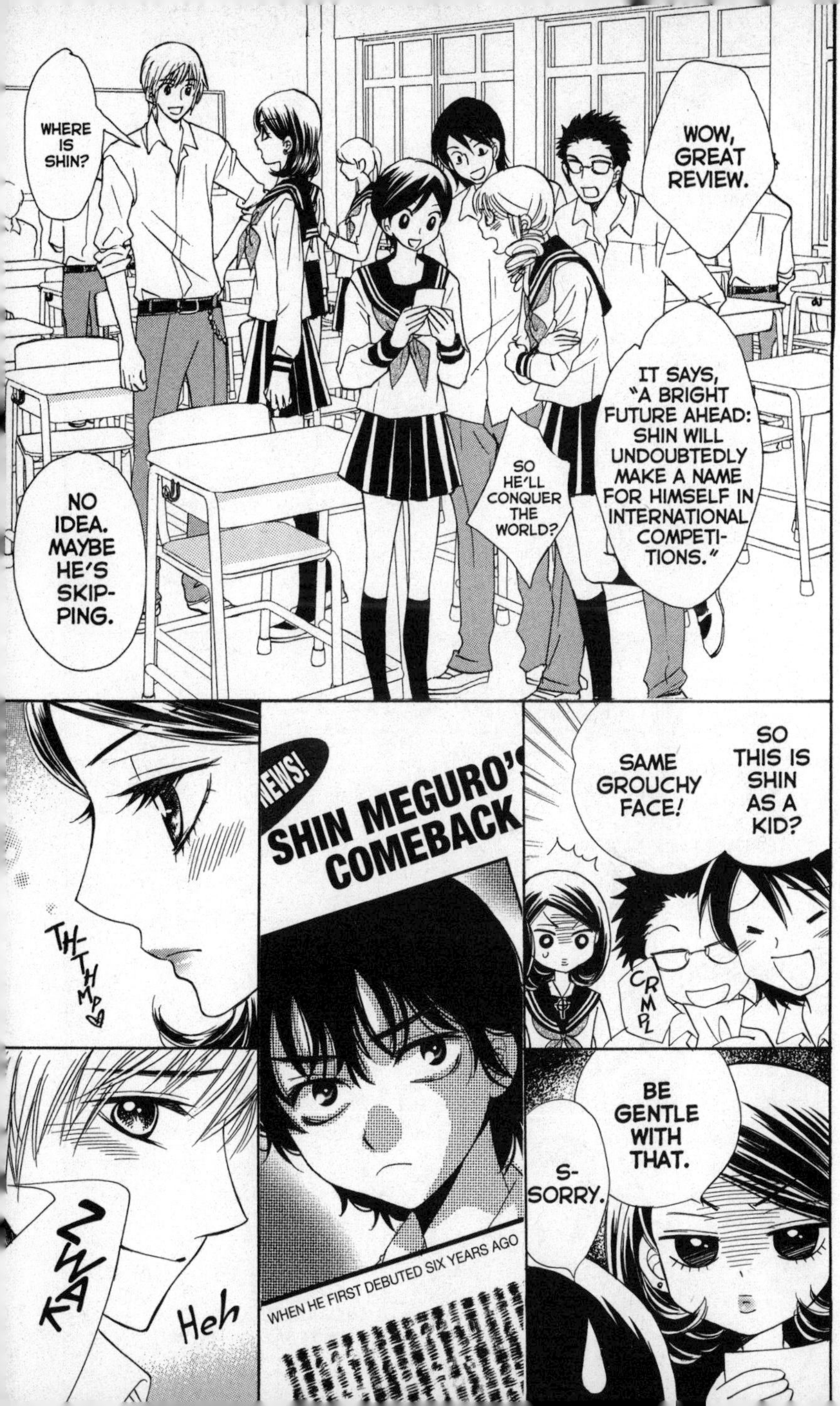
WOW, GREAT REVIEW.
IT SAYS, "A BRIGHT FUTURE AHEAD: SHIN WILL UNDOUBTEDLY MAKE A NAME FOR HIMSELF IN INTERNATIONAL COMPETI-TIONS."
SO HE'LL CONQUER THE WORLD?
WHERE IS SHIN?
NO IDEA. MAYBE HE'S SKIP-PING.
SO THIS IS SHIN AS A KID?
SAME GROUCHY FACE!
CRMPL
BE GENTLE WITH THAT.
S-SORRY.
NEWS!
SHIN MEGURO'S COMEBACK
WHEN HE FIRST DEBUTED SIX YEARS AGO
TH-THMP
ZWAK
Heh

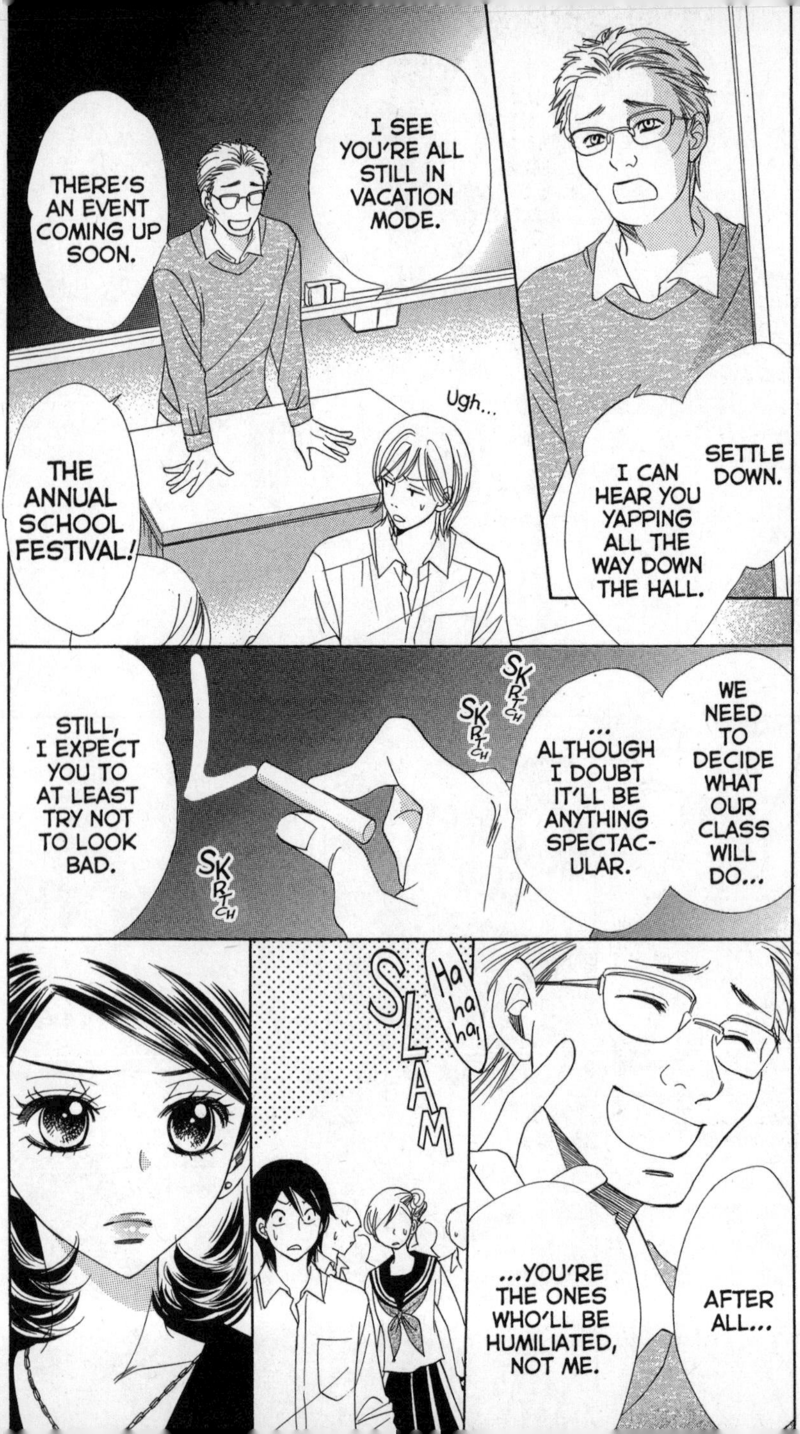
SETTLE DOWN.
I CAN HEAR YOU YAPPING ALL THE WAY DOWN THE HALL.
I SEE YOU'RE ALL STILL IN VACATION MODE.
THERE'S AN EVENT COMING UP SOON.
Ugh...
THE ANNUAL SCHOOL FESTIVAL!
WE NEED TO DECIDE WHAT OUR CLASS WILL DO...
...ALTHOUGH I DOUBT IT'LL BE ANYTHING SPECTACULAR.
SKRTCH
SKRTCH
STILL, I EXPECT YOU TO AT LEAST TRY NOT TO LOOK BAD.
SKRTCH
AFTER ALL...
...YOU'RE THE ONES WHO'LL BE HUMILIATED, NOT ME.
Ha ha ha!
SLAM

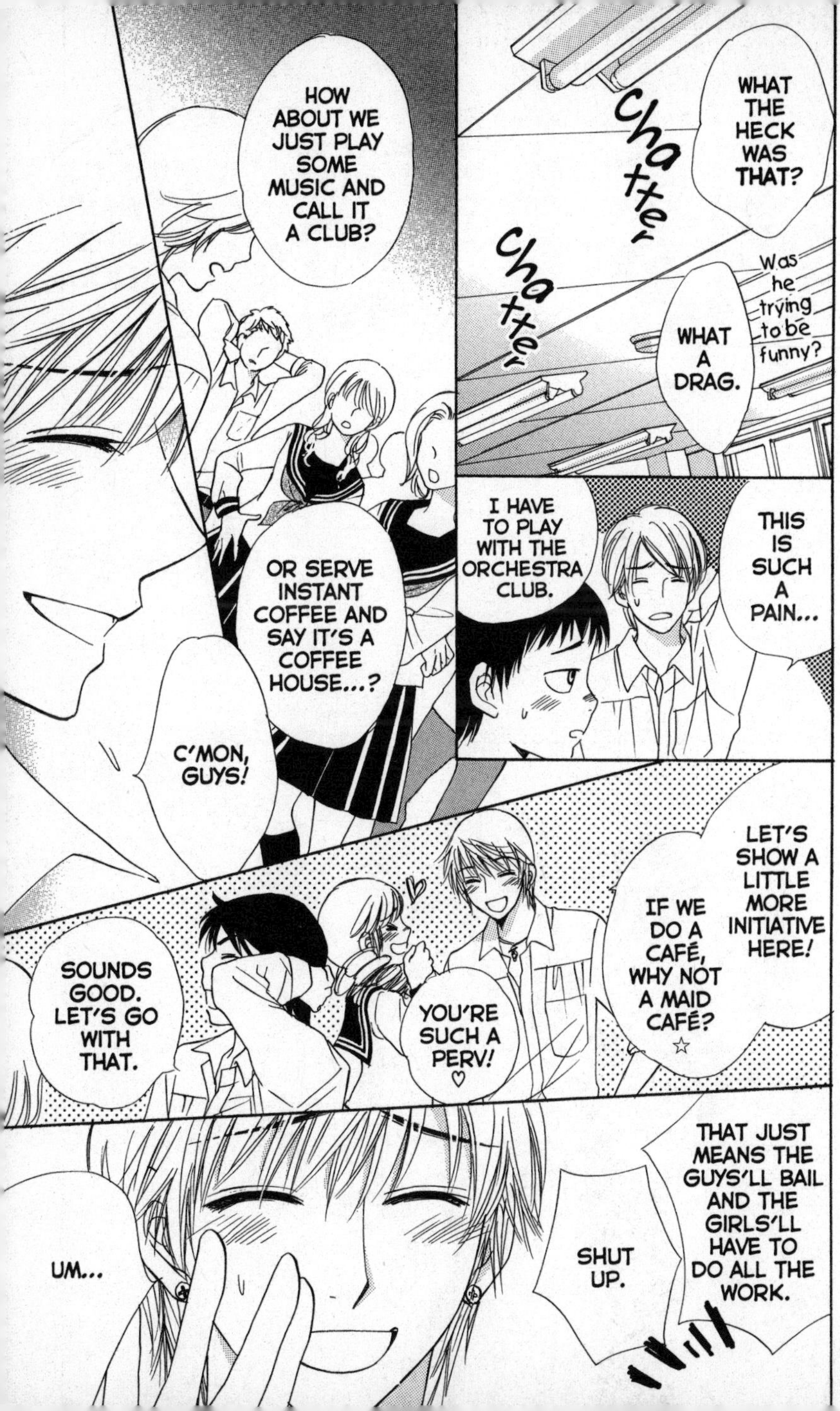
WHAT THE HECK WAS THAT?
Chatter
Chatter
Was he trying to be funny?
WHAT A DRAG.
THIS IS SUCH A PAIN...
I HAVE TO PLAY WITH THE ORCHESTRA CLUB.
HOW ABOUT WE JUST PLAY SOME MUSIC AND CALL IT A CLUB?
OR SERVE INSTANT COFFEE AND SAY IT'S A COFFEE HOUSE...?
C'MON, GUYS!
LET'S SHOW A LITTLE MORE INITIATIVE HERE!
IF WE DO A CAFÉ, WHY NOT A MAID CAFÉ? ☆
YOU'RE SUCH A PERV! ♡
SOUNDS GOOD. LET'S GO WITH THAT.
THAT JUST MEANS THE GUYS'LL BAIL AND THE GIRLS'LL HAVE TO DO ALL THE WORK.
SHUT UP.
UM...

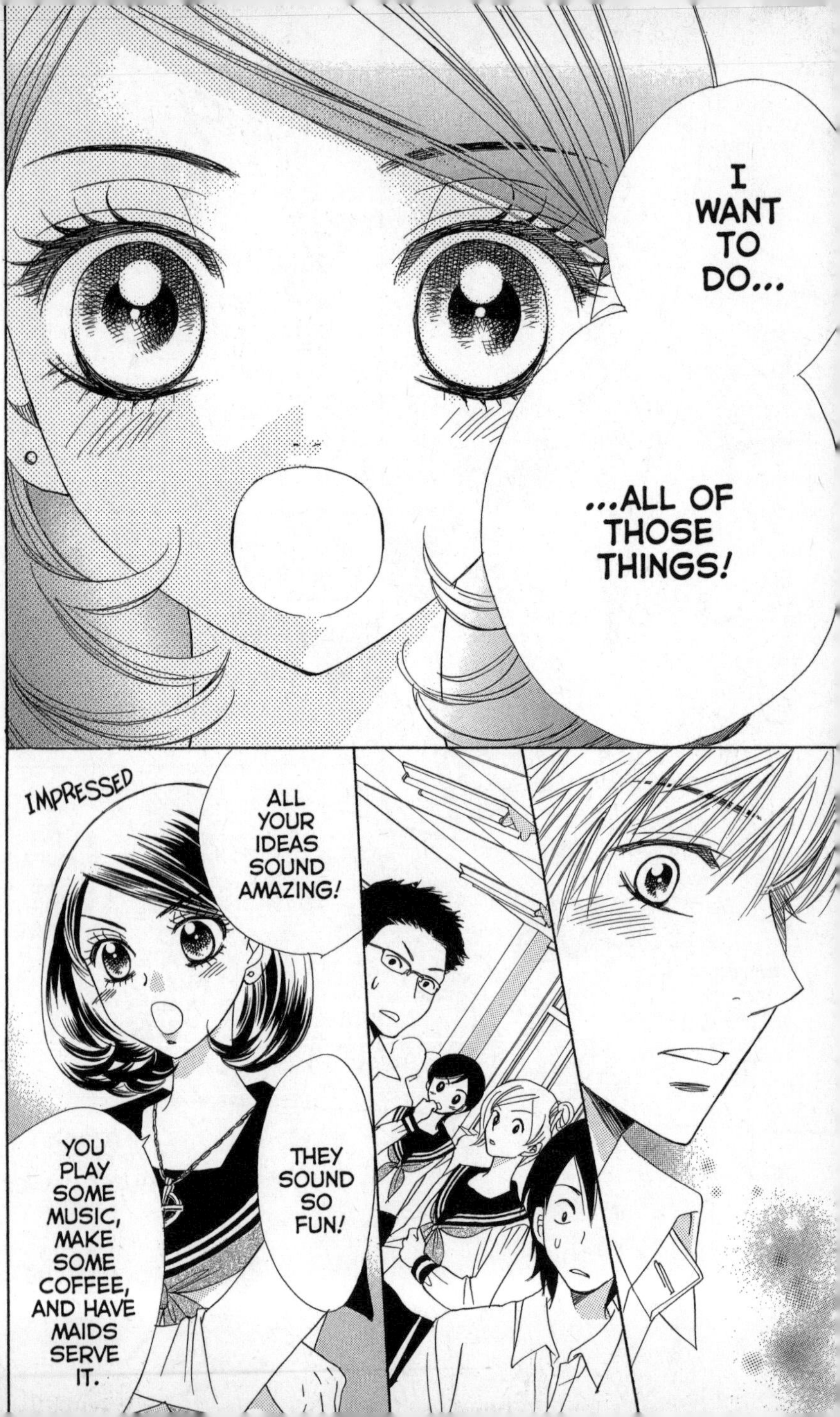
I WANT TO DO...
...ALL OF THOSE THINGS!
ALL YOUR IDEAS SOUND AMAZING!
IMPRESSED
THEY SOUND SO FUN!
YOU PLAY SOME MUSIC, MAKE SOME COFFEE, AND HAVE MAIDS SERVE IT.

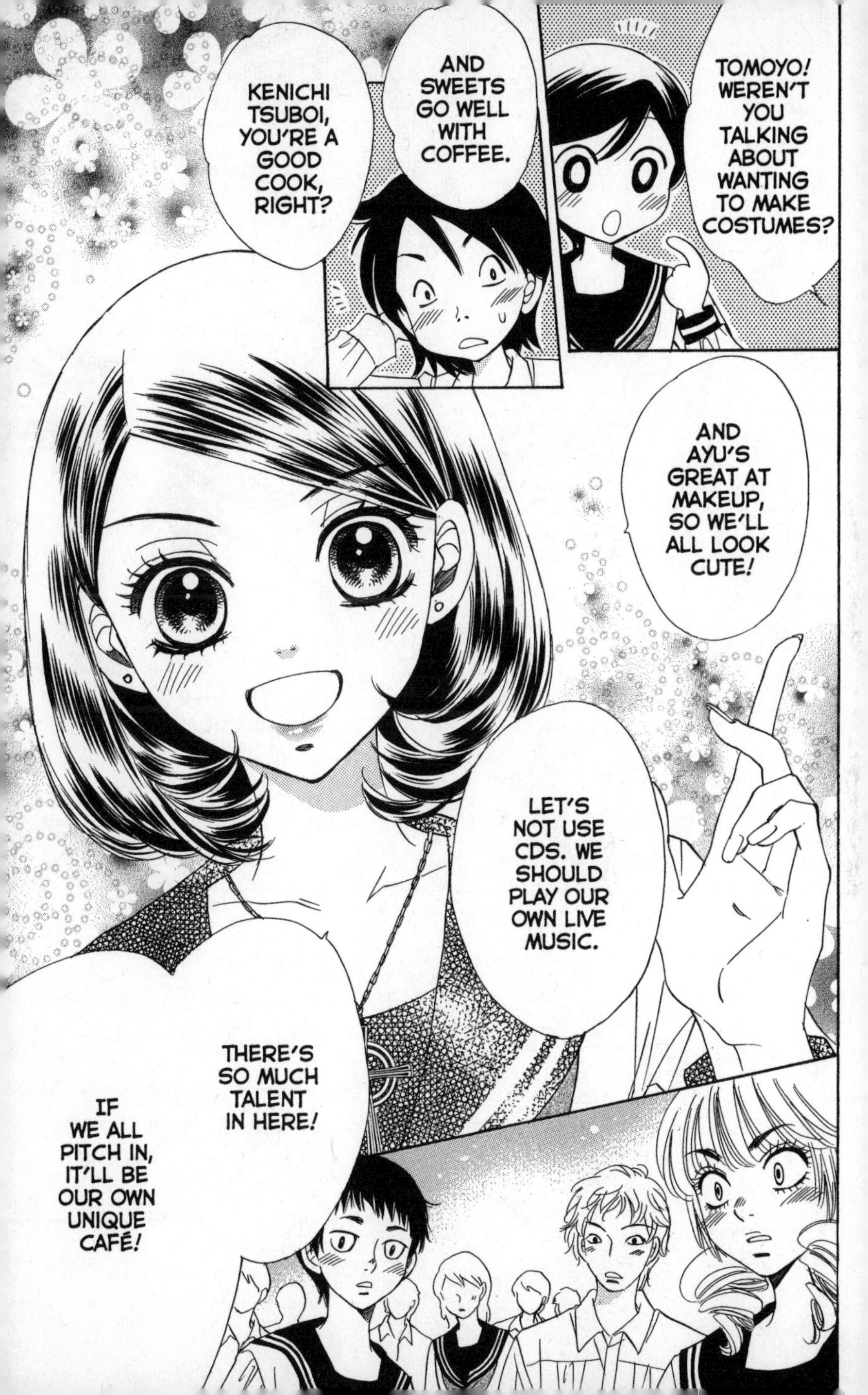
TOMOYO! WEREN'T YOU TALKING ABOUT WANTING TO MAKE COSTUMES?
KENICHI TSUBOI, YOU'RE A GOOD COOK, RIGHT?
AND SWEETS GO WELL WITH COFFEE.
AND AYU'S GREAT AT MAKEUP, SO WE'LL ALL LOOK CUTE!
LET'S NOT USE CDS. WE SHOULD PLAY OUR OWN LIVE MUSIC.
THERE'S SO MUCH TALENT IN HERE!
IF WE ALL PITCH IN, IT'LL BE OUR OWN UNIQUE CAFÉ!

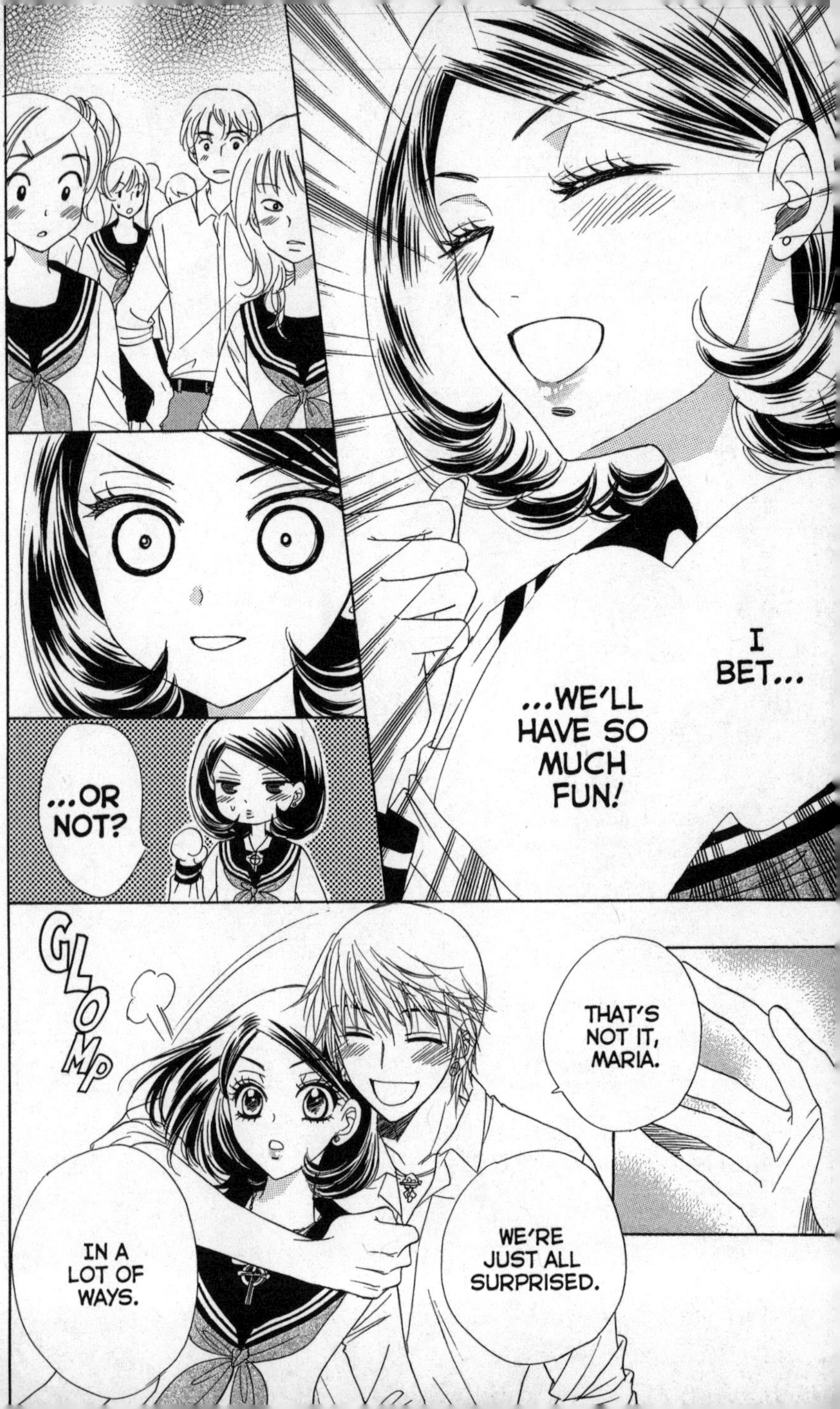
I BET...
...WE'LL HAVE SO MUCH FUN!
...OR NOT?
GLOMP
THAT'S NOT IT, MARIA.
WE'RE JUST ALL SURPRISED.
IN A LOT OF WAYS.

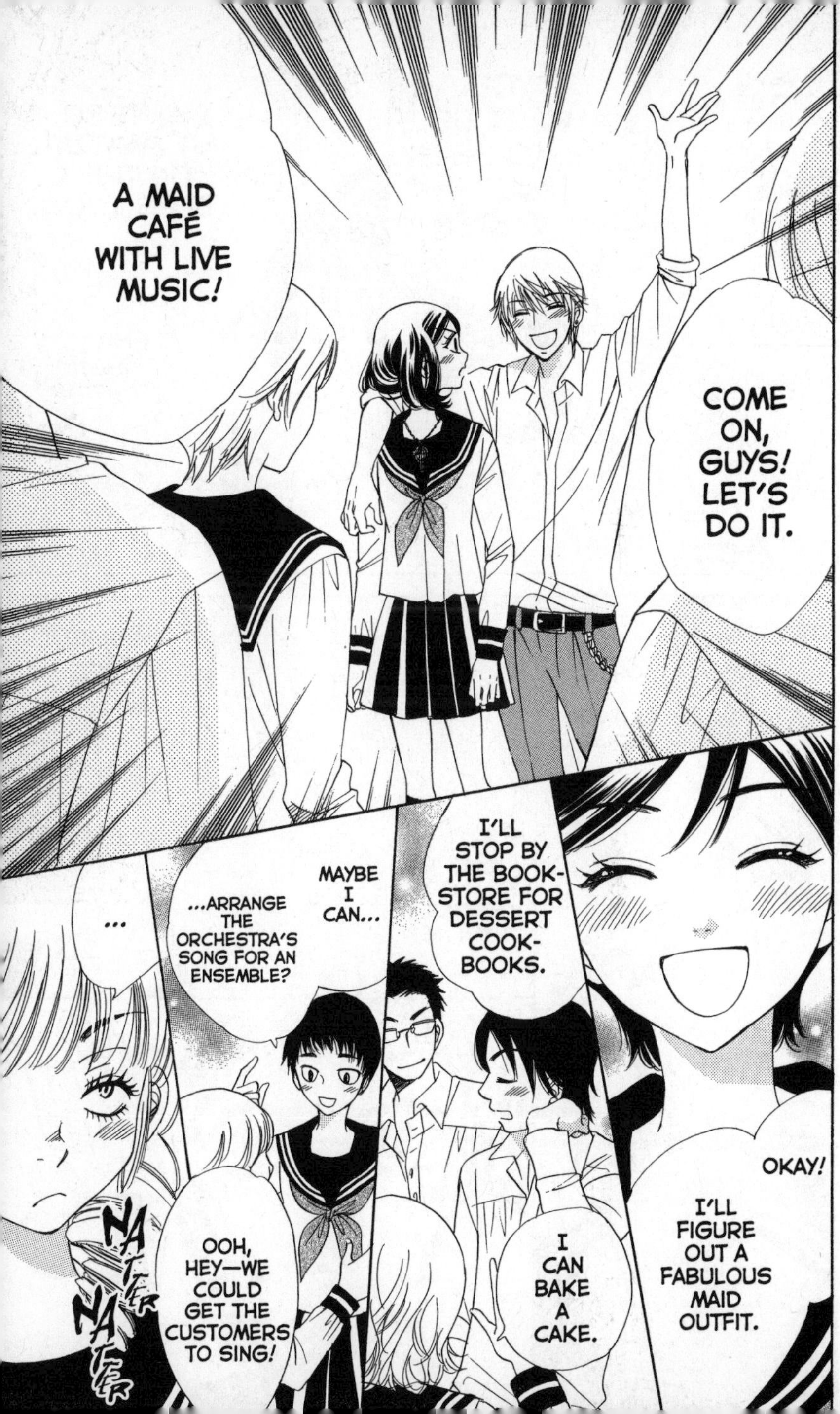

A MAID CAFÉ WITH LIVE MUSIC!
COME ON, GUYS! LET'S DO IT.
OKAY!
I'LL FIGURE OUT A FABULOUS MAID OUTFIT.
I'LL STOP BY THE BOOK-STORE FOR DESSERT COOK-BOOKS.
I CAN BAKE A CAKE.
MAYBE I CAN...
...ARRANGE THE ORCHESTRA'S SONG FOR AN ENSEMBLE?
OOH, HEY—WE COULD GET THE CUSTOMERS TO SING!
...
NATTER
NATTER

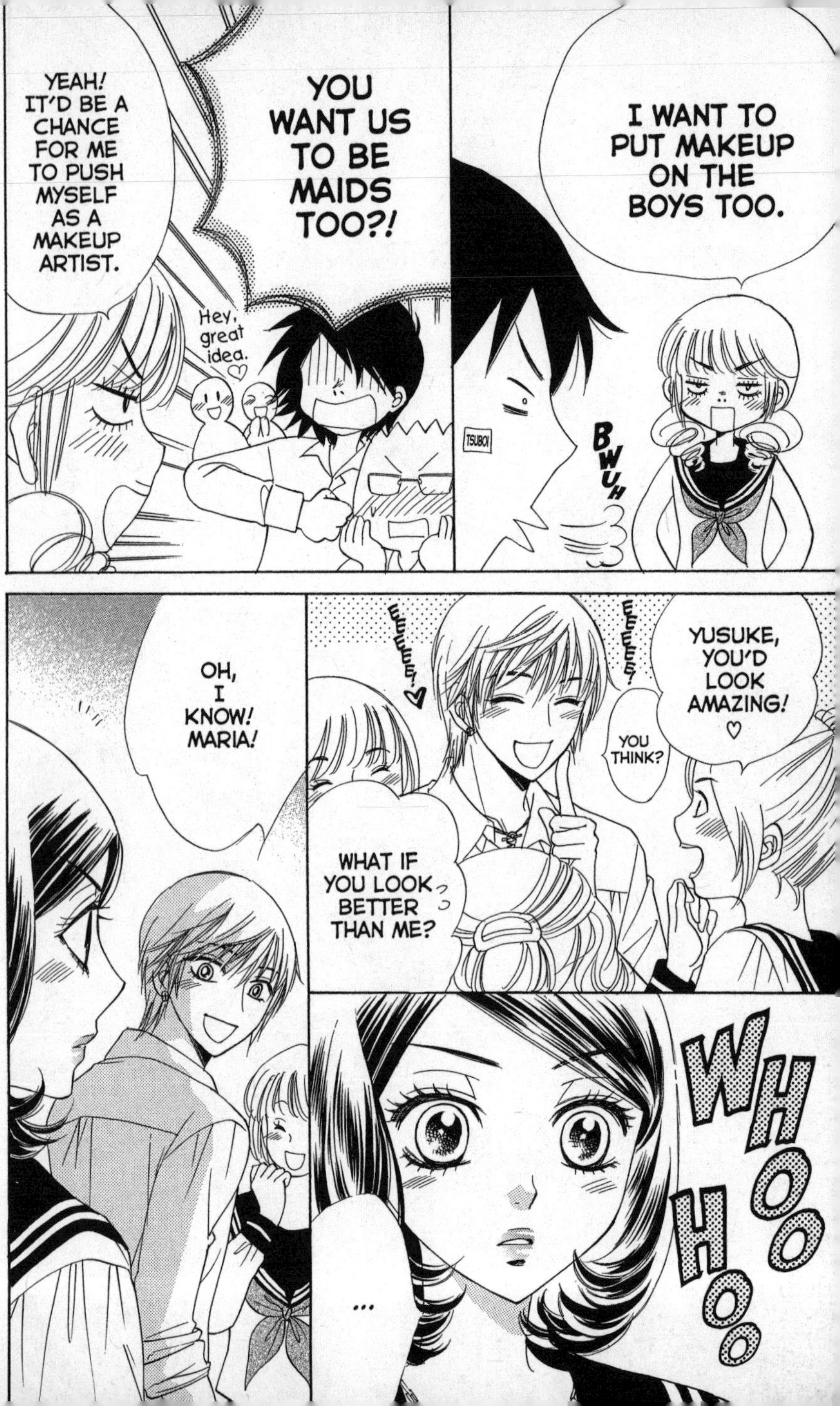
I WANT TO PUT MAKEUP ON THE BOYS TOO.
TSUBOI
BWUH
YOU WANT US TO BE MAIDS TOO?!
YEAH! IT'D BE A CHANCE FOR ME TO PUSH MYSELF AS A MAKEUP ARTIST.
Hey, great idea. ♡
YUSUKE, YOU'D LOOK AMAZING! ♡
EEEEE!
YOU THINK?
EEEEE! ♥
WHAT IF YOU LOOK BETTER THAN ME?
WHOOHOO
...
OH, I KNOW! MARIA!

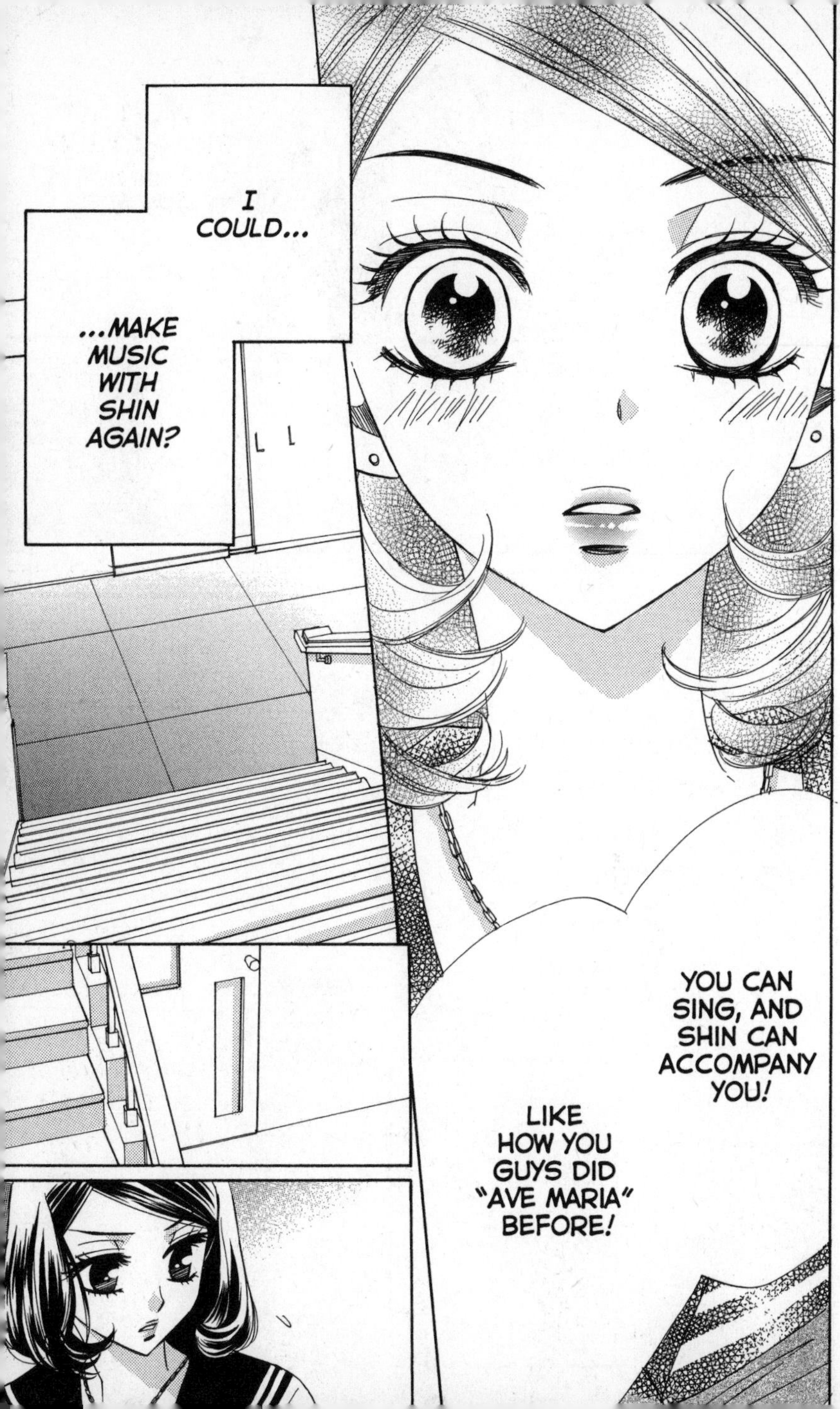
YOU CAN SING, AND SHIN CAN ACCOMPANY YOU!
LIKE HOW YOU GUYS DID "AVE MARIA" BEFORE!
I COULD...
...MAKE MUSIC WITH SHIN AGAIN?

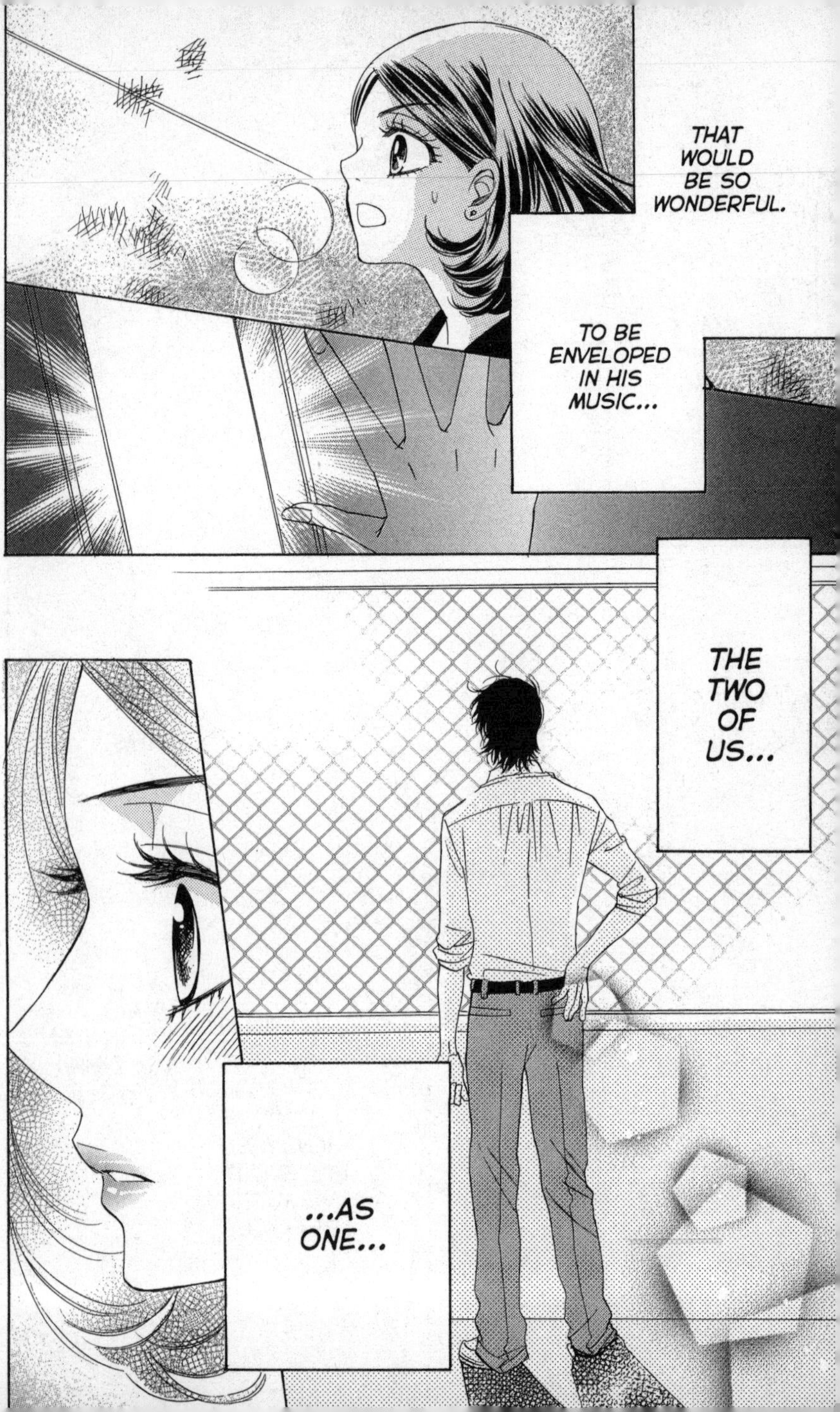
THAT WOULD BE SO WONDERFUL.
TO BE ENVELOPED IN HIS MUSIC...
THE TWO OF US...
...AS ONE...

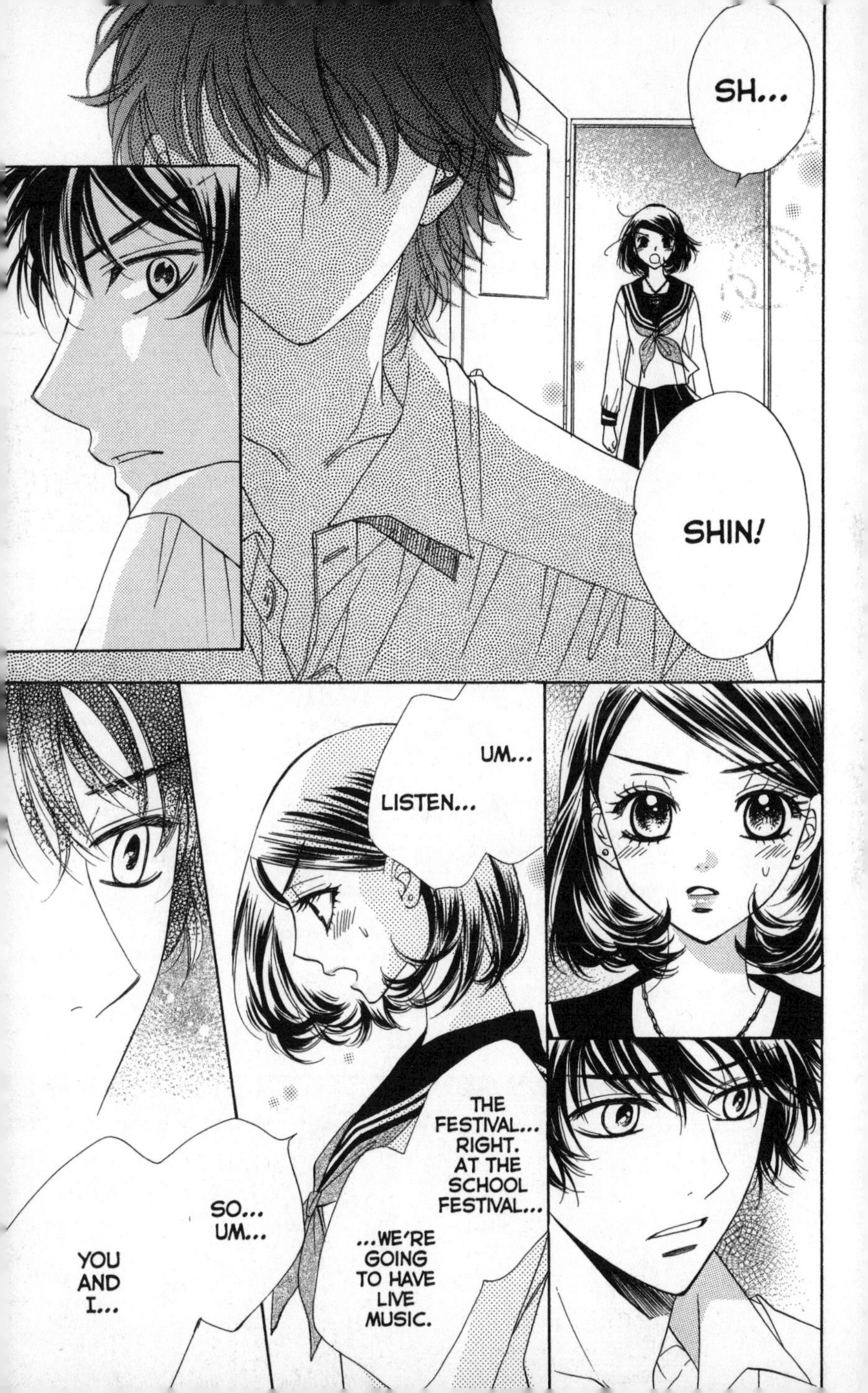
SH...
SHIN!
UM...
LISTEN...
THE FESTIVAL... RIGHT. AT THE SCHOOL FESTIVAL...
...WE'RE GOING TO HAVE LIVE MUSIC.
SO... UM...
YOU AND I...

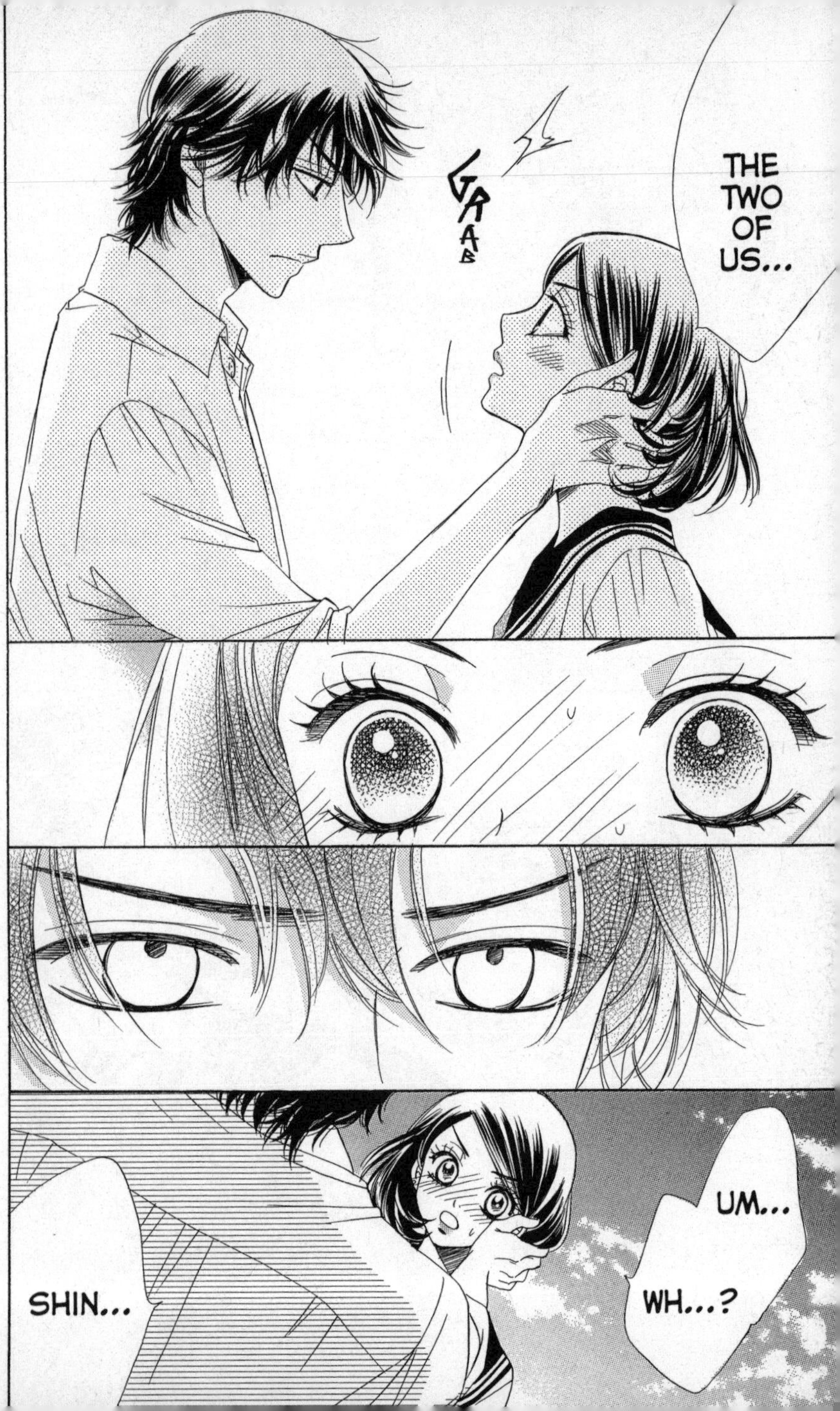
THE TWO OF US...
GRAB
UM... WH...?
SHIN...

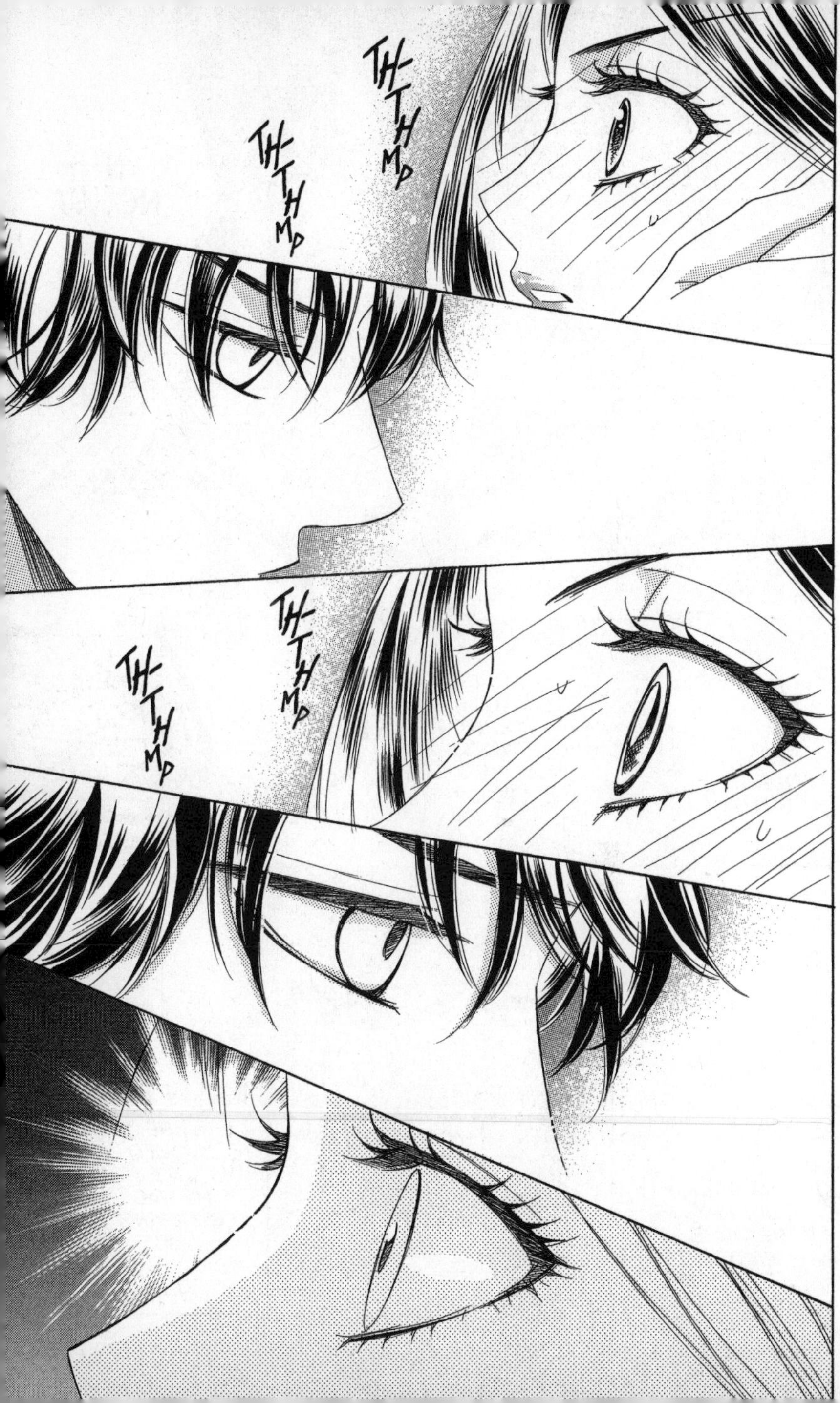
THTHMP
THTHMP
THTHMP
THTHMP

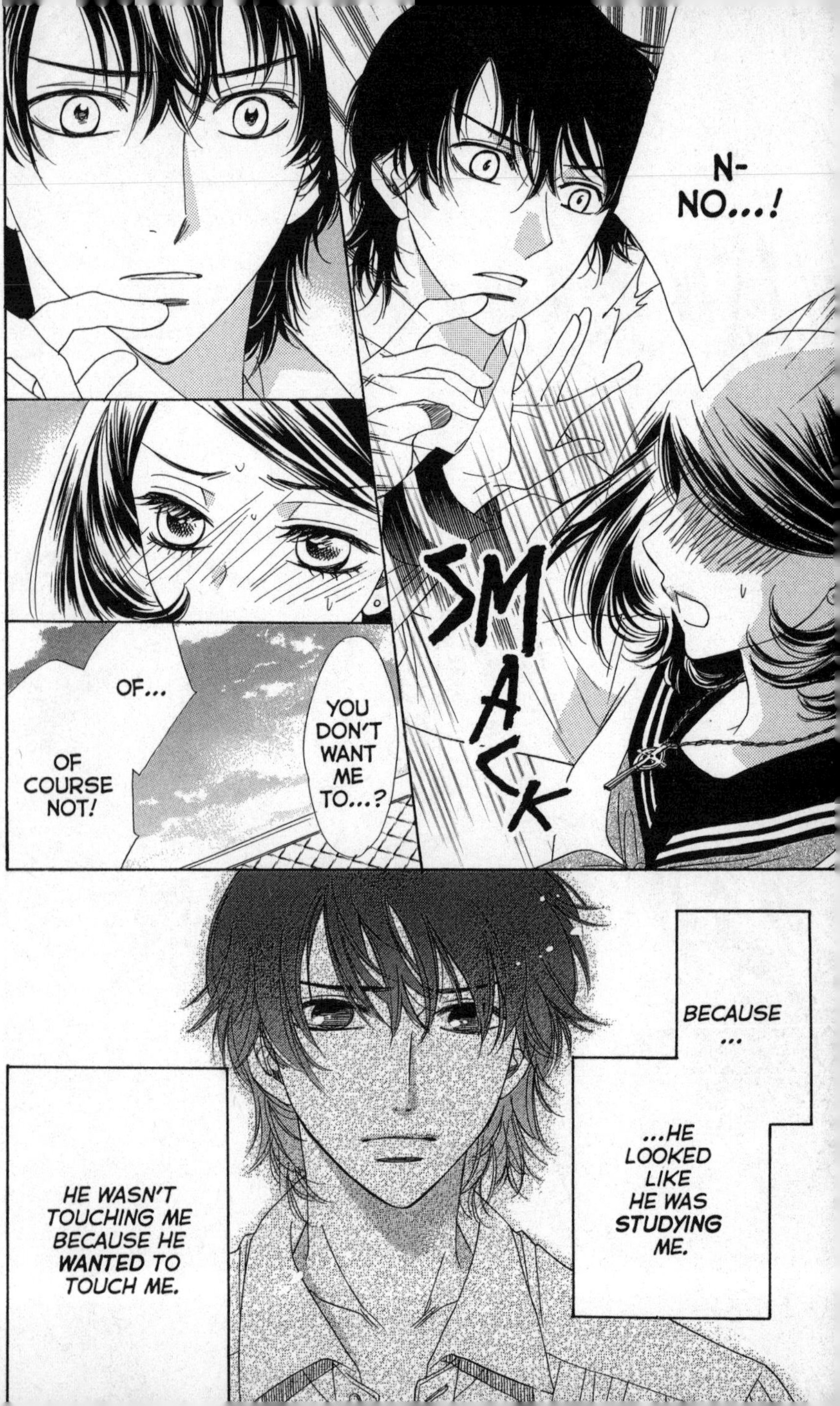
N-NO...!
SMACK
YOU DON'T WANT ME TO...?
OF...
OF COURSE NOT!
BECAUSE ...
...HE LOOKED LIKE HE WAS STUDYING ME.
HE WASN'T TOUCHING ME BECAUSE HE WANTED TO TOUCH ME.

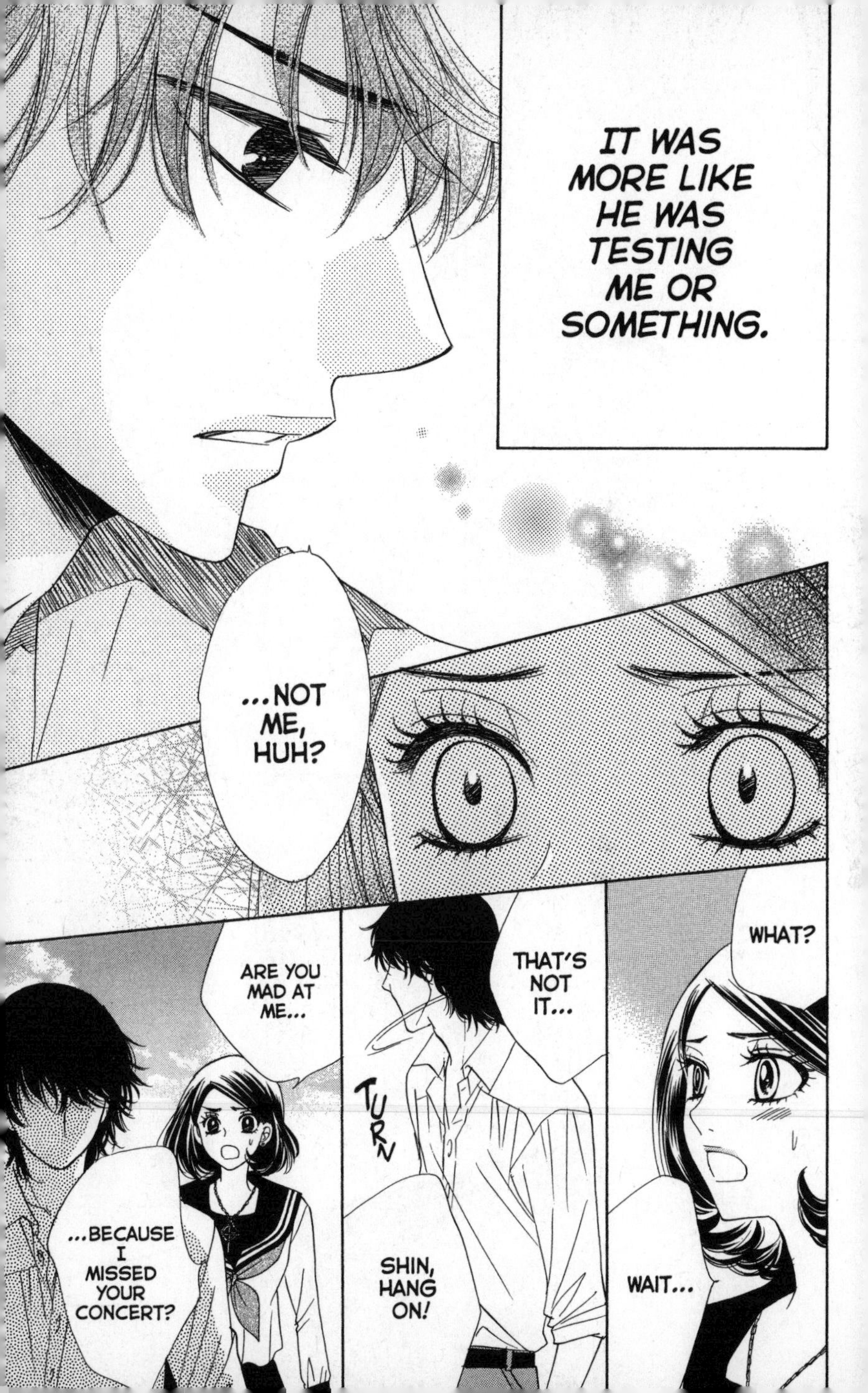
IT WAS MORE LIKE HE WAS TESTING ME OR SOMETHING.
...NOT ME, HUH?
WHAT?
WAIT...
THAT'S NOT IT...
TURN
SHIN, HANG ON!
ARE YOU MAD AT ME...
...BECAUSE I MISSED YOUR CONCERT?

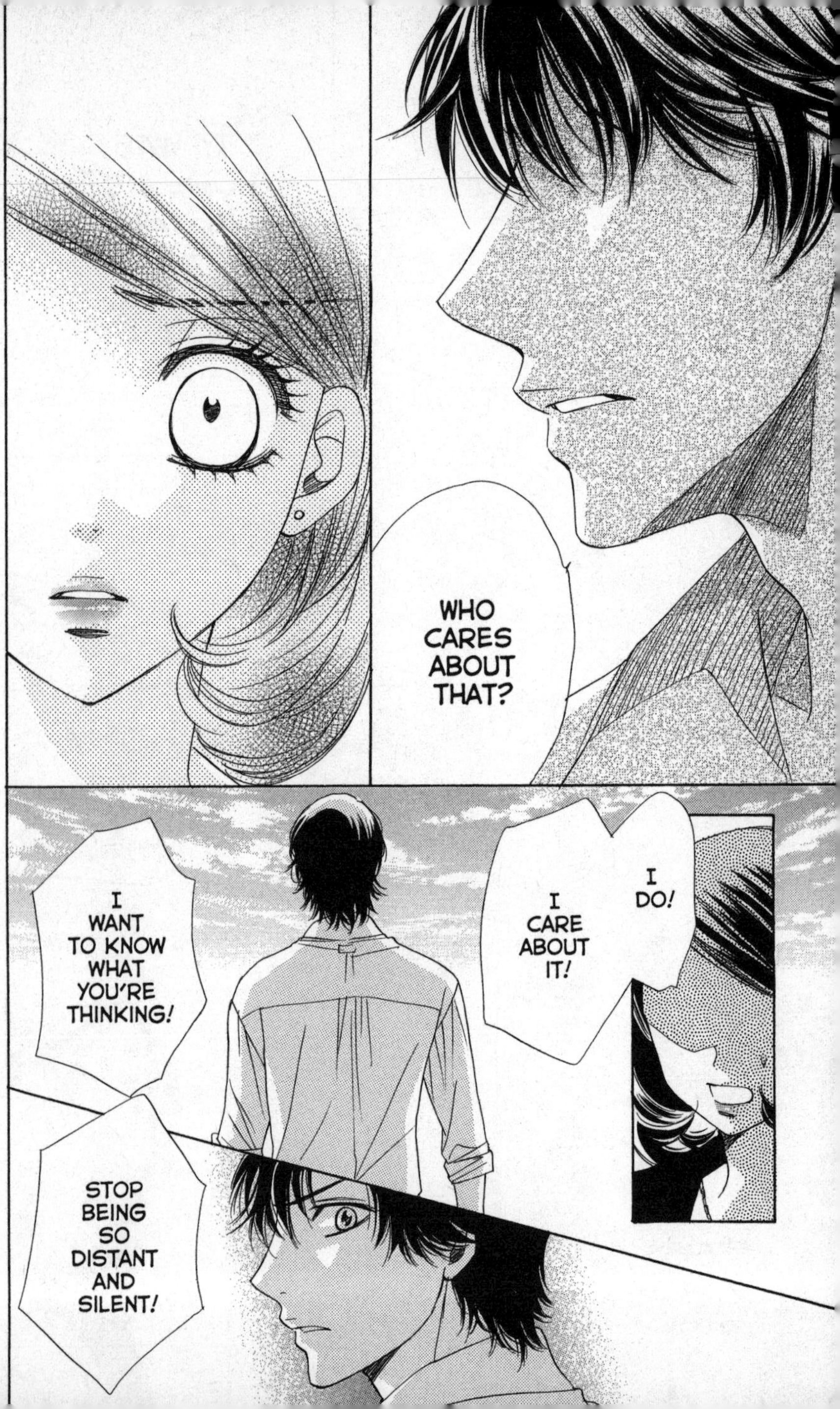
WHO CARES ABOUT THAT?
I DO!
I CARE ABOUT IT!
I WANT TO KNOW WHAT YOU'RE THINKING!
STOP BEING SO DISTANT AND SILENT!

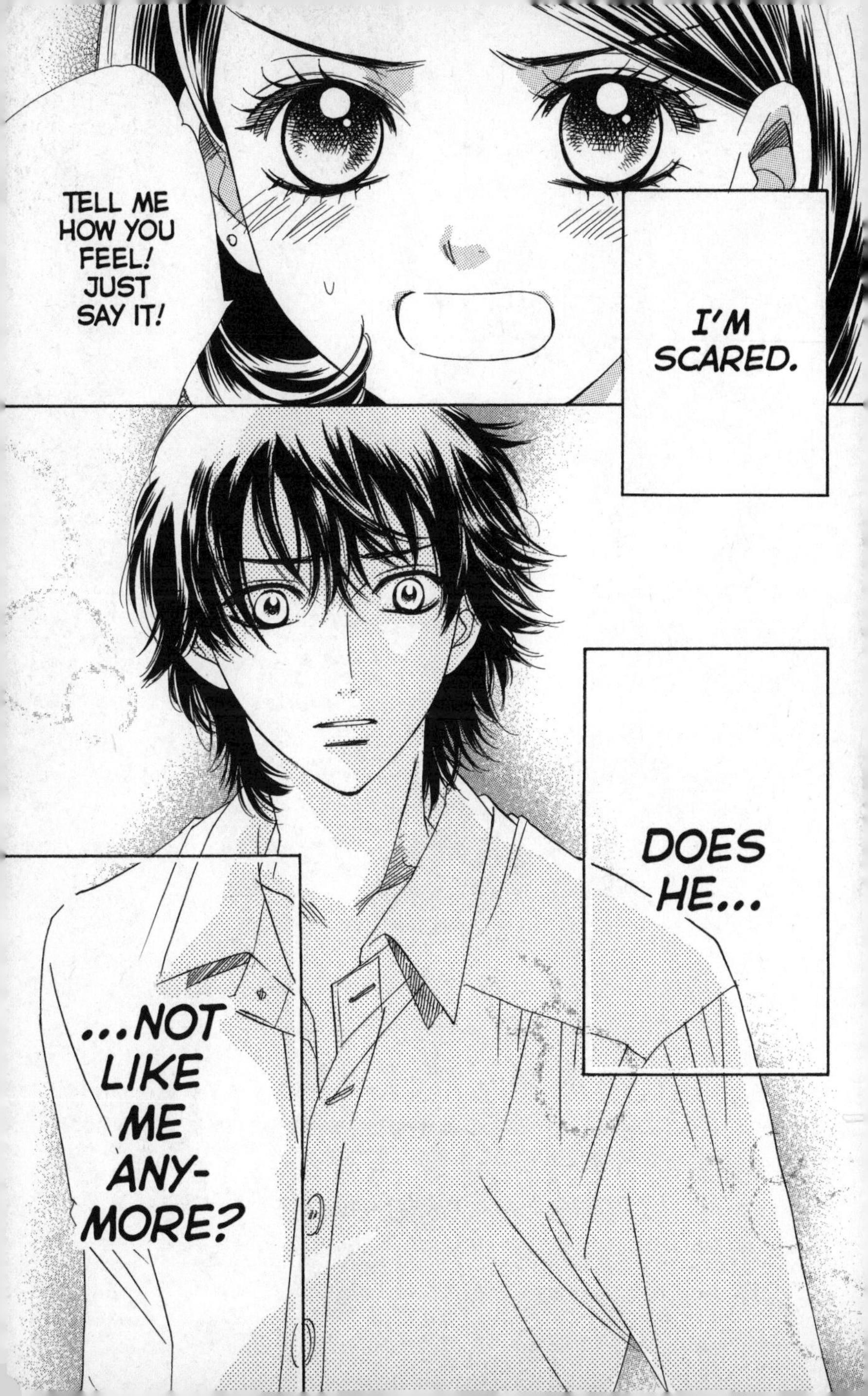
I'M SCARED.
TELL ME HOW YOU FEEL! JUST SAY IT!
DOES HE...
...NOT LIKE ME ANY-MORE?

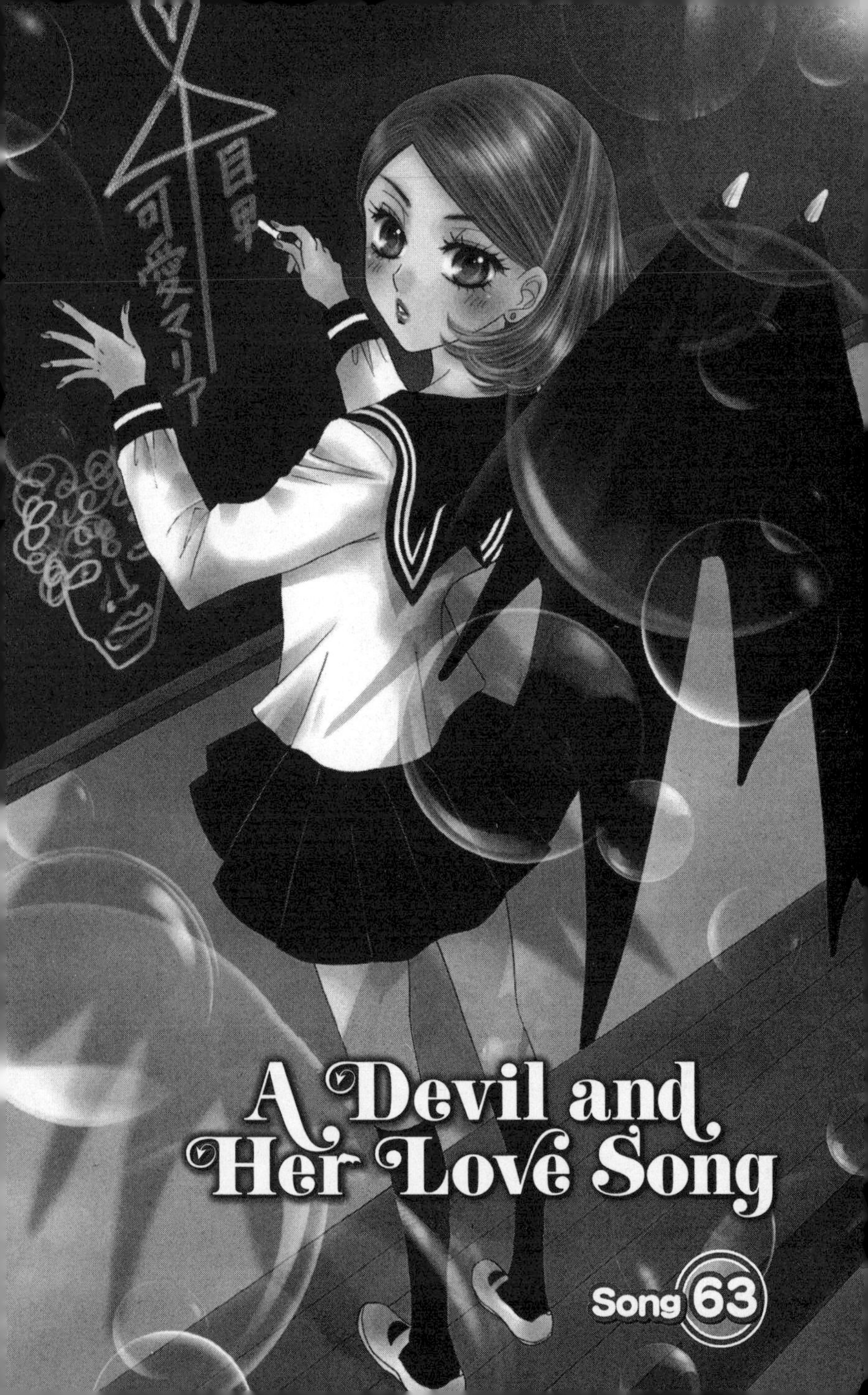
可愛マリア
A Devil and Her Love Song
Song 63

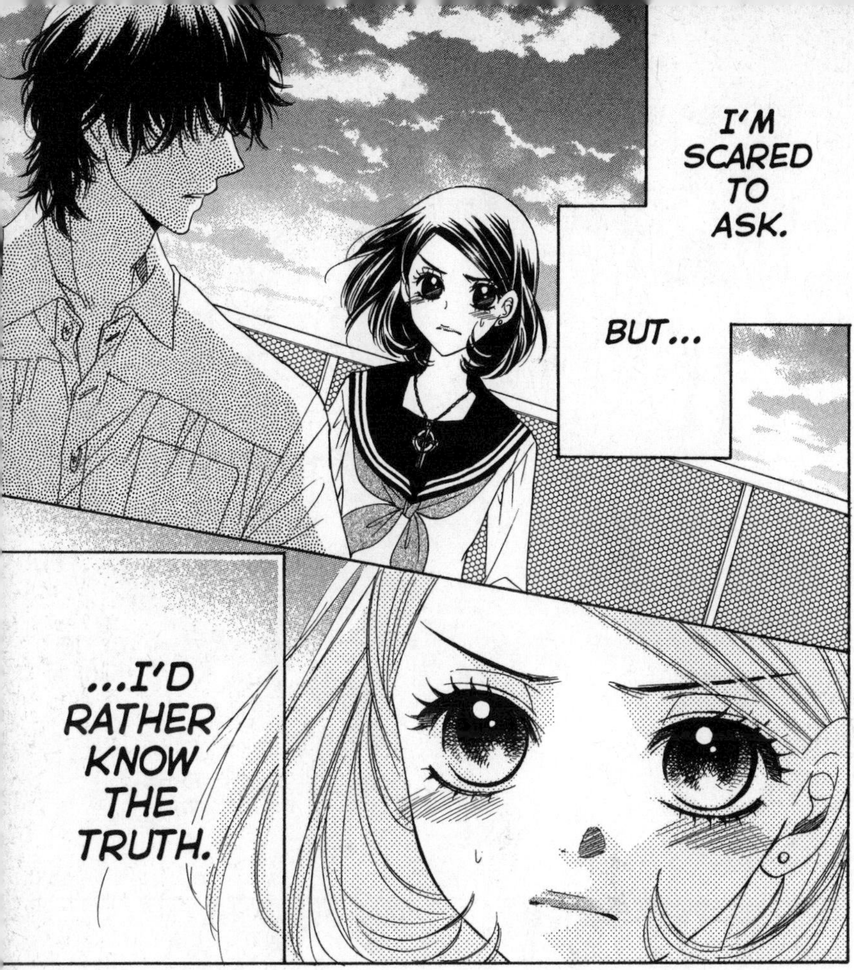
I'M SCARED TO ASK.
BUT...
...I'D RATHER KNOW THE TRUTH.

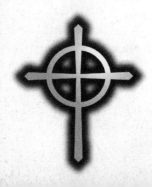

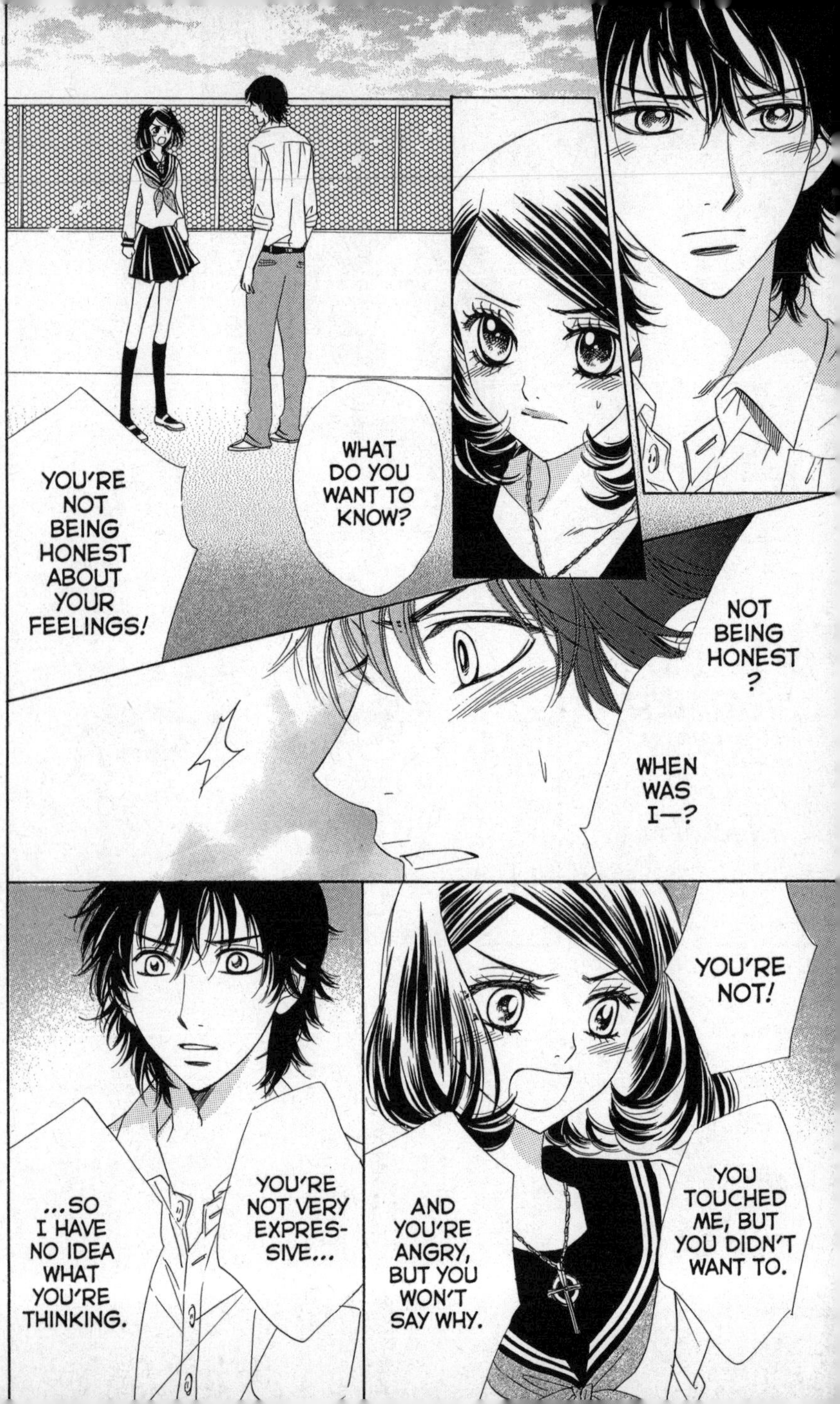
WHAT DO YOU WANT TO KNOW?
YOU'RE NOT BEING HONEST ABOUT YOUR FEELINGS!
NOT BEING HONEST?
WHEN WAS I—?
YOU'RE NOT!
YOU TOUCHED ME, BUT YOU DIDN'T WANT TO.
AND YOU'RE ANGRY, BUT YOU WON'T SAY WHY.
YOU'RE NOT VERY EXPRES-SIVE...
...SO I HAVE NO IDEA WHAT YOU'RE THINKING.

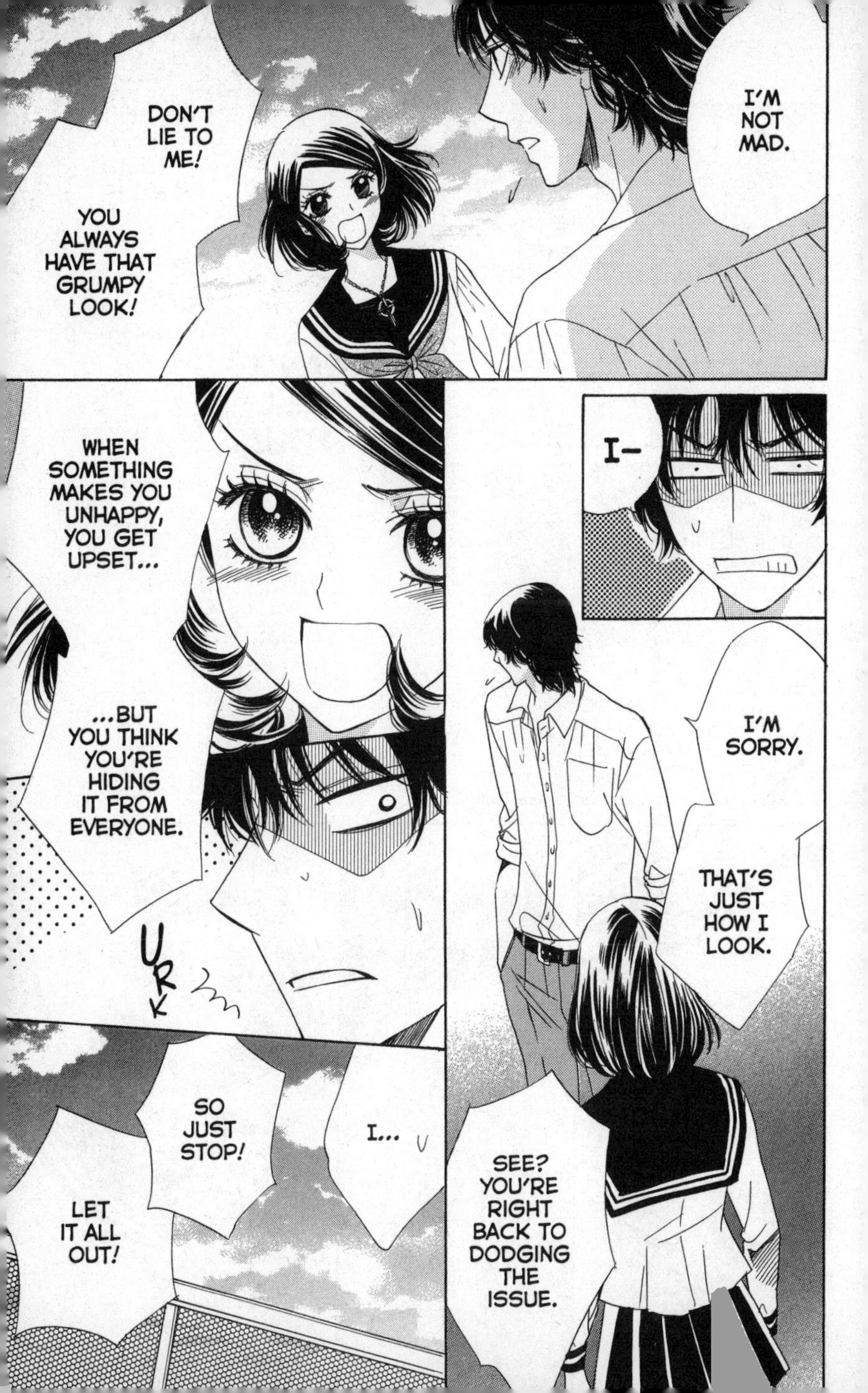
I'M NOT MAD.
DON'T LIE TO ME!
YOU ALWAYS HAVE THAT GRUMPY LOOK!
I–
I'M SORRY.
THAT'S JUST HOW I LOOK.
SEE? YOU'RE RIGHT BACK TO DODGING THE ISSUE.
WHEN SOMETHING MAKES YOU UNHAPPY, YOU GET UPSET...
...BUT YOU THINK YOU'RE HIDING IT FROM EVERYONE.
URK
I...
SO JUST STOP!
LET IT ALL OUT!

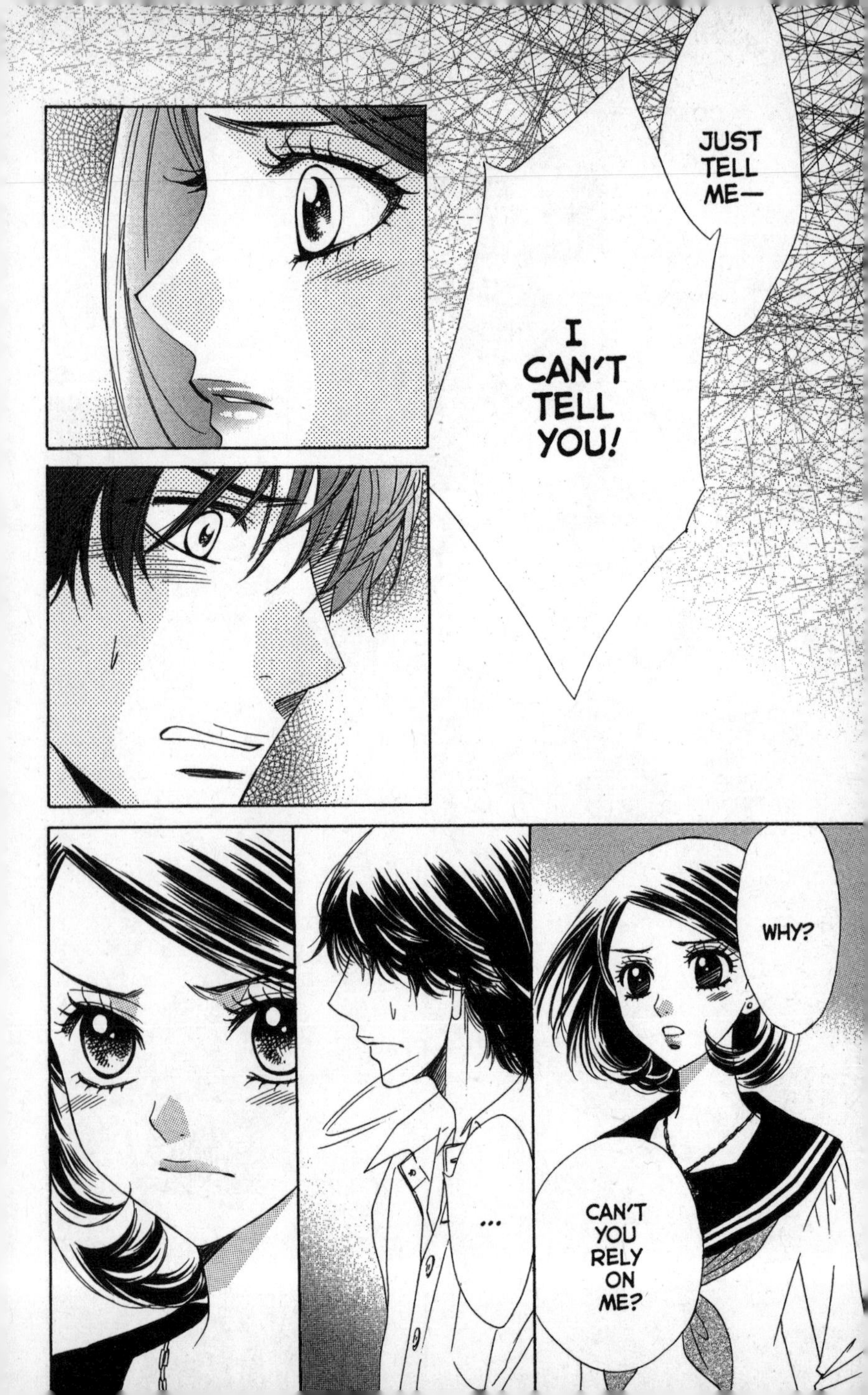
JUST TELL ME—
I CAN'T TELL YOU!
WHY?
CAN'T YOU RELY ON ME?
...

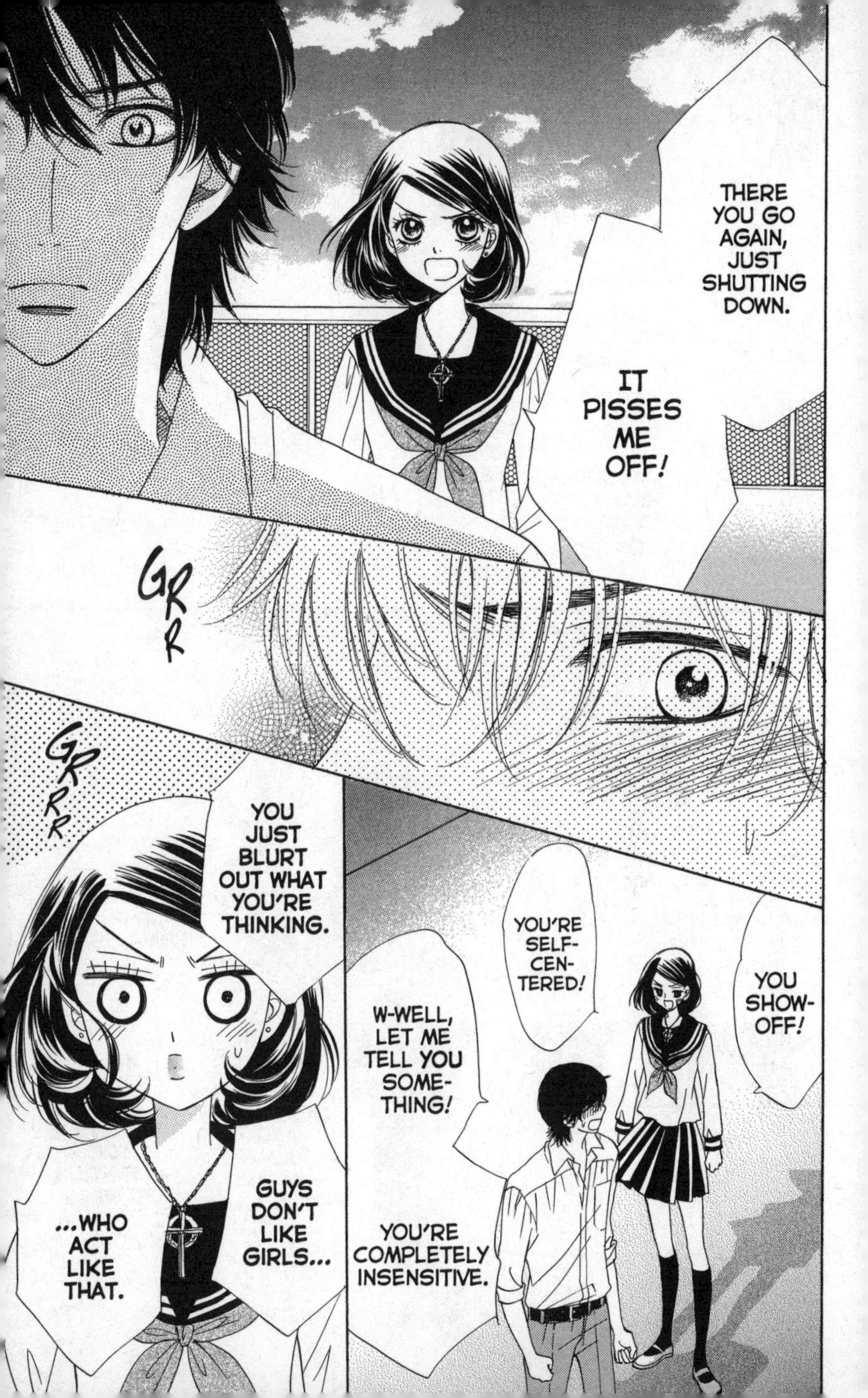
THERE YOU GO AGAIN, JUST SHUTTING DOWN.
IT PISSES ME OFF!
GRR
GRRR
YOU SHOW-OFF!
YOU'RE SELF-CENTERED!
W-WELL, LET ME TELL YOU SOME-THING!
YOU'RE COMPLETELY INSENSITIVE.
YOU JUST BLURT OUT WHAT YOU'RE THINKING.
GUYS DON'T LIKE GIRLS...
...WHO ACT LIKE THAT.

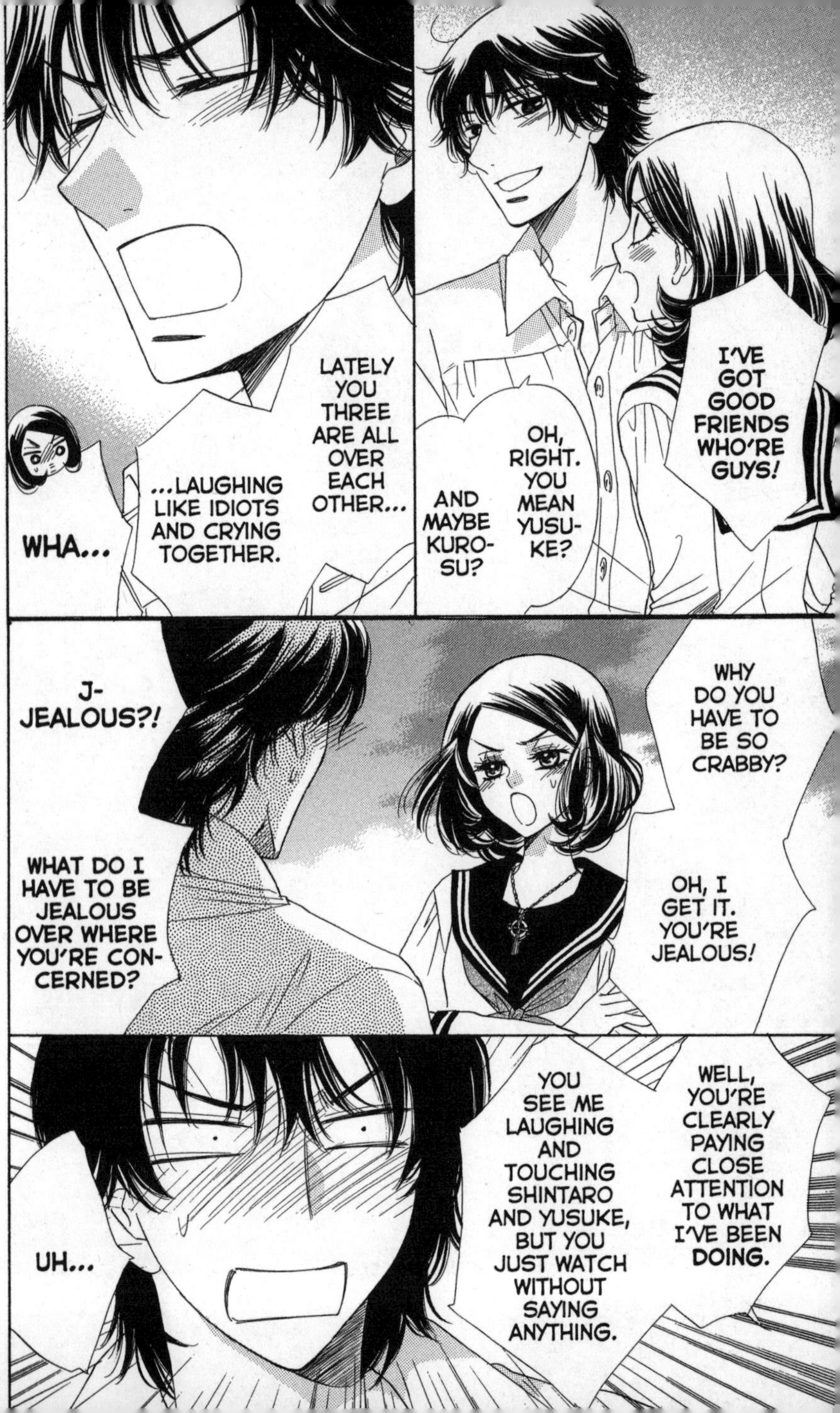
I'VE GOT GOOD FRIENDS WHO'RE GUYS!
OH, RIGHT. YOU MEAN YUSUKE?
AND MAYBE KUROSU?
LATELY YOU THREE ARE ALL OVER EACH OTHER...
...LAUGHING LIKE IDIOTS AND CRYING TOGETHER.
WHA...
WHY DO YOU HAVE TO BE SO CRABBY?
OH, I GET IT. YOU'RE JEALOUS!
J- JEALOUS?!
WHAT DO I HAVE TO BE JEALOUS OVER WHERE YOU'RE CONCERNED?
WELL, YOU'RE CLEARLY PAYING CLOSE ATTENTION TO WHAT I'VE BEEN DOING.
YOU SEE ME LAUGHING AND TOUCHING SHINTARO AND YUSUKE, BUT YOU JUST WATCH WITHOUT SAYING ANYTHING.
UH...

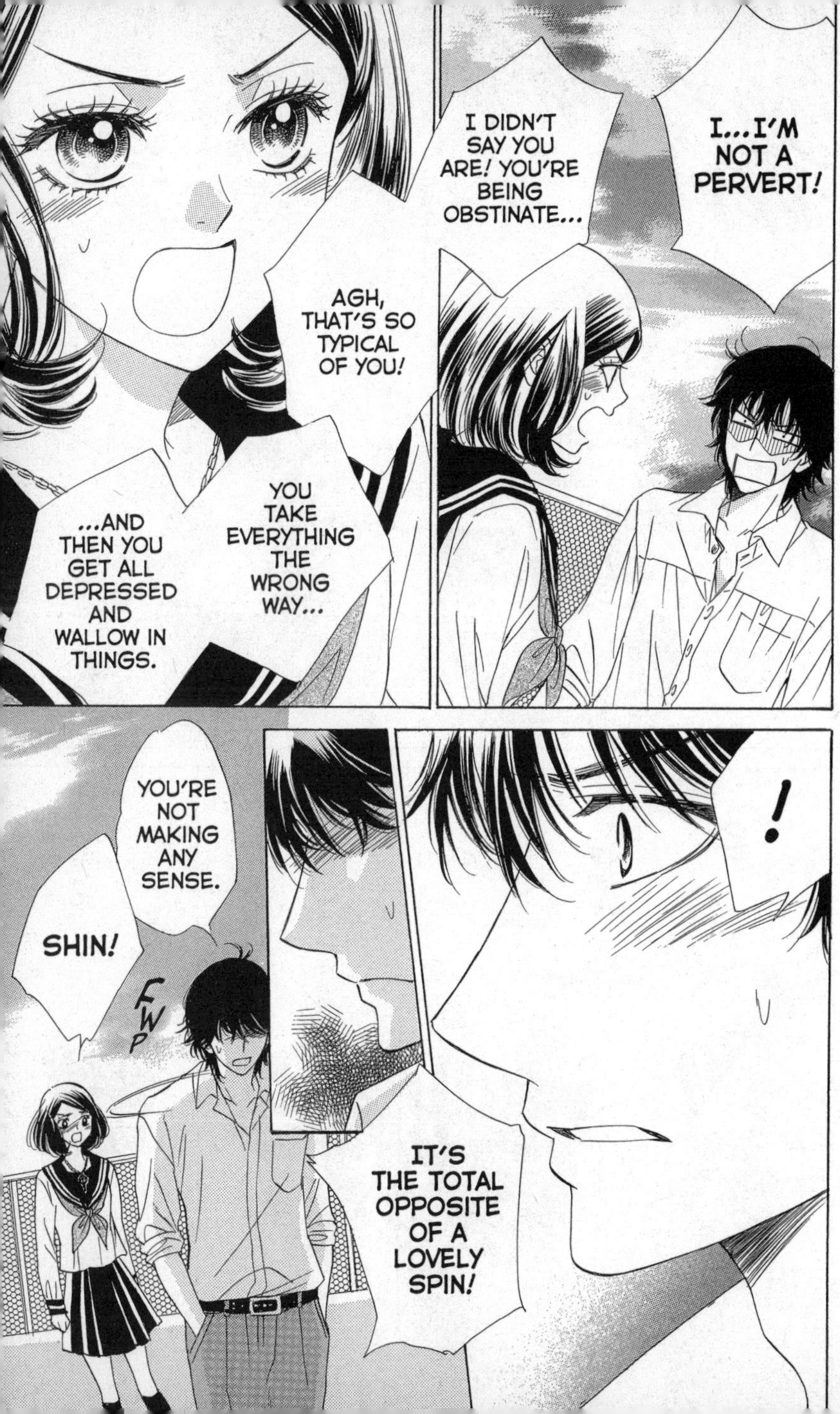
I...I'M NOT A PERVERT!
I DIDN'T SAY YOU ARE! YOU'RE BEING OBSTINATE...
AGH, THAT'S SO TYPICAL OF YOU!
YOU TAKE EVERYTHING THE WRONG WAY...
...AND THEN YOU GET ALL DEPRESSED AND WALLOW IN THINGS.
!
IT'S THE TOTAL OPPOSITE OF A LOVELY SPIN!
YOU'RE NOT MAKING ANY SENSE.
SHIN!
FWP

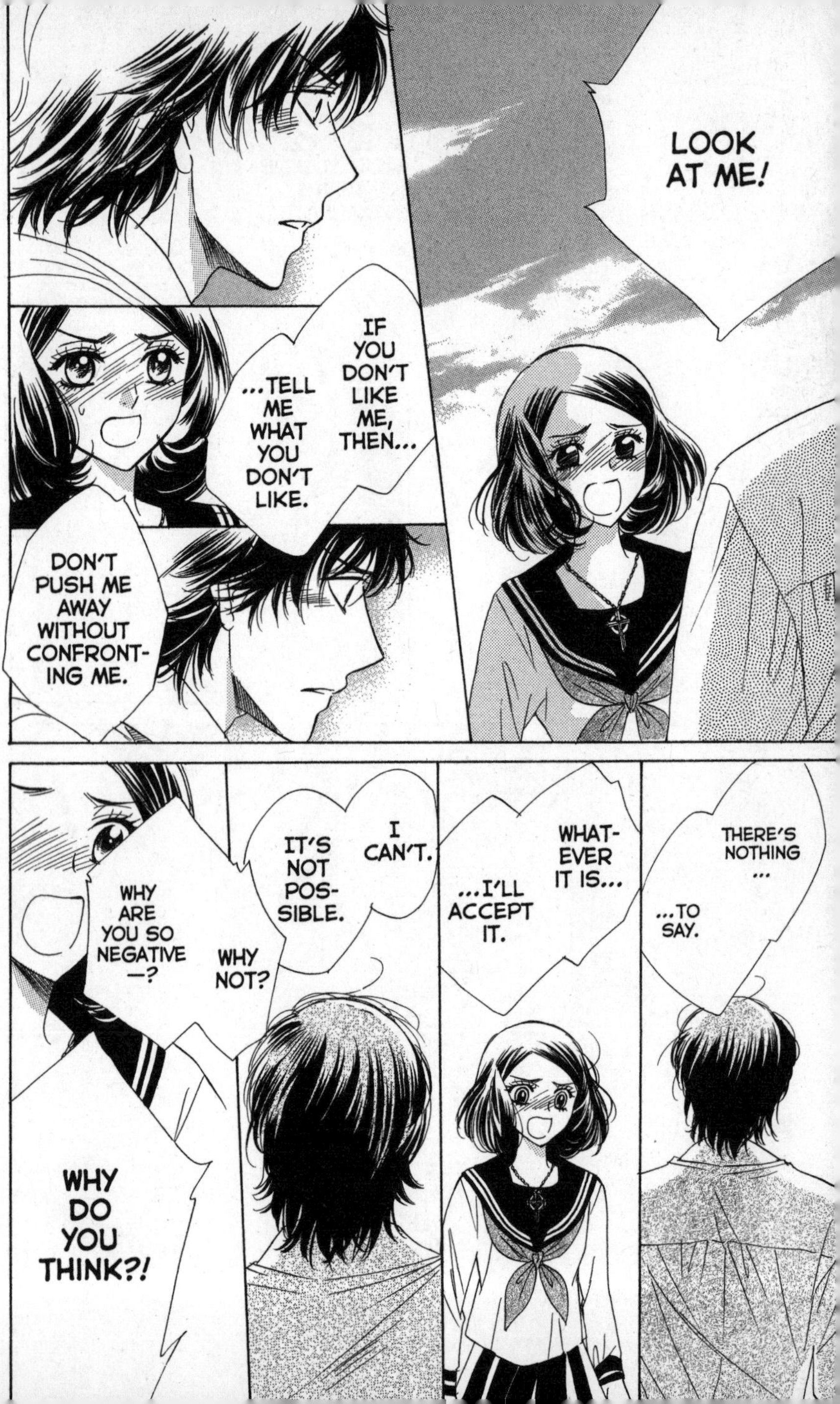
LOOK AT ME!
IF YOU DON'T LIKE ME, THEN...
...TELL ME WHAT YOU DON'T LIKE.
DON'T PUSH ME AWAY WITHOUT CONFRONTING ME.
THERE'S NOTHING ...
...TO SAY.
WHATEVER IT IS...
...I'LL ACCEPT IT.
I CAN'T.
IT'S NOT POSSIBLE.
WHY NOT?
WHY ARE YOU SO NEGATIVE—?
WHY DO YOU THINK?!

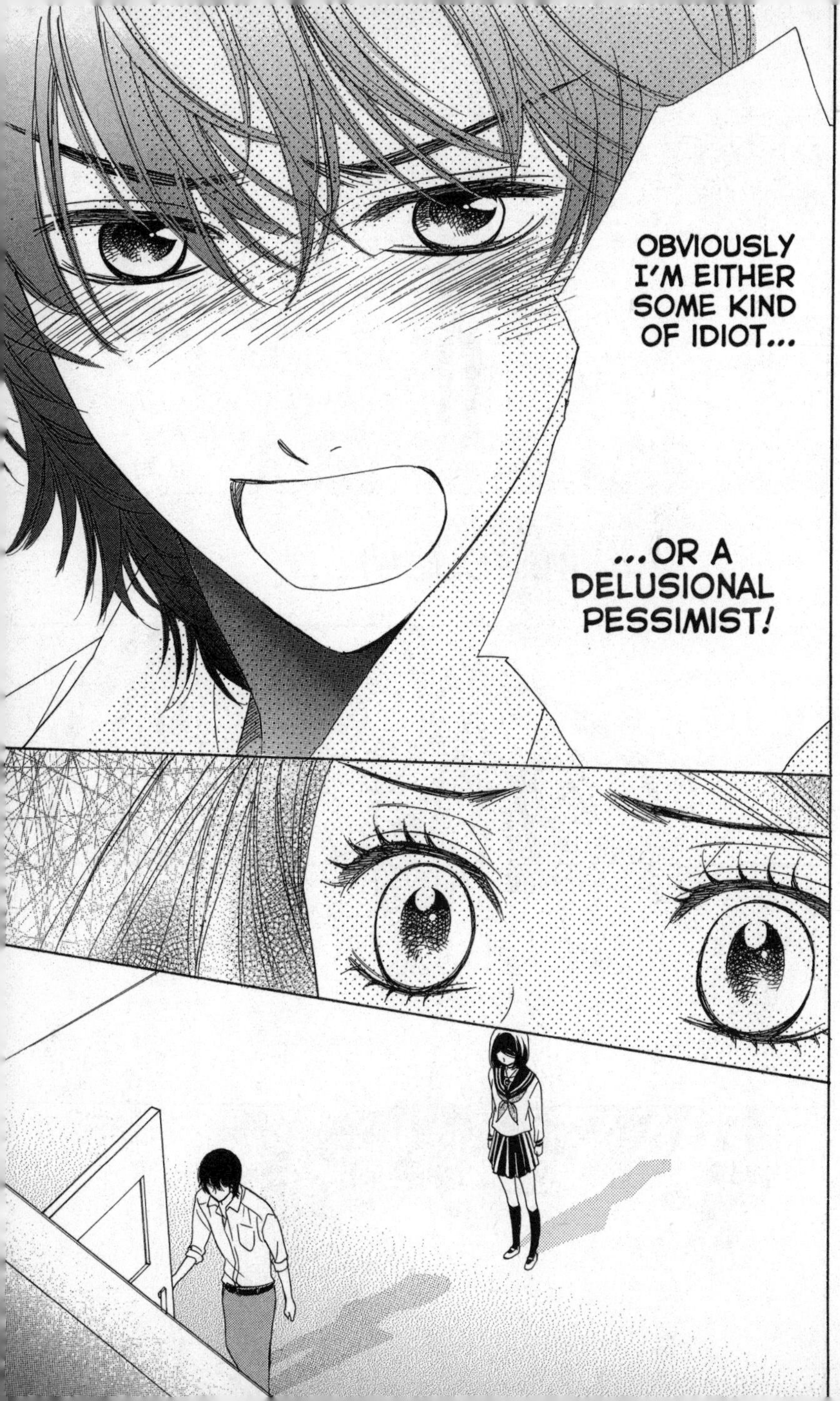
OBVIOUSLY I'M EITHER SOME KIND OF IDIOT...
...OR A DELUSIONAL PESSIMIST!

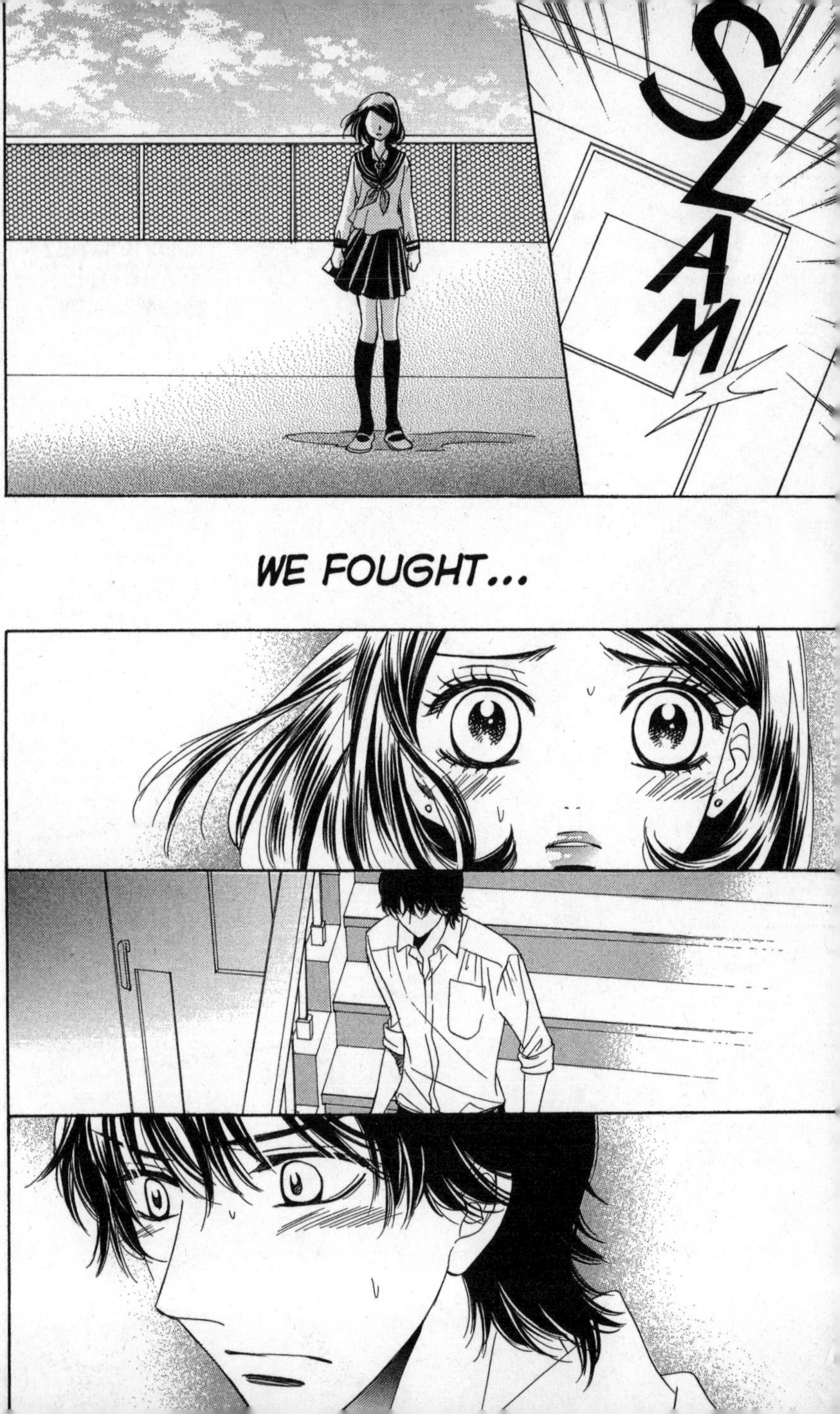
SLAM
WE FOUGHT...

WE HAD A REAL FIGHT.

I'M SO STUPID...

WE JUST PUT IT ALL OUT THERE.

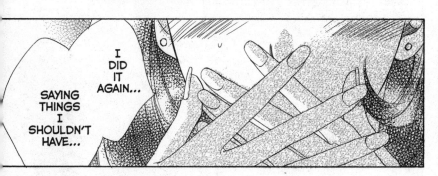

I DID IT AGAIN...

SAYING THINGS I SHOULDN'T HAVE...

HOW DID IT TURN OUT THIS WAY?

HA...

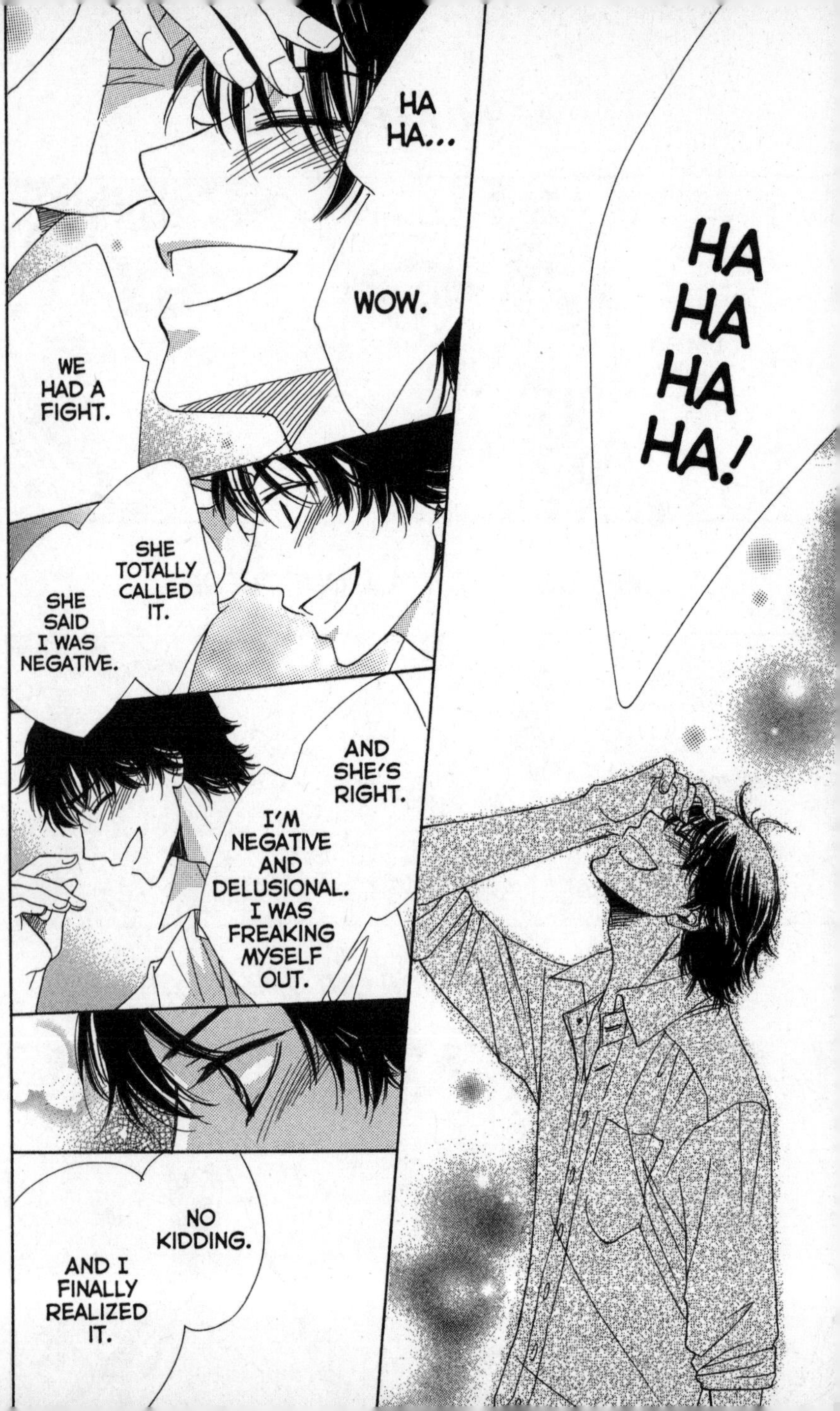
HA HA HA HA!
HA HA...
WOW.
WE HAD A FIGHT.
SHE TOTALLY CALLED IT.
SHE SAID I WAS NEGATIVE.
AND SHE'S RIGHT.
I'M NEGATIVE AND DELUSIONAL. I WAS FREAKING MYSELF OUT.
NO KIDDING.
AND I FINALLY REALIZED IT.

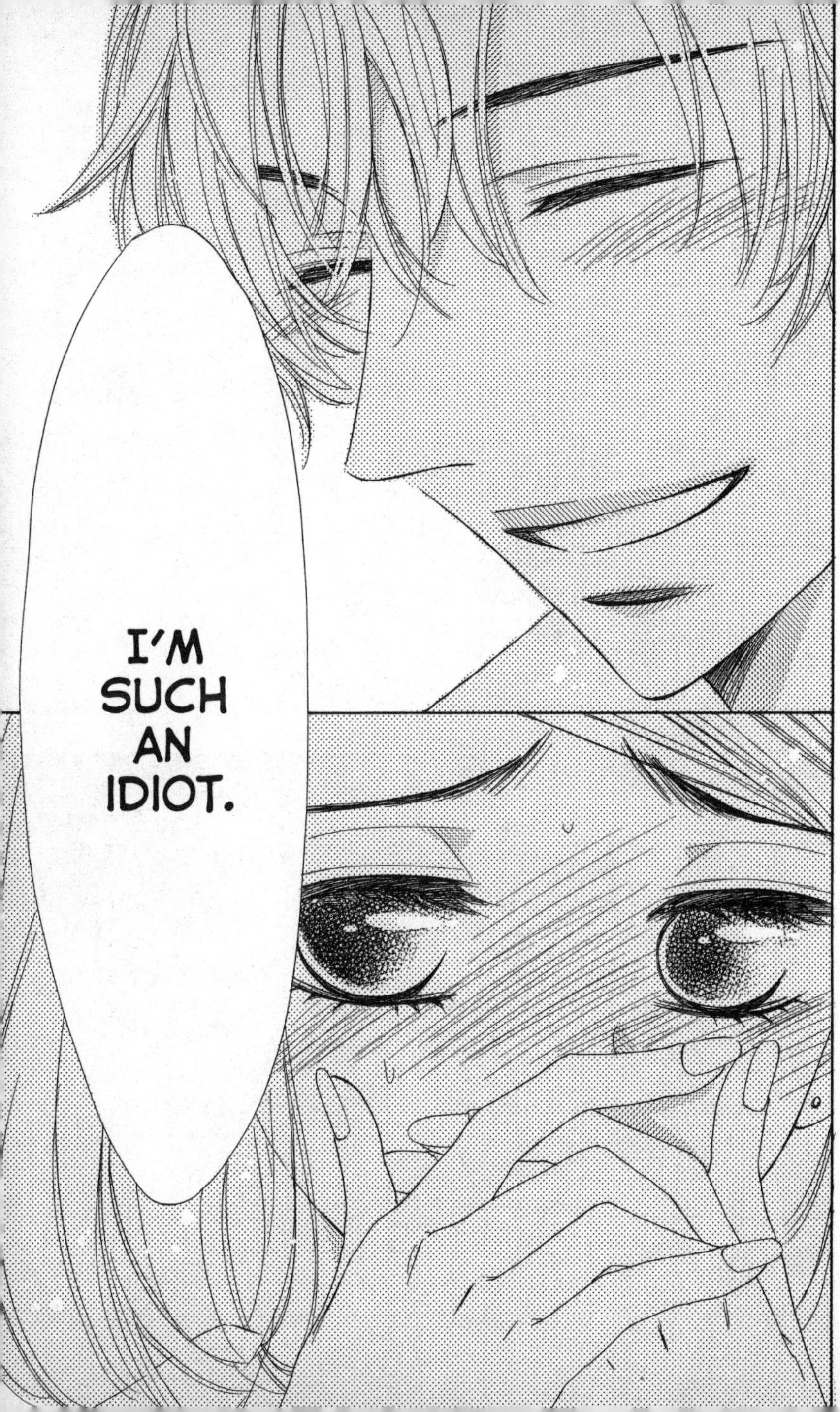
I'M SUCH AN IDIOT.

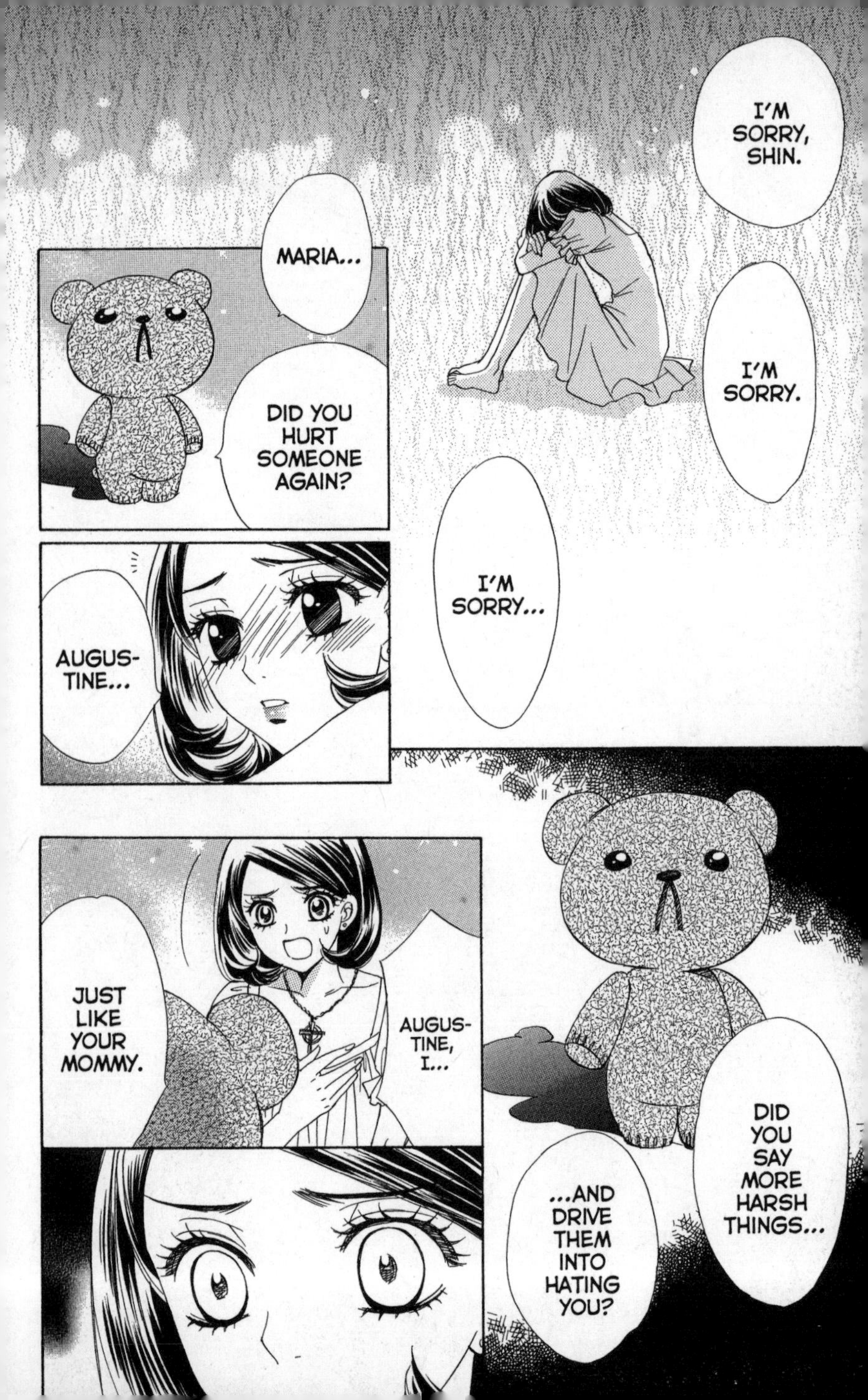
I'M SORRY, SHIN.
I'M SORRY.
I'M SORRY...
MARIA...
DID YOU HURT SOMEONE AGAIN?
AUGUSTINE...
DID YOU SAY MORE HARSH THINGS...
...AND DRIVE THEM INTO HATING YOU?
AUGUSTINE, I...
JUST LIKE YOUR MOMMY.

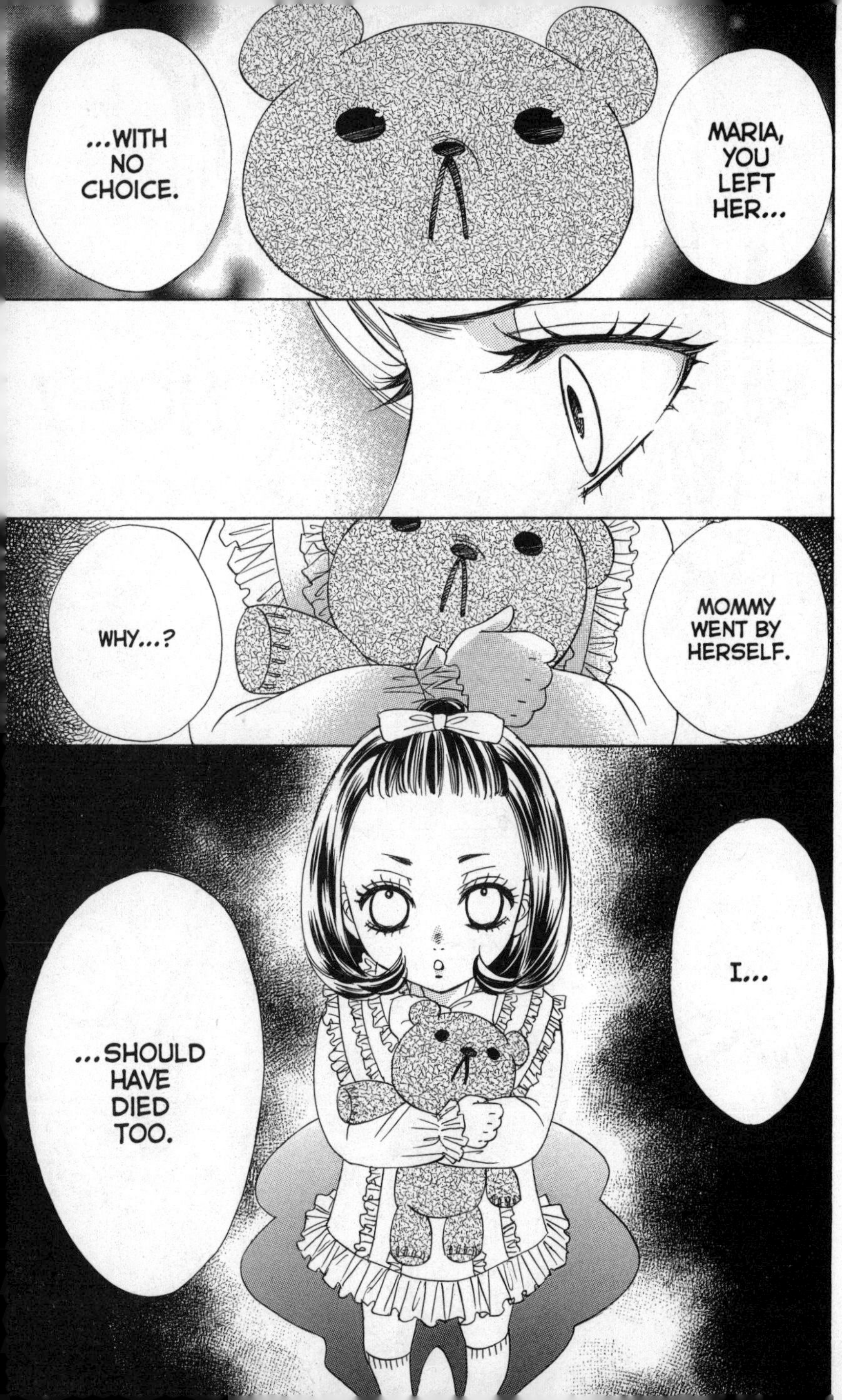
MARIA, YOU LEFT HER...
...WITH NO CHOICE.
MOMMY WENT BY HERSELF.
WHY...?
I...
...SHOULD HAVE DIED TOO.

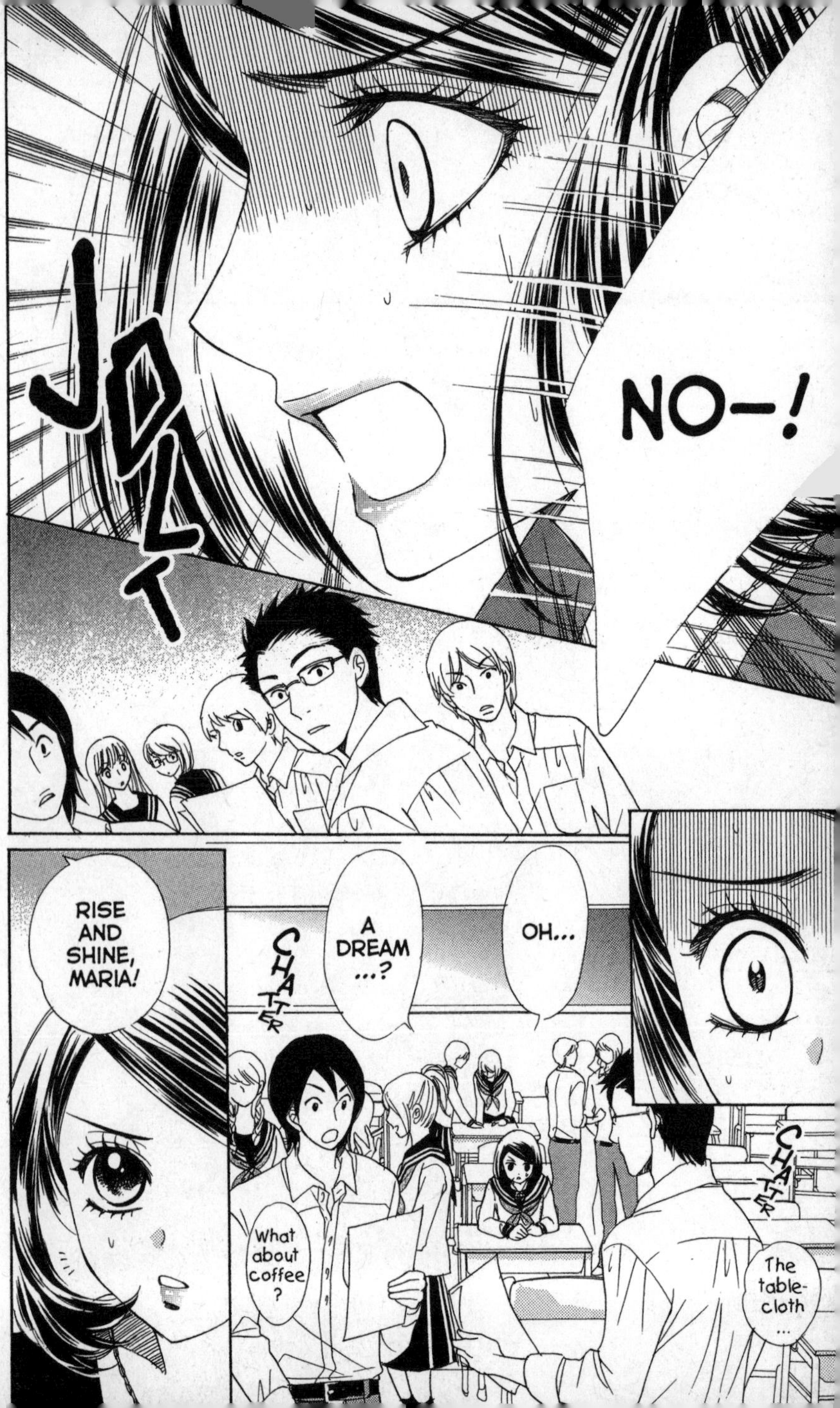
NO--!
JOLT
OH...
A DREAM ...?
CHATTER
CHATTER
The table-cloth ...
What about coffee ?
RISE AND SHINE, MARIA!

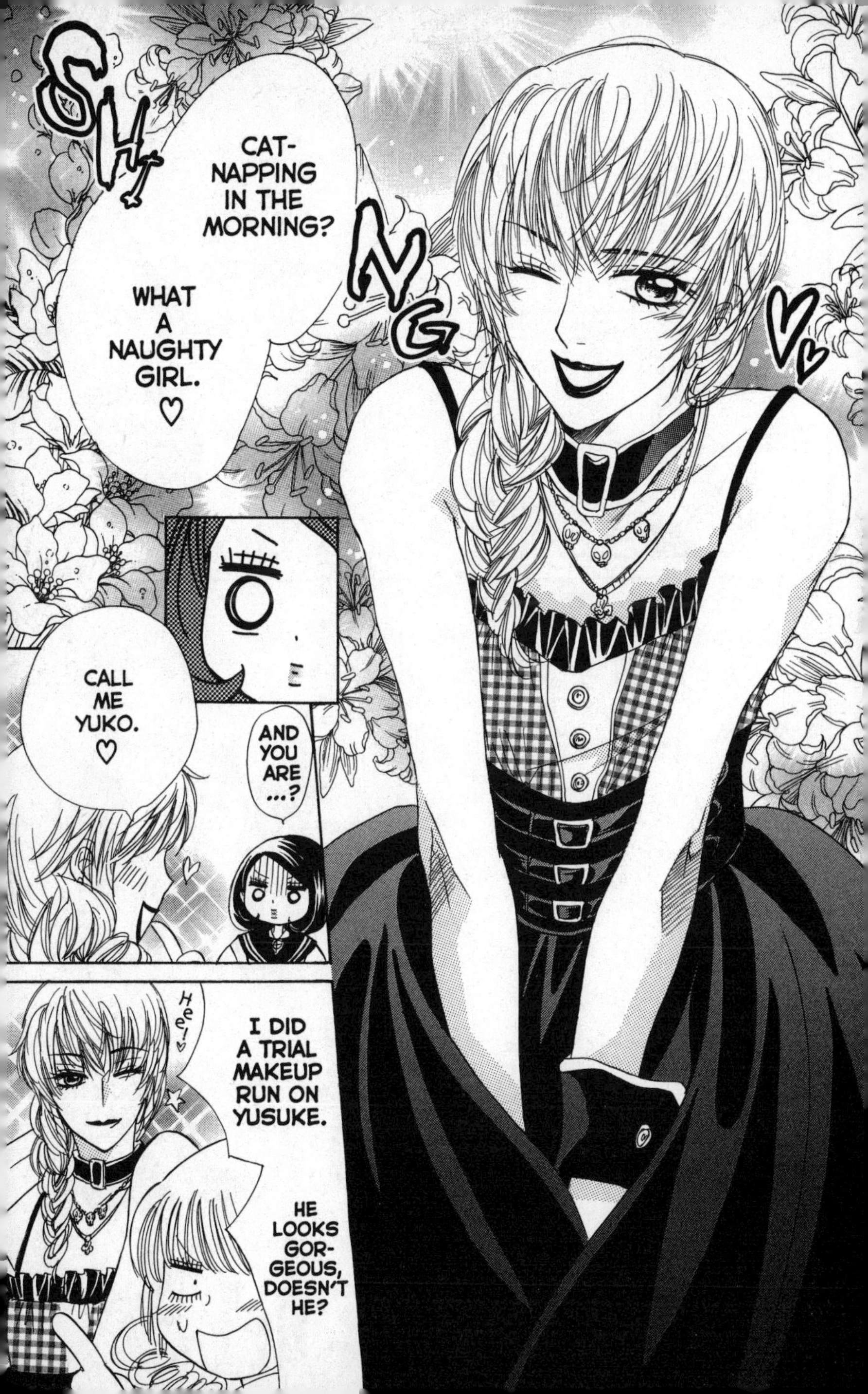
SHING
CAT-NAPPING IN THE MORNING?
WHAT A NAUGHTY GIRL. ♡
AND YOU ARE ...?
CALL ME YUKO. ♡
I DID A TRIAL MAKEUP RUN ON YUSUKE.
Hee!♡
HE LOOKS GORGEOUS, DOESN'T HE?

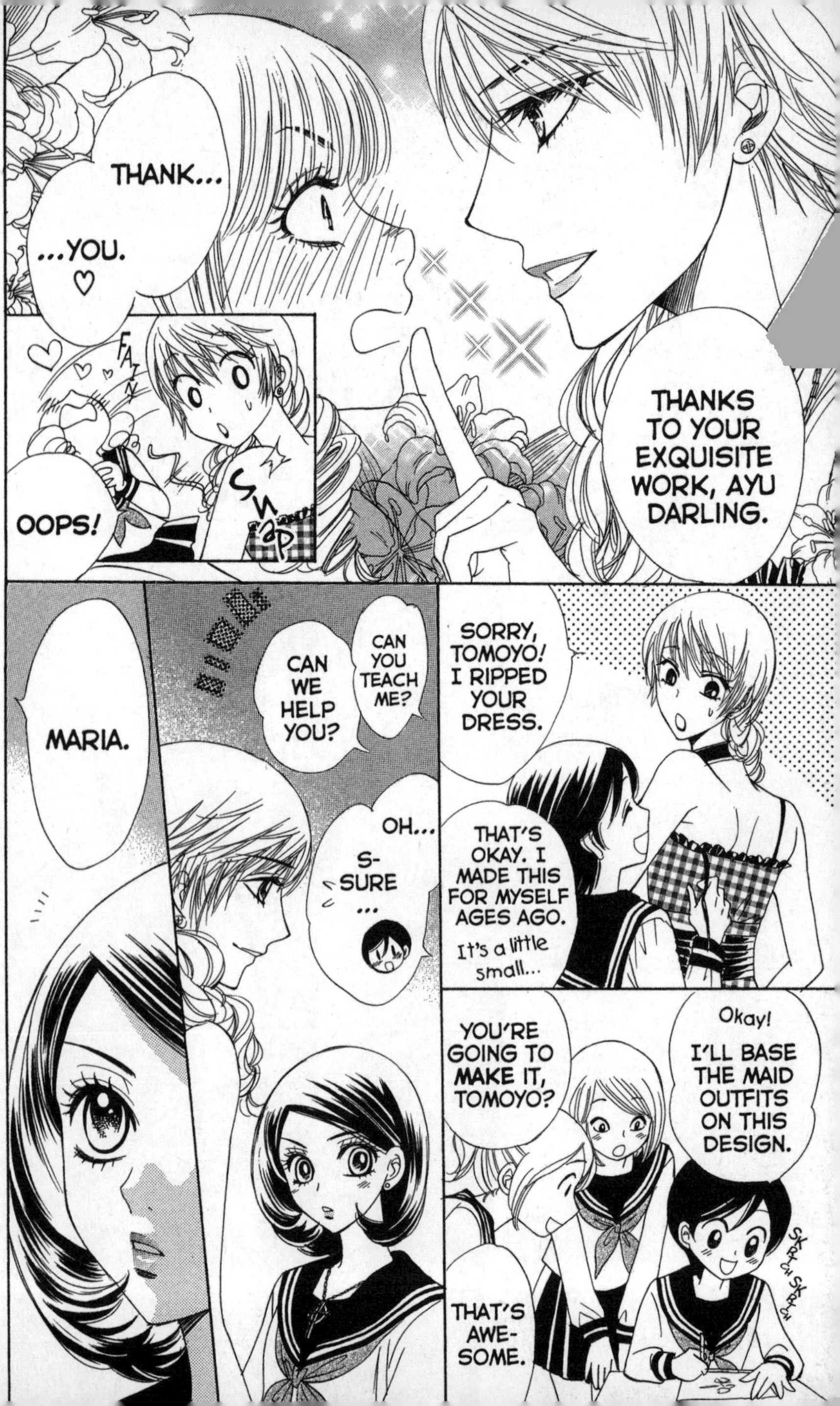
THANKS TO YOUR EXQUISITE WORK, AYU DARLING.
THANK...
...YOU. ♡
FAINT
OOPS!
SNAP
SORRY, TOMOYO! I RIPPED YOUR DRESS.
THAT'S OKAY. I MADE THIS FOR MYSELF AGES AGO.
It's a little small...
Okay!
I'LL BASE THE MAID OUTFITS ON THIS DESIGN.
YOU'RE GOING TO MAKE IT, TOMOYO?
THAT'S AWESOME.
SKRTCH SKRTCH
CAN YOU TEACH ME?
CAN WE HELP YOU?
OH...
S-SURE...
MARIA.

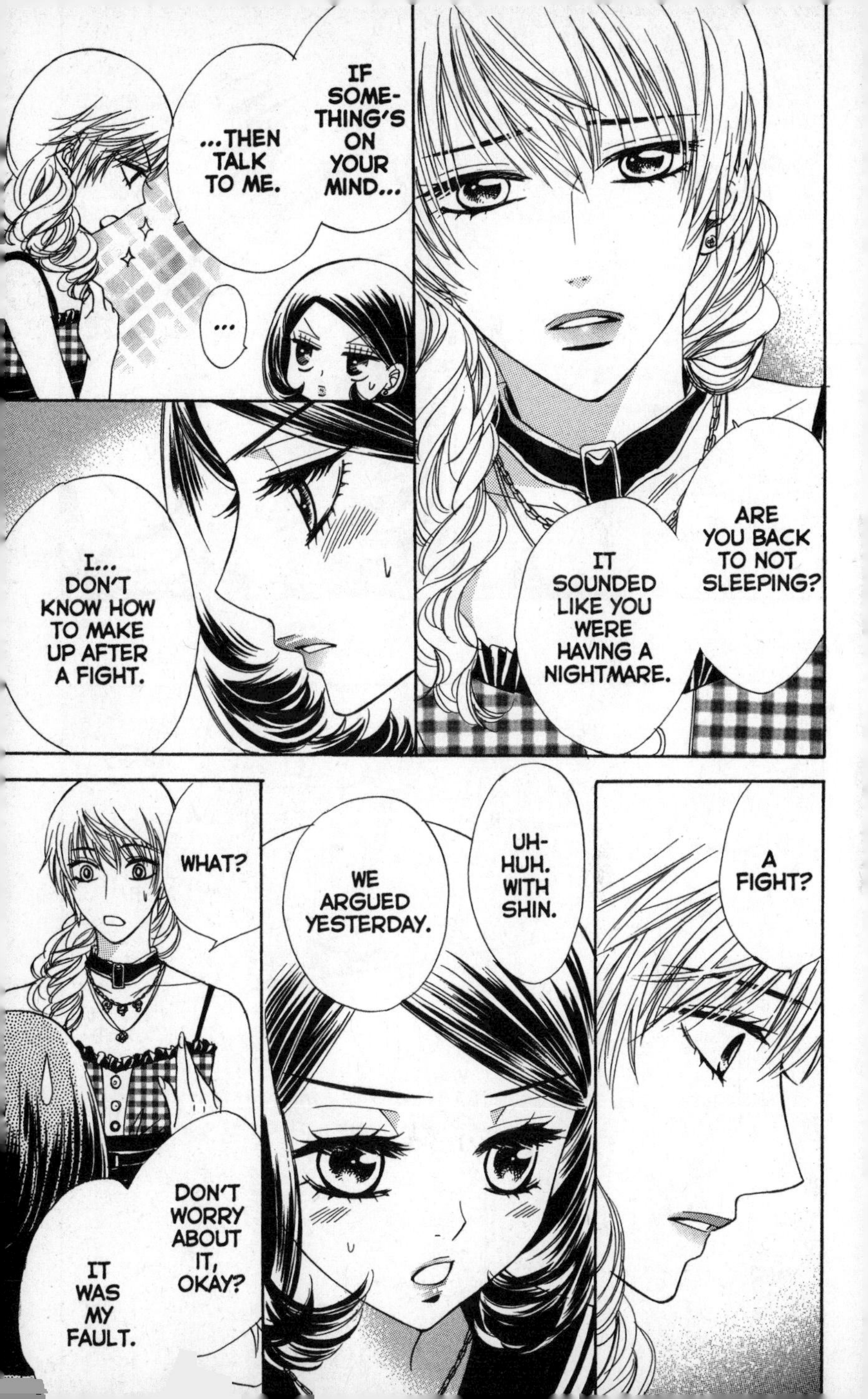
ARE YOU BACK TO NOT SLEEPING?
IT SOUNDED LIKE YOU WERE HAVING A NIGHTMARE.
IF SOMETHING'S ON YOUR MIND...
...THEN TALK TO ME.
...
I... DON'T KNOW HOW TO MAKE UP AFTER A FIGHT.
A FIGHT?
UH-HUH. WITH SHIN.
WE ARGUED YESTERDAY.
WHAT?
DON'T WORRY ABOUT IT, OKAY?
IT WAS MY FAULT.

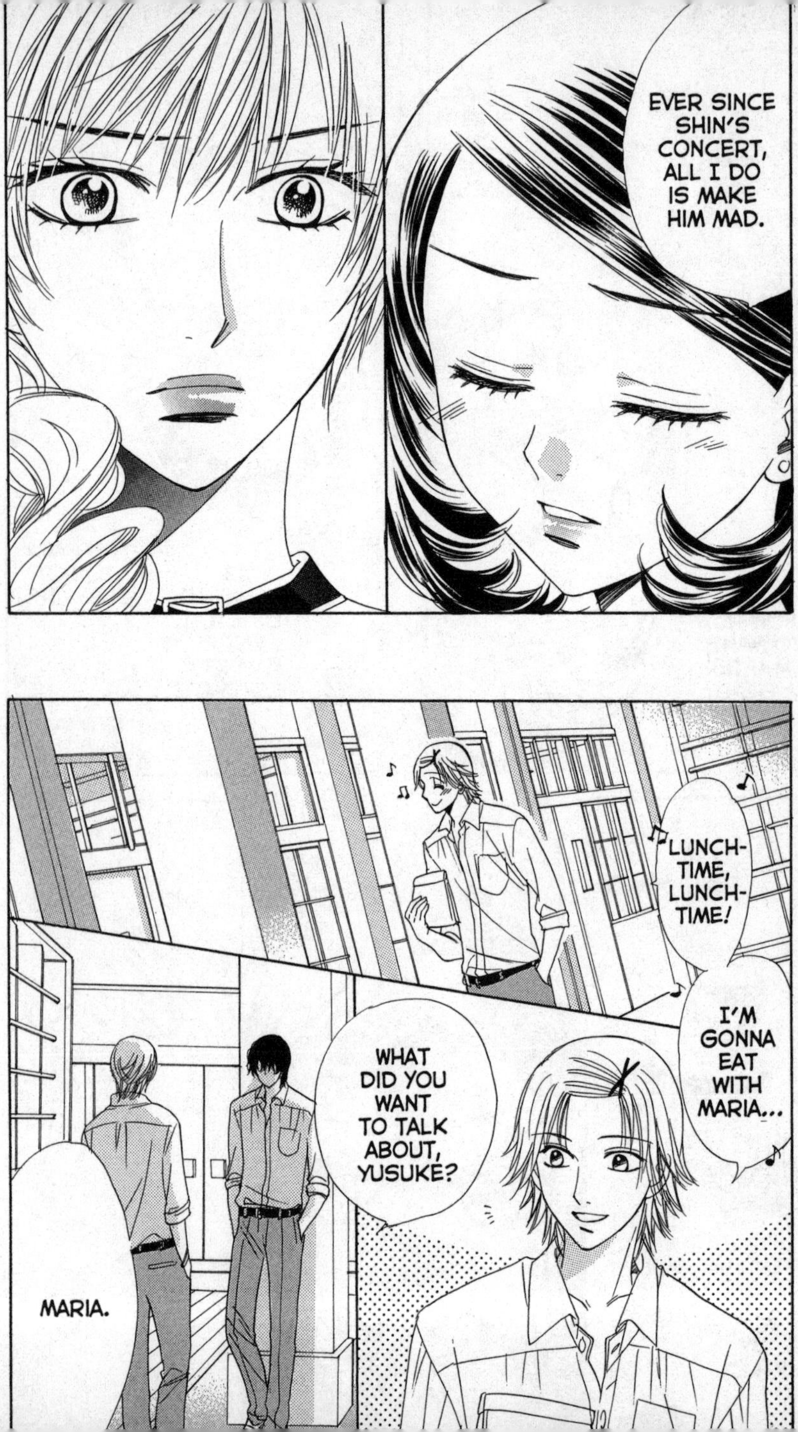
EVER SINCE SHIN'S CONCERT, ALL I DO IS MAKE HIM MAD.
LUNCH-TIME, LUNCH-TIME!
I'M GONNA EAT WITH MARIA...
WHAT DID YOU WANT TO TALK ABOUT, YUSUKE?
MARIA.

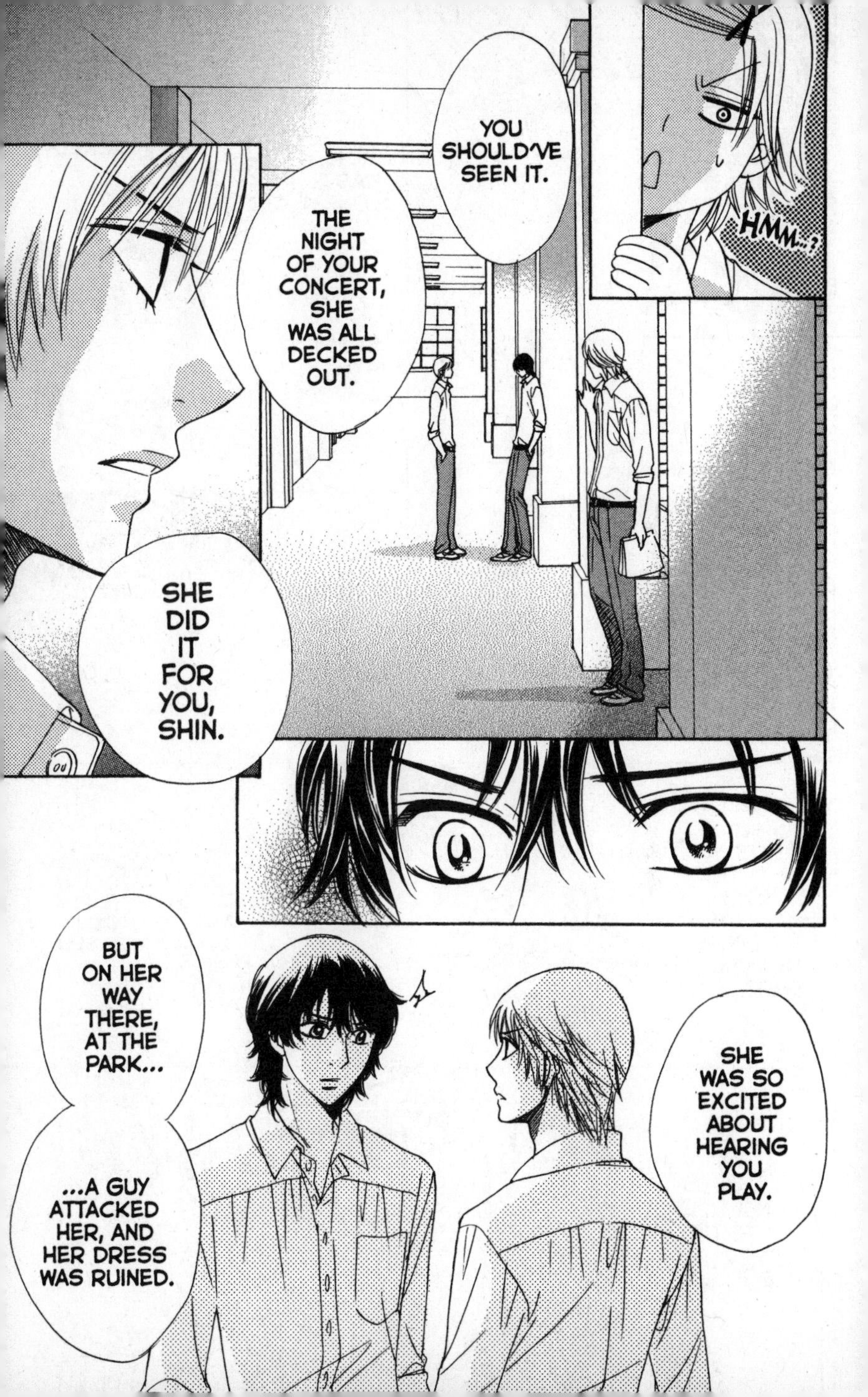
HMM...?
YOU SHOULD'VE SEEN IT.
THE NIGHT OF YOUR CONCERT, SHE WAS ALL DECKED OUT.
SHE DID IT FOR YOU, SHIN.
SHE WAS SO EXCITED ABOUT HEARING YOU PLAY.
BUT ON HER WAY THERE, AT THE PARK...
...A GUY ATTACKED HER, AND HER DRESS WAS RUINED.

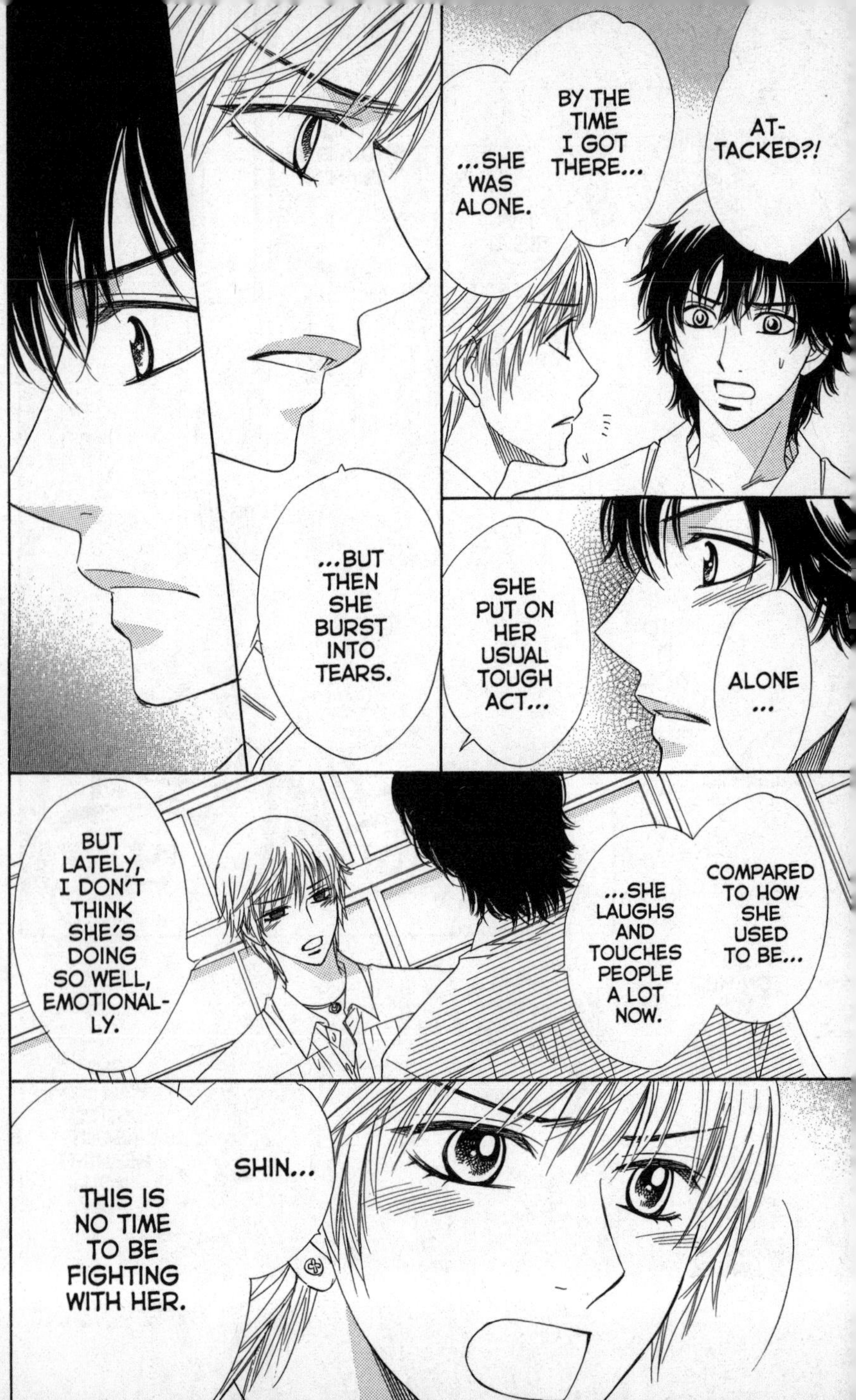

AT-TACKED?!
BY THE TIME I GOT THERE...
...SHE WAS ALONE.
ALONE...
SHE PUT ON HER USUAL TOUGH ACT...
...BUT THEN SHE BURST INTO TEARS.
COMPARED TO HOW SHE USED TO BE...
...SHE LAUGHS AND TOUCHES PEOPLE A LOT NOW.
BUT LATELY, I DON'T THINK SHE'S DOING SO WELL, EMOTIONALLY.
SHIN...
THIS IS NO TIME TO BE FIGHTING WITH HER.

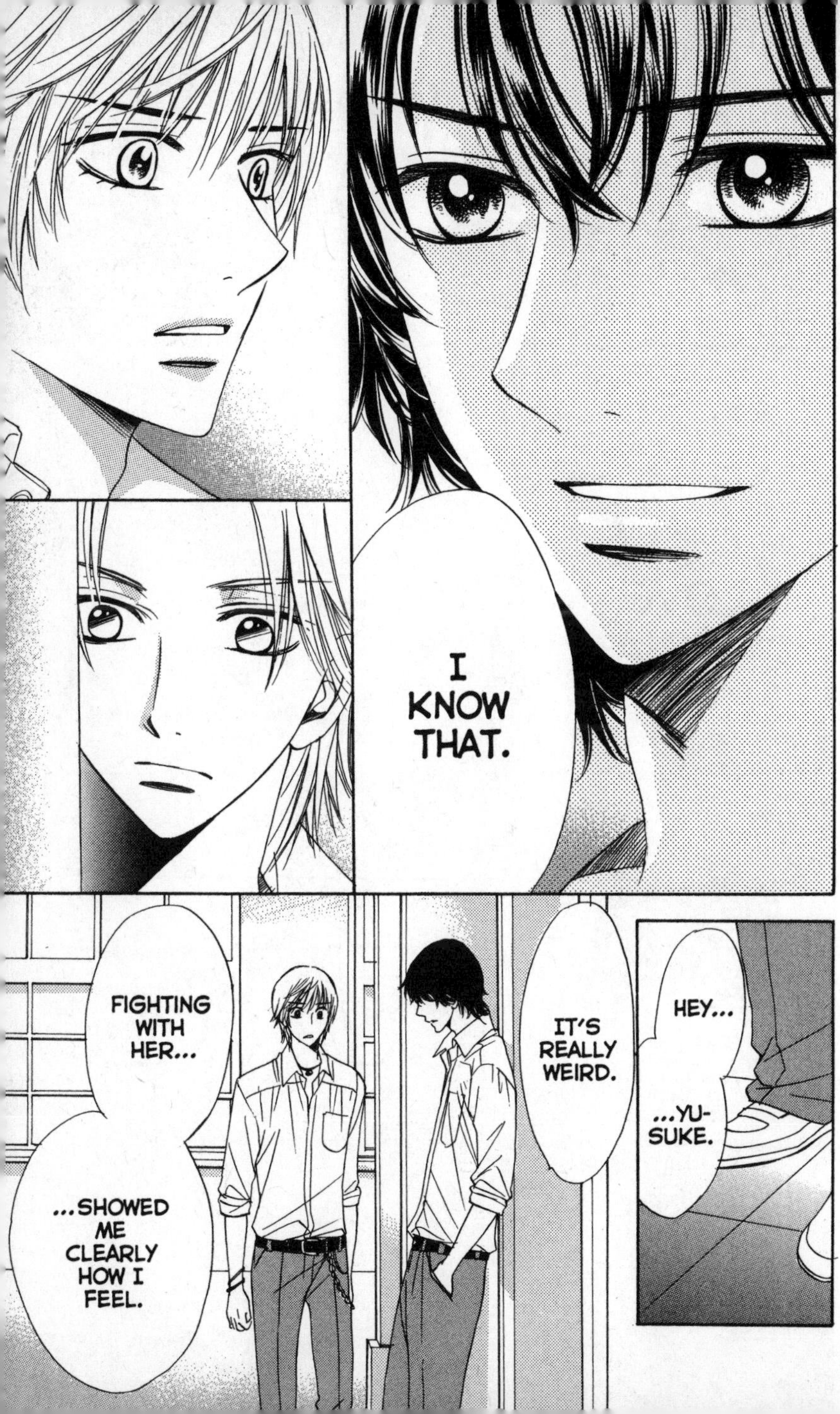
I KNOW THAT.
HEY...
...YU-SUKE.
IT'S REALLY WEIRD.
FIGHTING WITH HER...
...SHOWED ME CLEARLY HOW I FEEL.

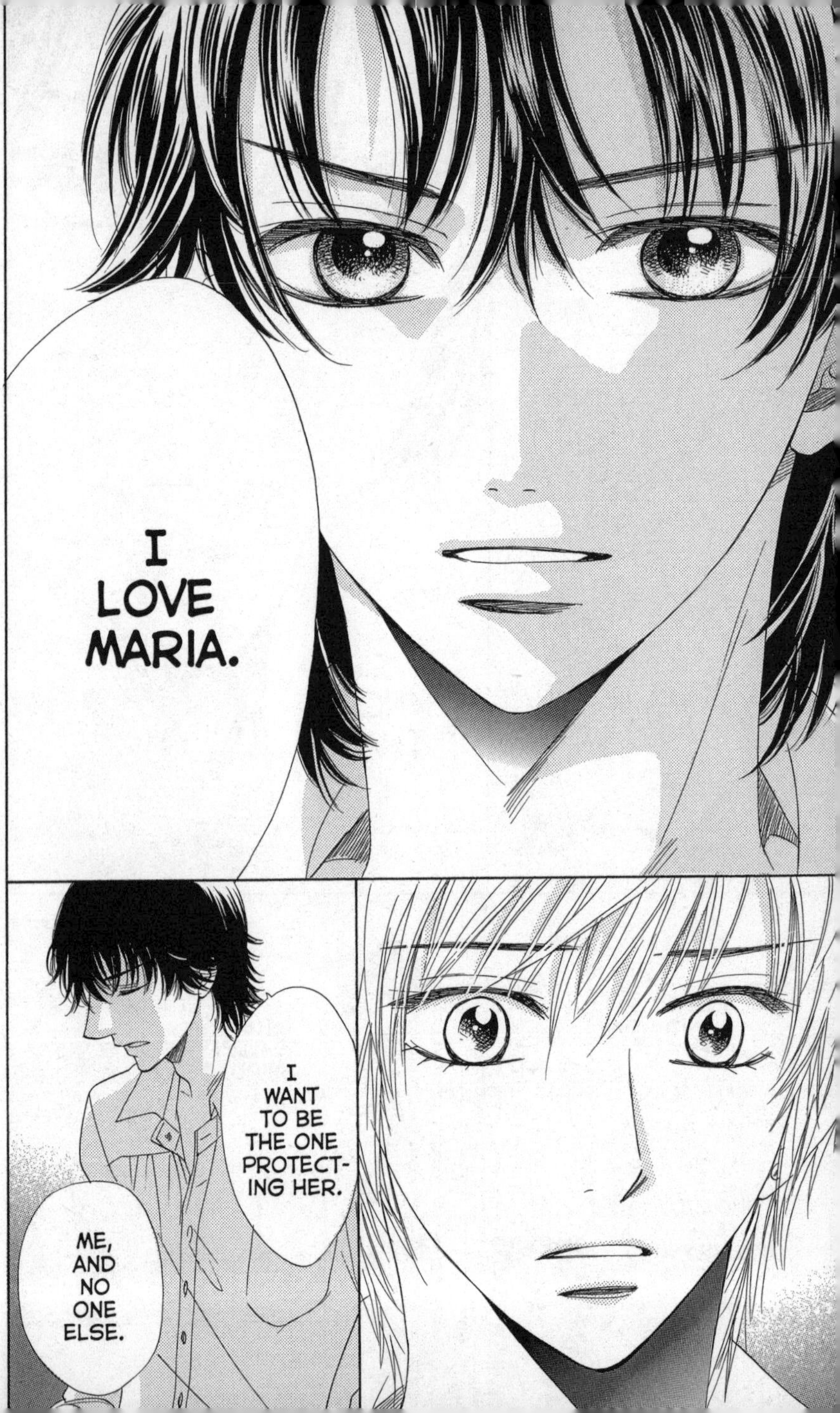
I LOVE MARIA.
I WANT TO BE THE ONE PROTECTING HER.
ME, AND NO ONE ELSE.

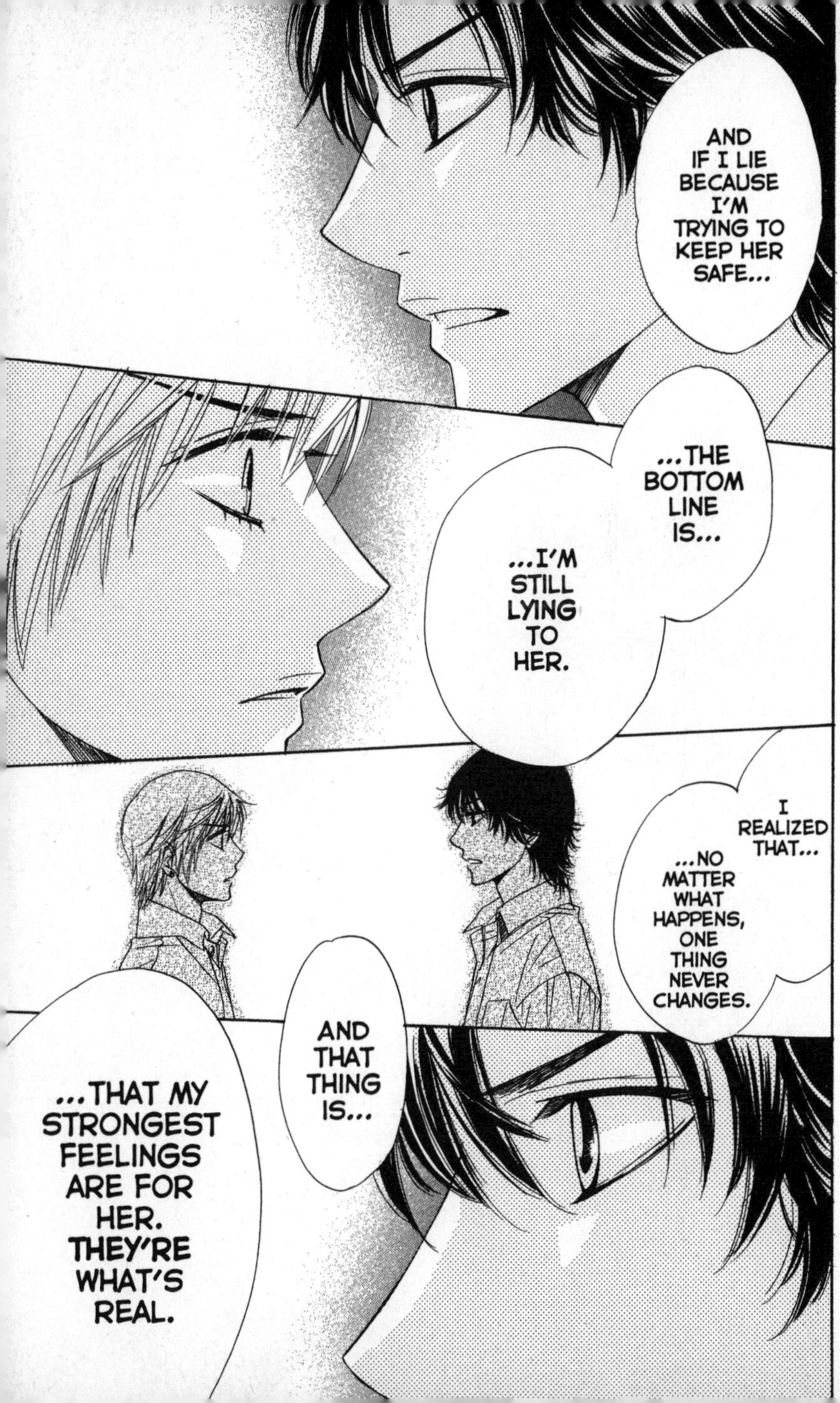
AND IF I LIE BECAUSE I'M TRYING TO KEEP HER SAFE...
...THE BOTTOM LINE IS...
...I'M STILL LYING TO HER.
I REALIZED THAT...
...NO MATTER WHAT HAPPENS, ONE THING NEVER CHANGES.
AND THAT THING IS...
...THAT MY STRONGEST FEELINGS ARE FOR HER. THEY'RE WHAT'S REAL.

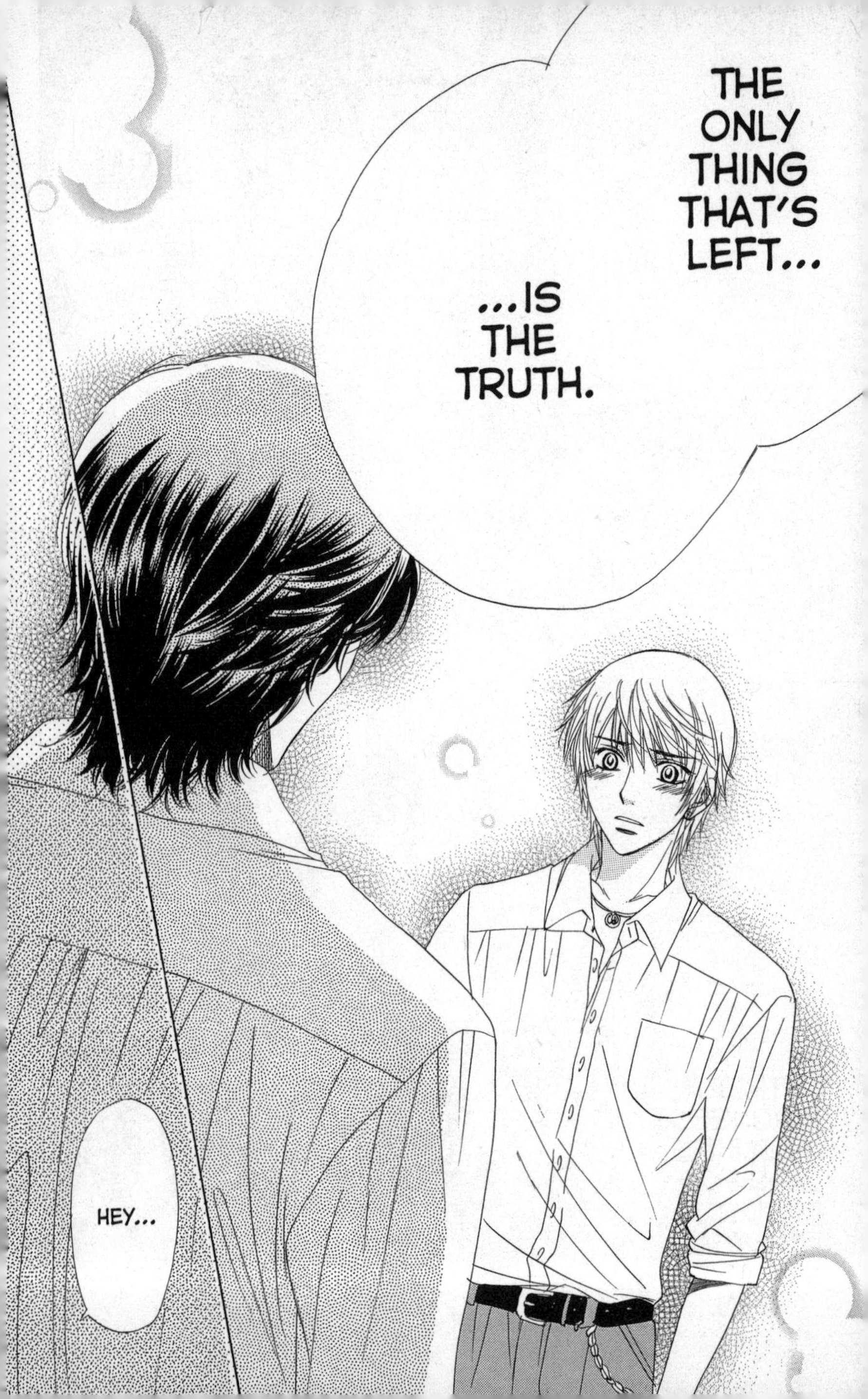
THE ONLY THING THAT'S LEFT...
...IS THE TRUTH.
HEY...

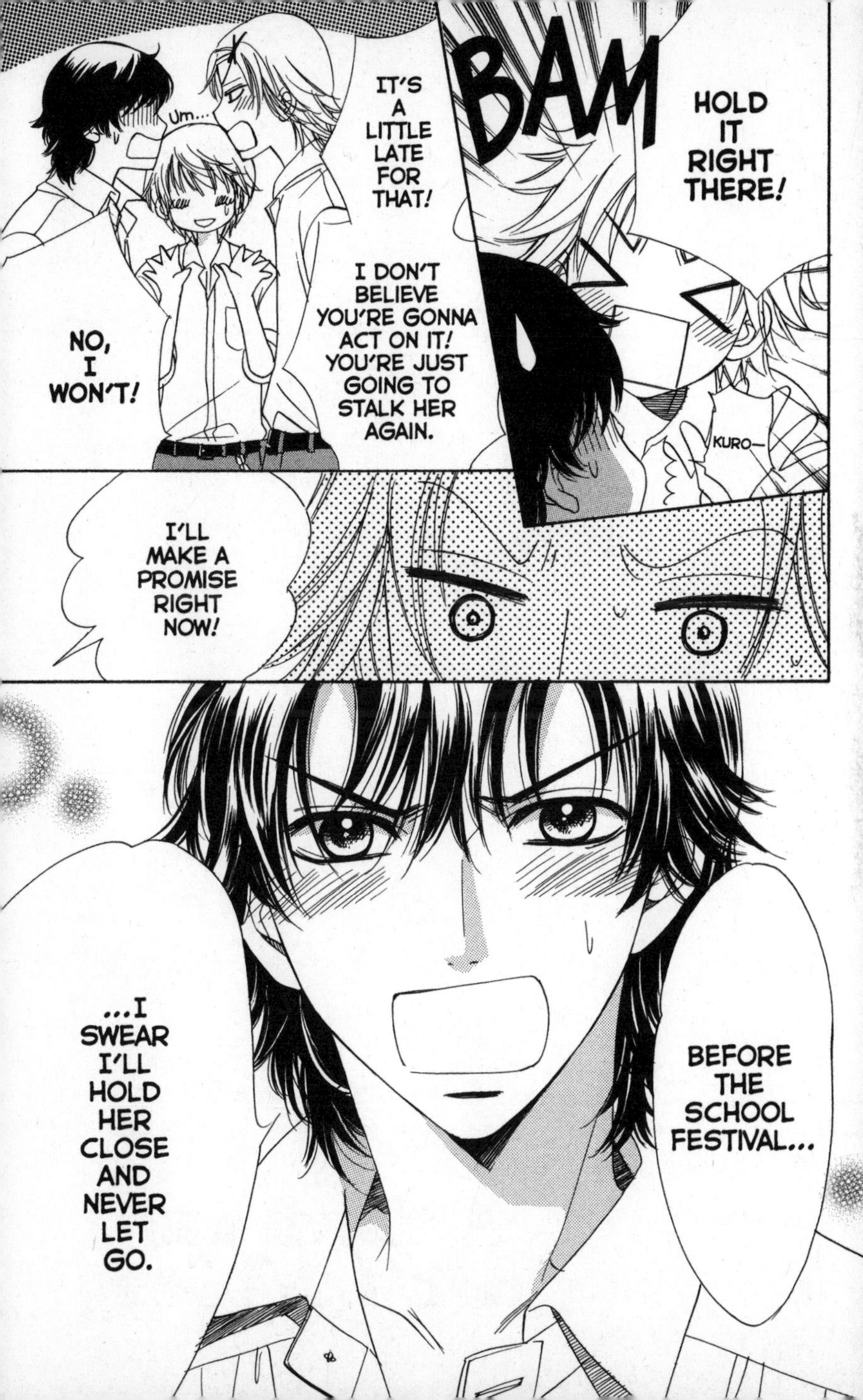
BAM
HOLD IT RIGHT THERE!
KURO—
IT'S A LITTLE LATE FOR THAT!
Um...
I DON'T BELIEVE YOU'RE GONNA ACT ON IT! YOU'RE JUST GOING TO STALK HER AGAIN.
NO, I WON'T!
I'LL MAKE A PROMISE RIGHT NOW!
BEFORE THE SCHOOL FESTIVAL...
...I SWEAR I'LL HOLD HER CLOSE AND NEVER LET GO.

A Devil and
Her Love Song

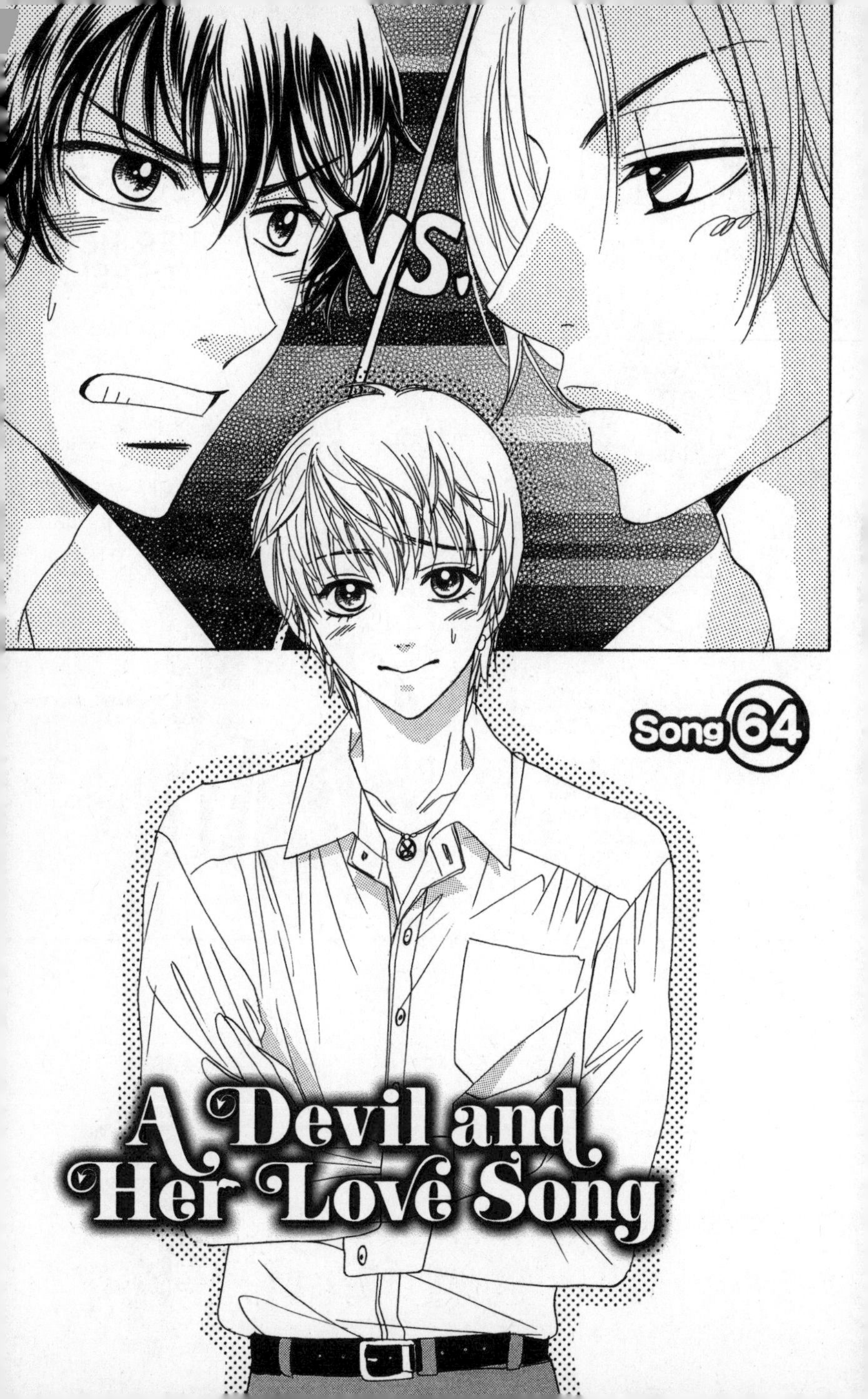
VS.
Song 64
A Devil and Her Love Song

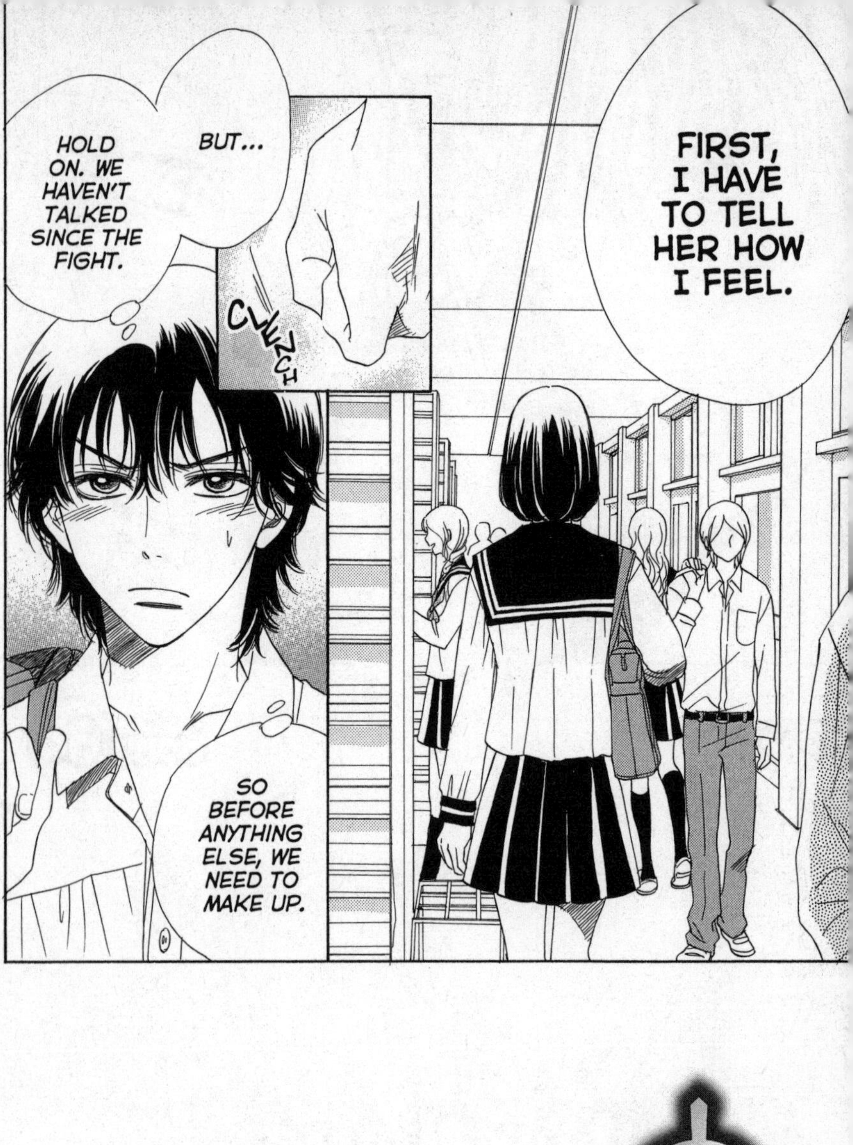
FIRST, I HAVE TO TELL HER HOW I FEEL.
CLENCH
BUT...
HOLD ON. WE HAVEN'T TALKED SINCE THE FIGHT.
SO BEFORE ANYTHING ELSE, WE NEED TO MAKE UP.

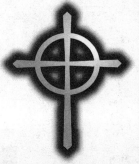

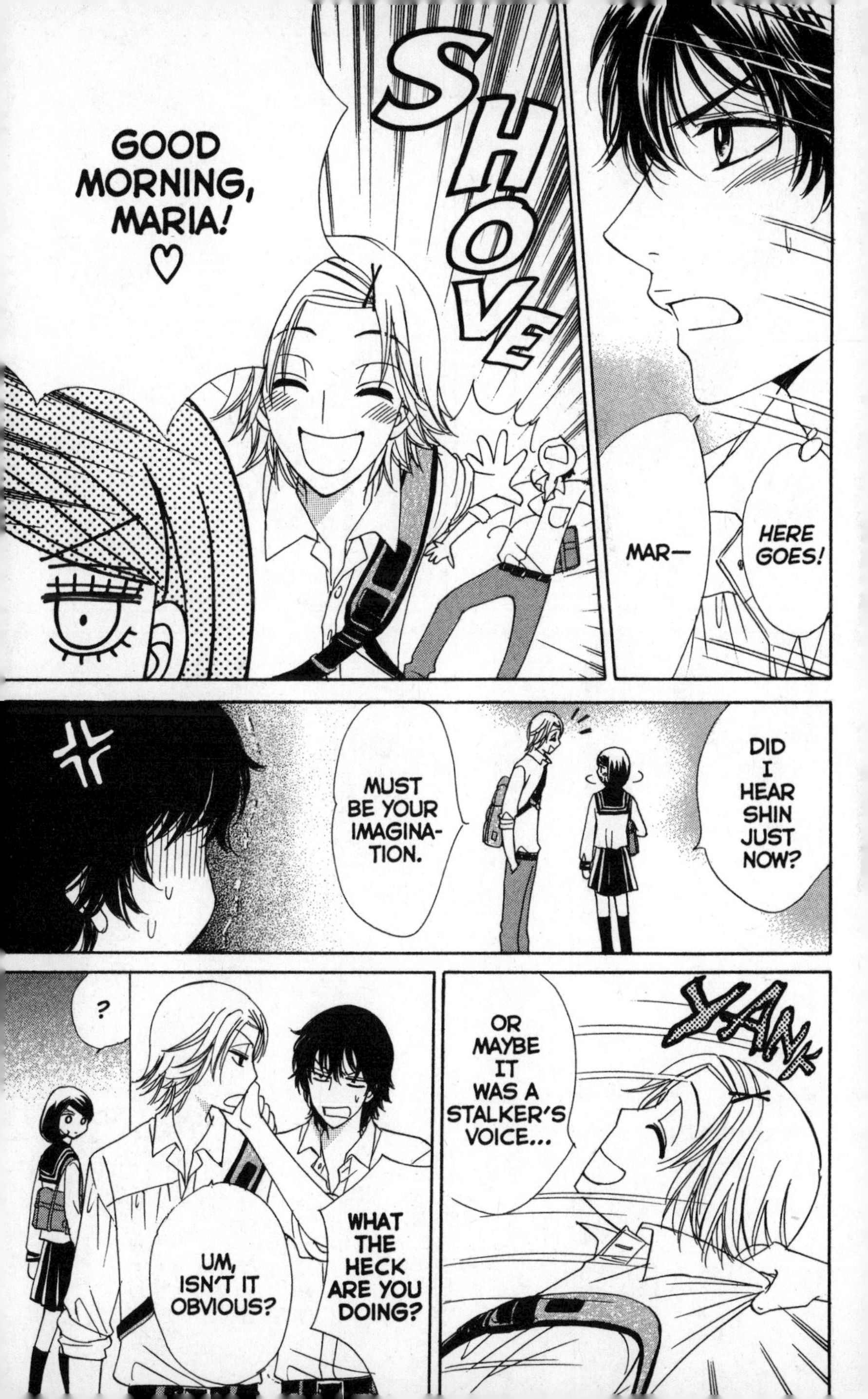
HERE GOES!
MAR—
SHOVE
GOOD MORNING, MARIA! ♡
DID I HEAR SHIN JUST NOW?
MUST BE YOUR IMAGINATION.
YANK
OR MAYBE IT WAS A STALKER'S VOICE...
?
WHAT THE HECK ARE YOU DOING?
UM, ISN'T IT OBVIOUS?

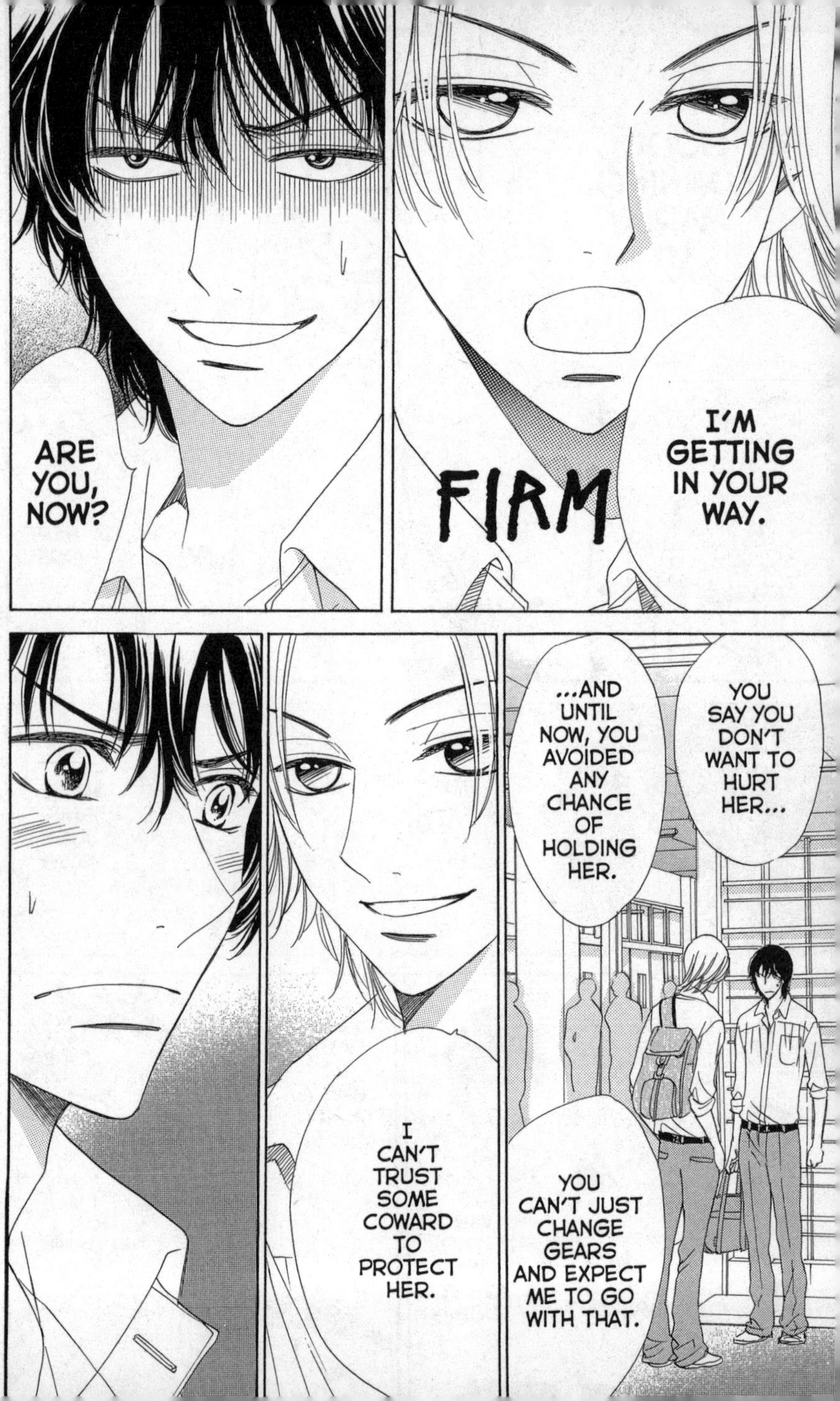
I'M GETTING IN YOUR WAY.
FIRM
ARE YOU, NOW?
YOU SAY YOU DON'T WANT TO HURT HER...
...AND UNTIL NOW, YOU AVOIDED ANY CHANCE OF HOLDING HER.
YOU CAN'T JUST CHANGE GEARS AND EXPECT ME TO GO WITH THAT.
I CAN'T TRUST SOME COWARD TO PROTECT HER.

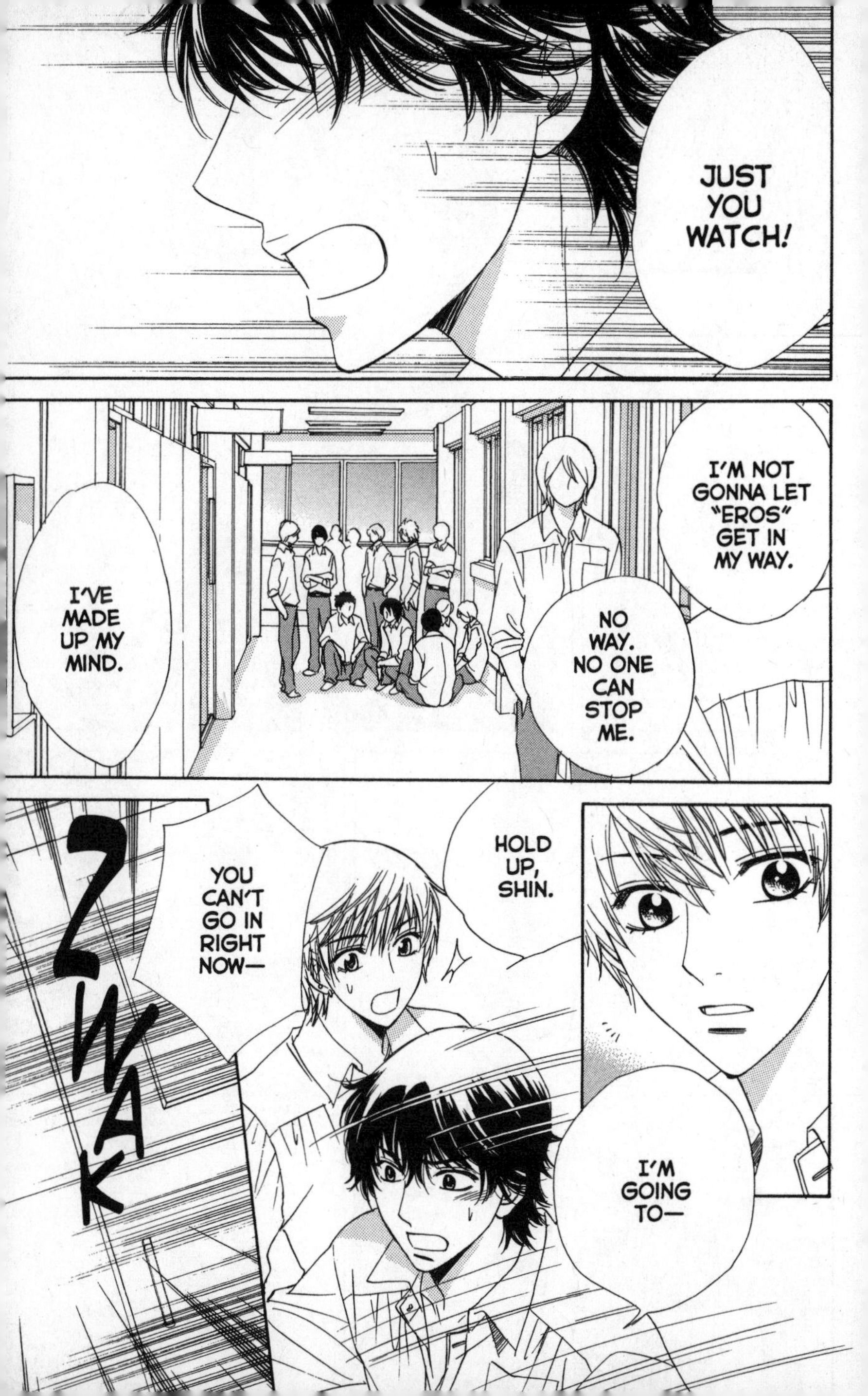
JUST YOU WATCH!
I'M NOT GONNA LET "EROS" GET IN MY WAY.
NO WAY. NO ONE CAN STOP ME.
I'VE MADE UP MY MIND.
HOLD UP, SHIN.
YOU CAN'T GO IN RIGHT NOW—
I'M GOING TO—
ZWAK

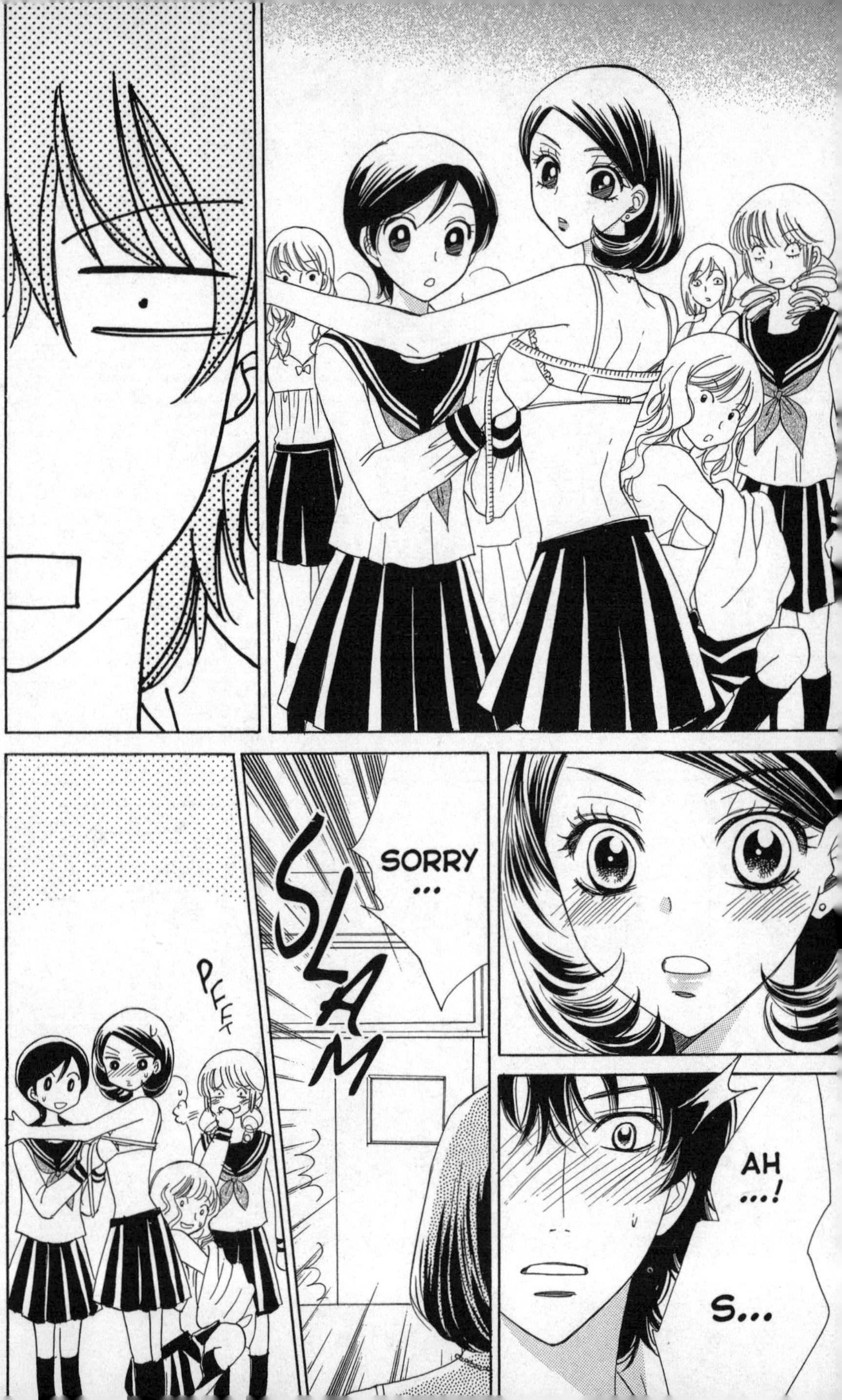
AH ...!
S...
SORRY ...
SLAM
PFFT

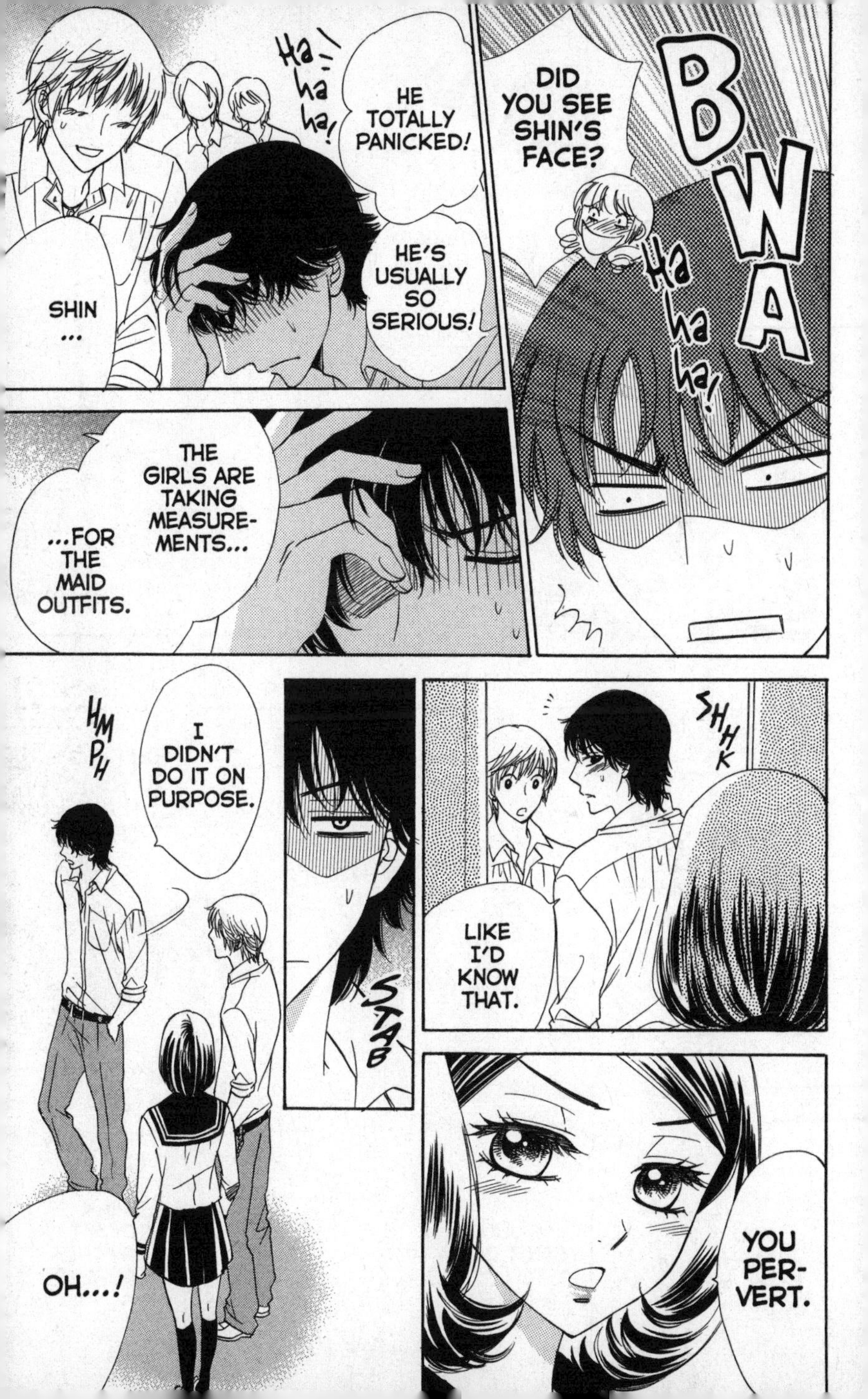
BWA
Ha ha ha!
DID YOU SEE SHIN'S FACE?
Ha ha ha!
HE TOTALLY PANICKED!
HE'S USUALLY SO SERIOUS!
SHIN...
THE GIRLS ARE TAKING MEASUREMENTS...
...FOR THE MAID OUTFITS.
SHHK
LIKE I'D KNOW THAT.
YOU PERVERT.
STAB
HMPH
I DIDN'T DO IT ON PURPOSE.
OH...!

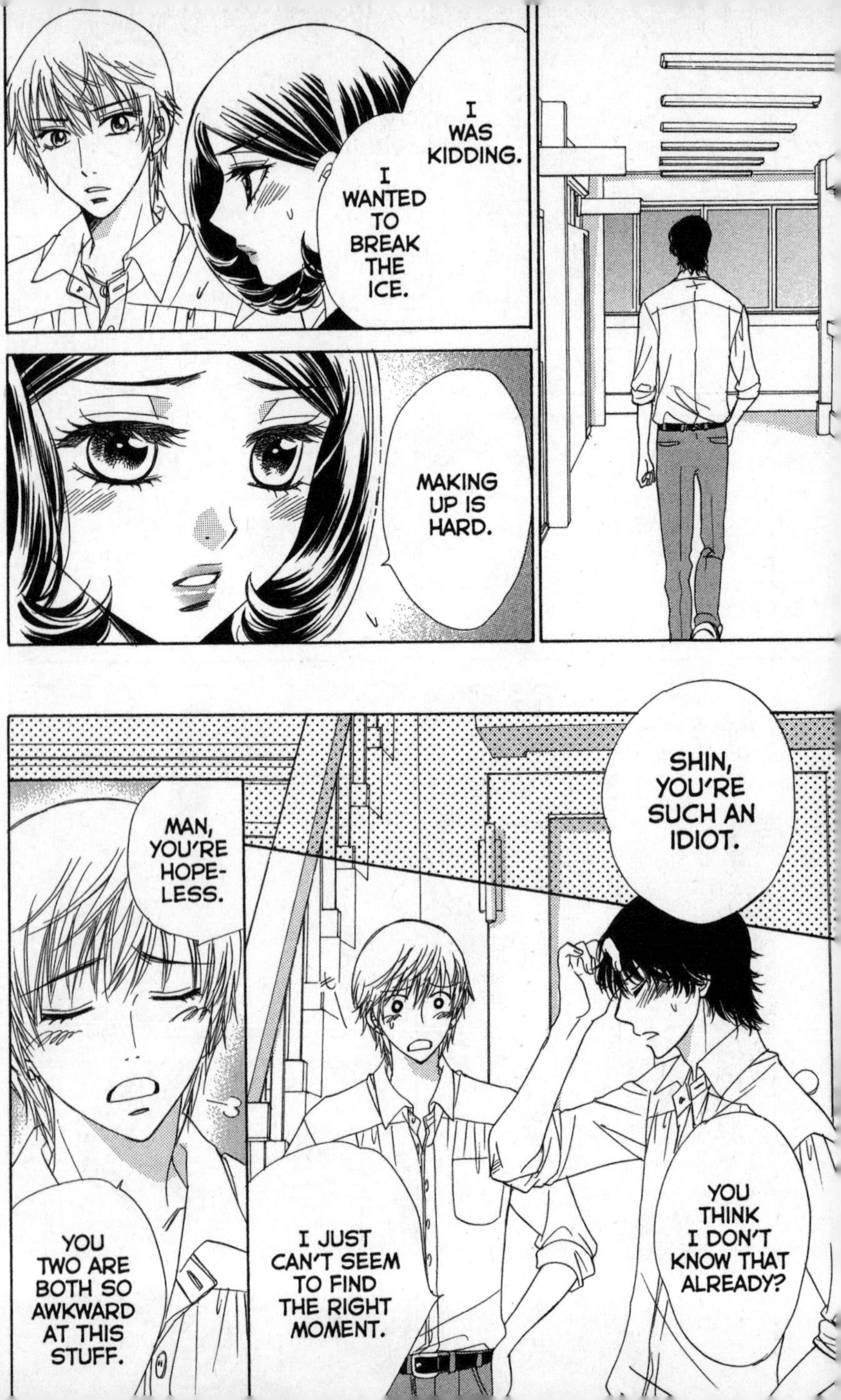
I WAS KIDDING.
I WANTED TO BREAK THE ICE.
MAKING UP IS HARD.
SHIN, YOU'RE SUCH AN IDIOT.
YOU THINK I DON'T KNOW THAT ALREADY?
MAN, YOU'RE HOPE-LESS.
I JUST CAN'T SEEM TO FIND THE RIGHT MOMENT.
YOU TWO ARE BOTH SO AWKWARD AT THIS STUFF.

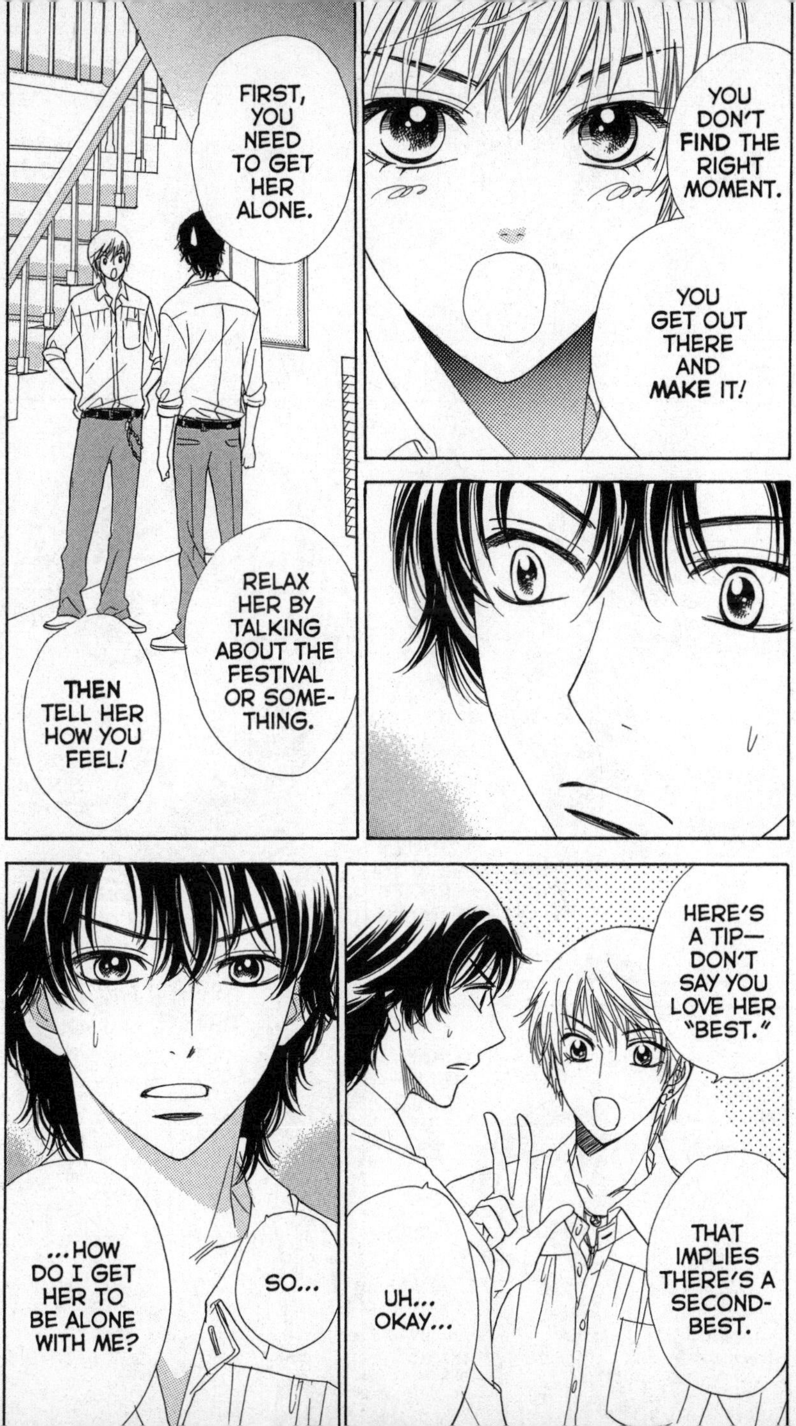
YOU DON'T FIND THE RIGHT MOMENT.
YOU GET OUT THERE AND MAKE IT!
FIRST, YOU NEED TO GET HER ALONE.
RELAX HER BY TALKING ABOUT THE FESTIVAL OR SOME-THING.
THEN TELL HER HOW YOU FEEL!
HERE'S A TIP—DON'T SAY YOU LOVE HER "BEST."
THAT IMPLIES THERE'S A SECOND-BEST.
UH... OKAY...
SO...
...HOW DO I GET HER TO BE ALONE WITH ME?

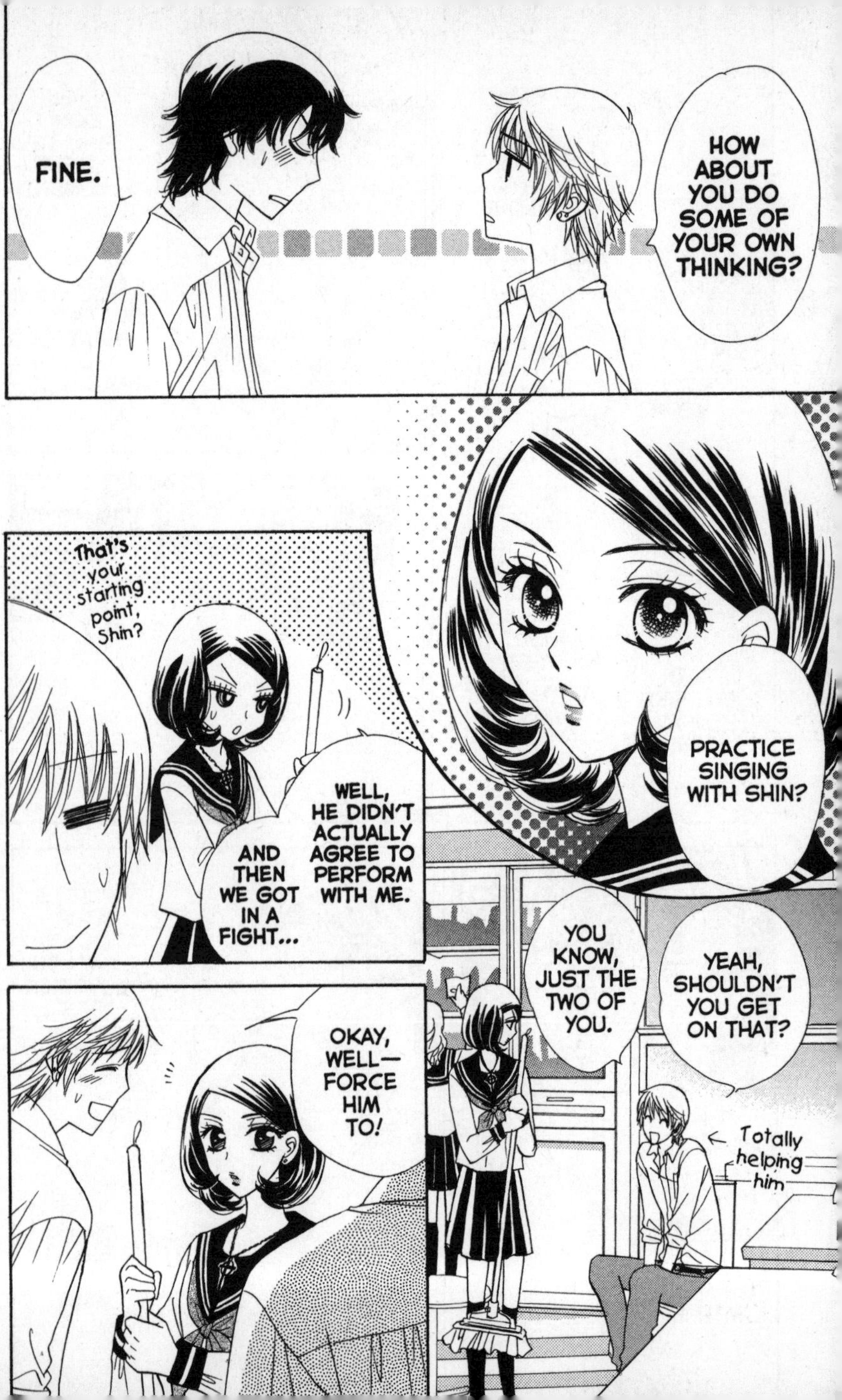
HOW ABOUT YOU DO SOME OF YOUR OWN THINKING?
FINE.
PRACTICE SINGING WITH SHIN?
YEAH, SHOULDN'T YOU GET ON THAT?
YOU KNOW, JUST THE TWO OF YOU.
Totally helping him
That's your starting point, Shin?
WELL, HE DIDN'T ACTUALLY AGREE TO PERFORM WITH ME.
AND THEN WE GOT IN A FIGHT...
OKAY, WELL— FORCE HIM TO!

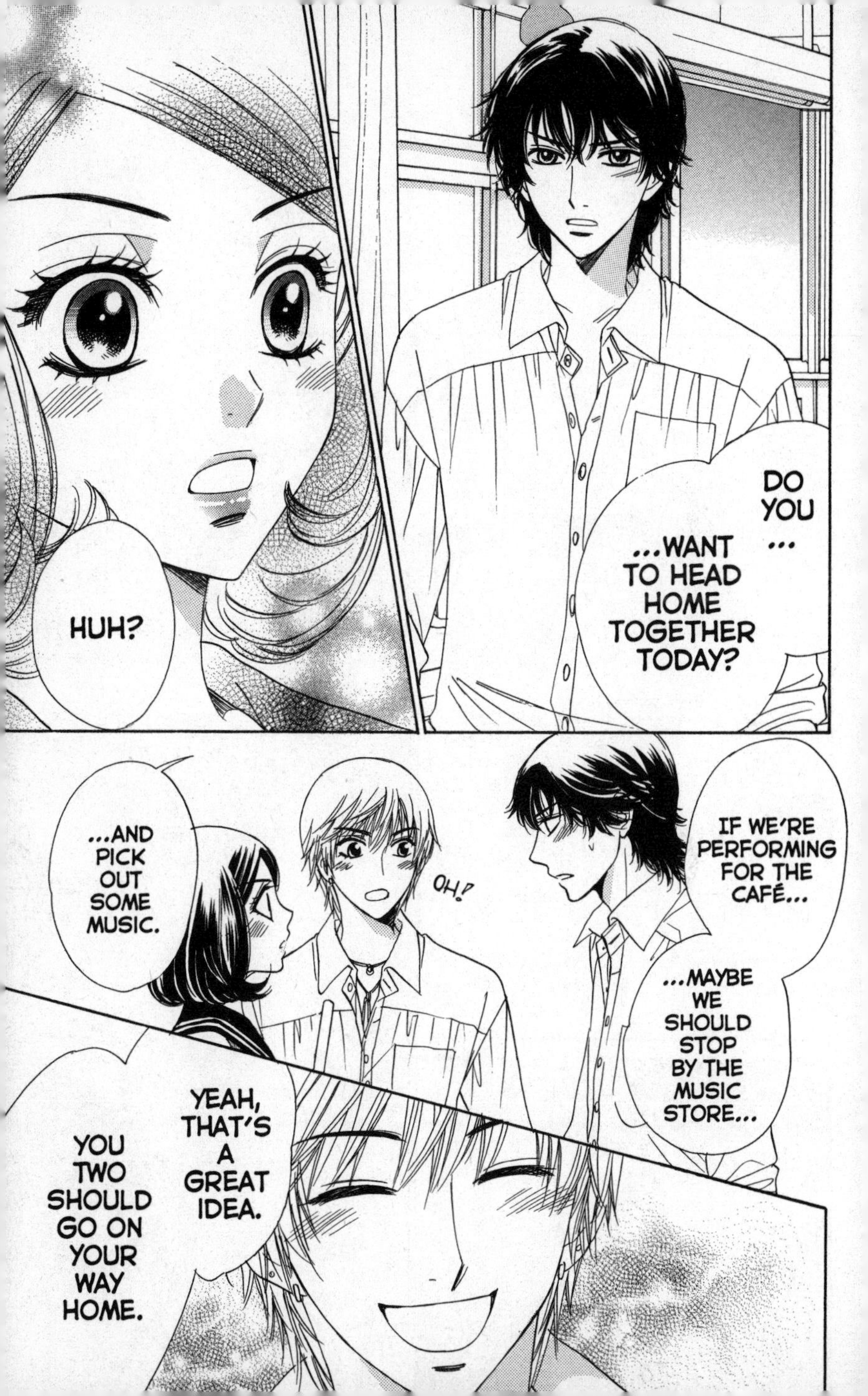
DO YOU...
...WANT TO HEAD HOME TOGETHER TODAY?
HUH?
IF WE'RE PERFORMING FOR THE CAFÉ...
...MAYBE WE SHOULD STOP BY THE MUSIC STORE...
OH!
...AND PICK OUT SOME MUSIC.
YEAH, THAT'S A GREAT IDEA.
YOU TWO SHOULD GO ON YOUR WAY HOME.

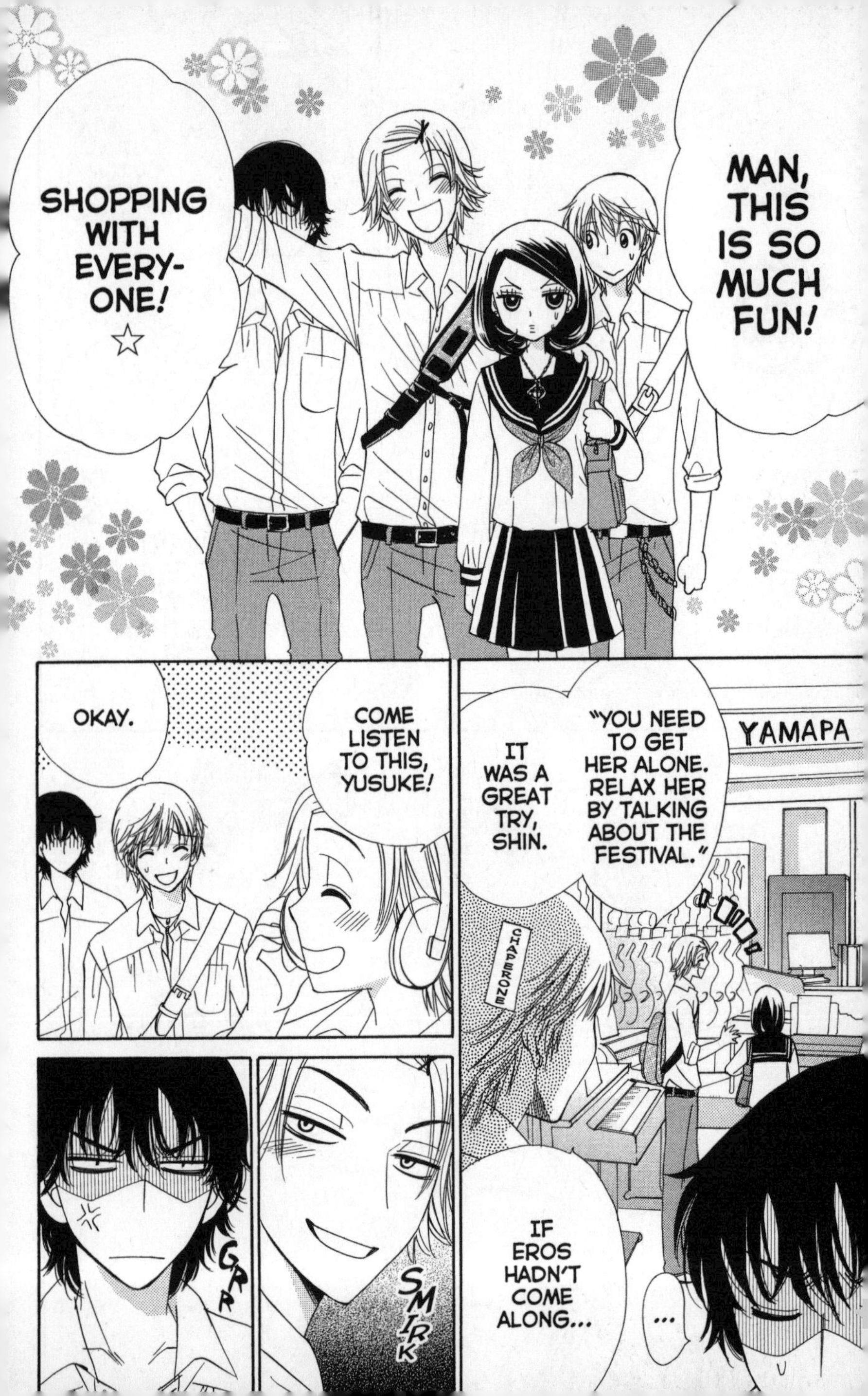
MAN, THIS IS SO MUCH FUN!
SHOPPING WITH EVERY-ONE! ☆
YAMAPA
"YOU NEED TO GET HER ALONE. RELAX HER BY TALKING ABOUT THE FESTIVAL."
IT WAS A GREAT TRY, SHIN.
CHAPERONE
IF EROS HADN'T COME ALONG...
...
COME LISTEN TO THIS, YUSUKE!
OKAY.
SMIRK
GRR

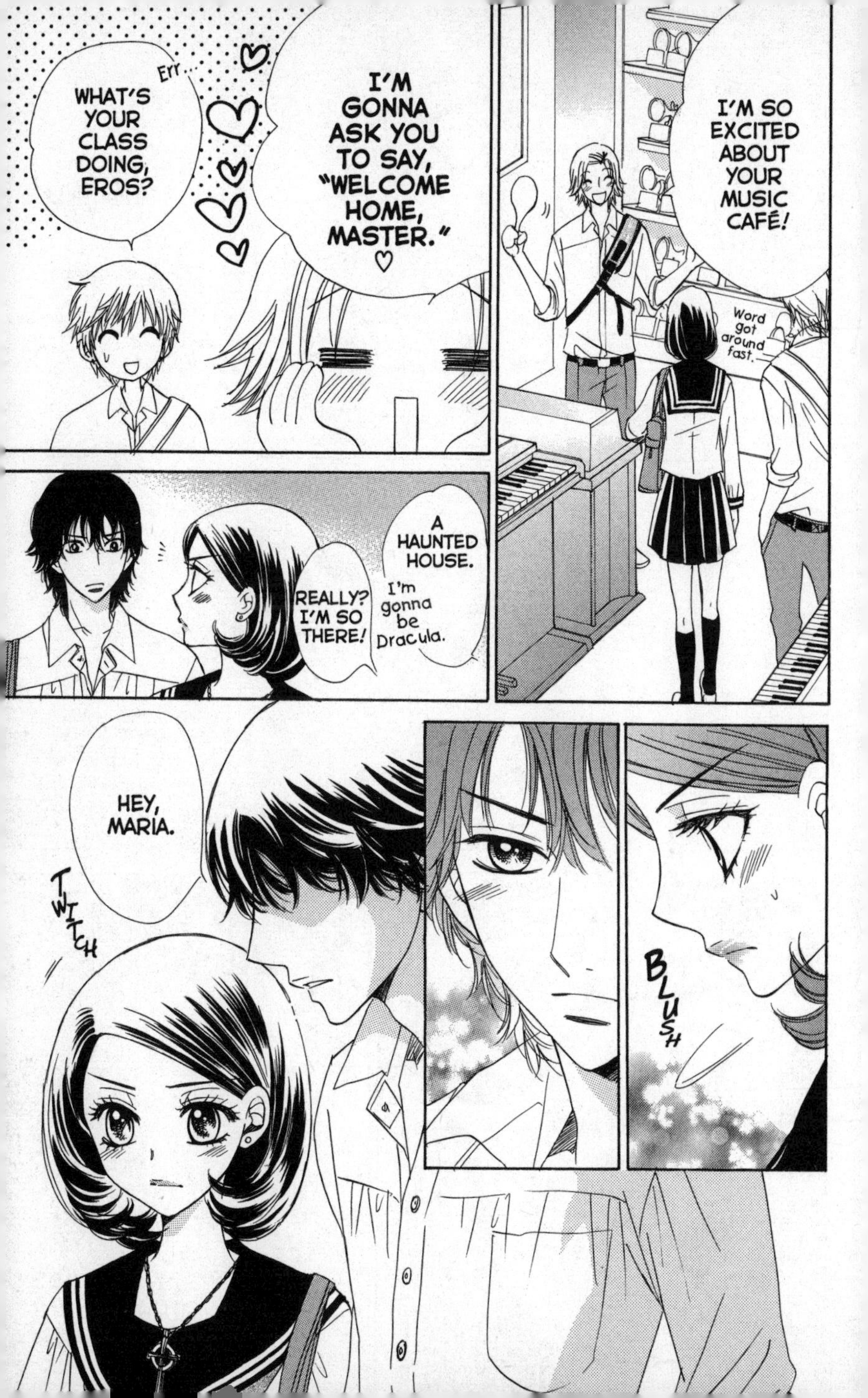
I'M SO EXCITED ABOUT YOUR MUSIC CAFÉ!
Word got around fast.
I'M GONNA ASK YOU TO SAY, "WELCOME HOME, MASTER." ♡
Err...
WHAT'S YOUR CLASS DOING, EROS?
A HAUNTED HOUSE.
I'm gonna be Dracula.
REALLY? I'M SO THERE!
BLUSH
HEY, MARIA.
TWITCH

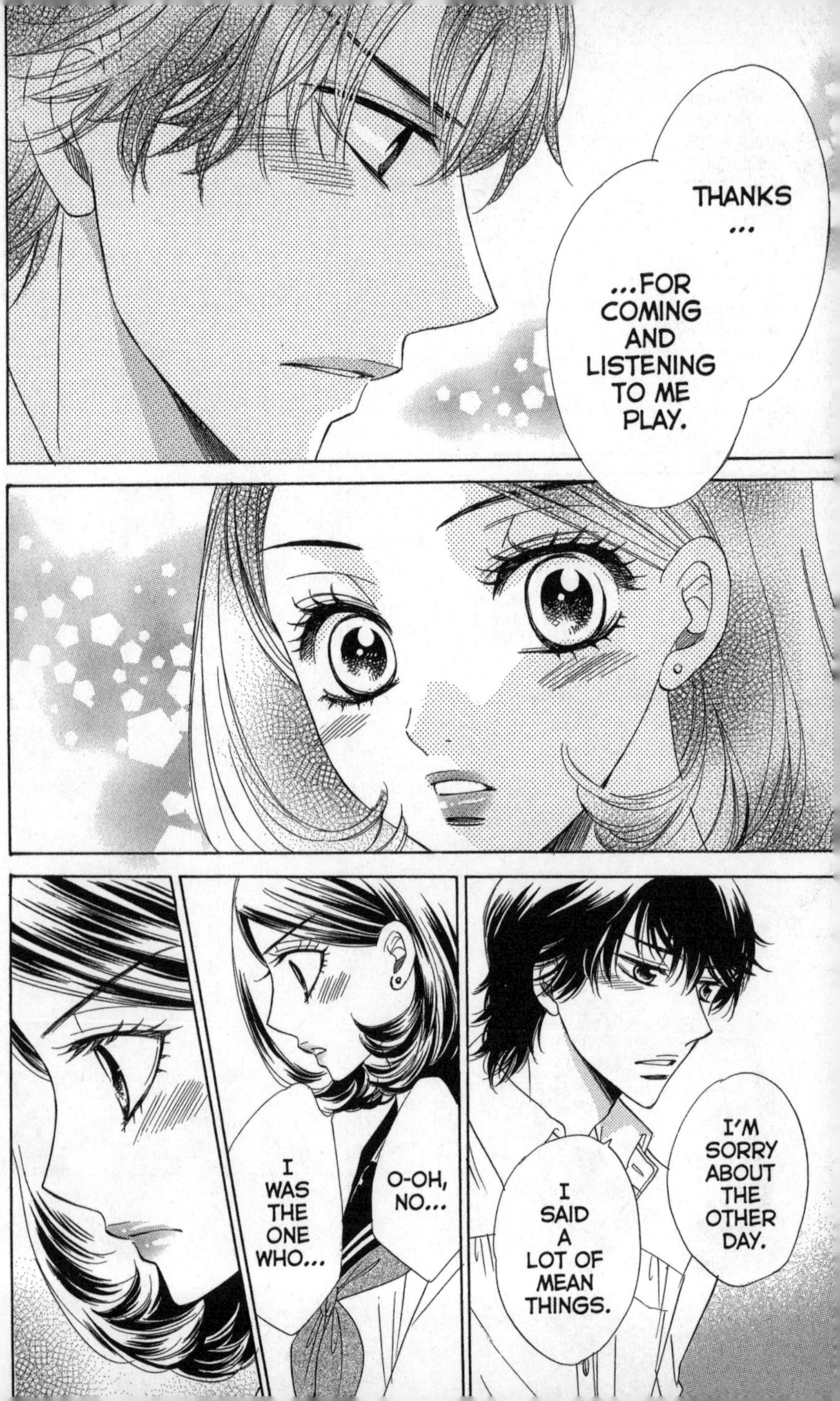
THANKS...
...FOR COMING AND LISTENING TO ME PLAY.
I'M SORRY ABOUT THE OTHER DAY.
I SAID A LOT OF MEAN THINGS.
O-OH, NO...
I WAS THE ONE WHO...

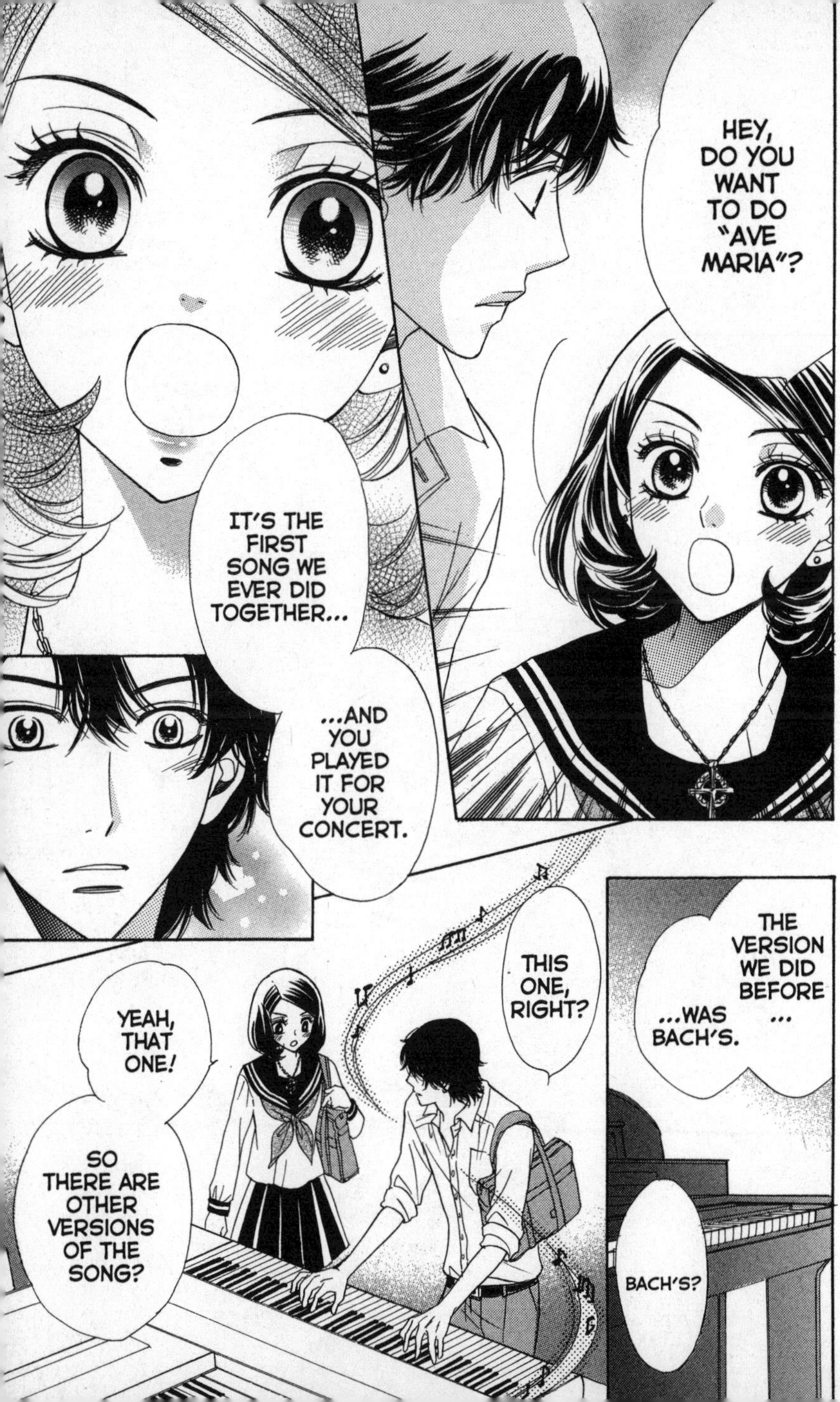
HEY, DO YOU WANT TO DO "AVE MARIA"?
IT'S THE FIRST SONG WE EVER DID TOGETHER...
...AND YOU PLAYED IT FOR YOUR CONCERT.
THE VERSION WE DID BEFORE ...
...WAS BACH'S.
BACH'S?
THIS ONE, RIGHT?
YEAH, THAT ONE!
SO THERE ARE OTHER VERSIONS OF THE SONG?

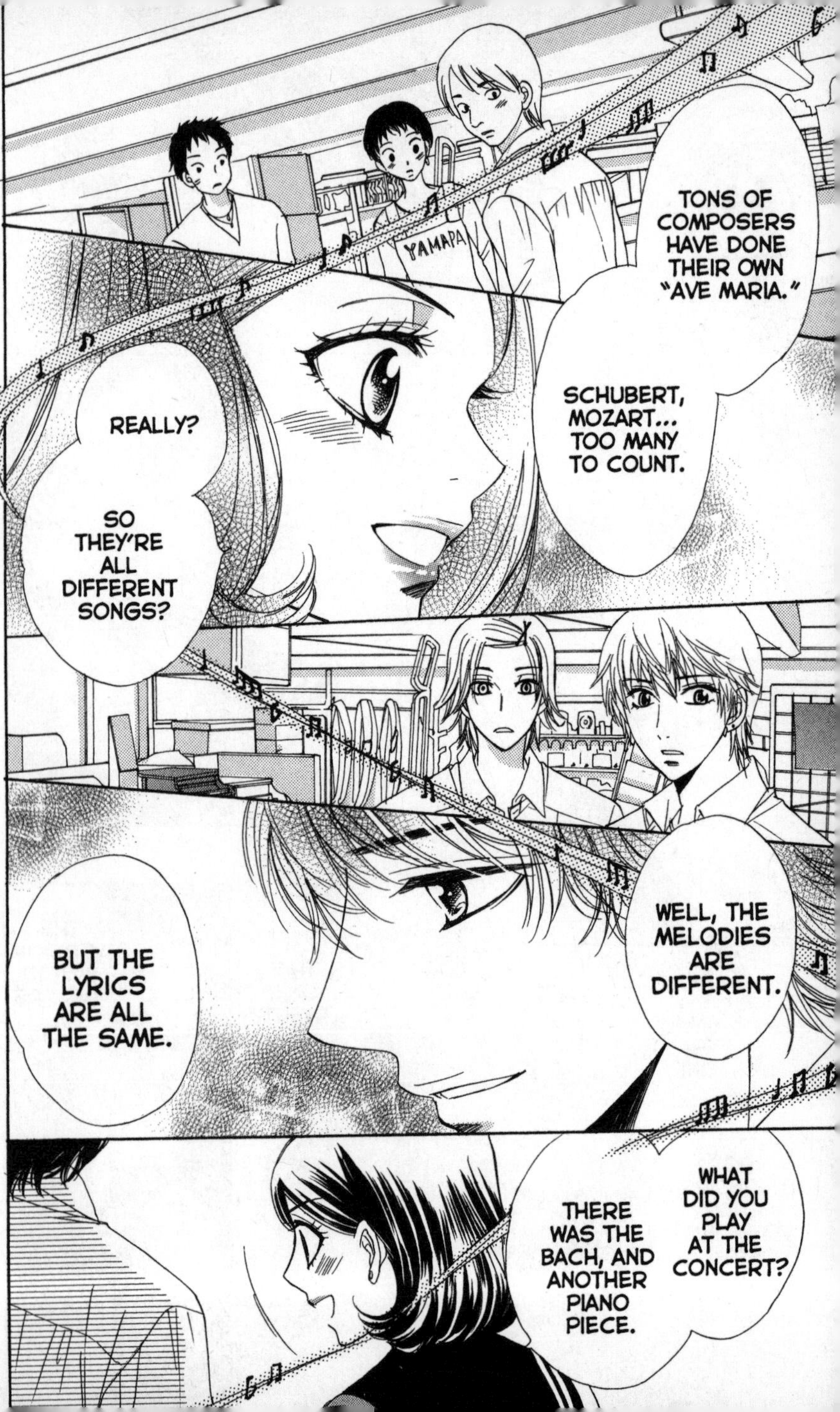
TONS OF COMPOSERS HAVE DONE THEIR OWN "AVE MARIA."
YAMAPA
SCHUBERT, MOZART... TOO MANY TO COUNT.
REALLY?
SO THEY'RE ALL DIFFERENT SONGS?
WELL, THE MELODIES ARE DIFFERENT.
BUT THE LYRICS ARE ALL THE SAME.
WHAT DID YOU PLAY AT THE CONCERT?
THERE WAS THE BACH, AND ANOTHER PIANO PIECE.

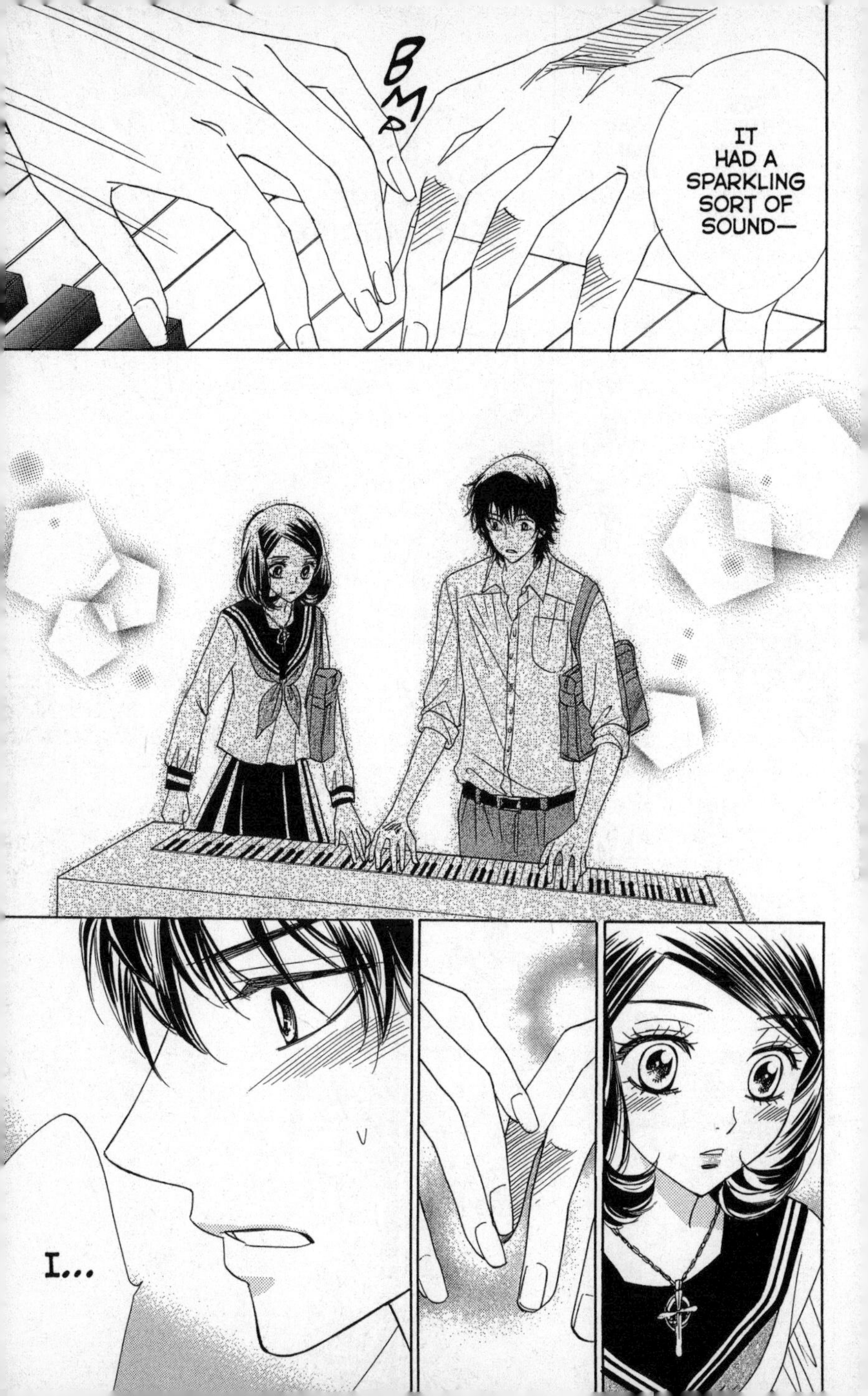
BMP
IT HAD A SPARKLING SORT OF SOUND—
I...

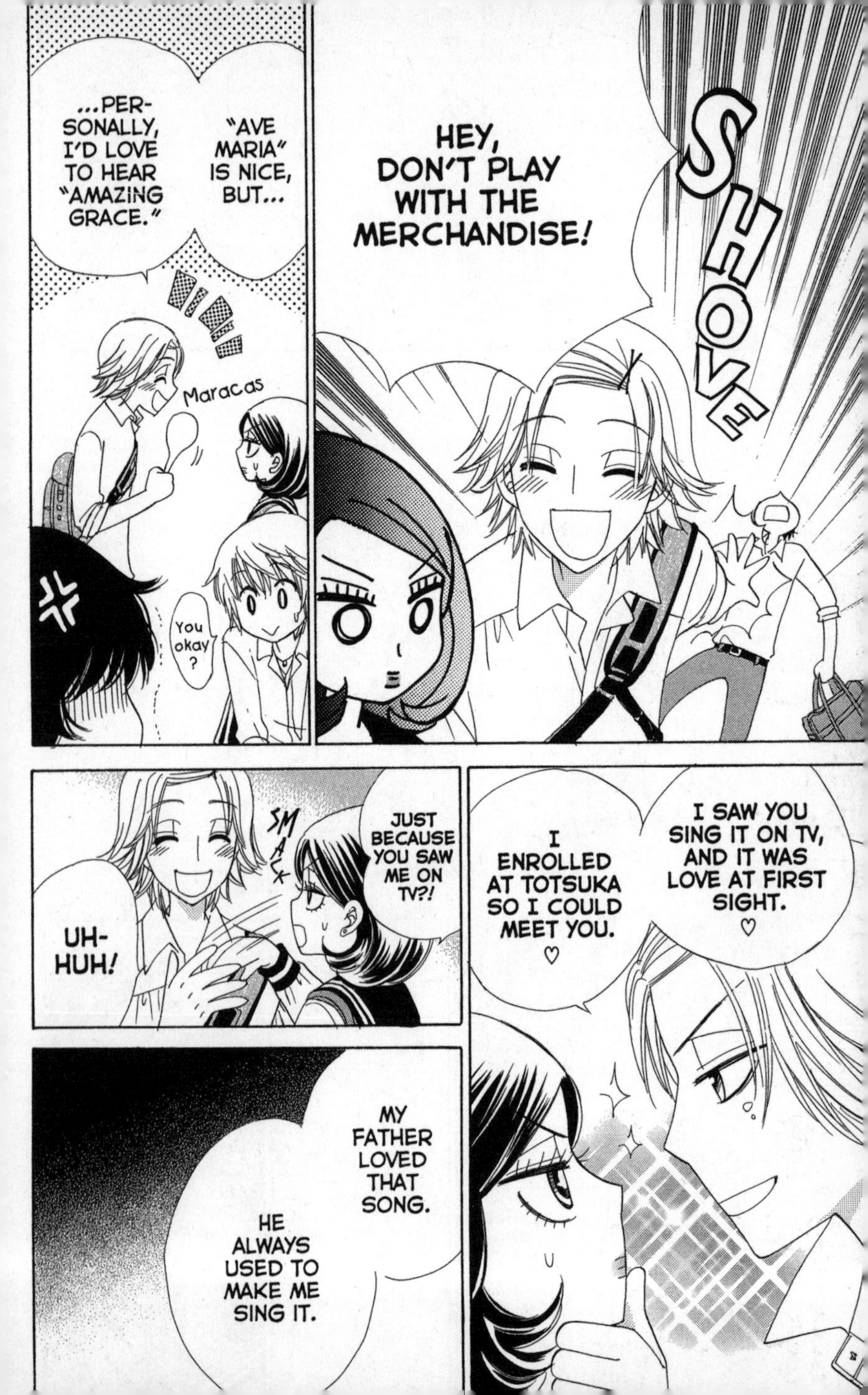
SHOVE
HEY, DON'T PLAY WITH THE MERCHANDISE!
"AVE MARIA" IS NICE, BUT...
...PERSONALLY, I'D LOVE TO HEAR "AMAZING GRACE."
Maracas
You okay?
I SAW YOU SING IT ON TV, AND IT WAS LOVE AT FIRST SIGHT. ♡
I ENROLLED AT TOTSUKA SO I COULD MEET YOU. ♡
JUST BECAUSE YOU SAW ME ON TV?!
SMACK
UH-HUH!
MY FATHER LOVED THAT SONG.
HE ALWAYS USED TO MAKE ME SING IT.

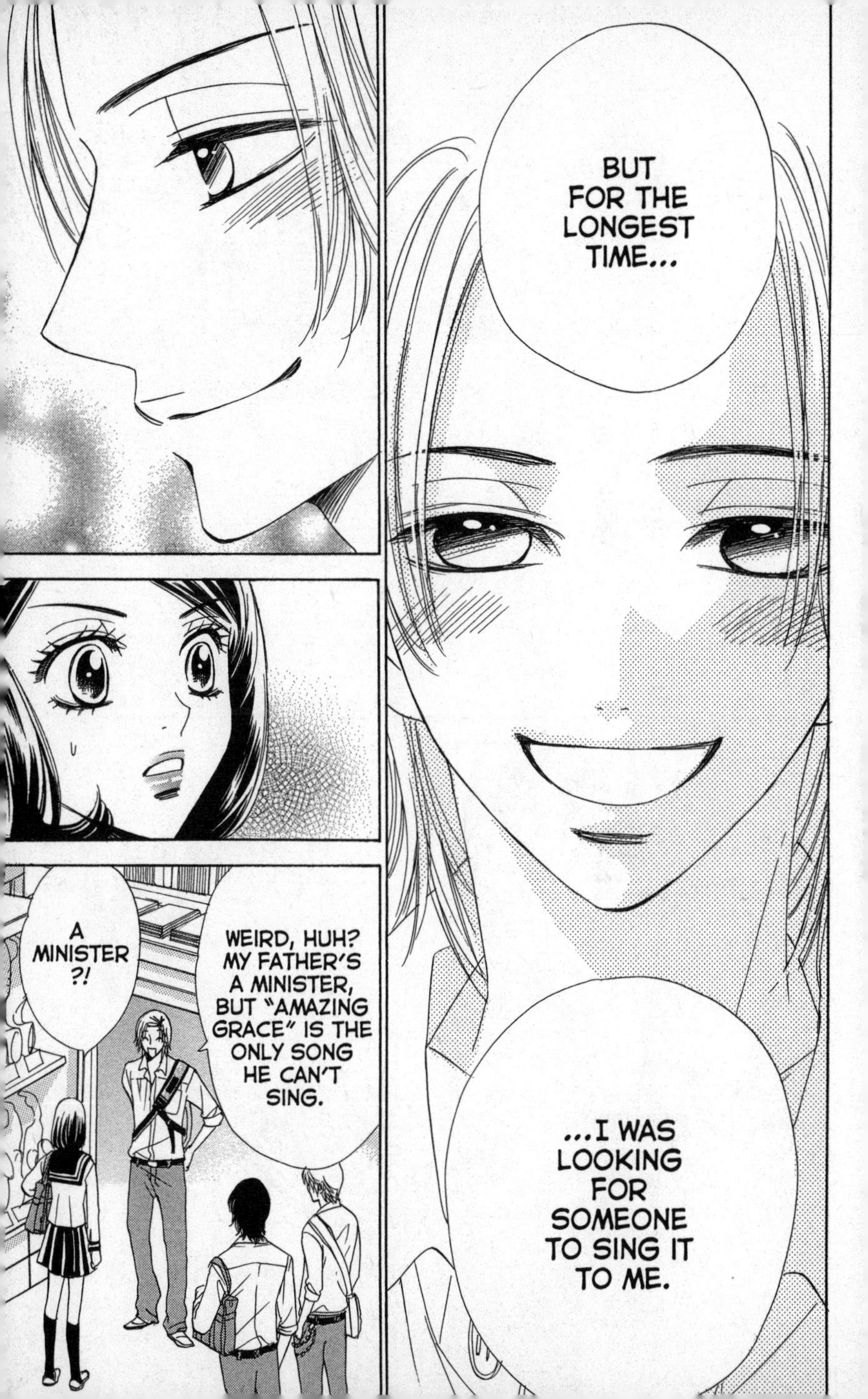
WEIRD, HUH? MY FATHER'S A MINISTER, BUT "AMAZING GRACE" IS THE ONLY SONG HE CAN'T SING.
A MINISTER ?!
BUT FOR THE LONGEST TIME...
...I WAS LOOKING FOR SOMEONE TO SING IT TO ME.

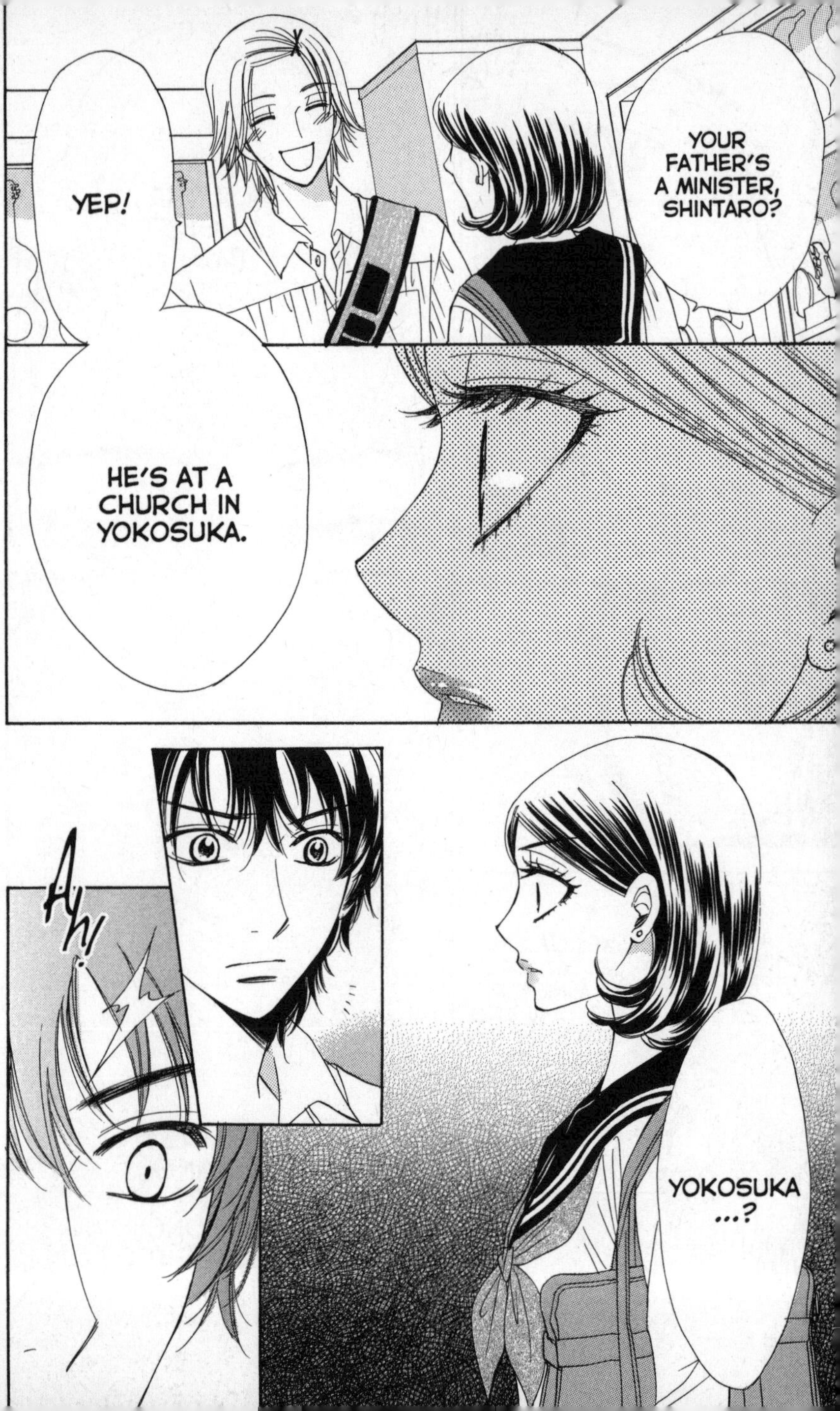
YOUR FATHER'S A MINISTER, SHINTARO?
YEP!
HE'S AT A CHURCH IN YOKOSUKA.
YOKOSUKA ...?
AH!

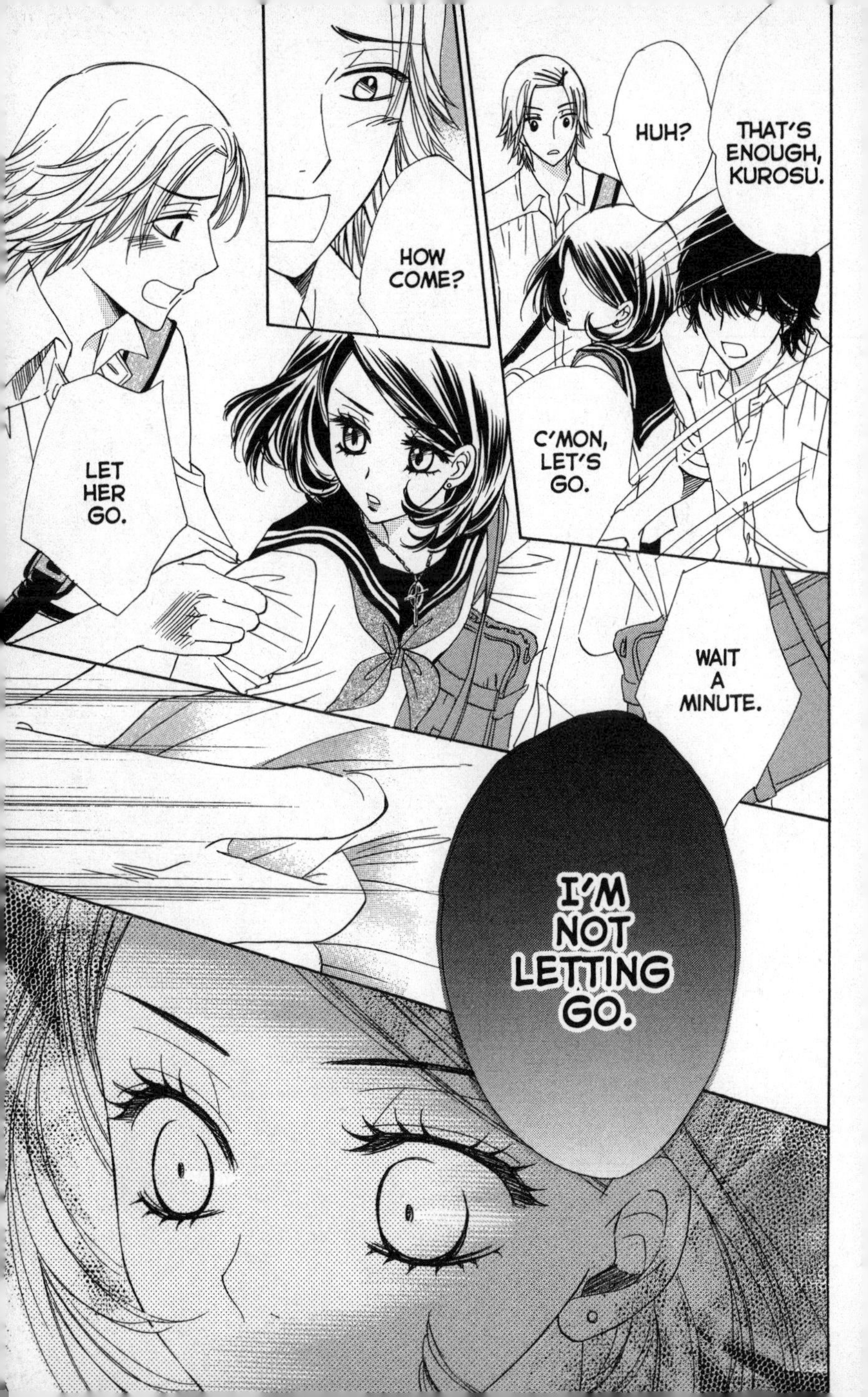

THAT'S ENOUGH, KUROSU.
HUH?
C'MON, LET'S GO.
HOW COME?
LET HER GO.
WAIT A MINUTE.
I'M NOT LETTING GO.

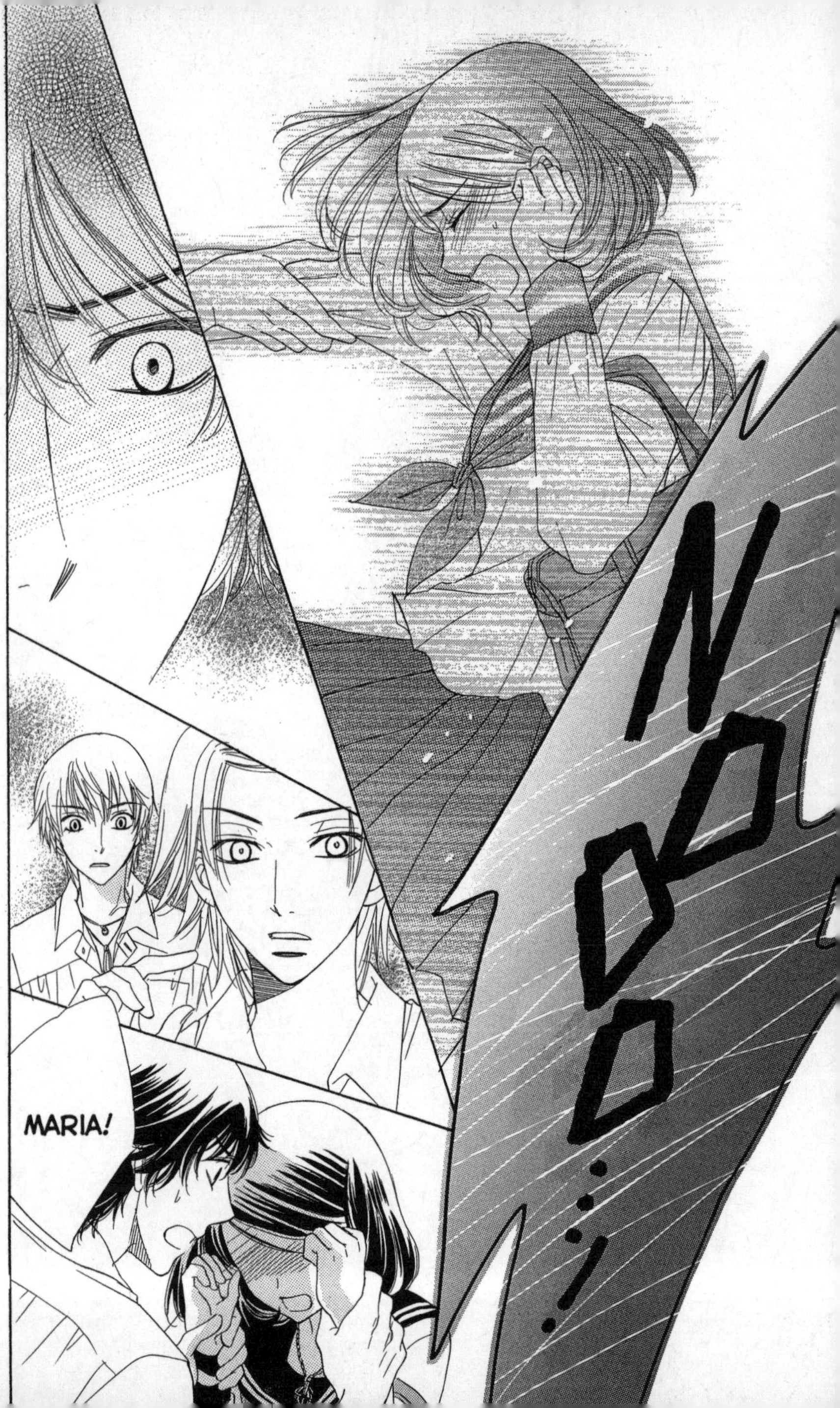
NOOO...!
MARIA!

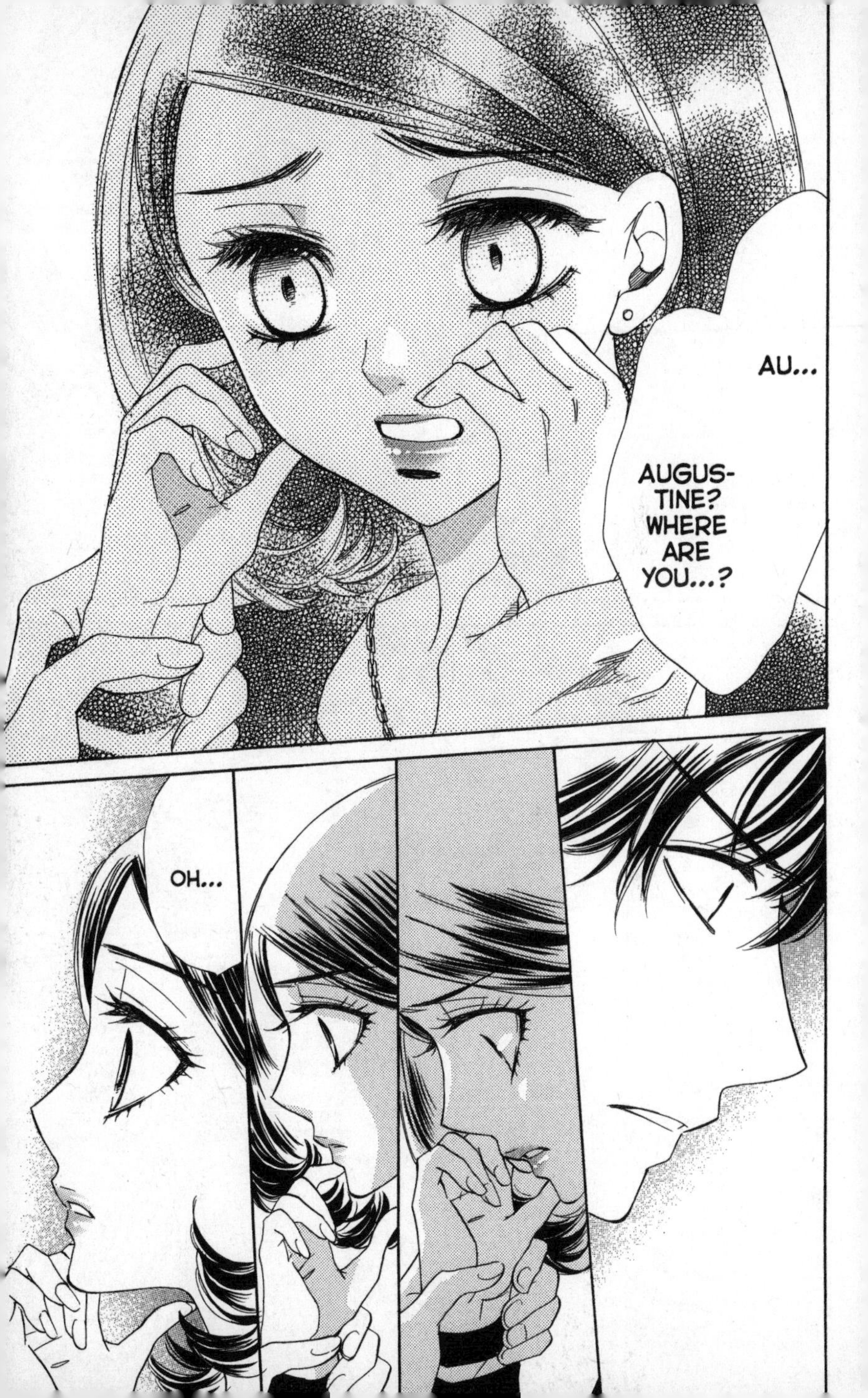
AU...
AUGUS-TINE? WHERE ARE YOU...?
OH...

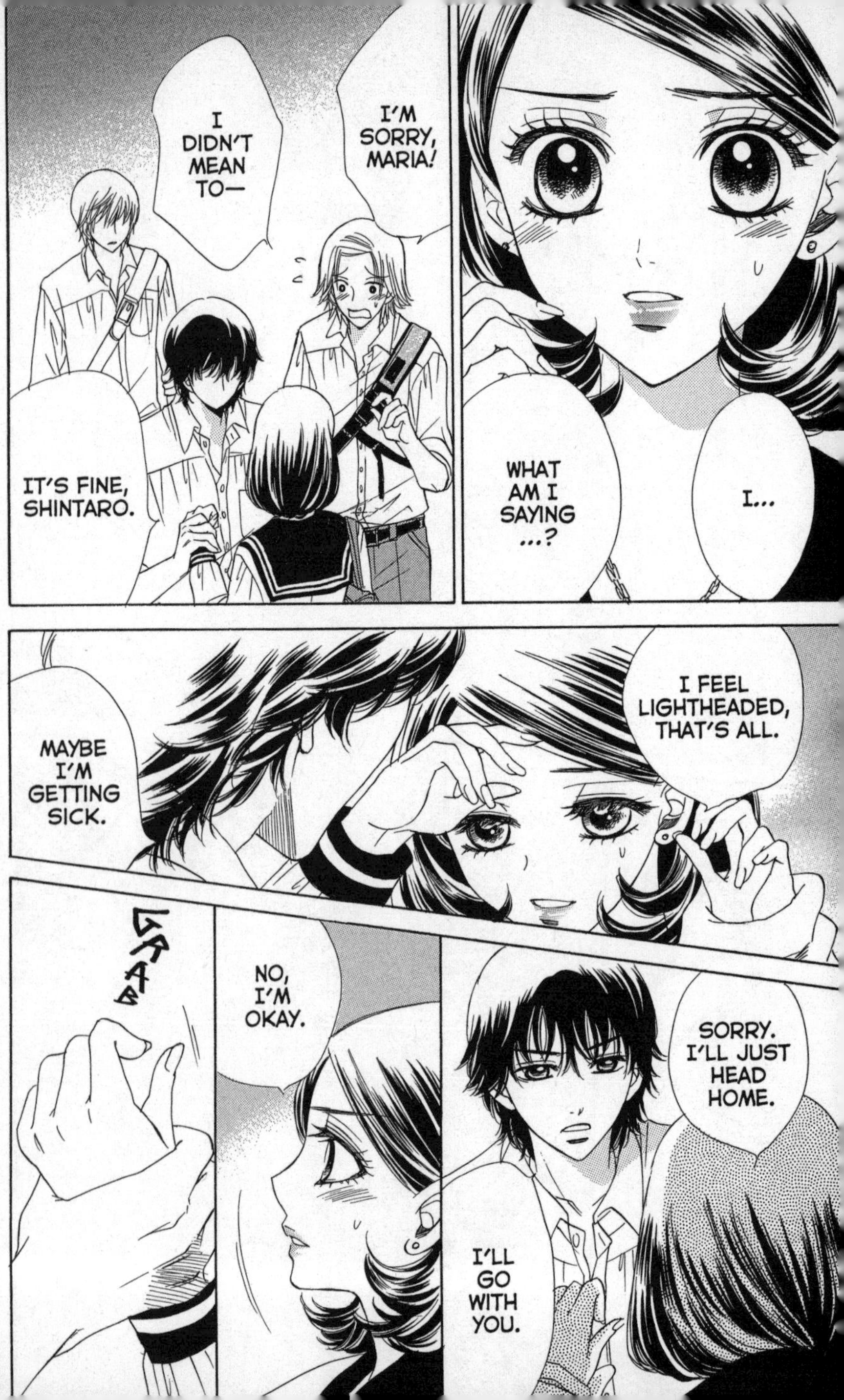
I...
WHAT AM I SAYING ...?
I'M SORRY, MARIA!
I DIDN'T MEAN TO—
IT'S FINE, SHINTARO.
I FEEL LIGHTHEADED, THAT'S ALL.
MAYBE I'M GETTING SICK.
SORRY. I'LL JUST HEAD HOME.
I'LL GO WITH YOU.
NO, I'M OKAY.
GRAB

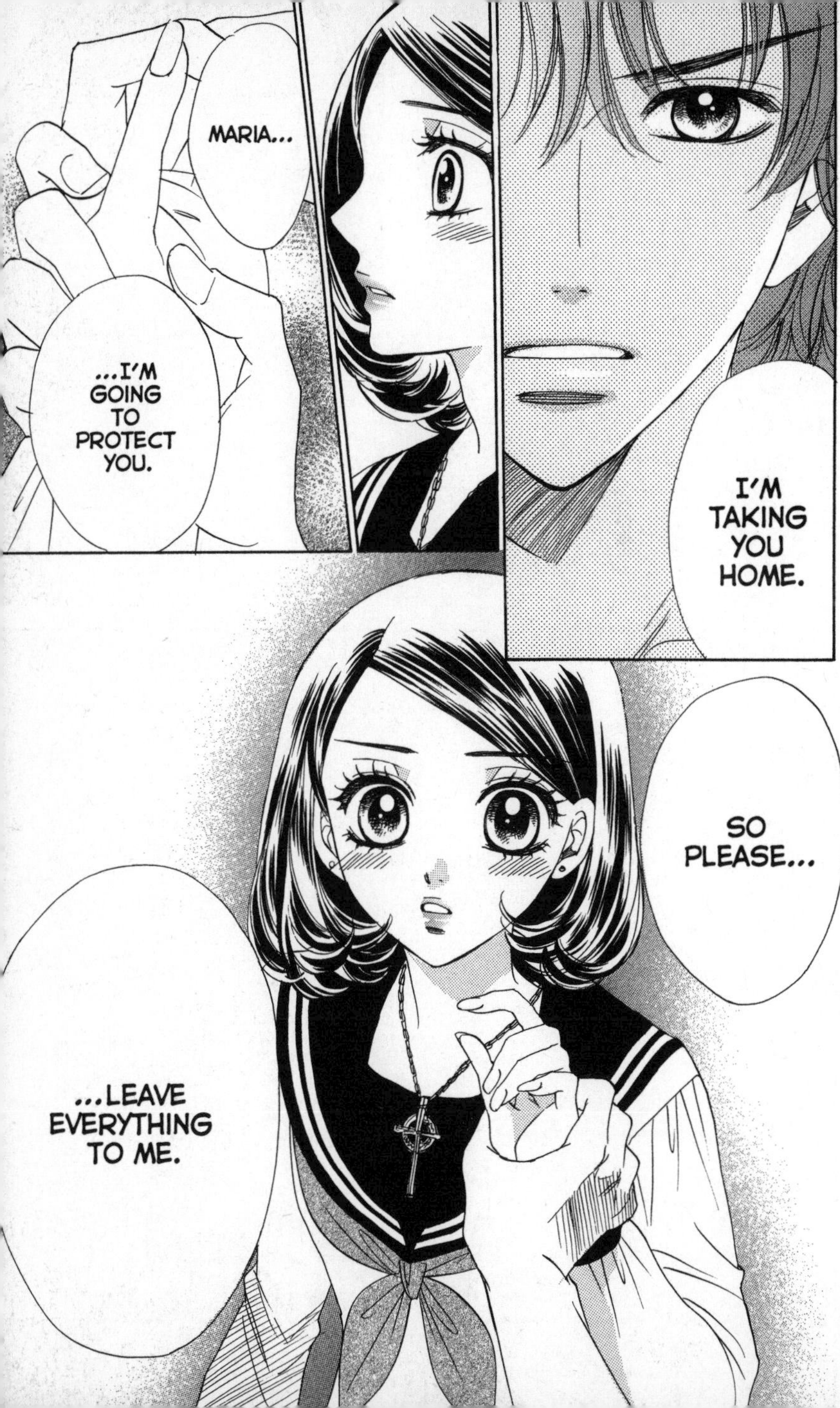
I'M TAKING YOU HOME.
MARIA...
...I'M GOING TO PROTECT YOU.
SO PLEASE...
...LEAVE EVERYTHING TO ME.

A Devil and
Her Love Song

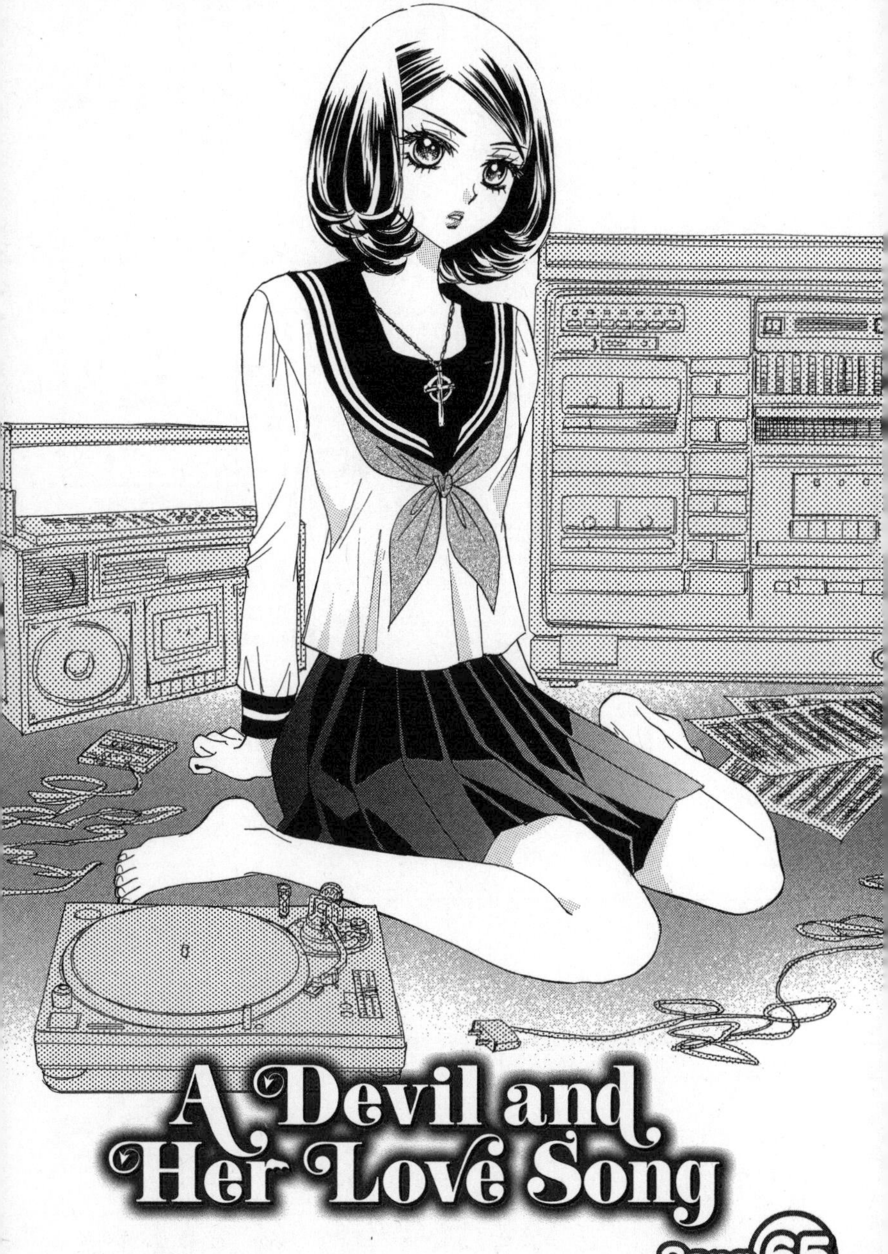
A Devil and Her Love Song
Song 65

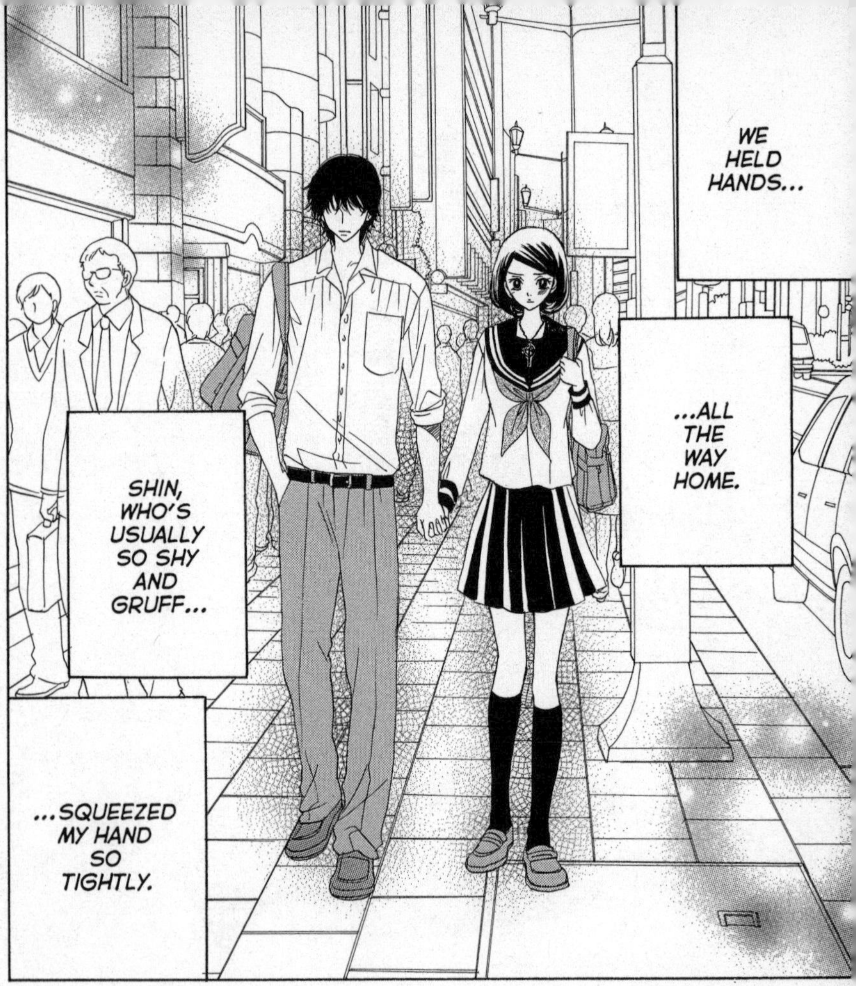
WE HELD HANDS...
...ALL THE WAY HOME.
SHIN, WHO'S USUALLY SO SHY AND GRUFF...
...SQUEEZED MY HAND SO TIGHTLY.

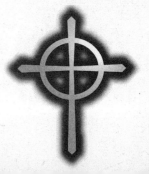

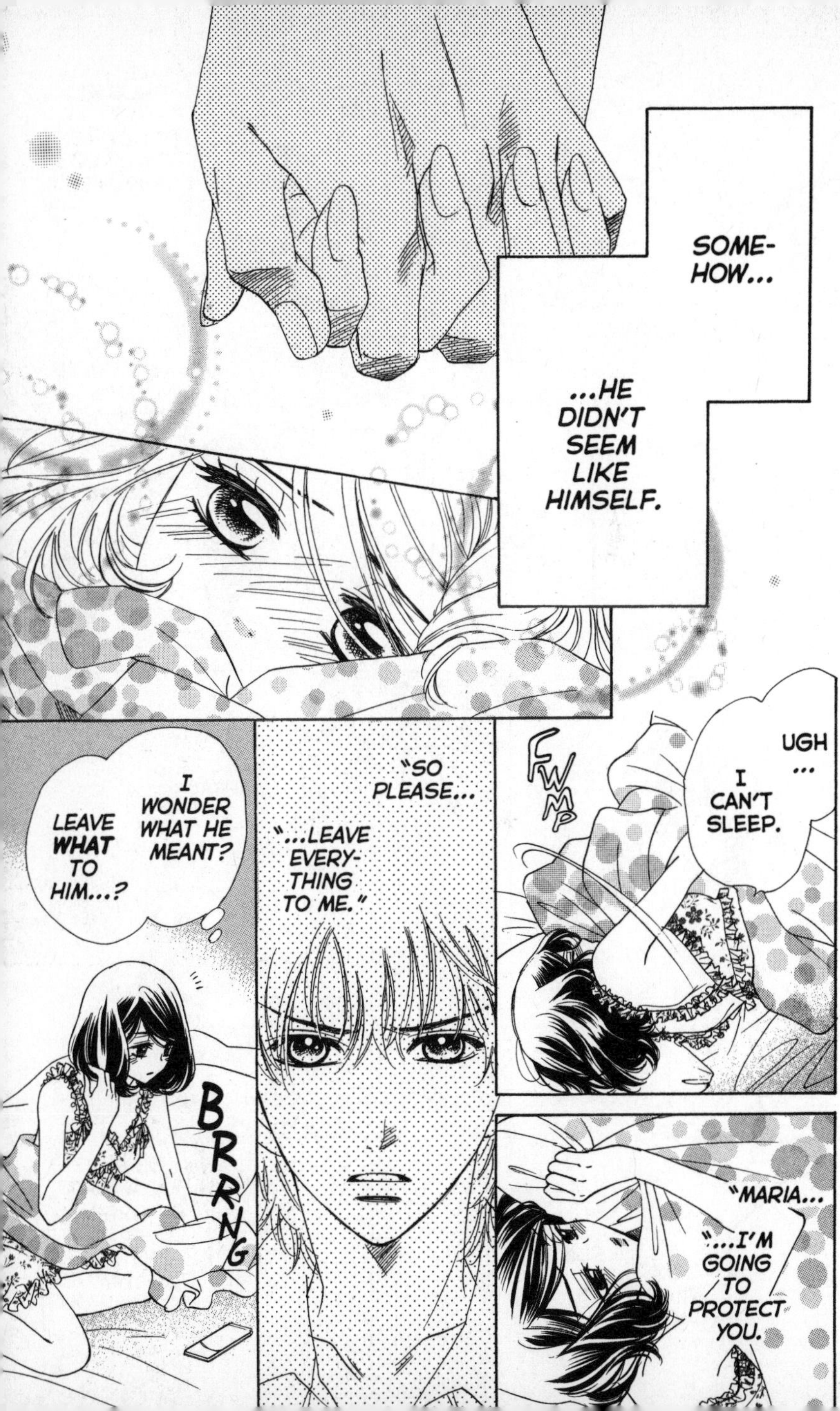
SOME-HOW...
...HE DIDN'T SEEM LIKE HIMSELF.
FWMP
UGH... I CAN'T SLEEP.
"MARIA...
"...I'M GOING TO PROTECT YOU.
"SO PLEASE...
"...LEAVE EVERYTHING TO ME."
I WONDER WHAT HE MEANT? LEAVE WHAT TO HIM...?
BRRNG

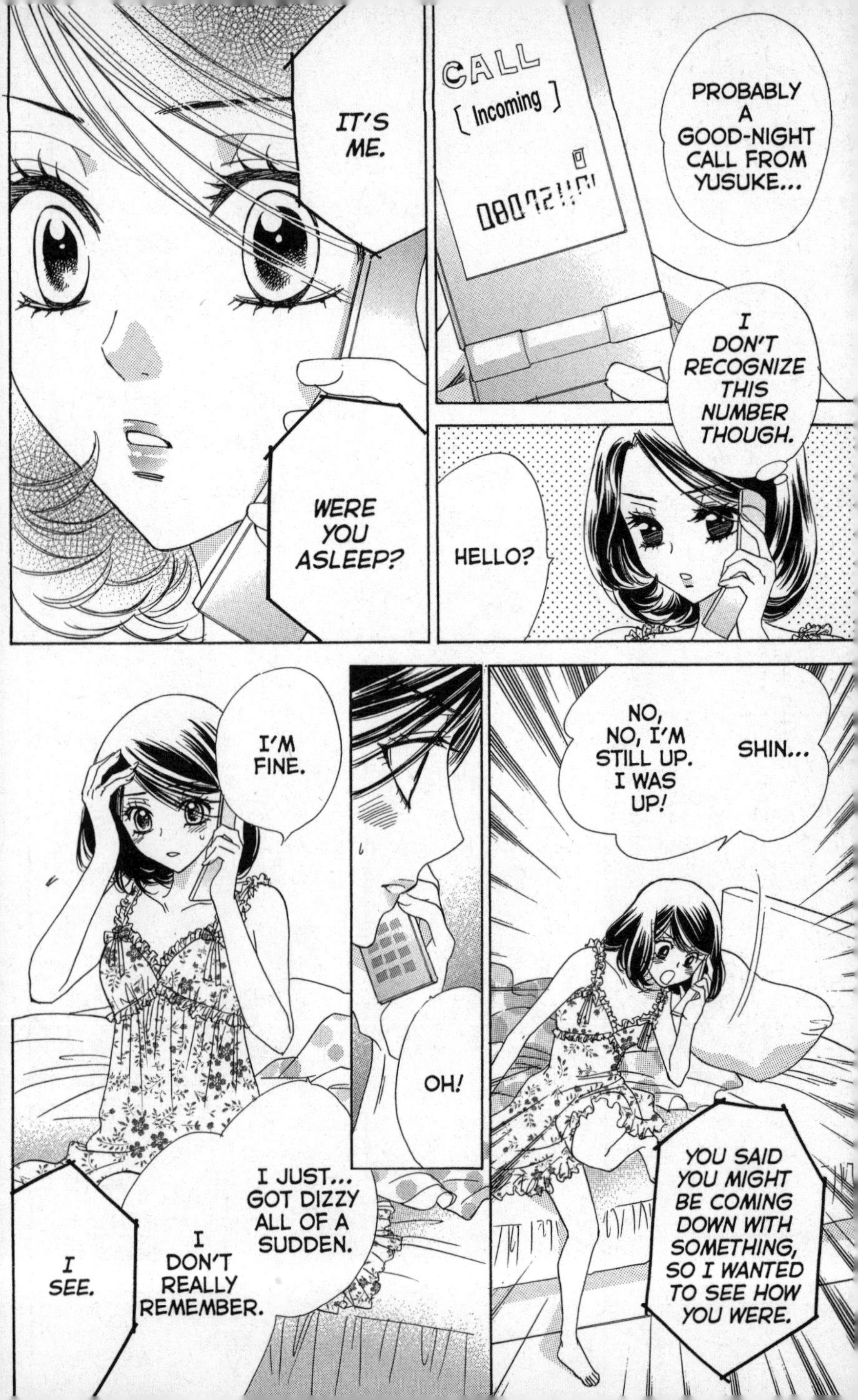
CALL
[Incoming]
PROBABLY A GOOD-NIGHT CALL FROM YUSUKE...
I DON'T RECOGNIZE THIS NUMBER THOUGH.
HELLO?
IT'S ME.
WERE YOU ASLEEP?
SHIN...
NO, NO, I'M STILL UP. I WAS UP!
YOU SAID YOU MIGHT BE COMING DOWN WITH SOMETHING, SO I WANTED TO SEE HOW YOU WERE.
OH!
I'M FINE.
I JUST... GOT DIZZY ALL OF A SUDDEN.
I DON'T REALLY REMEMBER.
I SEE.

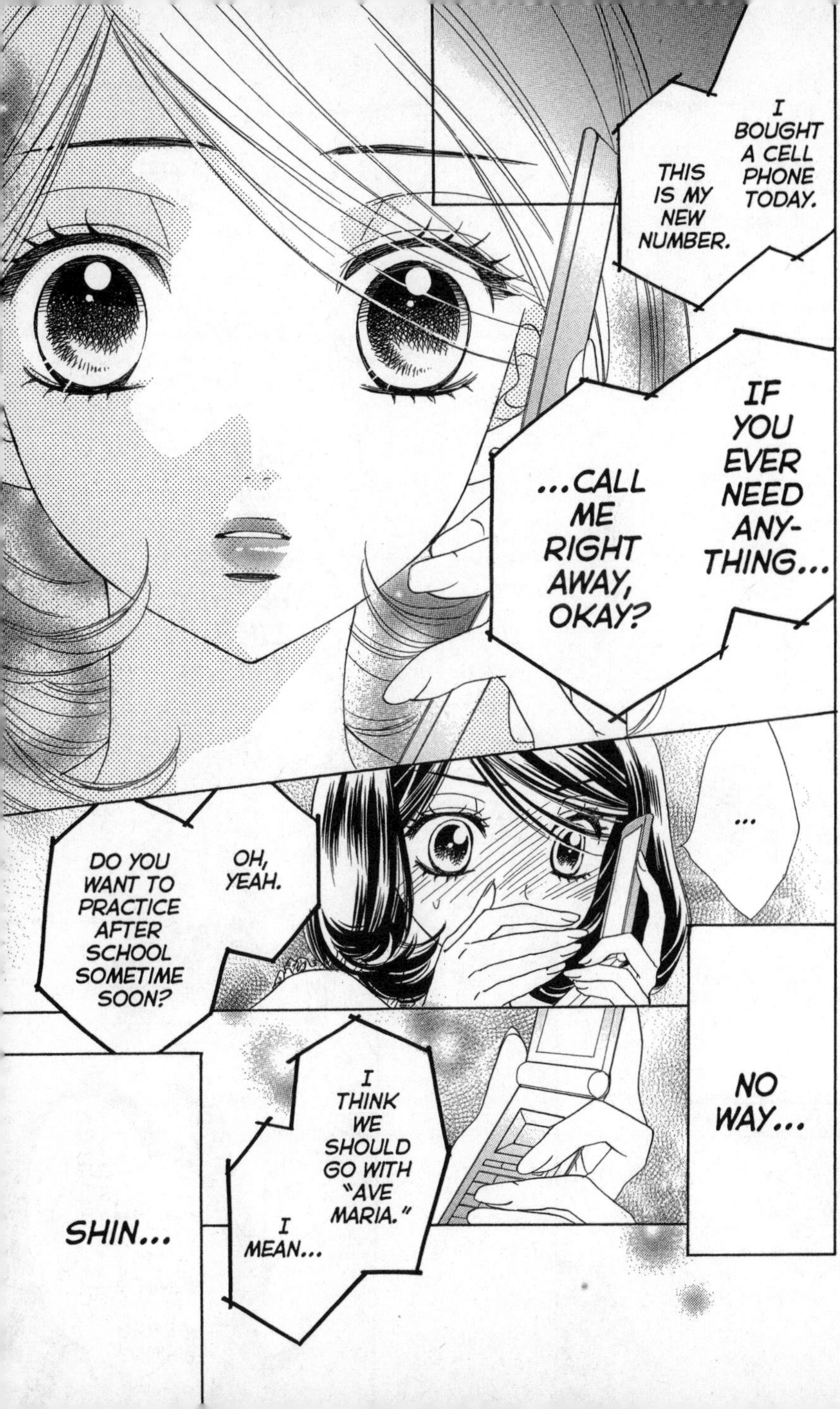
I BOUGHT A CELL PHONE TODAY.
THIS IS MY NEW NUMBER.
IF YOU EVER NEED ANYTHING...
...CALL ME RIGHT AWAY, OKAY?
...
OH, YEAH.
DO YOU WANT TO PRACTICE AFTER SCHOOL SOMETIME SOON?
NO WAY...
I THINK WE SHOULD GO WITH "AVE MARIA."
I MEAN...
SHIN...

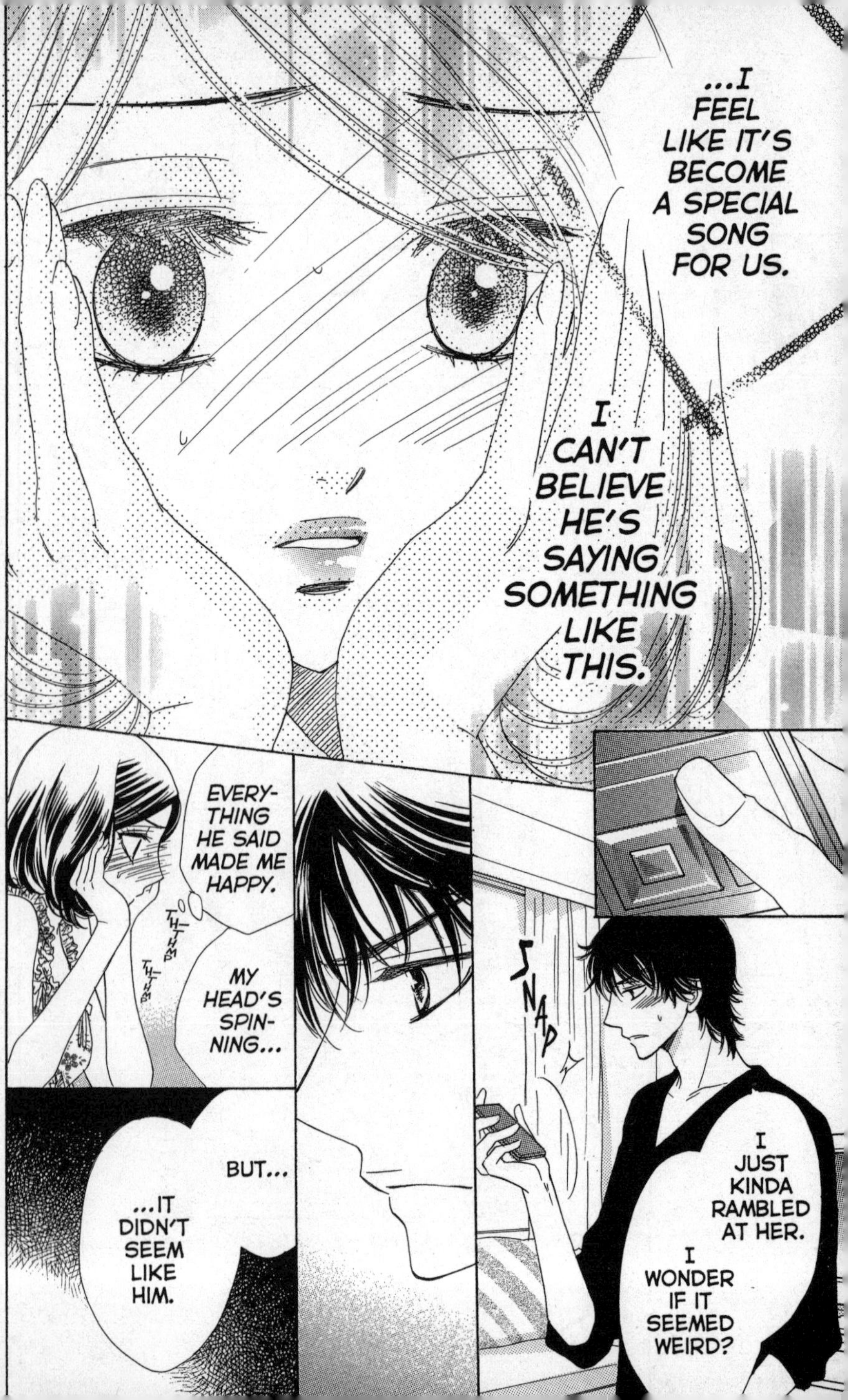
...I FEEL LIKE IT'S BECOME A SPECIAL SONG FOR US.
I CAN'T BELIEVE HE'S SAYING SOMETHING LIKE THIS.
SNAP
I JUST KINDA RAMBLED AT HER.
I WONDER IF IT SEEMED WEIRD?
EVERY-THING HE SAID MADE ME HAPPY.
TH-THMP
TH-THMP
MY HEAD'S SPIN-NING...
BUT...
...IT DIDN'T SEEM LIKE HIM.

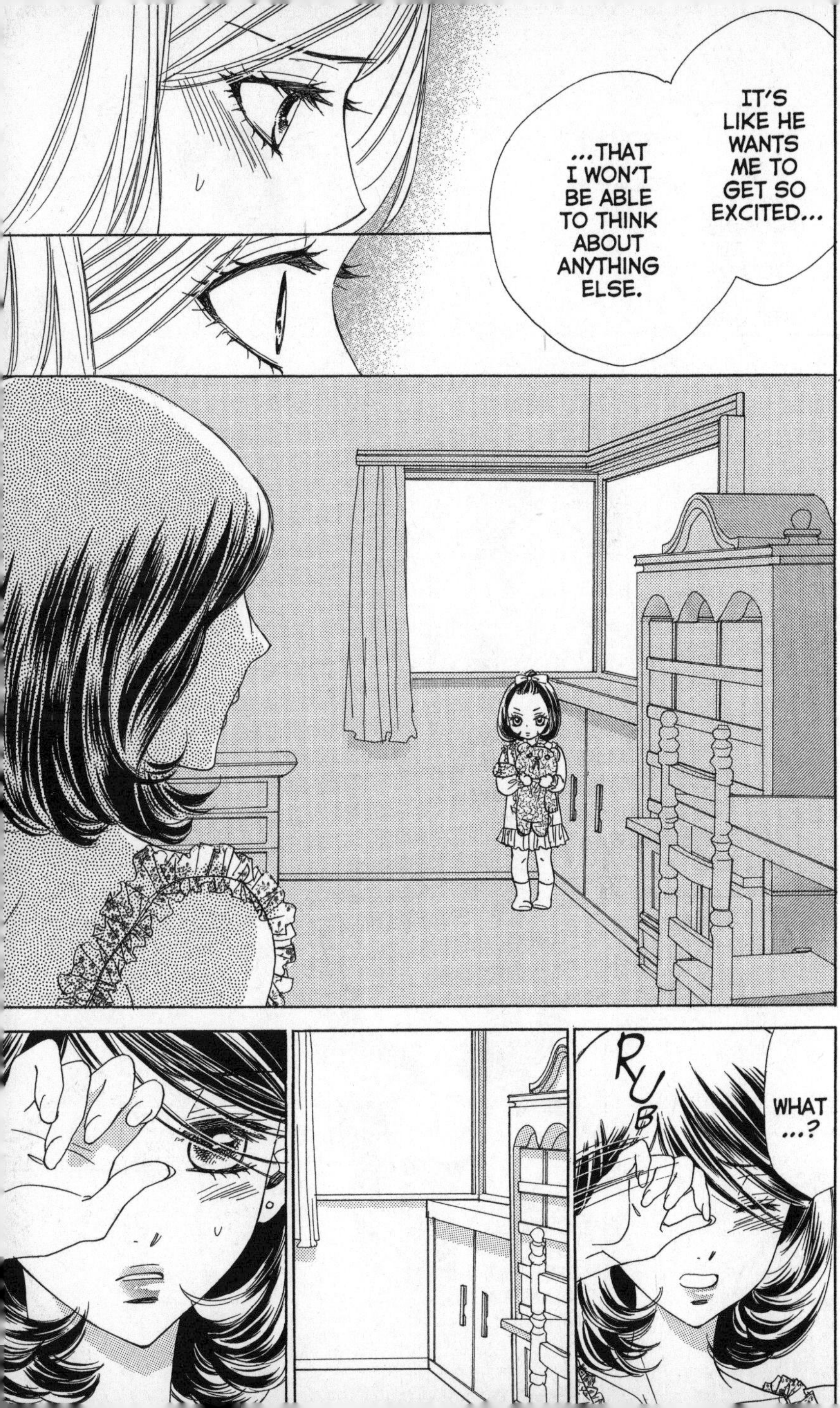
IT'S LIKE HE WANTS ME TO GET SO EXCITED...
...THAT I WON'T BE ABLE TO THINK ABOUT ANYTHING ELSE.
WHAT ...?
RUB

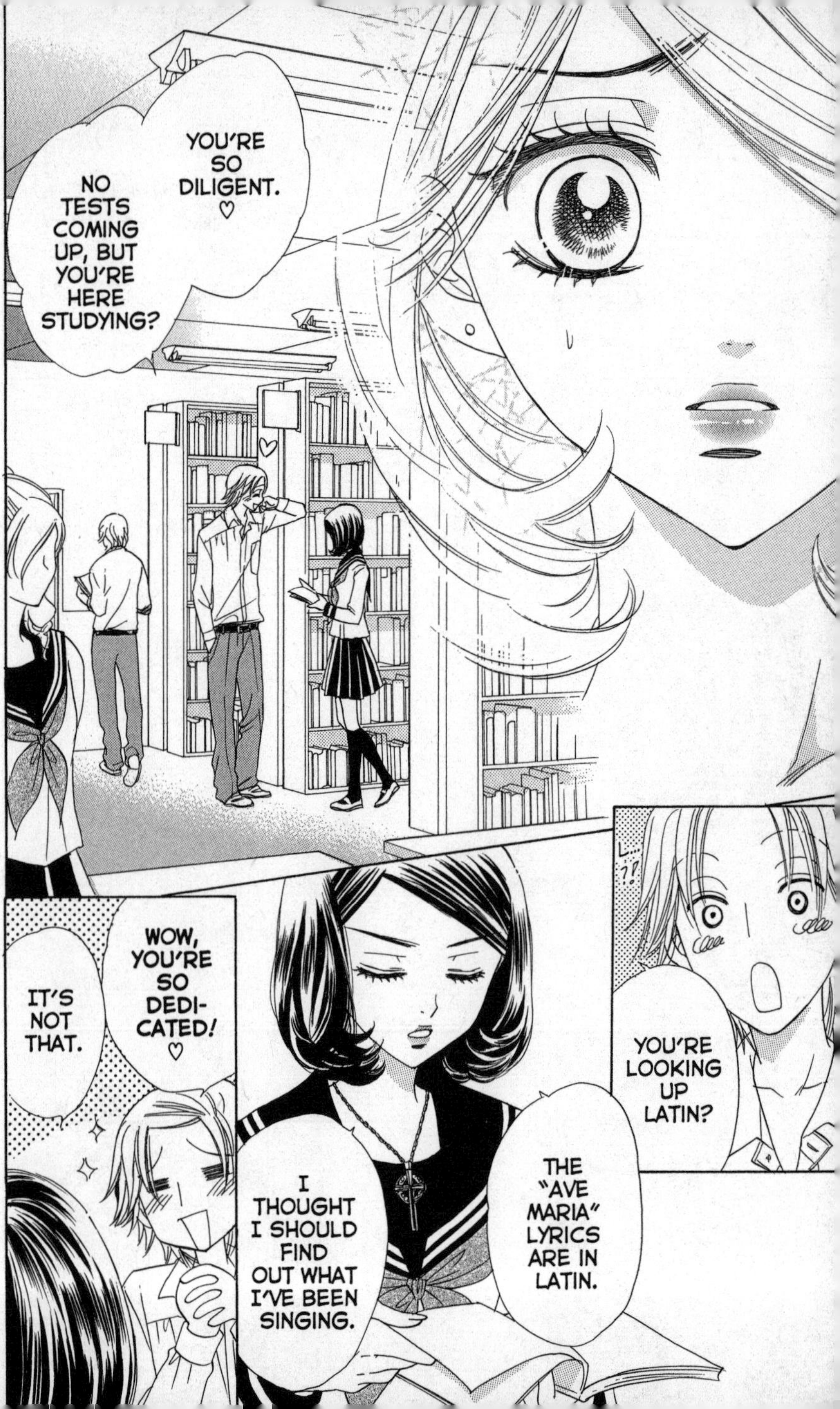
YOU'RE SO DILIGENT. ♡
NO TESTS COMING UP, BUT YOU'RE HERE STUDYING?
L...?!
YOU'RE LOOKING UP LATIN?
THE "AVE MARIA" LYRICS ARE IN LATIN.
I THOUGHT I SHOULD FIND OUT WHAT I'VE BEEN SINGING.
WOW, YOU'RE SO DEDICATED! ♡
IT'S NOT THAT.

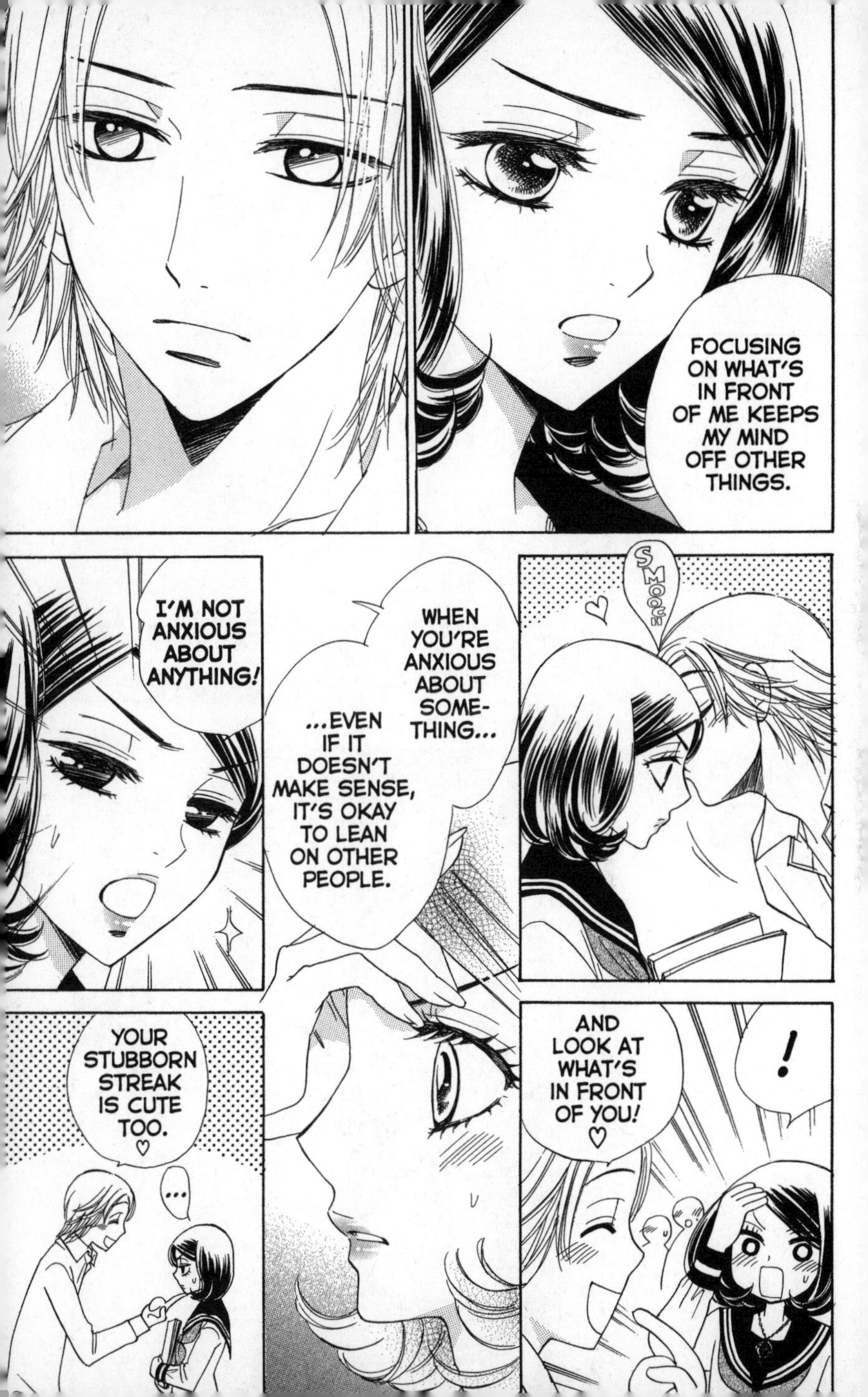
FOCUSING ON WHAT'S IN FRONT OF ME KEEPS MY MIND OFF OTHER THINGS.
SMOOCH
♡
WHEN YOU'RE ANXIOUS ABOUT SOME-THING...
...EVEN IF IT DOESN'T MAKE SENSE, IT'S OKAY TO LEAN ON OTHER PEOPLE.
I'M NOT ANXIOUS ABOUT ANYTHING!
AND LOOK AT WHAT'S IN FRONT OF YOU! ♡
!
YOUR STUBBORN STREAK IS CUTE TOO. ♡
...

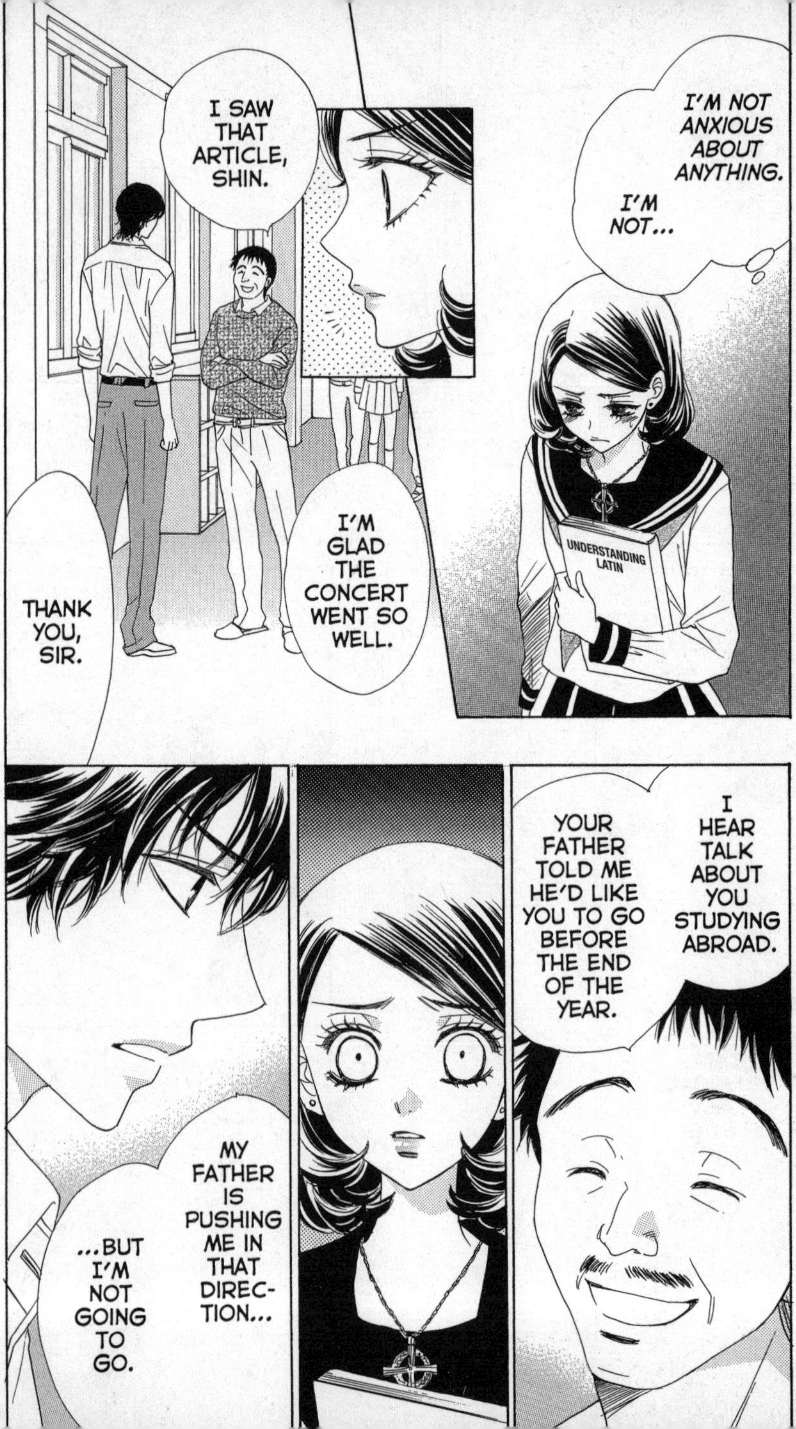
I'M NOT ANXIOUS ABOUT ANYTHING.
I'M NOT...
UNDERSTANDING LATIN
I SAW THAT ARTICLE, SHIN.
I'M GLAD THE CONCERT WENT SO WELL.
THANK YOU, SIR.
I HEAR TALK ABOUT YOU STUDYING ABROAD.
YOUR FATHER TOLD ME HE'D LIKE YOU TO GO BEFORE THE END OF THE YEAR.
MY FATHER IS PUSHING ME IN THAT DIREC-TION...
...BUT I'M NOT GOING TO GO.

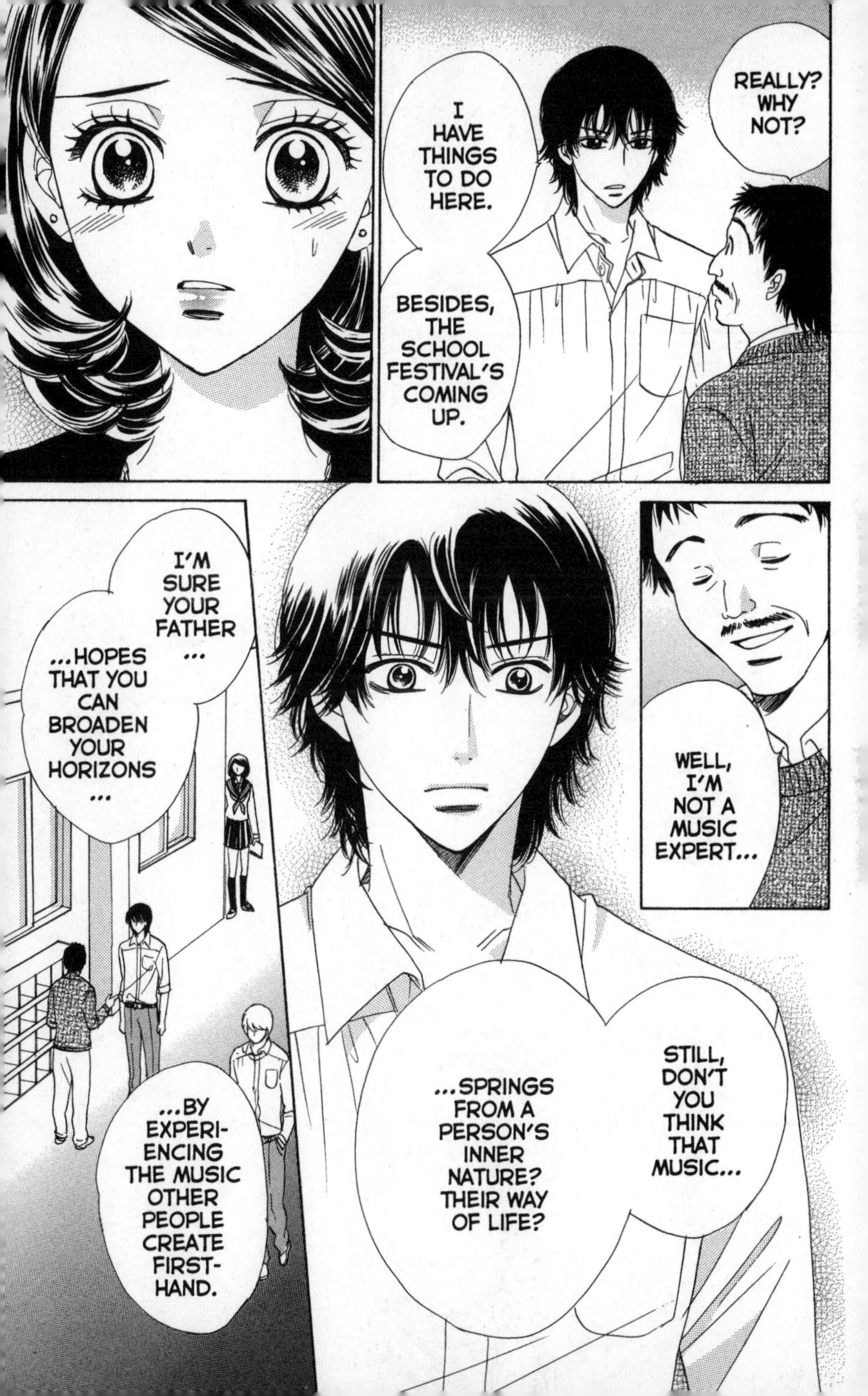
REALLY? WHY NOT?
I HAVE THINGS TO DO HERE.
BESIDES, THE SCHOOL FESTIVAL'S COMING UP.
WELL, I'M NOT A MUSIC EXPERT...
STILL, DON'T YOU THINK THAT MUSIC...
...SPRINGS FROM A PERSON'S INNER NATURE? THEIR WAY OF LIFE?
I'M SURE YOUR FATHER...
...HOPES THAT YOU CAN BROADEN YOUR HORIZONS...
...BY EXPERIENCING THE MUSIC OTHER PEOPLE CREATE FIRST-HAND.

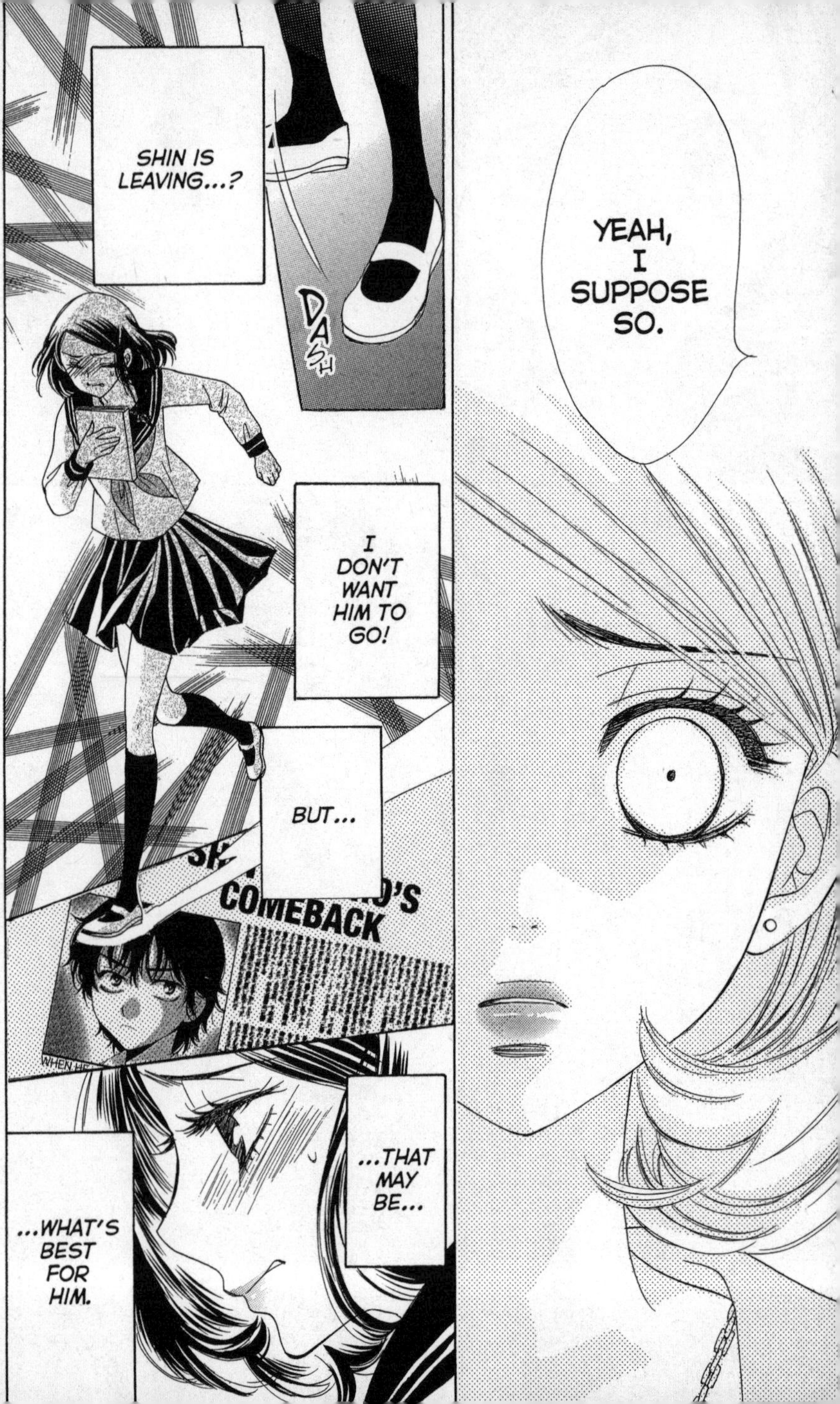
YEAH, I SUPPOSE SO.
DASH
SHIN IS LEAVING...?
I DON'T WANT HIM TO GO!
BUT...
COMEBACK
...THAT MAY BE...
...WHAT'S BEST FOR HIM.

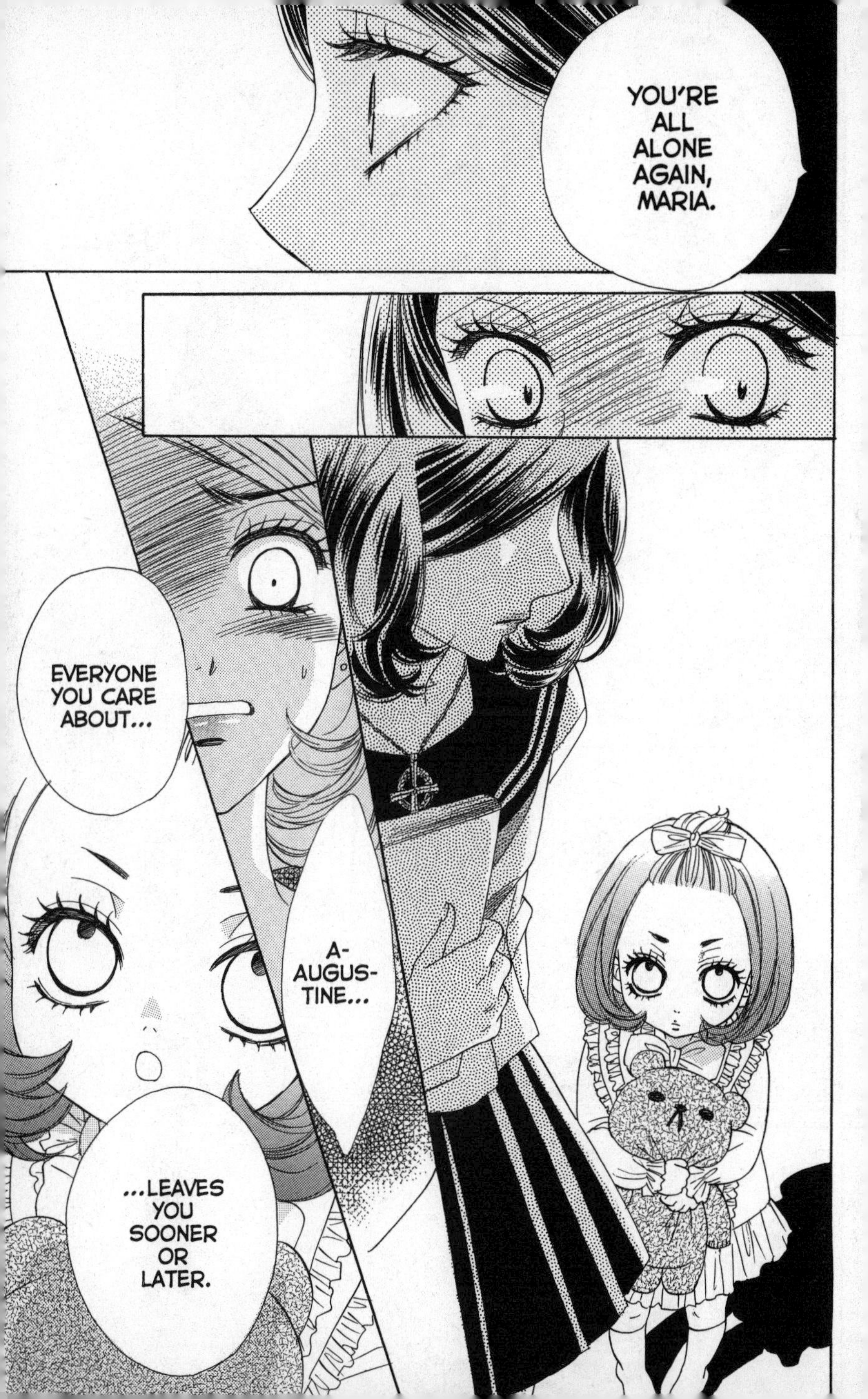
YOU'RE ALL ALONE AGAIN, MARIA.
EVERYONE YOU CARE ABOUT...
A-AUGUSTINE...
...LEAVES YOU SOONER OR LATER.

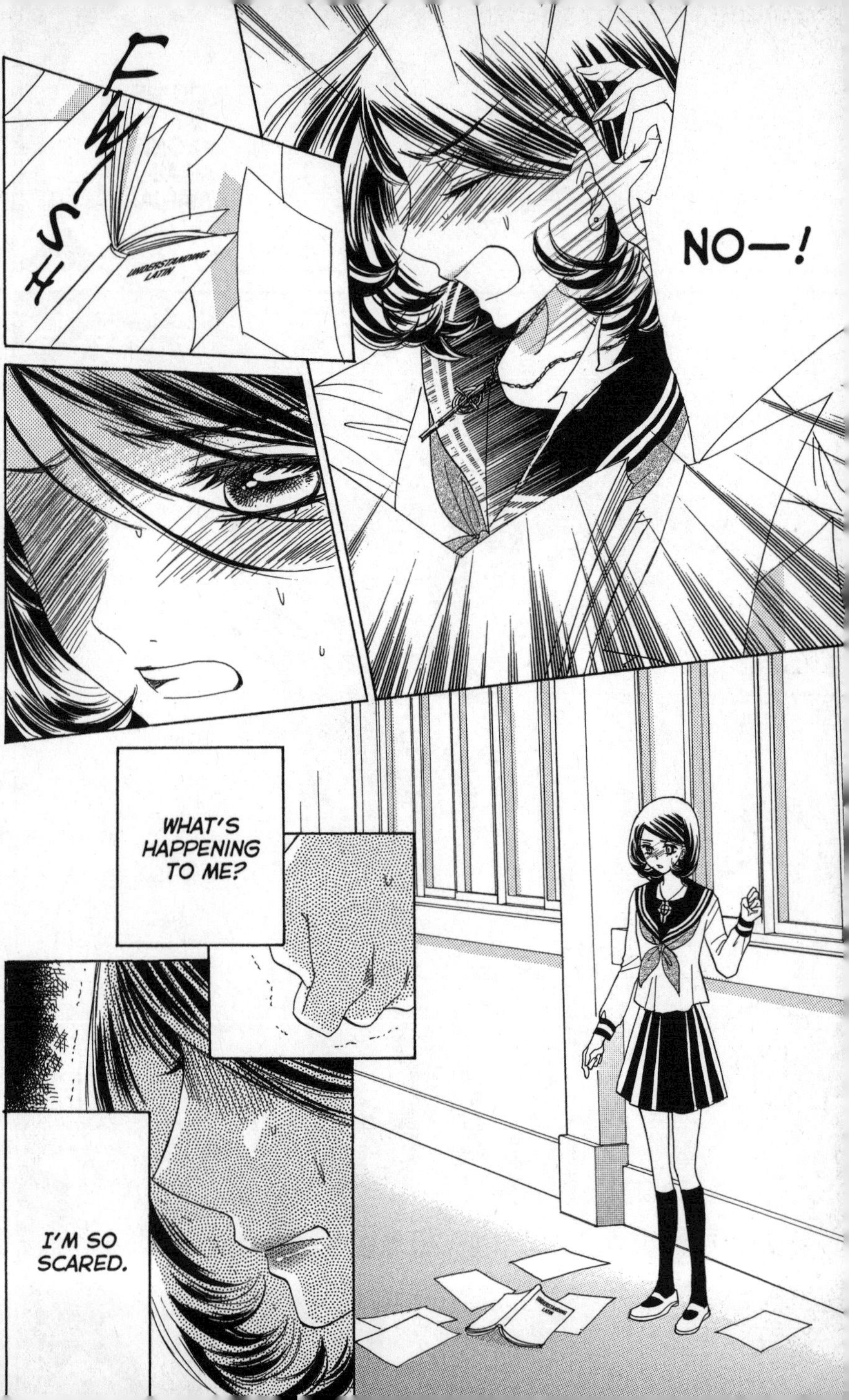
NO—!
FWISH
UNDERSTANDING LATIN
WHAT'S HAPPENING TO ME?
I'M SO SCARED.

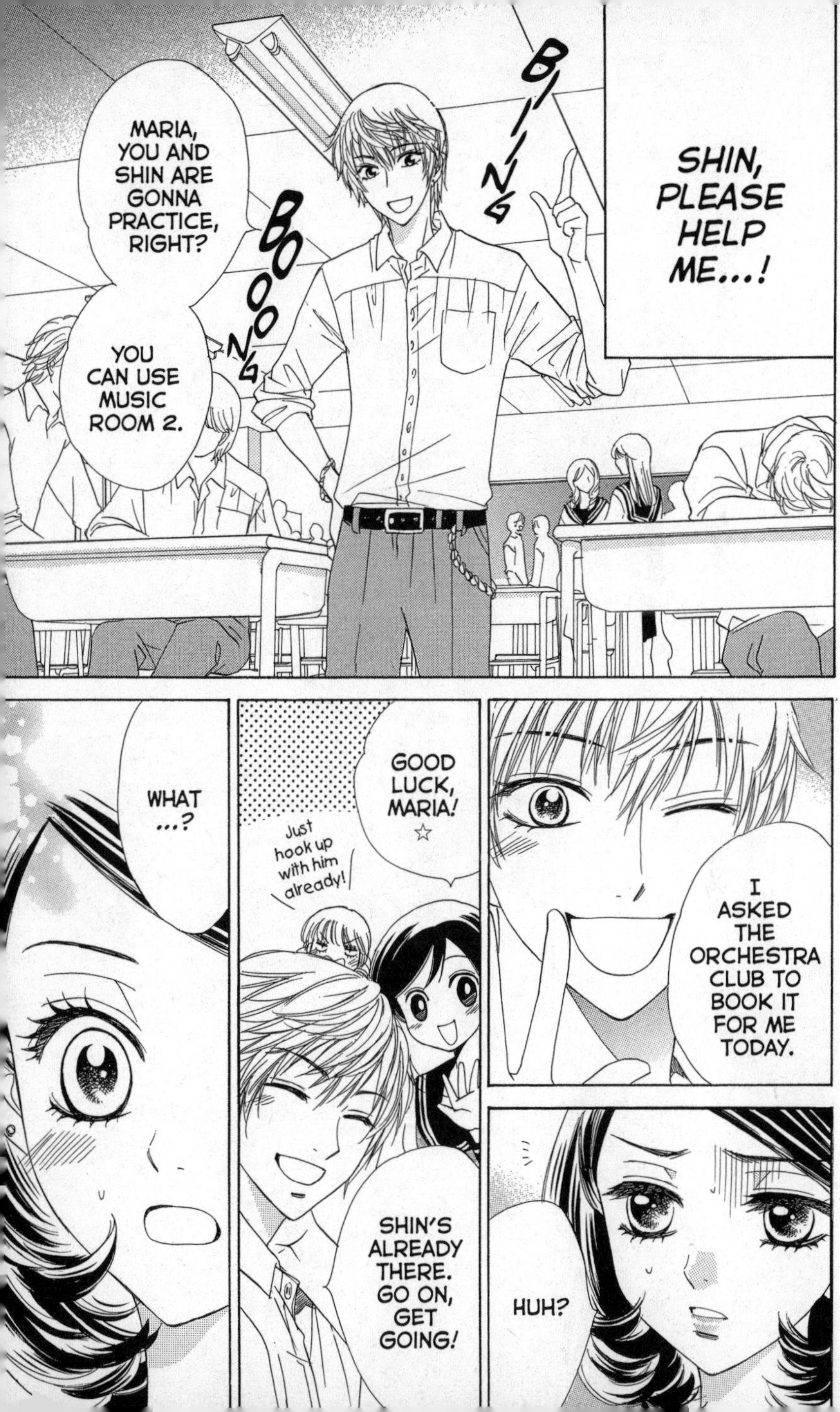
SHIN, PLEASE HELP ME...!
BIIING
BOOONG
MARIA, YOU AND SHIN ARE GONNA PRACTICE, RIGHT?
YOU CAN USE MUSIC ROOM 2.
I ASKED THE ORCHESTRA CLUB TO BOOK IT FOR ME TODAY.
HUH?
GOOD LUCK, MARIA! ☆
Just hook up with him already!
SHIN'S ALREADY THERE. GO ON, GET GOING!
WHAT ...?

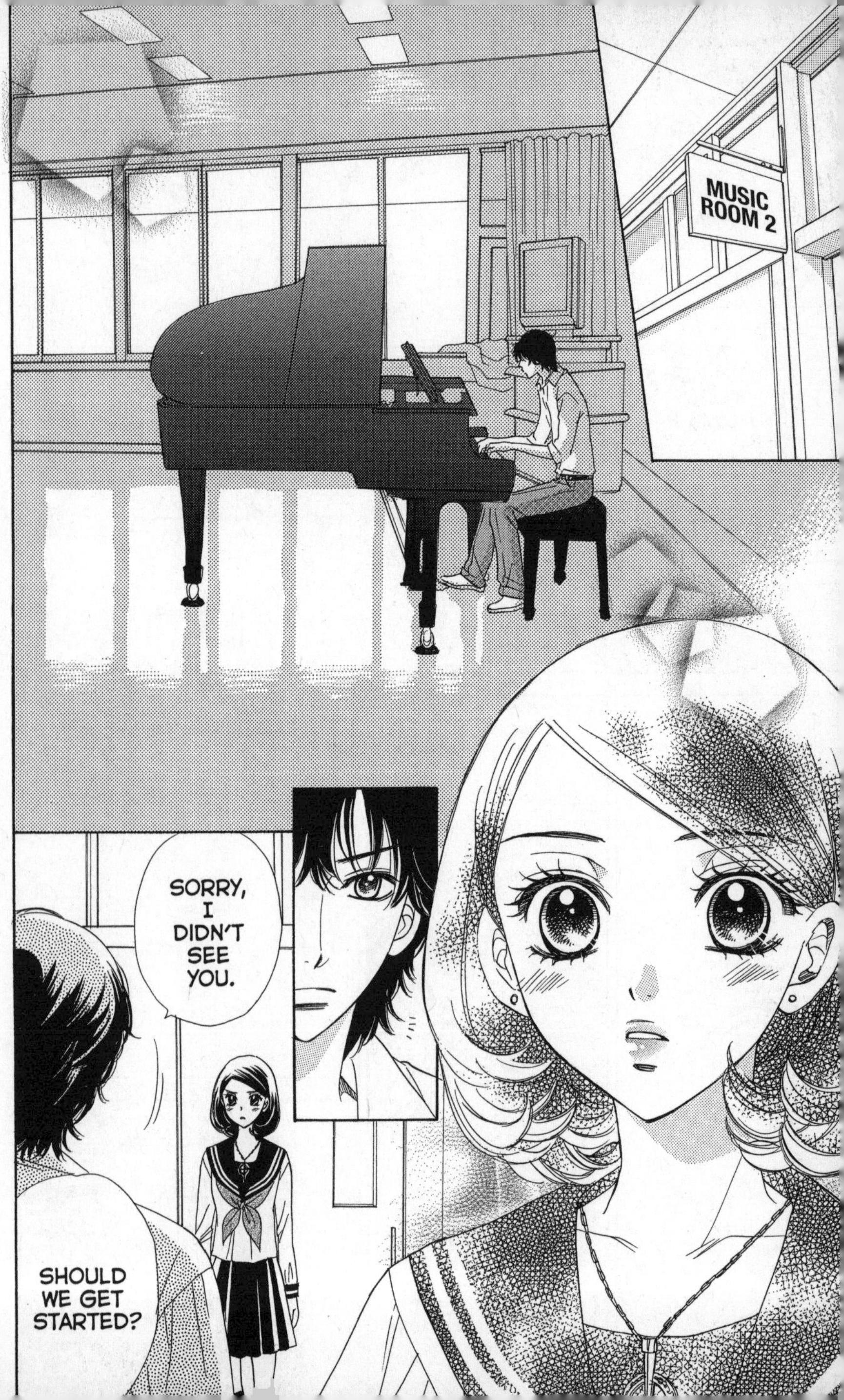
MUSIC ROOM 2
SORRY, I DIDN'T SEE YOU.
SHOULD WE GET STARTED?

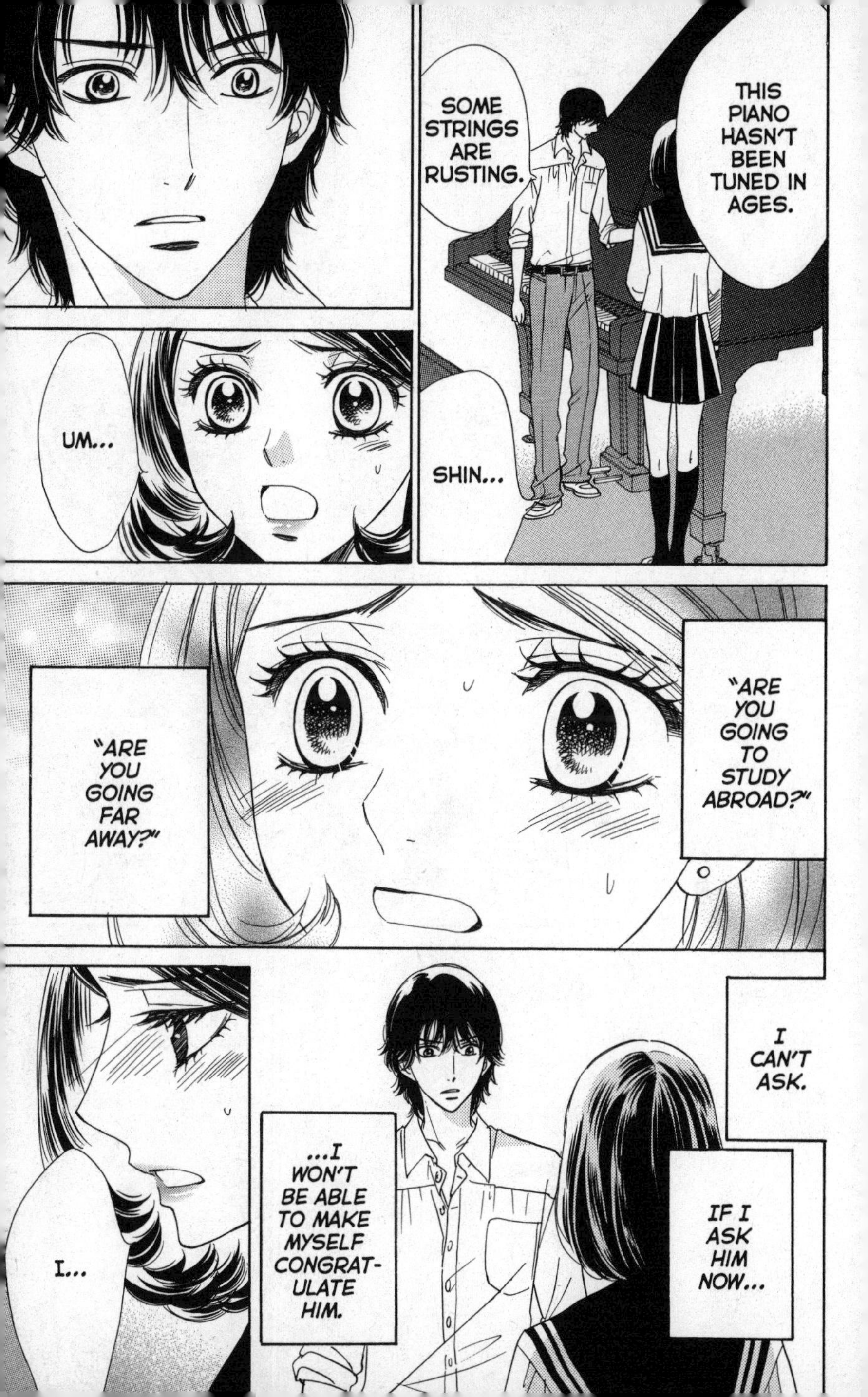
THIS PIANO HASN'T BEEN TUNED IN AGES.
SOME STRINGS ARE RUSTING.
SHIN...
UM...
"ARE YOU GOING TO STUDY ABROAD?"
"ARE YOU GOING FAR AWAY?"
I CAN'T ASK.
IF I ASK HIM NOW...
...I WON'T BE ABLE TO MAKE MYSELF CONGRAT-ULATE HIM.
I...

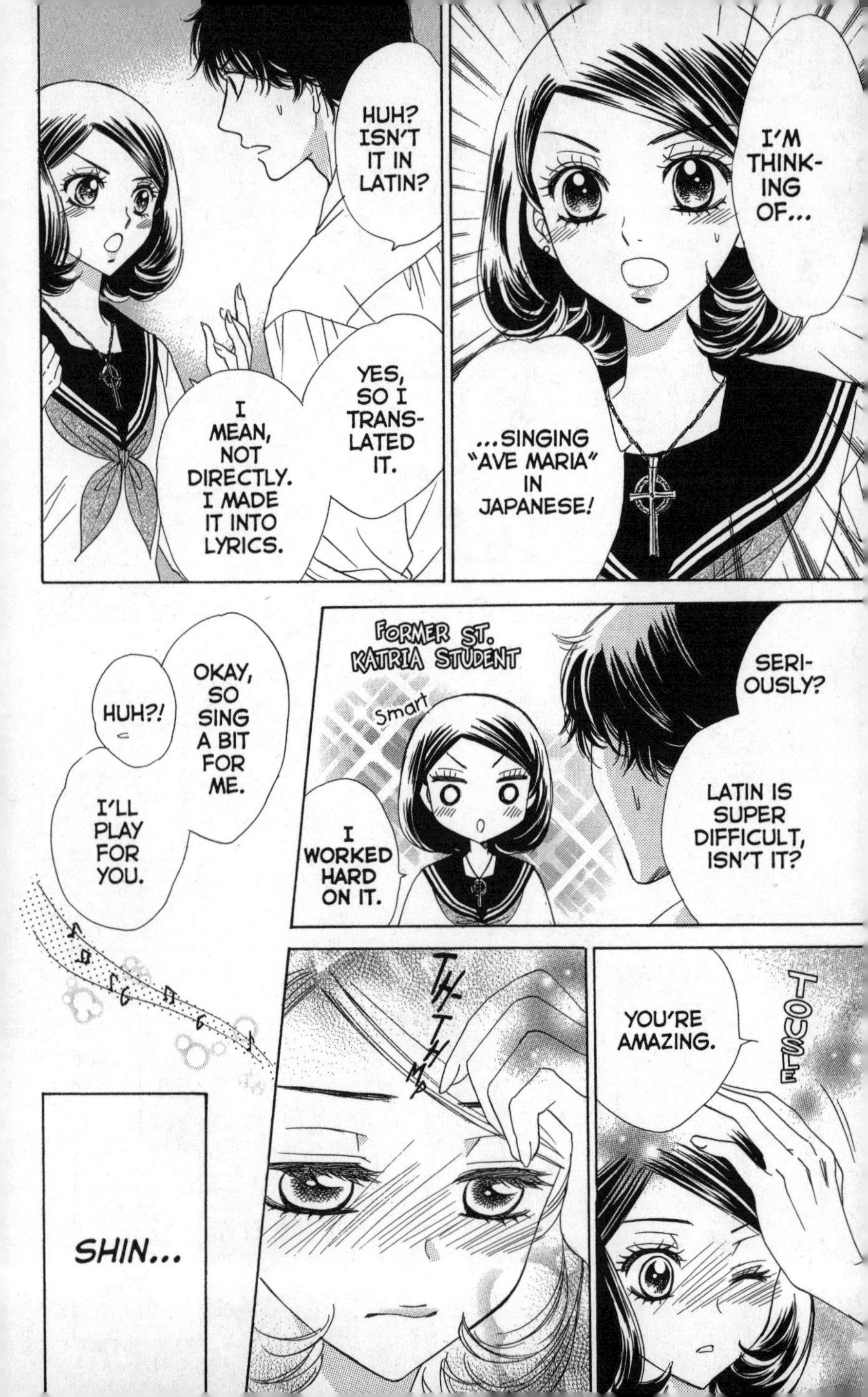
I'M THINKING-ING OF...
...SINGING "AVE MARIA" IN JAPANESE!
HUH? ISN'T IT IN LATIN?
YES, SO I TRANSLATED IT.
I MEAN, NOT DIRECTLY. I MADE IT INTO LYRICS.
SERIOUSLY?
LATIN IS SUPER DIFFICULT, ISN'T IT?
FORMER ST. KATRIA STUDENT
Smart
I WORKED HARD ON IT.
OKAY, SO SING A BIT FOR ME.
HUH?!
I'LL PLAY FOR YOU.
TOUSLE
YOU'RE AMAZING.
TH-THMP
SHIN...

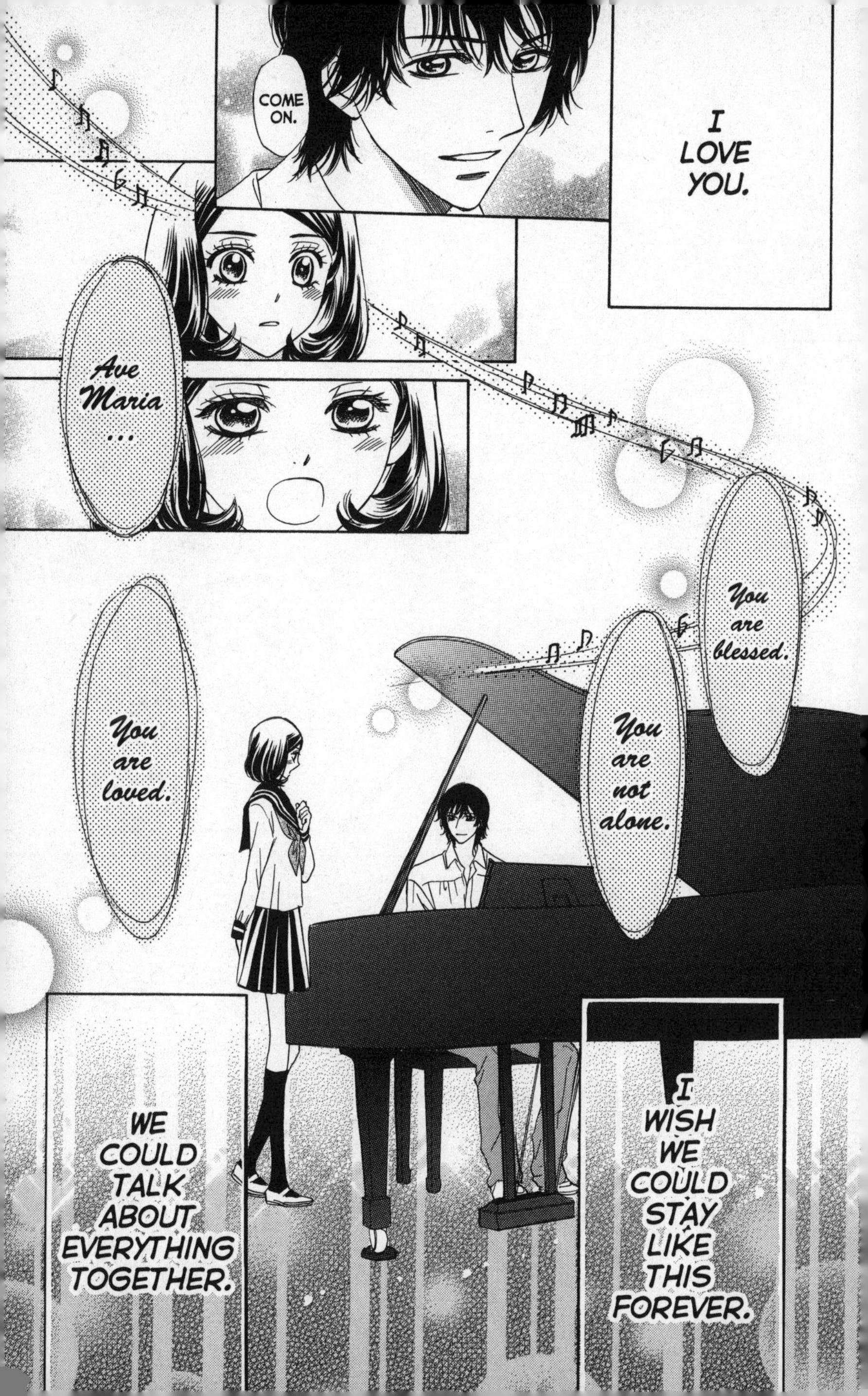
I LOVE YOU.
COME ON.
Ave Maria...
You are blessed.
You are not alone.
You are loved.
I WISH WE COULD STAY LIKE THIS FOREVER.
WE COULD TALK ABOUT EVERYTHING TOGETHER.

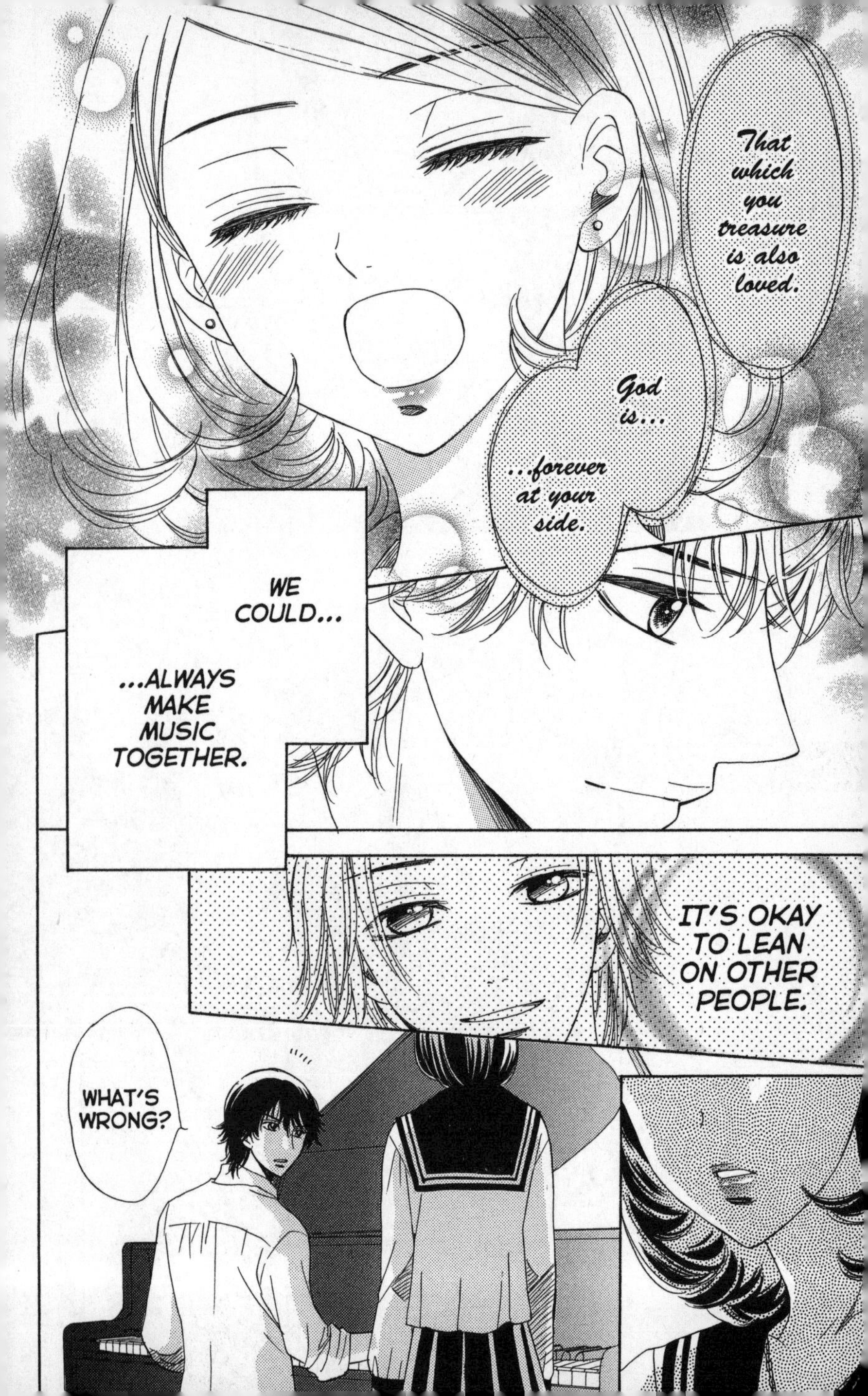
That which you treasure is also loved.
God is...
...forever at your side.
WE COULD...
...ALWAYS MAKE MUSIC TOGETHER.
IT'S OKAY TO LEAN ON OTHER PEOPLE.
WHAT'S WRONG?

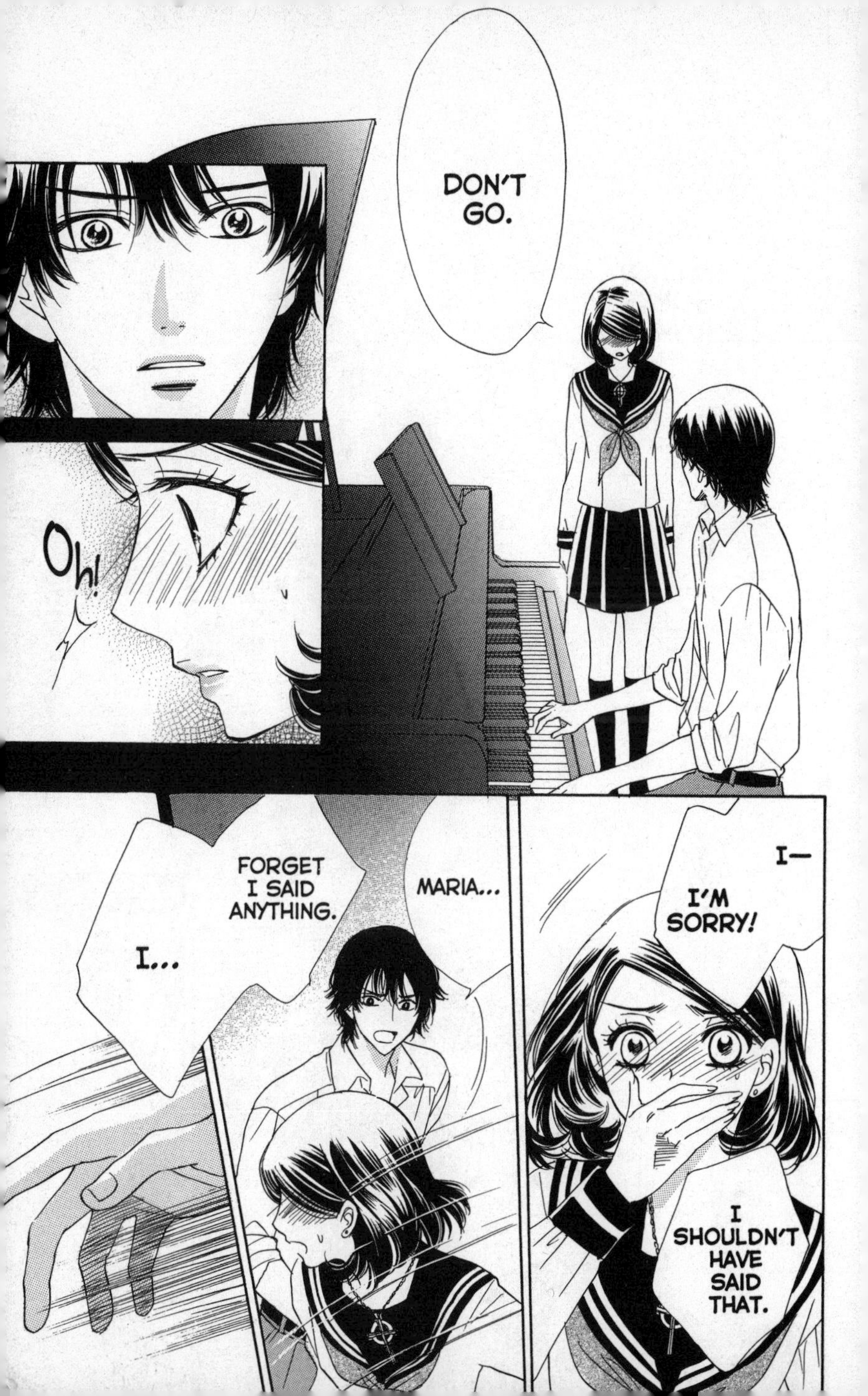
DON'T GO.
Oh!
I—
I'M SORRY!
I SHOULDN'T HAVE SAID THAT.
MARIA...
FORGET I SAID ANYTHING.
I...

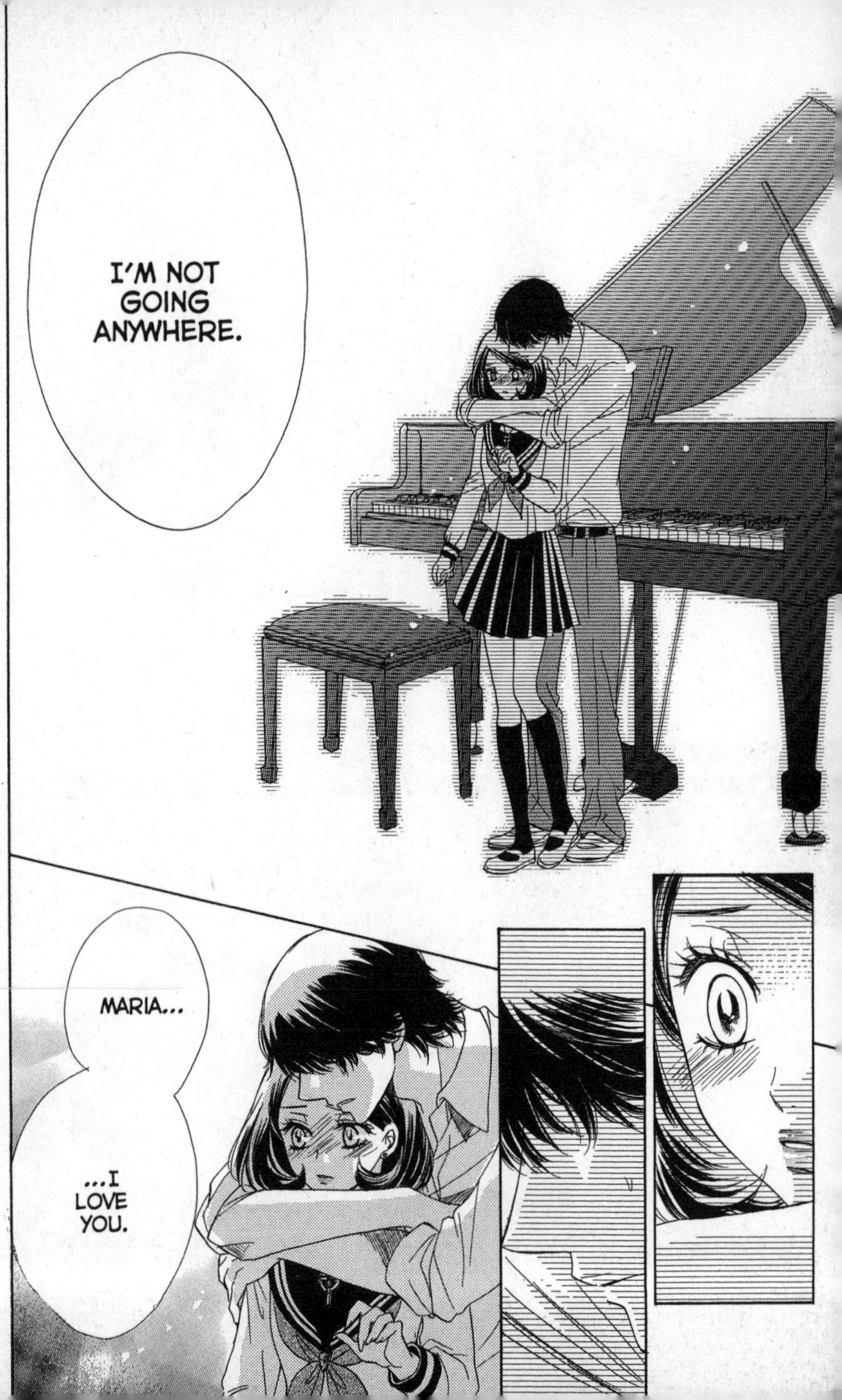
I'M NOT GOING ANYWHERE.
MARIA...
...I LOVE YOU.

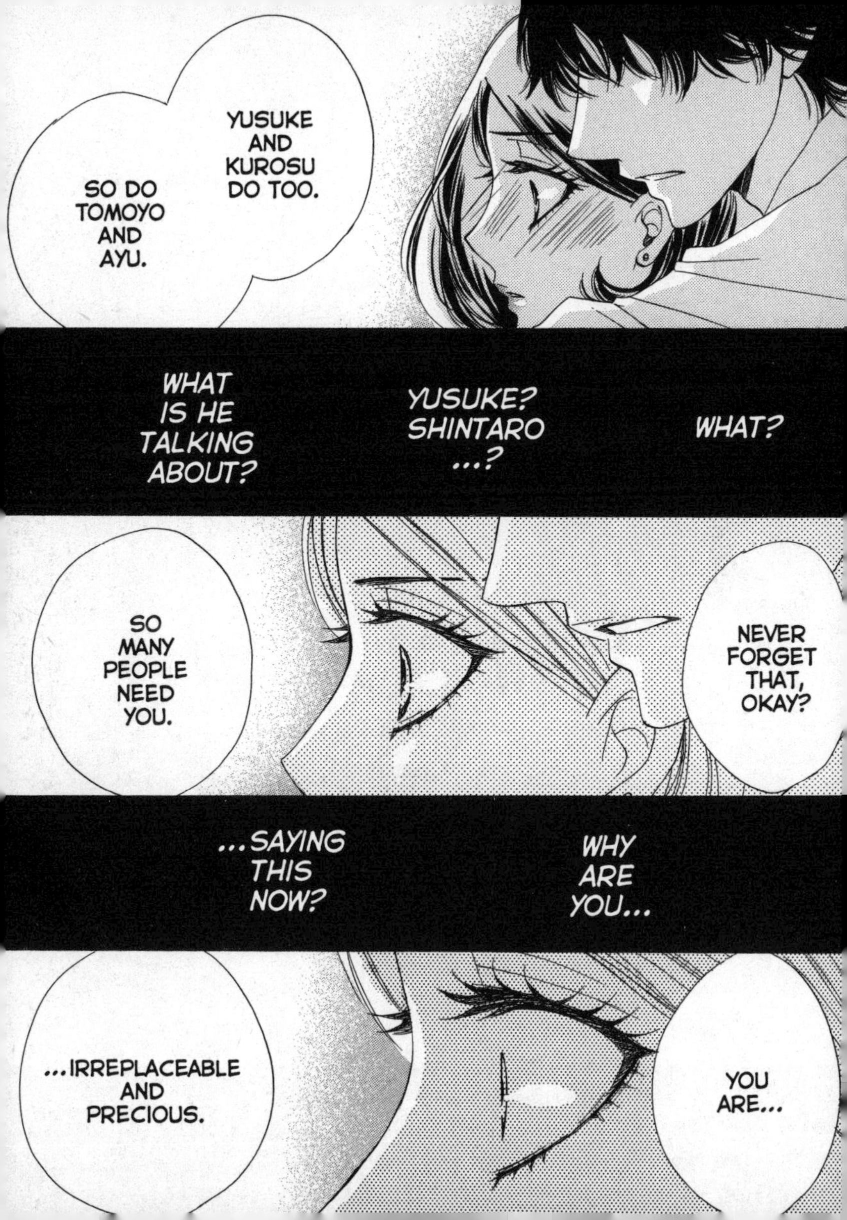
YUSUKE AND KUROSU DO TOO.
SO DO TOMOYO AND AYU.
WHAT?
YUSUKE? SHINTARO ...?
WHAT IS HE TALKING ABOUT?
NEVER FORGET THAT, OKAY?
SO MANY PEOPLE NEED YOU.
WHY ARE YOU...
...SAYING THIS NOW?
YOU ARE...
...IRREPLACEABLE AND PRECIOUS.

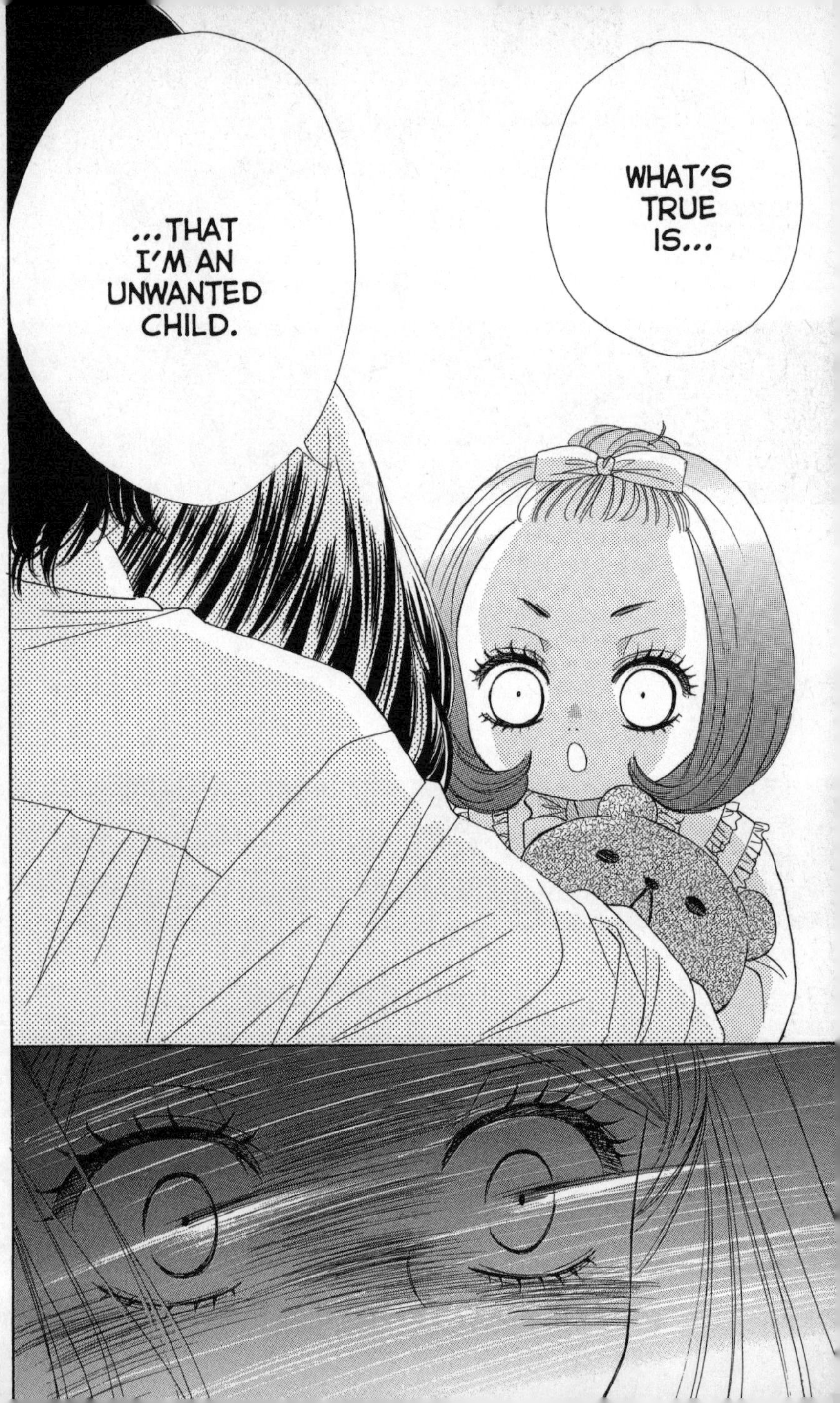
WHAT'S TRUE IS...
...THAT I'M AN UNWANTED CHILD.

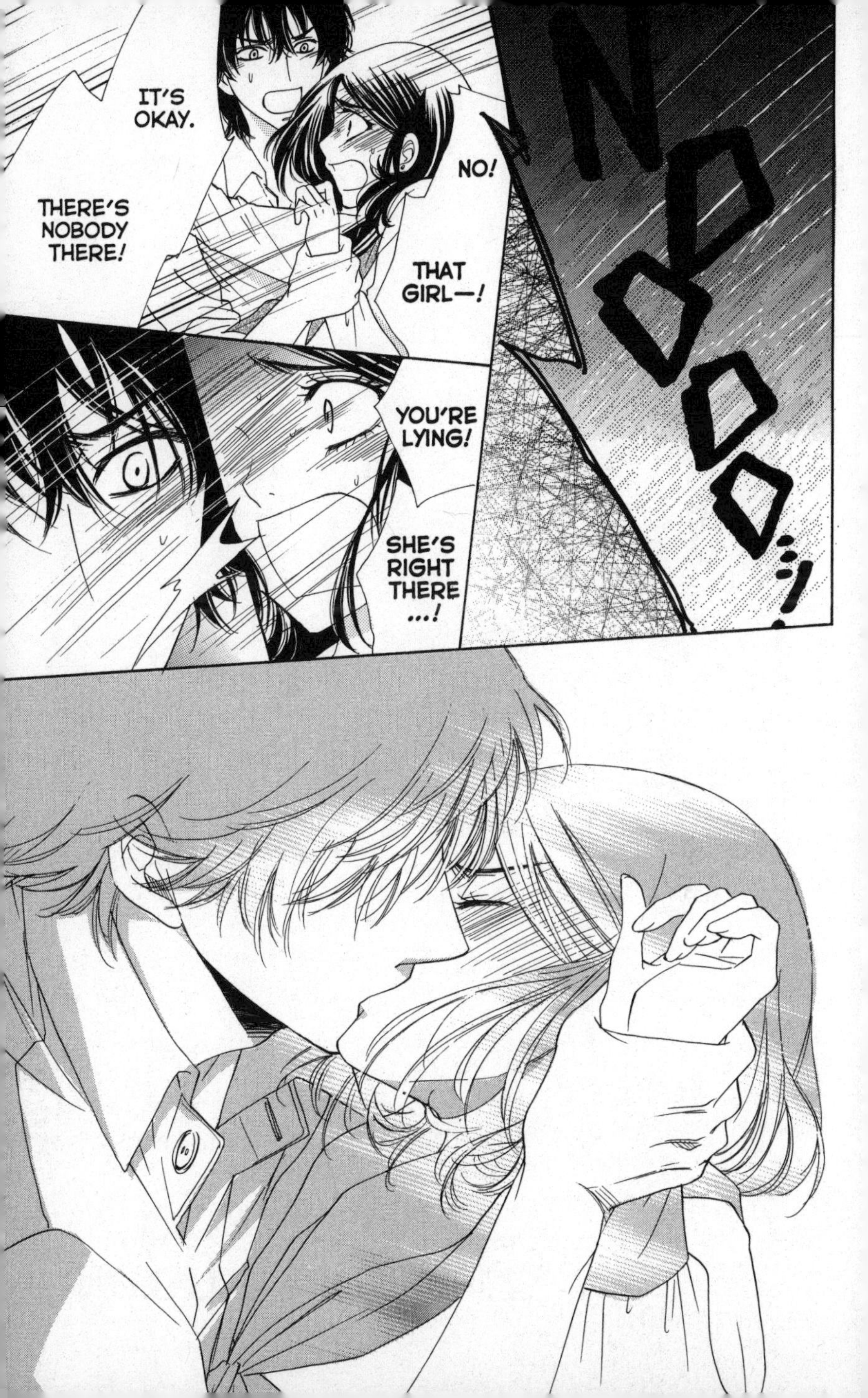
NOOOOO...!!
NO!
THAT GIRL—!
IT'S OKAY.
THERE'S NOBODY THERE!
YOU'RE LYING!
SHE'S RIGHT THERE ...!

A Devil and
Her Love Song

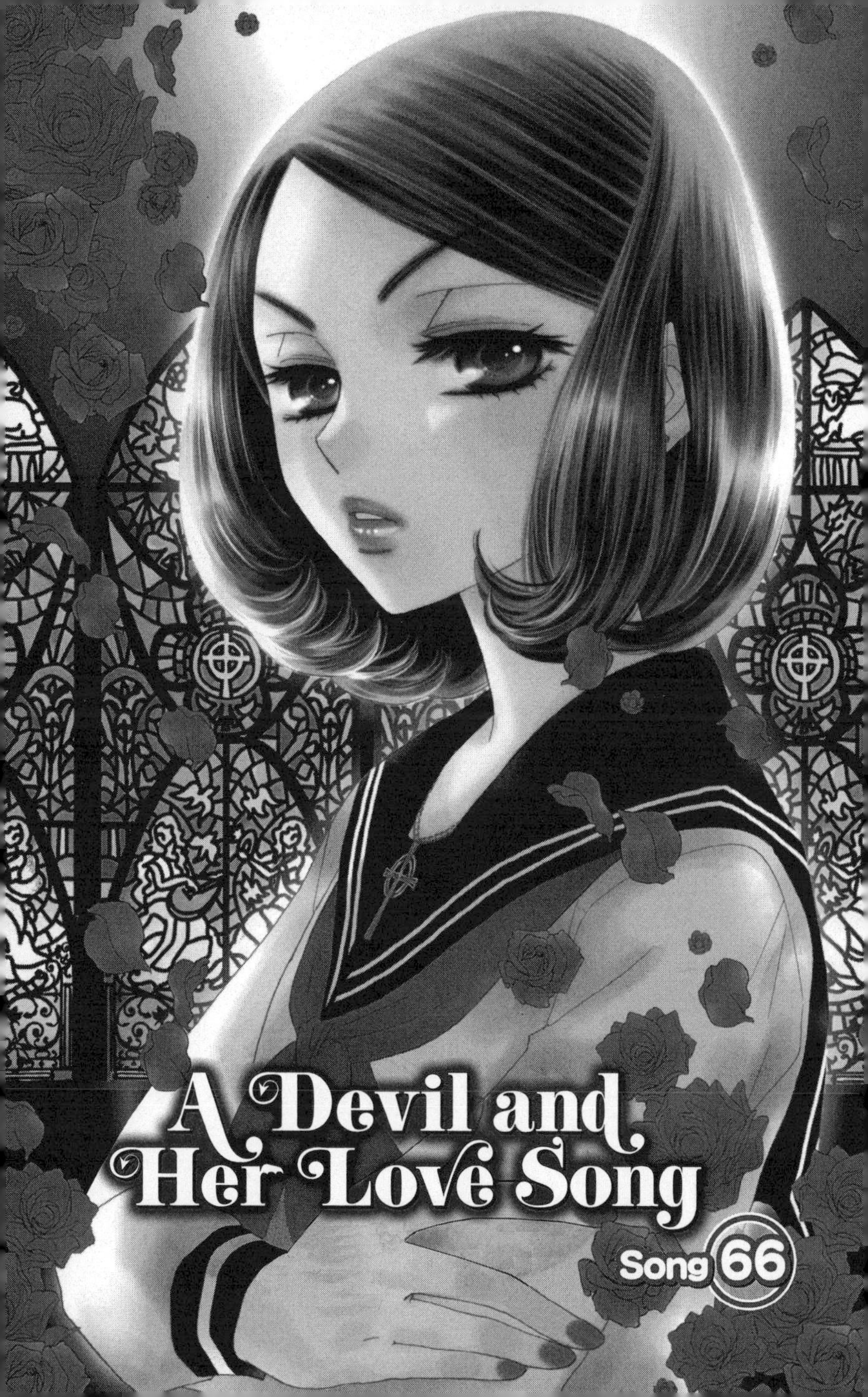
A Devil and Her Love Song
Song 66

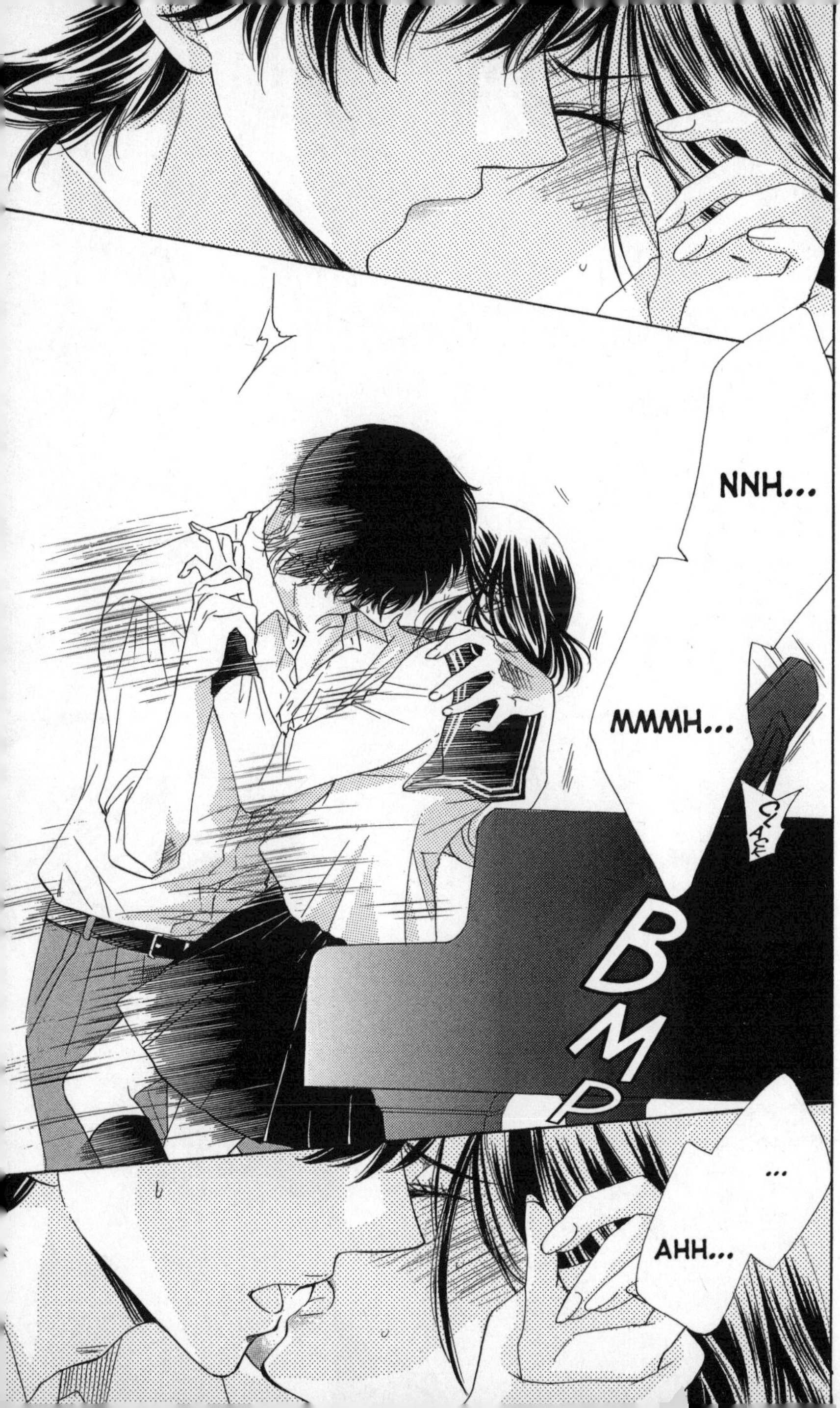
NNH...
MMMH...
CLACK
BMP
...
AHH...

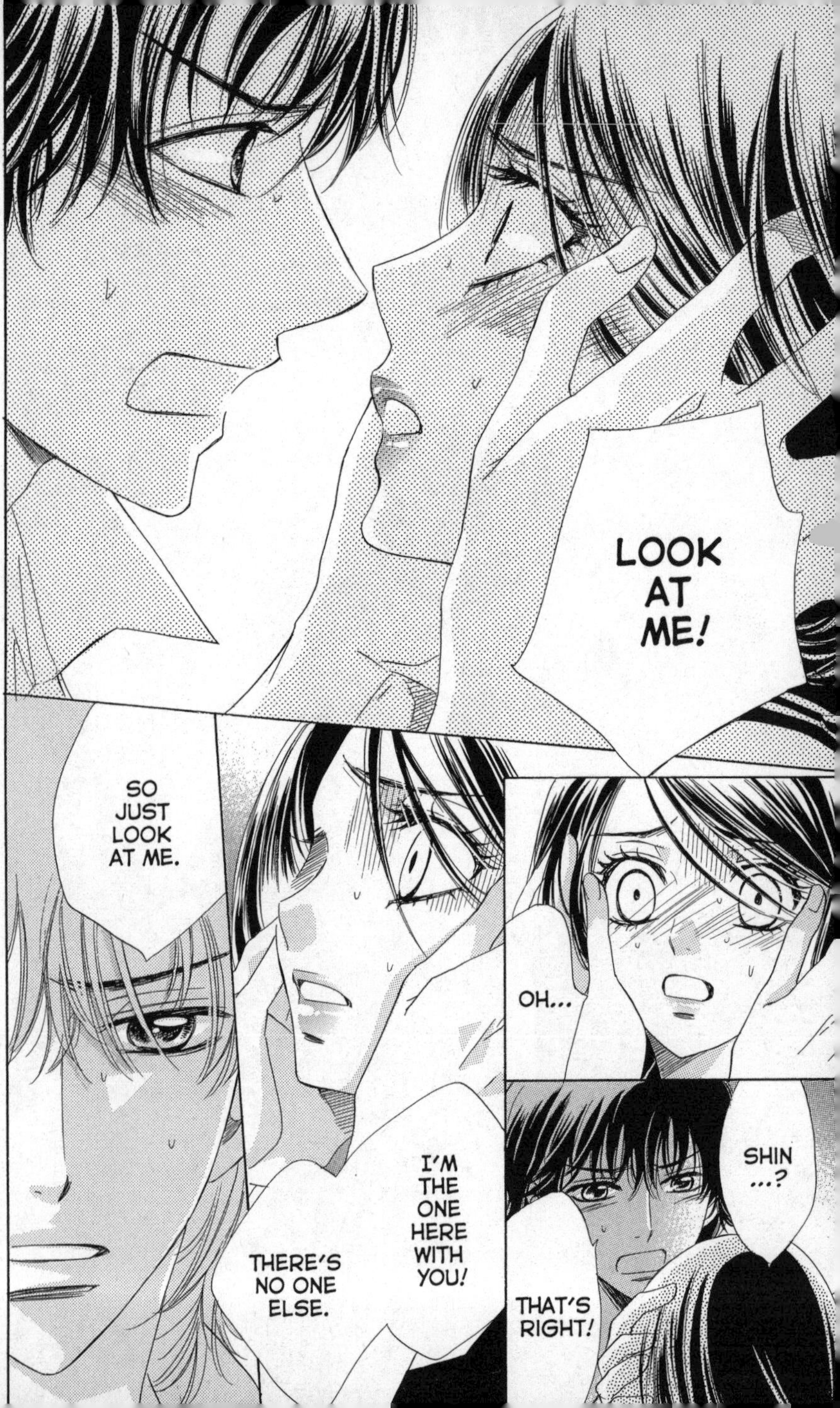
LOOK AT ME!
OH...
SHIN ...?
THAT'S RIGHT!
I'M THE ONE HERE WITH YOU!
THERE'S NO ONE ELSE.
SO JUST LOOK AT ME.

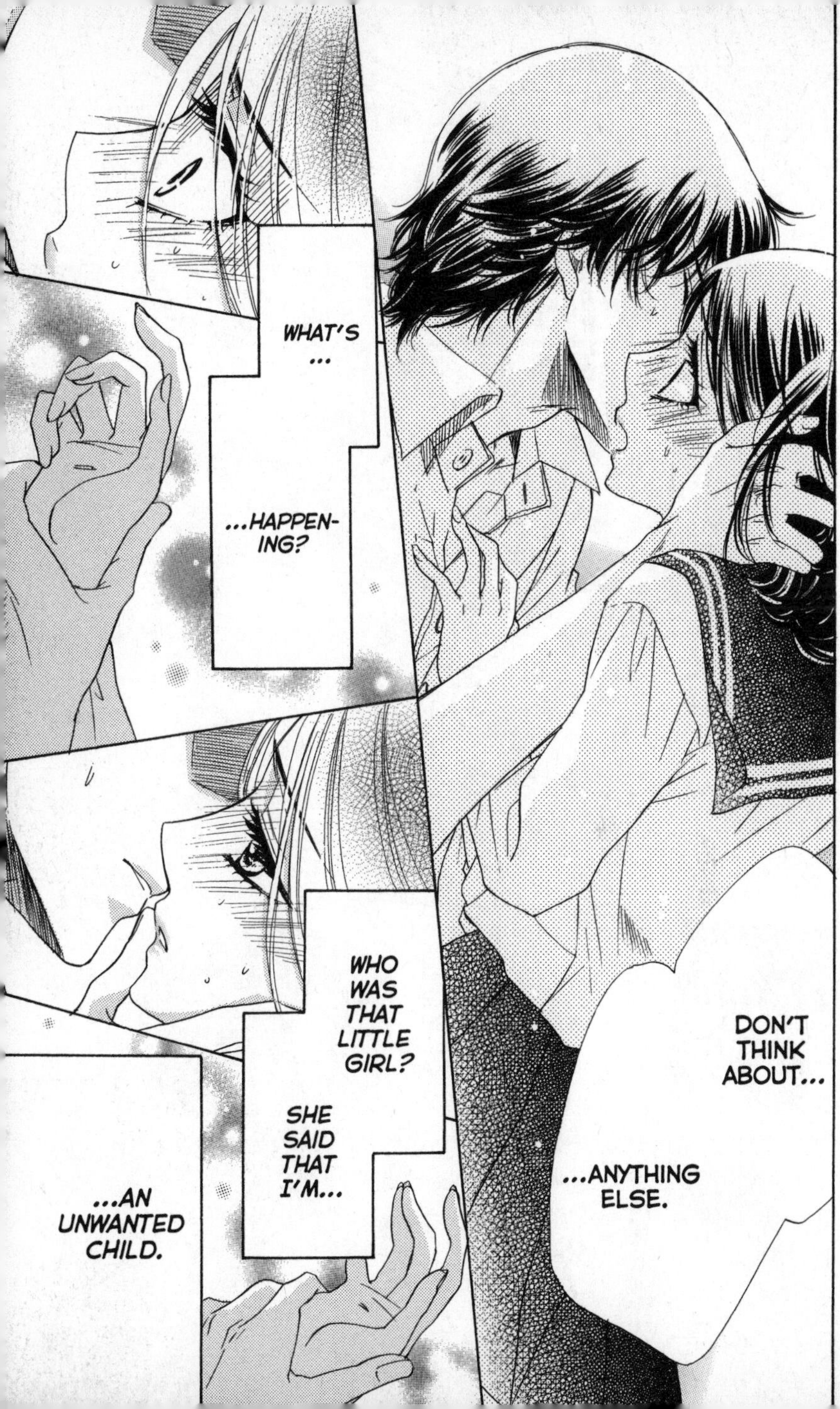
DON'T THINK ABOUT...
...ANYTHING ELSE.
WHAT'S ...
...HAPPEN-ING?
WHO WAS THAT LITTLE GIRL?
SHE SAID THAT I'M...
...AN UNWANTED CHILD.

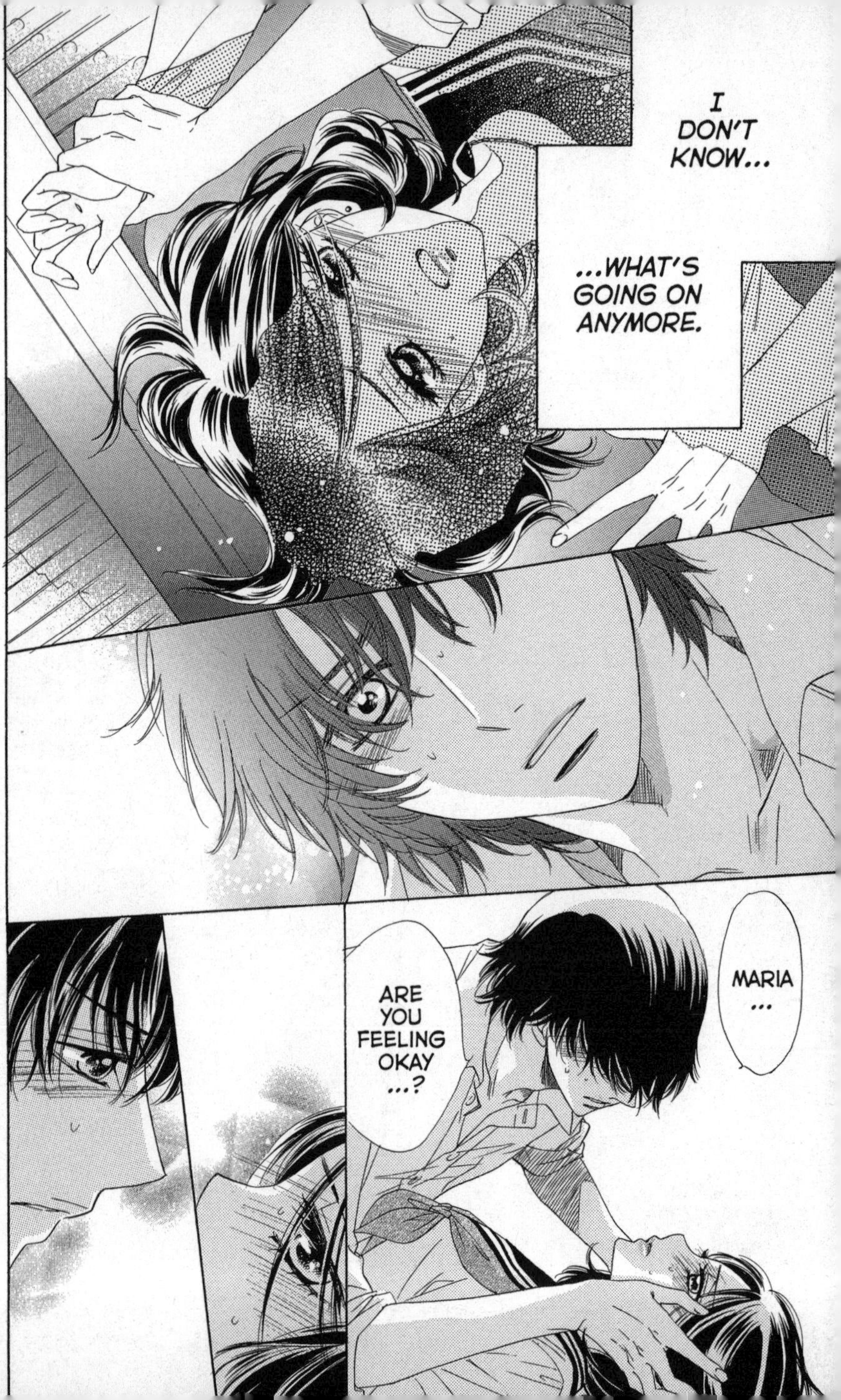
I DON'T KNOW...
...WHAT'S GOING ON ANYMORE.
MARIA...
ARE YOU FEELING OKAY...?

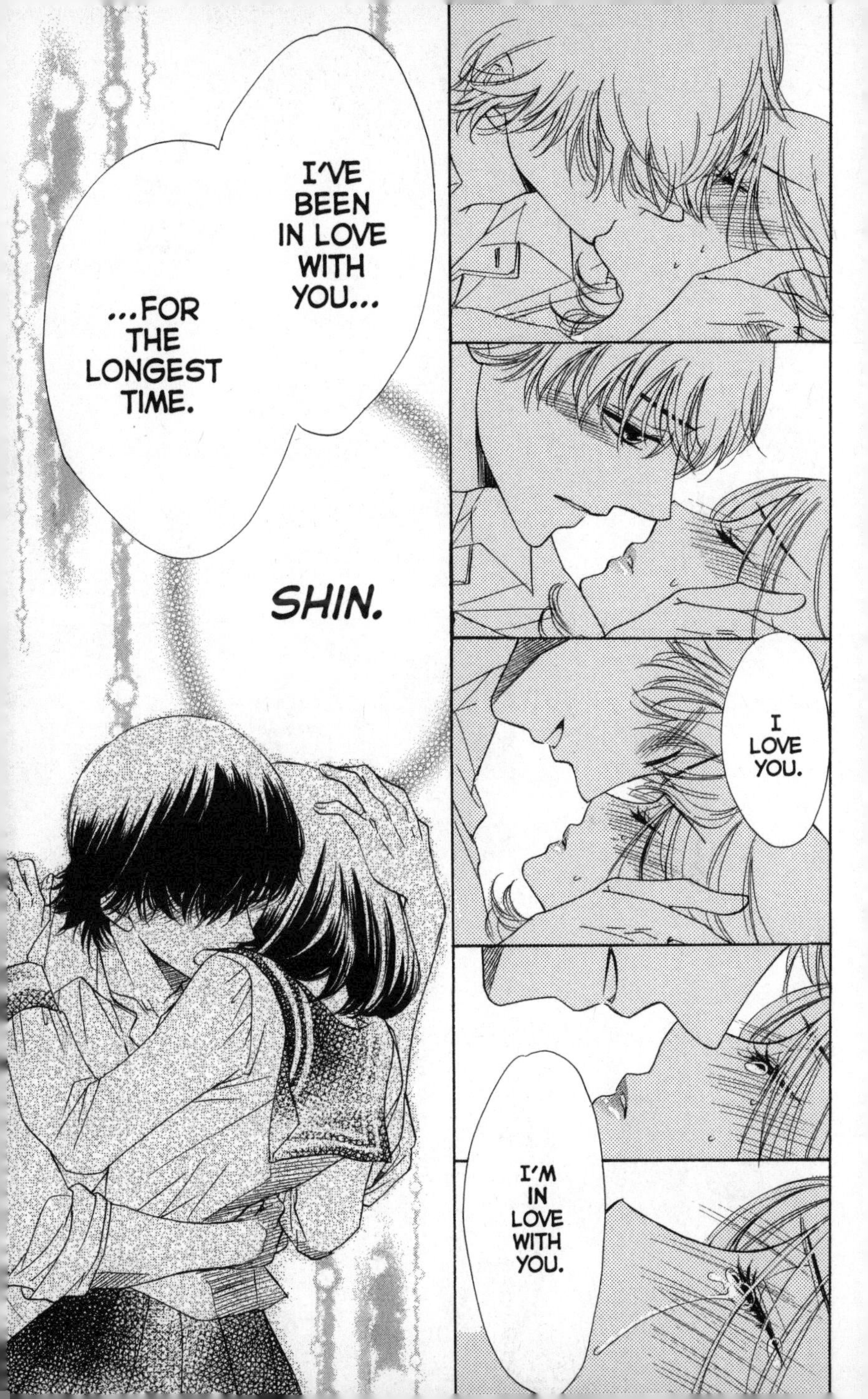
I LOVE YOU.
I'M IN LOVE WITH YOU.
I'VE BEEN IN LOVE WITH YOU...
...FOR THE LONGEST TIME.
SHIN.

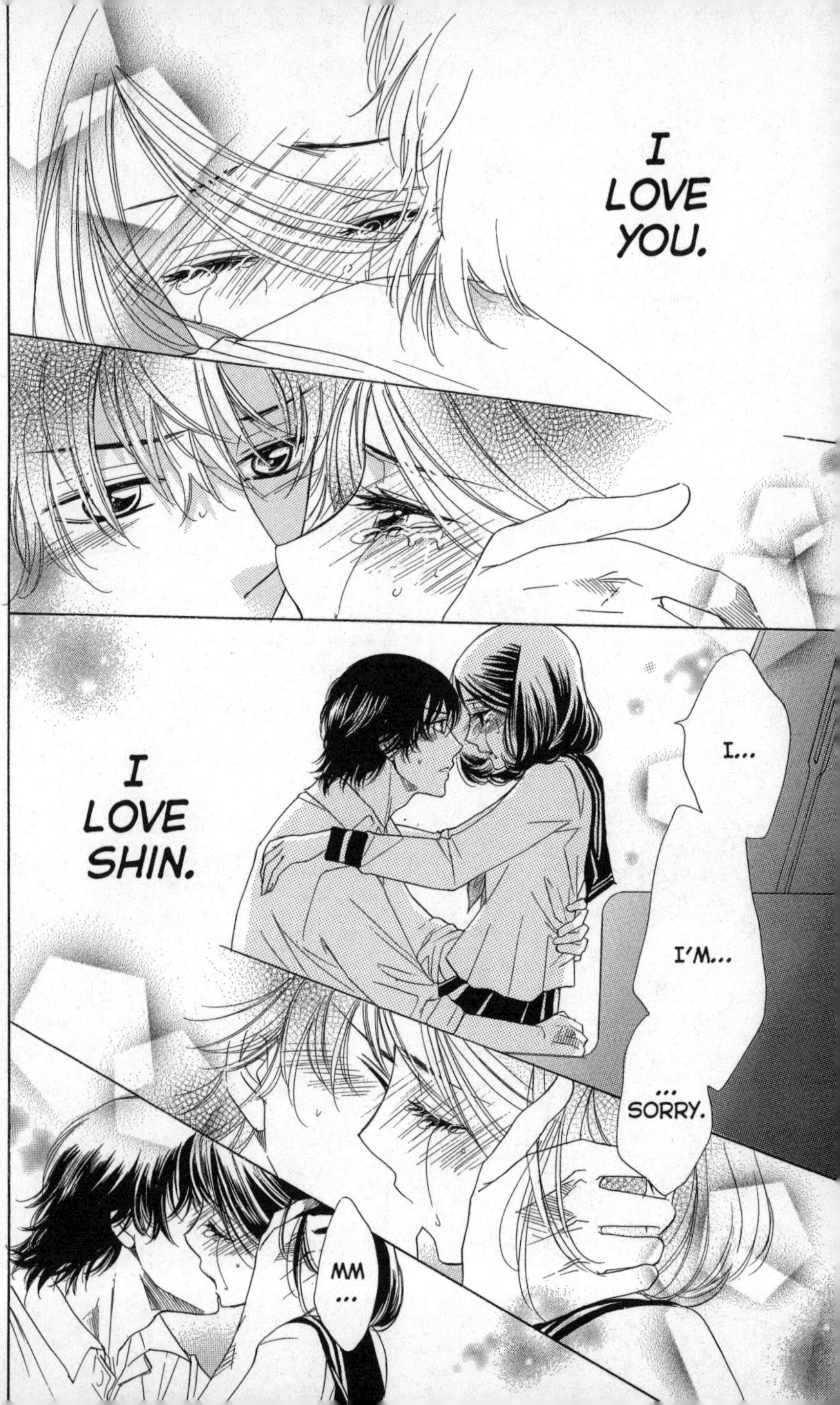
I LOVE YOU.
I... I'M... ...SORRY.
I LOVE SHIN.
MM ...

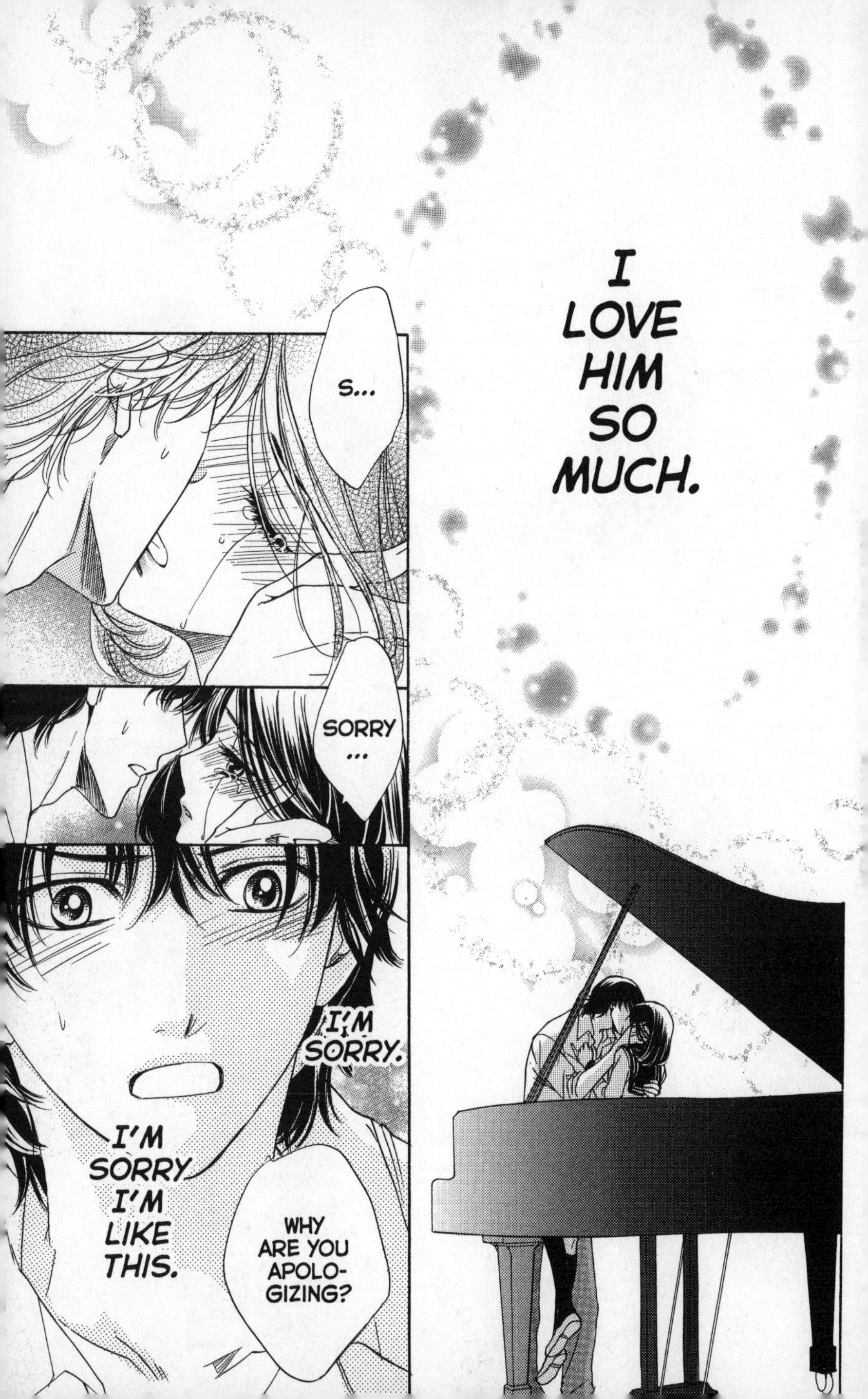
I LOVE HIM SO MUCH.
S...
SORRY...
I'M SORRY.
I'M SORRY I'M LIKE THIS.
WHY ARE YOU APOLOGIZING?

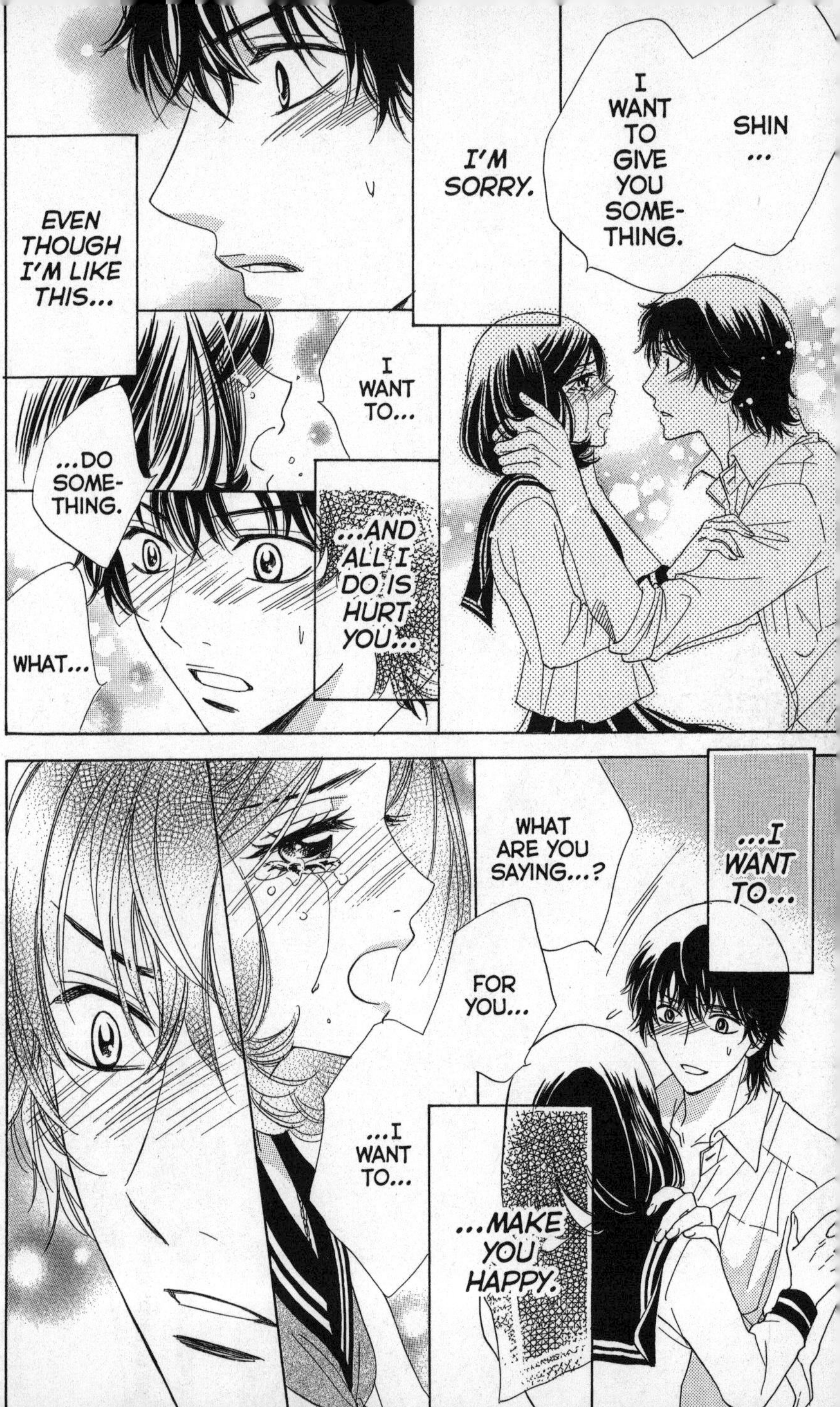
SHIN...
I WANT TO GIVE YOU SOMETHING.
I'M SORRY.
EVEN THOUGH I'M LIKE THIS...
...AND ALL I DO IS HURT YOU...
I WANT TO...
...DO SOMETHING.
WHAT...
...I WANT TO...
WHAT ARE YOU SAYING...?
FOR YOU...
...I WANT TO...
...MAKE YOU HAPPY.

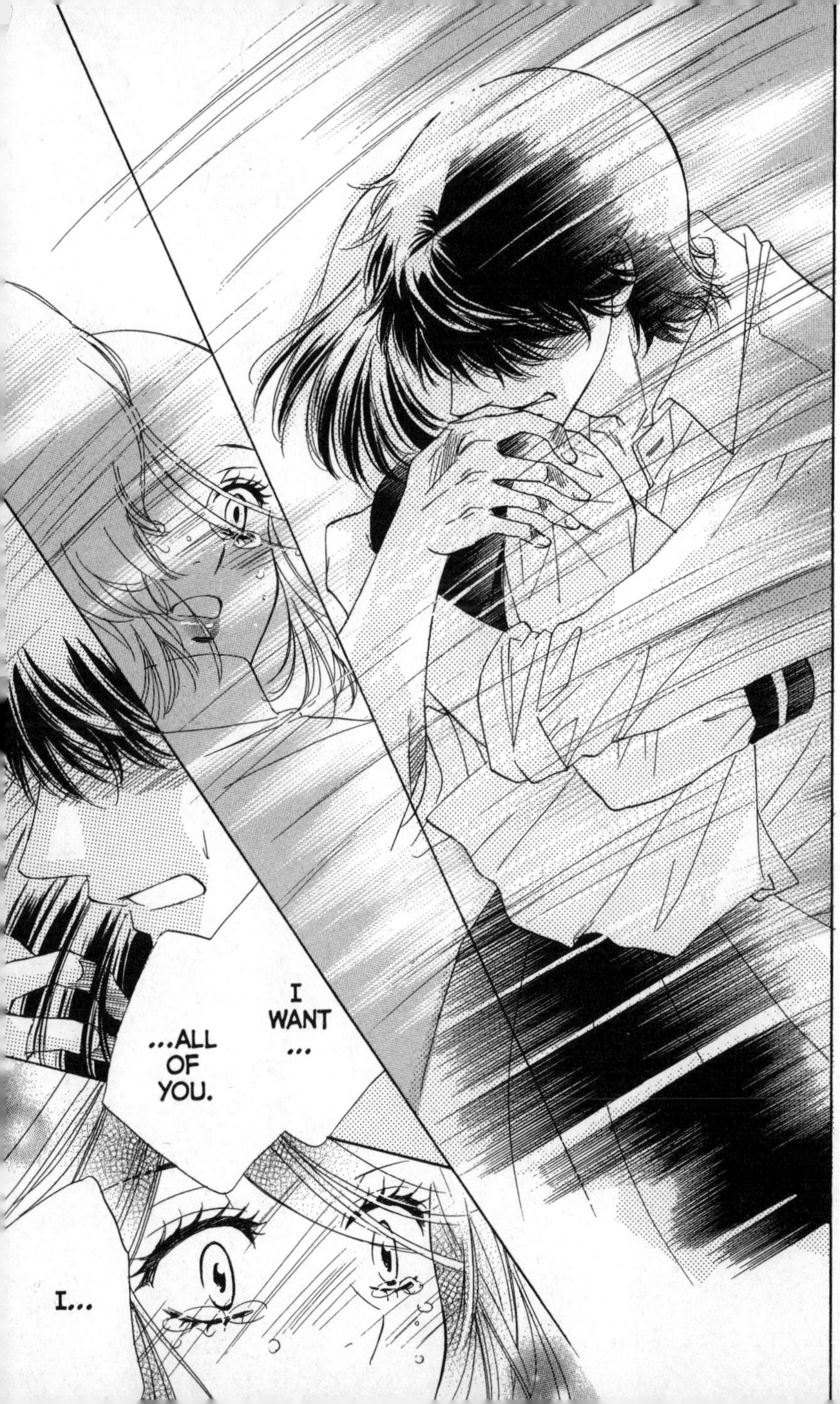
I WANT...
...ALL OF YOU.
I...

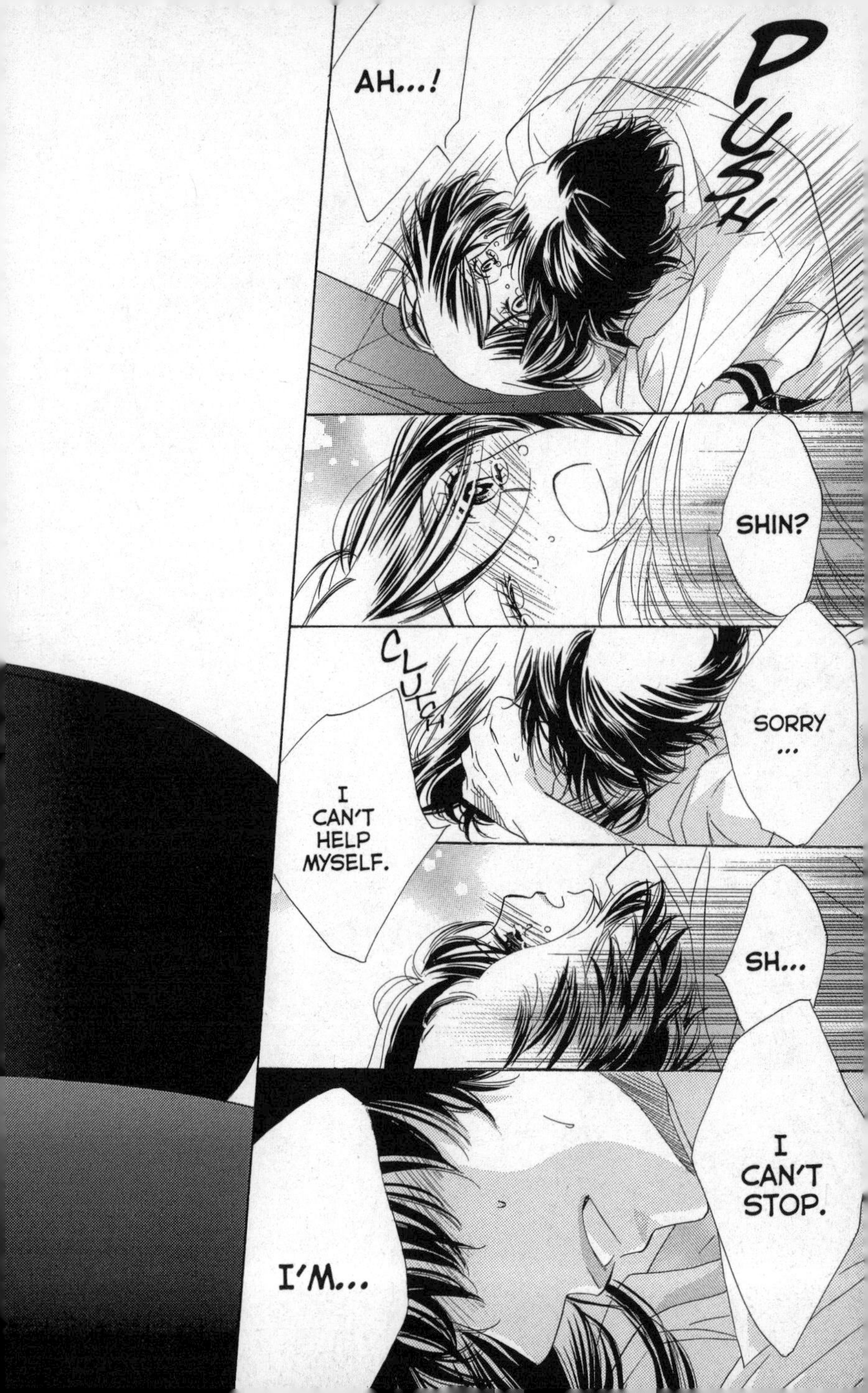
PUSH
AH...!
SHIN?
SORRY ...
CLUTCH
I CAN'T HELP MYSELF.
SH...
I CAN'T STOP.
I'M...

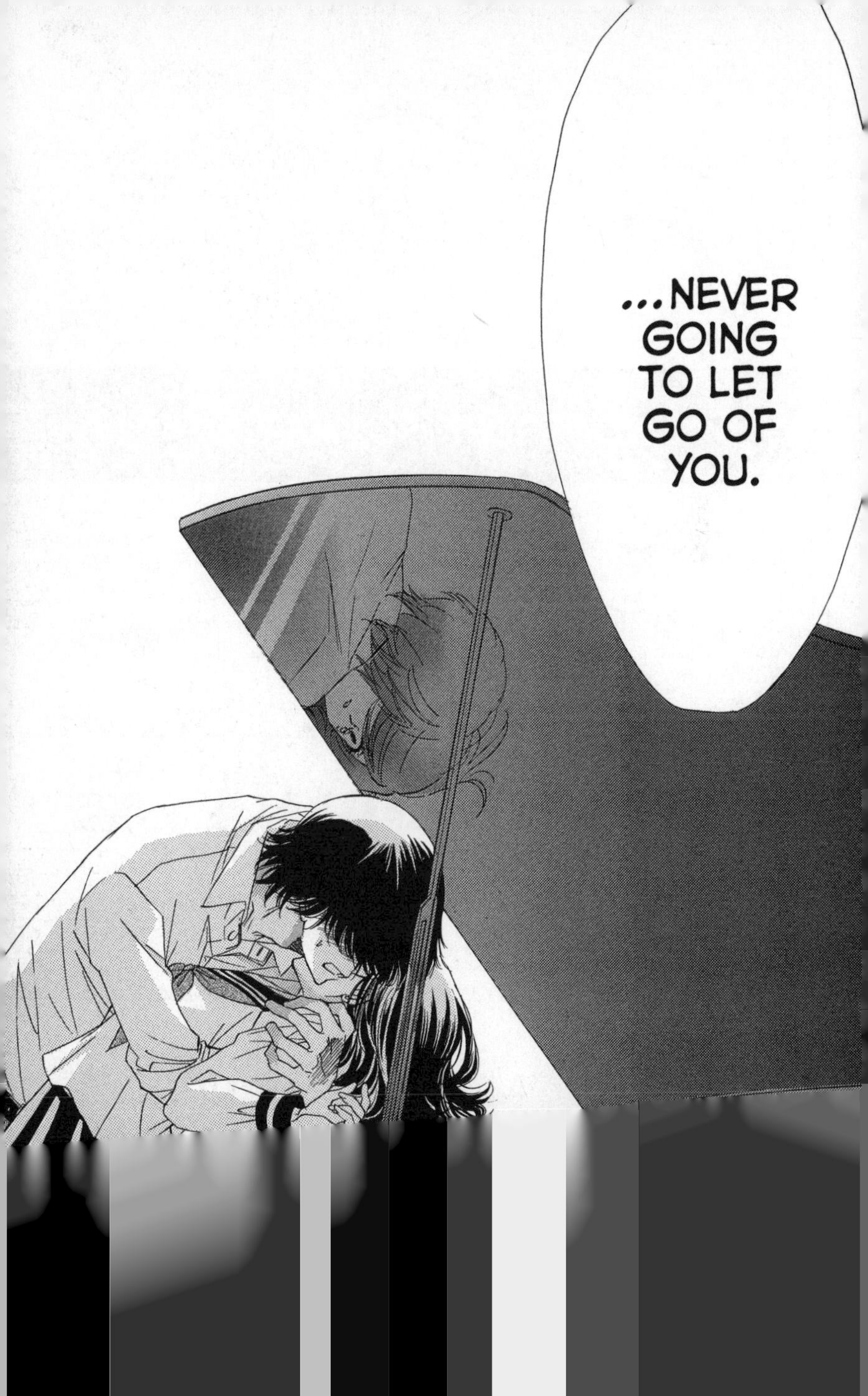
...NEVER GOING TO LET GO OF YOU.

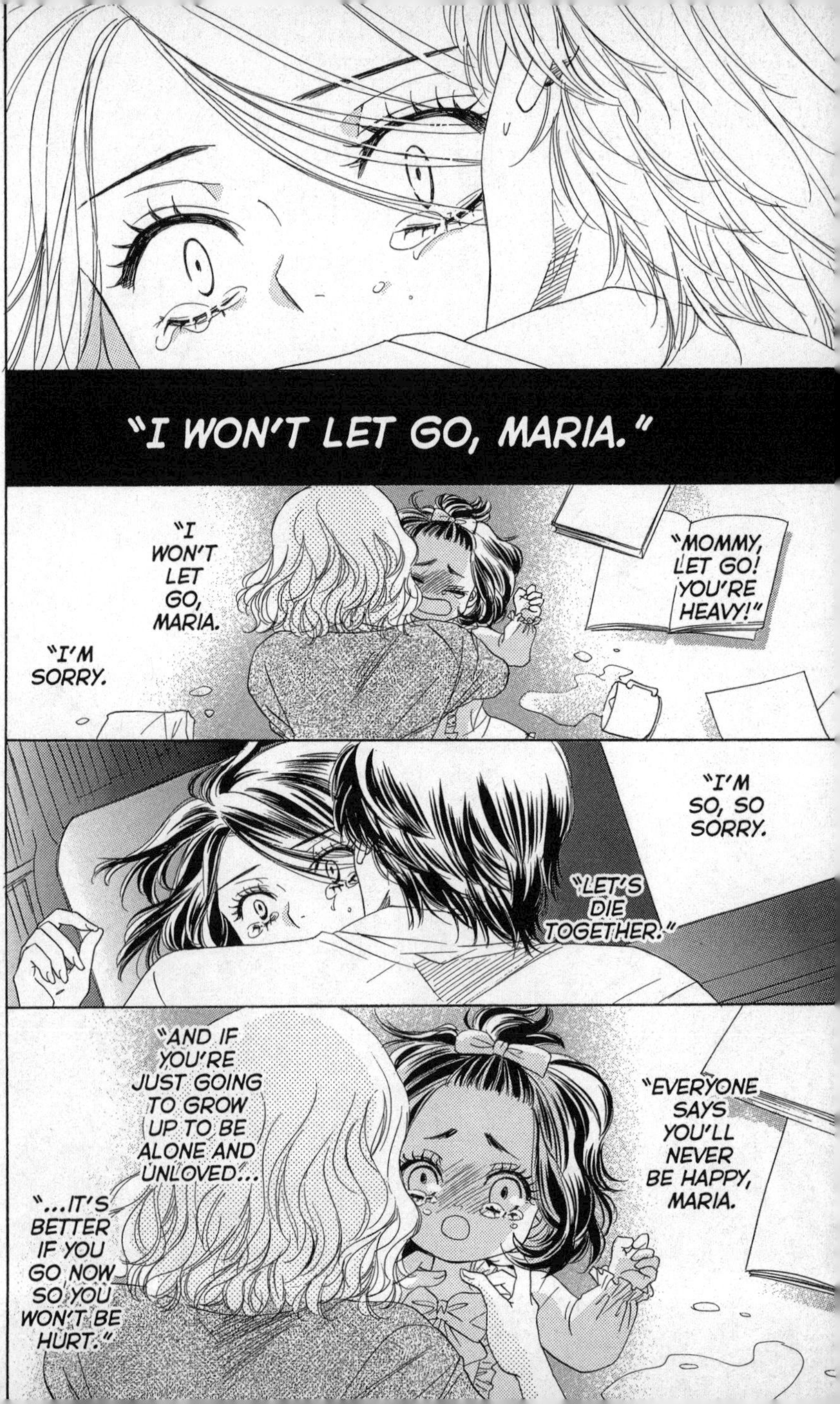
"I WON'T LET GO, MARIA."
"MOMMY, LET GO! YOU'RE HEAVY!"
"I WON'T LET GO, MARIA.
"I'M SORRY.
"I'M SO, SO SORRY.
"LET'S DIE TOGETHER."
"EVERYONE SAYS YOU'LL NEVER BE HAPPY, MARIA.
"AND IF YOU'RE JUST GOING TO GROW UP TO BE ALONE AND UNLOVED...
"...IT'S BETTER IF YOU GO NOW SO YOU WON'T BE HURT."

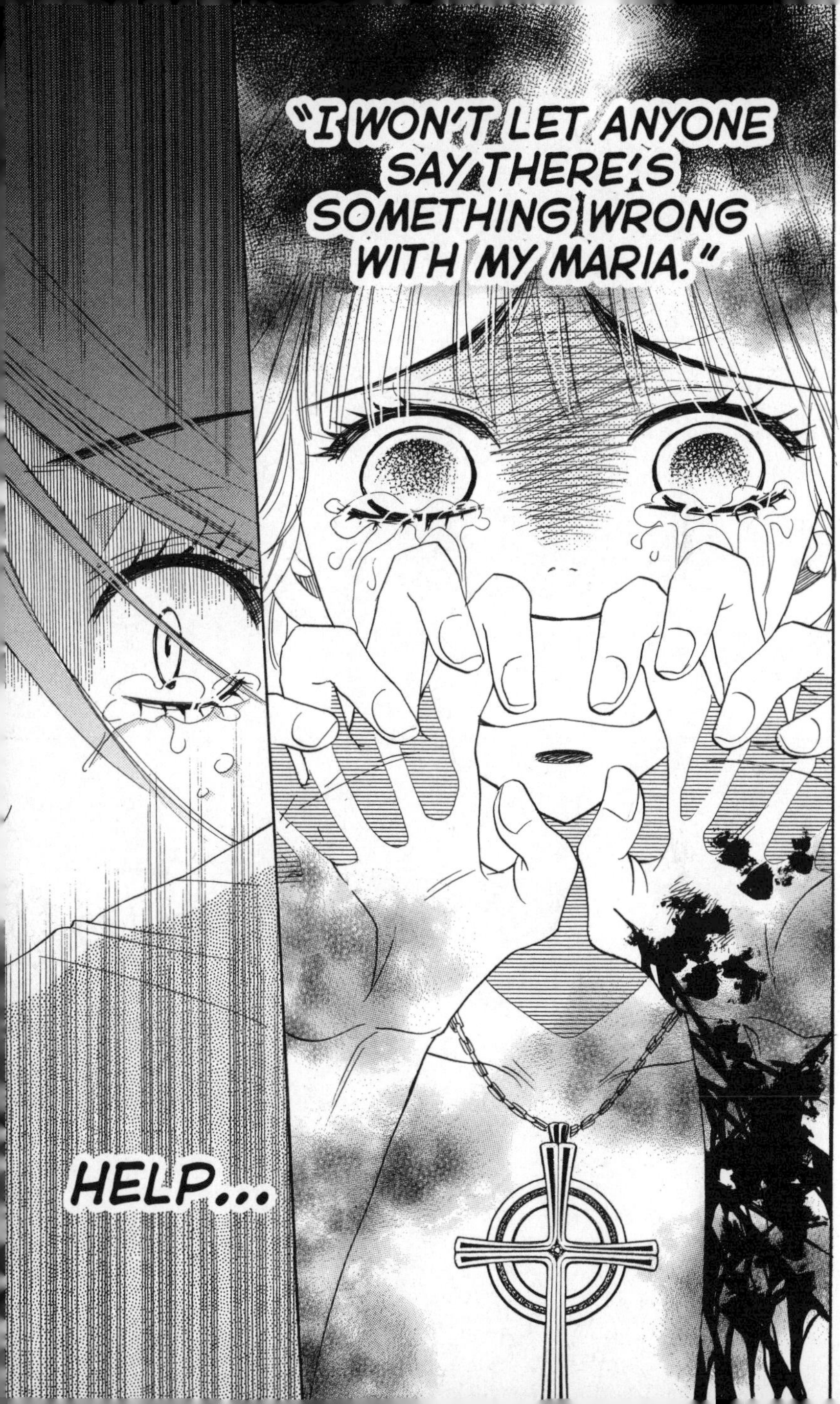
"I WON'T LET ANYONE SAY THERE'S SOMETHING WRONG WITH MY MARIA."
HELP...

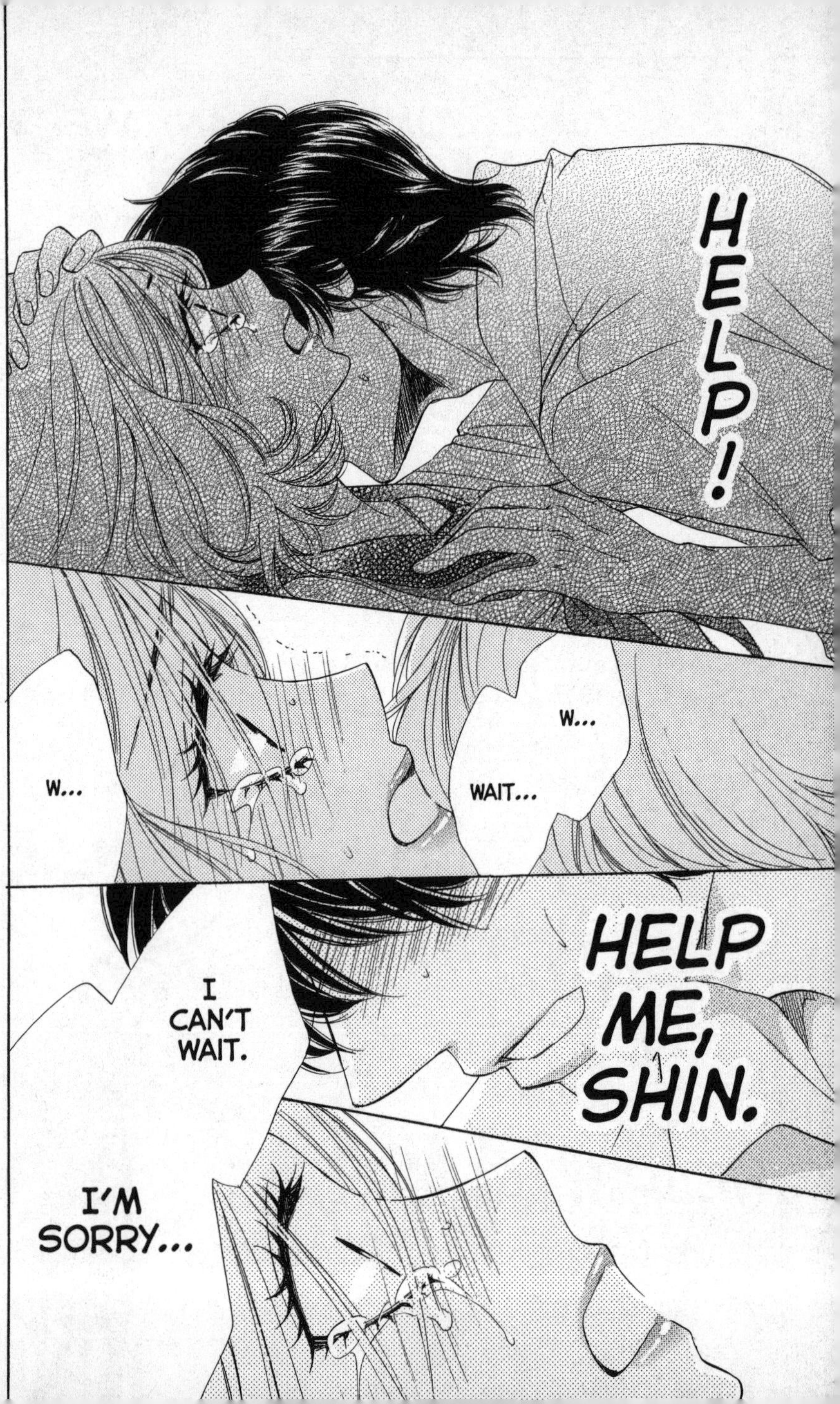
HELP!
W...
WAIT...
W...
HELP ME, SHIN.
I CAN'T WAIT.
I'M SORRY...

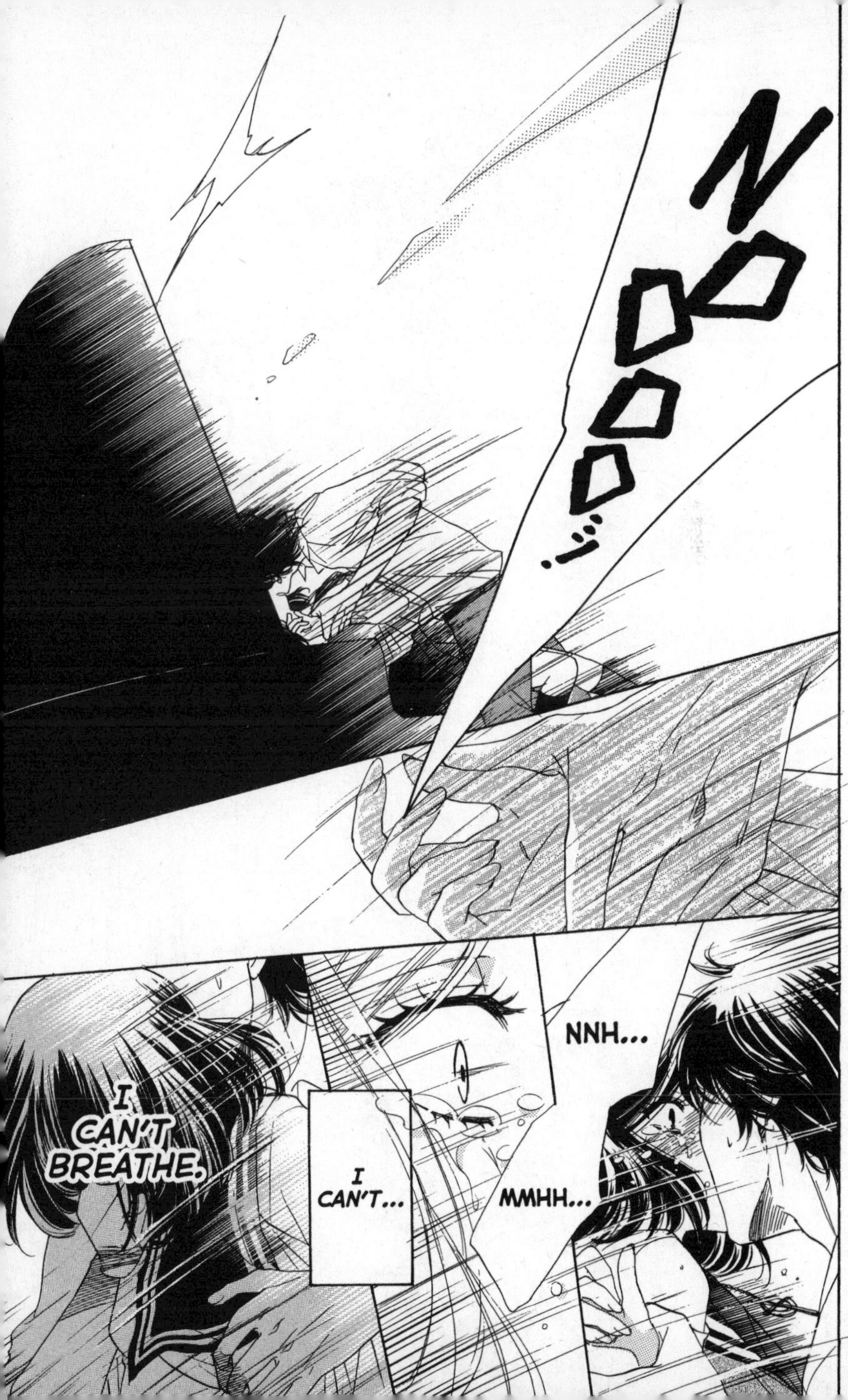
NOOOOッ
NNH...
MMHH...
I CAN'T...
I CAN'T BREATHE.

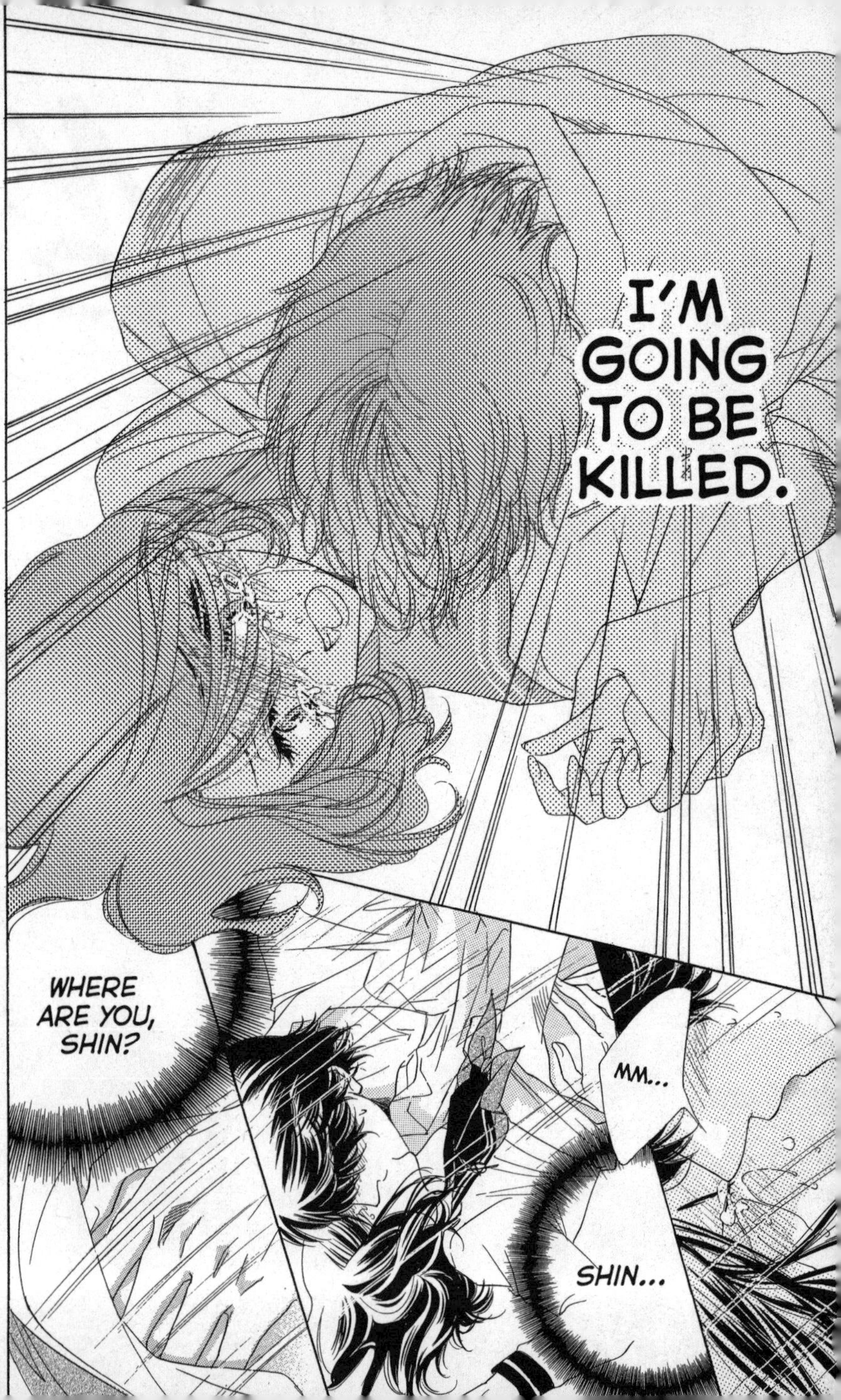
I'M GOING TO BE KILLED.
MM...
SHIN...
WHERE ARE YOU, SHIN?

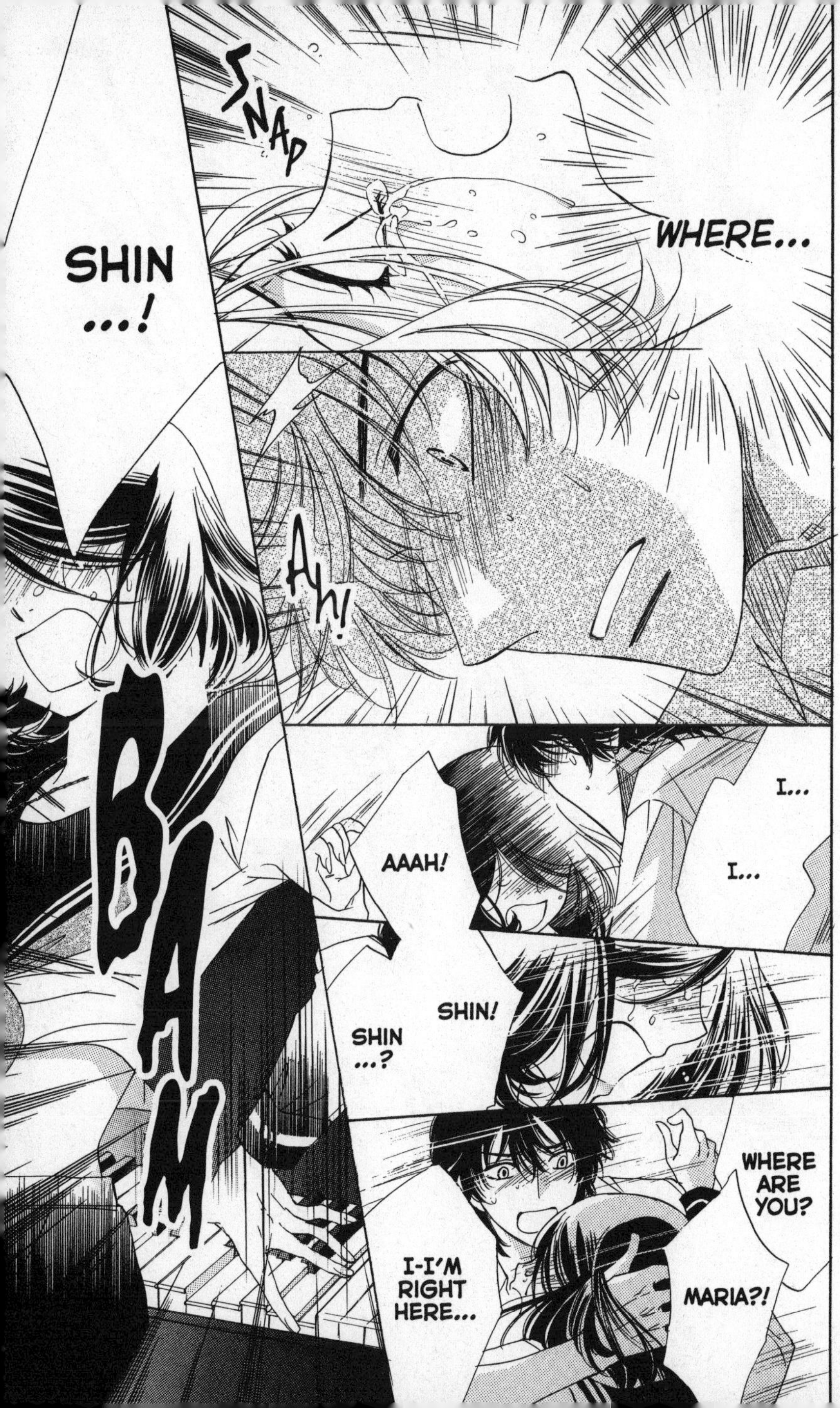
SNAP
WHERE...
Ah!
I...
I...
AAAH!
SHIN!
SHIN ...?
WHERE ARE YOU?
MARIA?!
I-I'M RIGHT HERE...
SHIN ...!
BAM

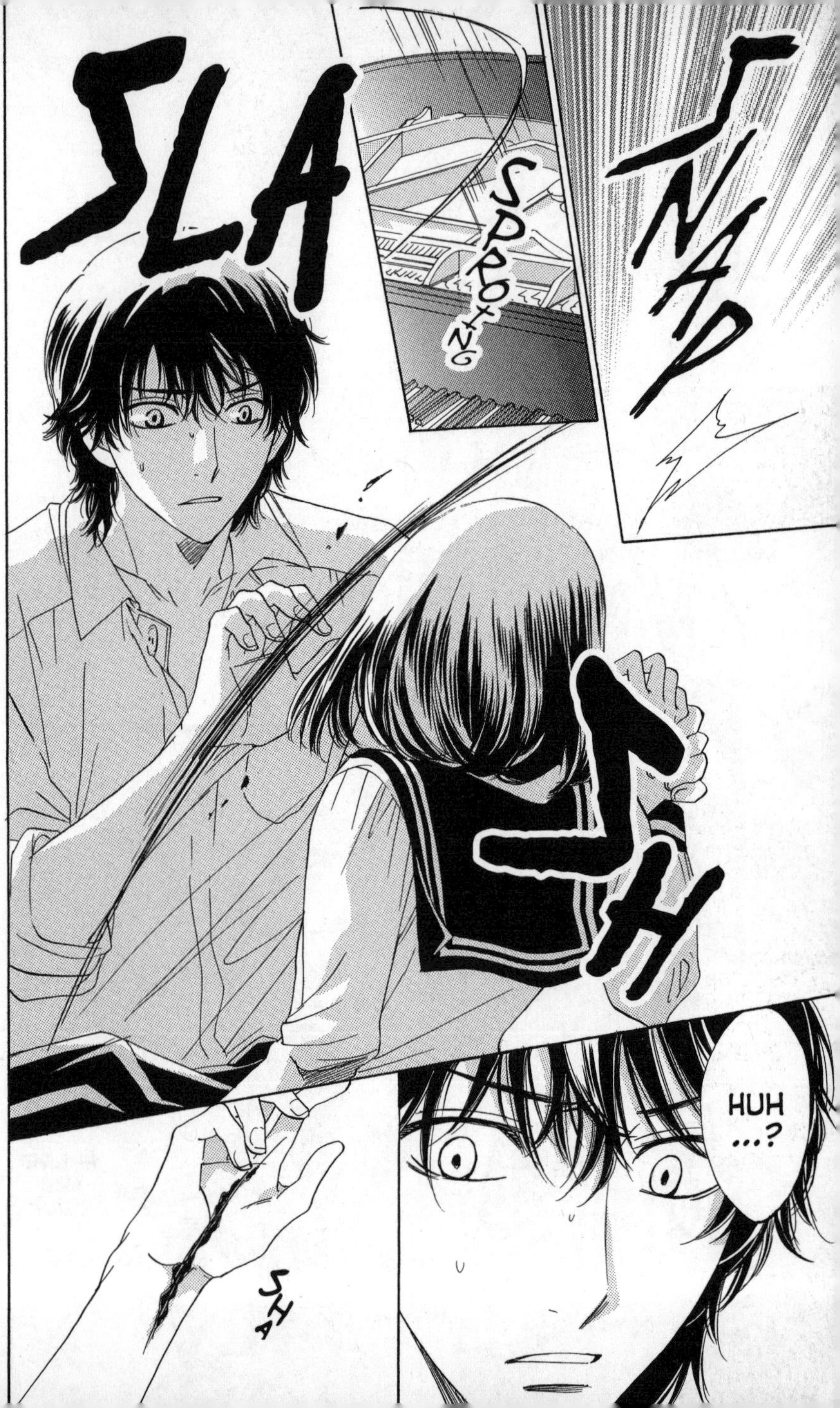
SNAP
SPROING
SLA
SH
HUH ...?
SHA

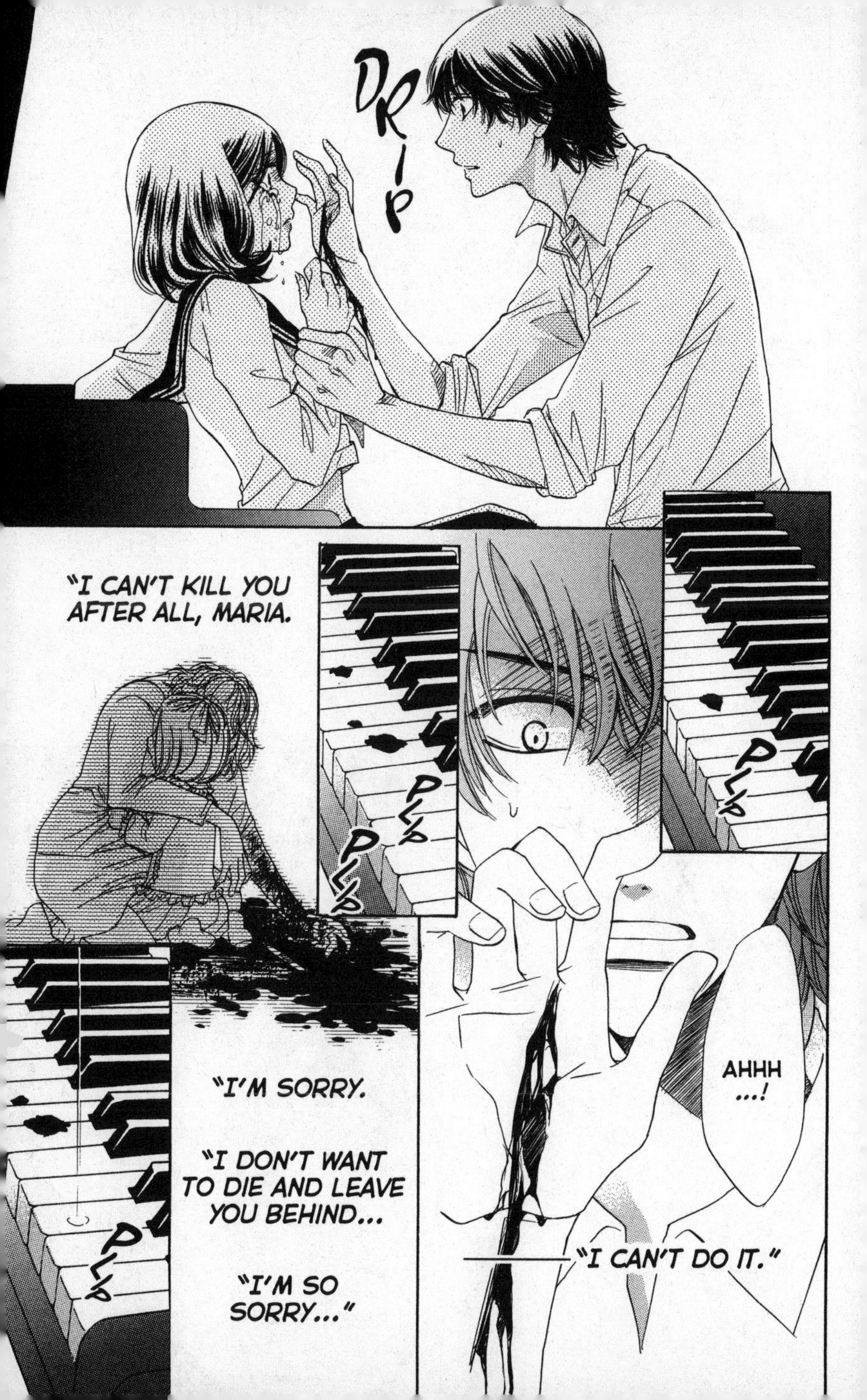

DRIP
PLIP
AHHH ...!
"I CAN'T DO IT."
PLIP
PLIP
"I CAN'T KILL YOU AFTER ALL, MARIA.
"I'M SORRY.
"I DON'T WANT TO DIE AND LEAVE YOU BEHIND...
"I'M SO SORRY..."
PLIP

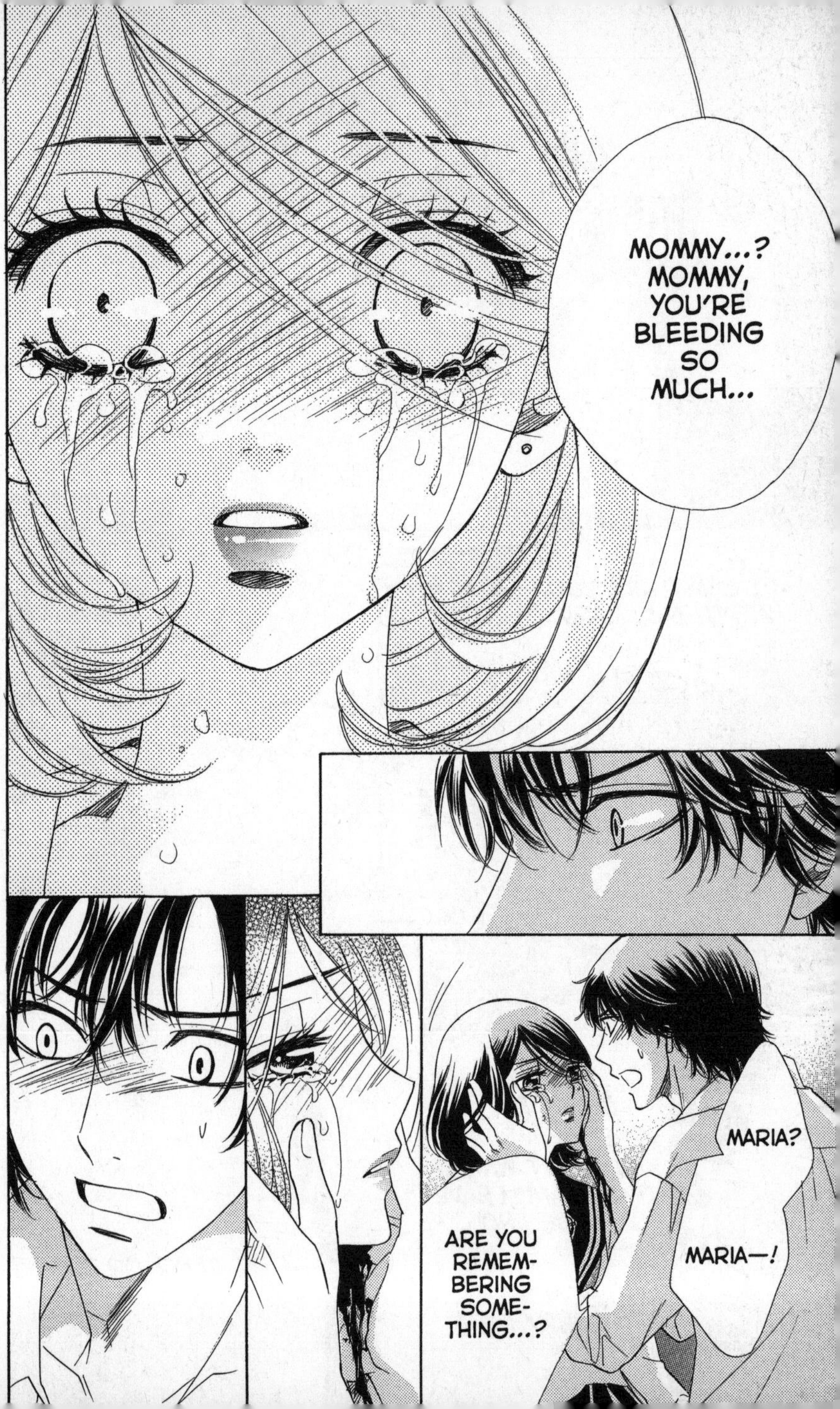
MOMMY...? MOMMY, YOU'RE BLEEDING SO MUCH...
MARIA?
MARIA—!
ARE YOU REMEMBERING SOMETHING...?

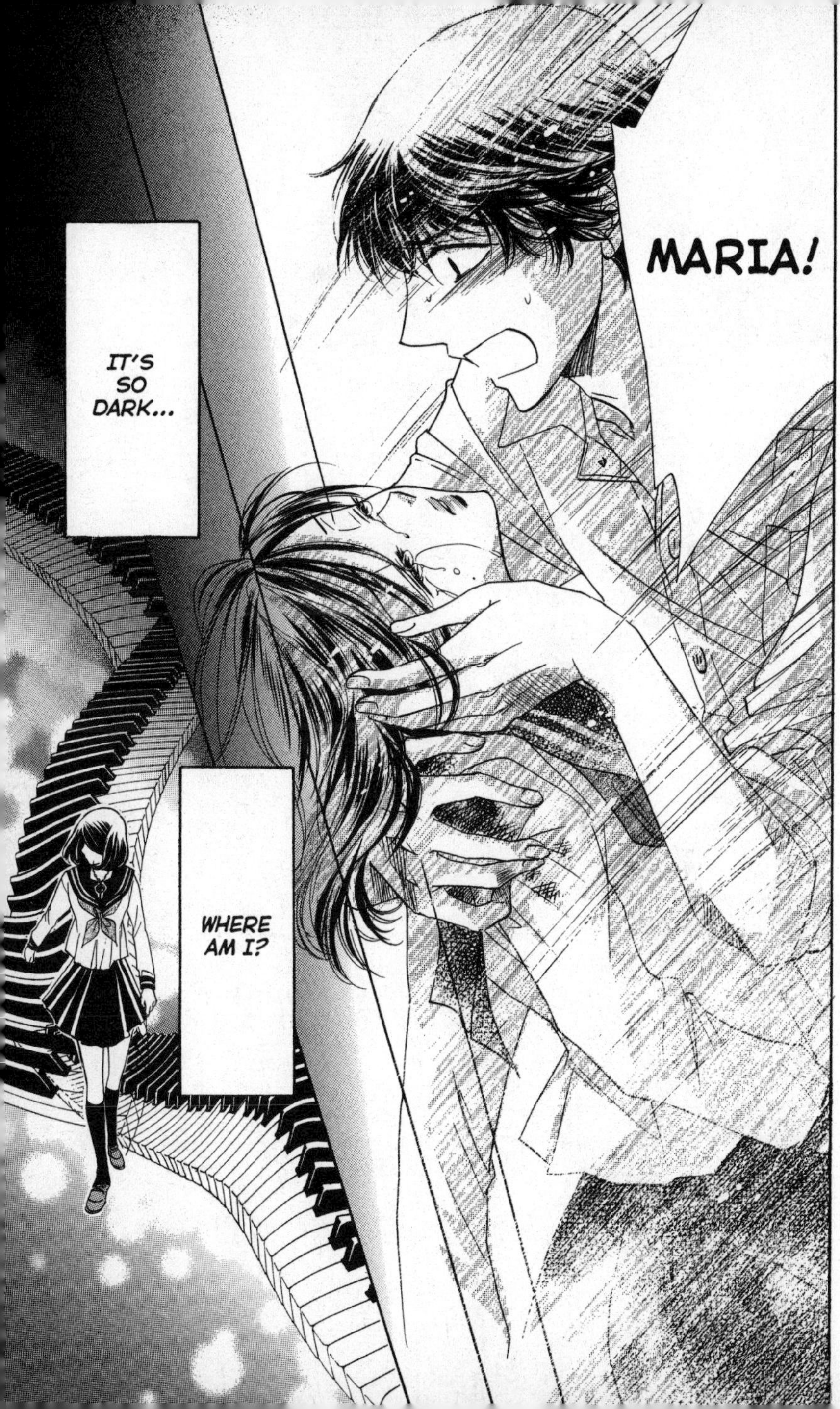
MARIA!
IT'S SO DARK...
WHERE AM I?

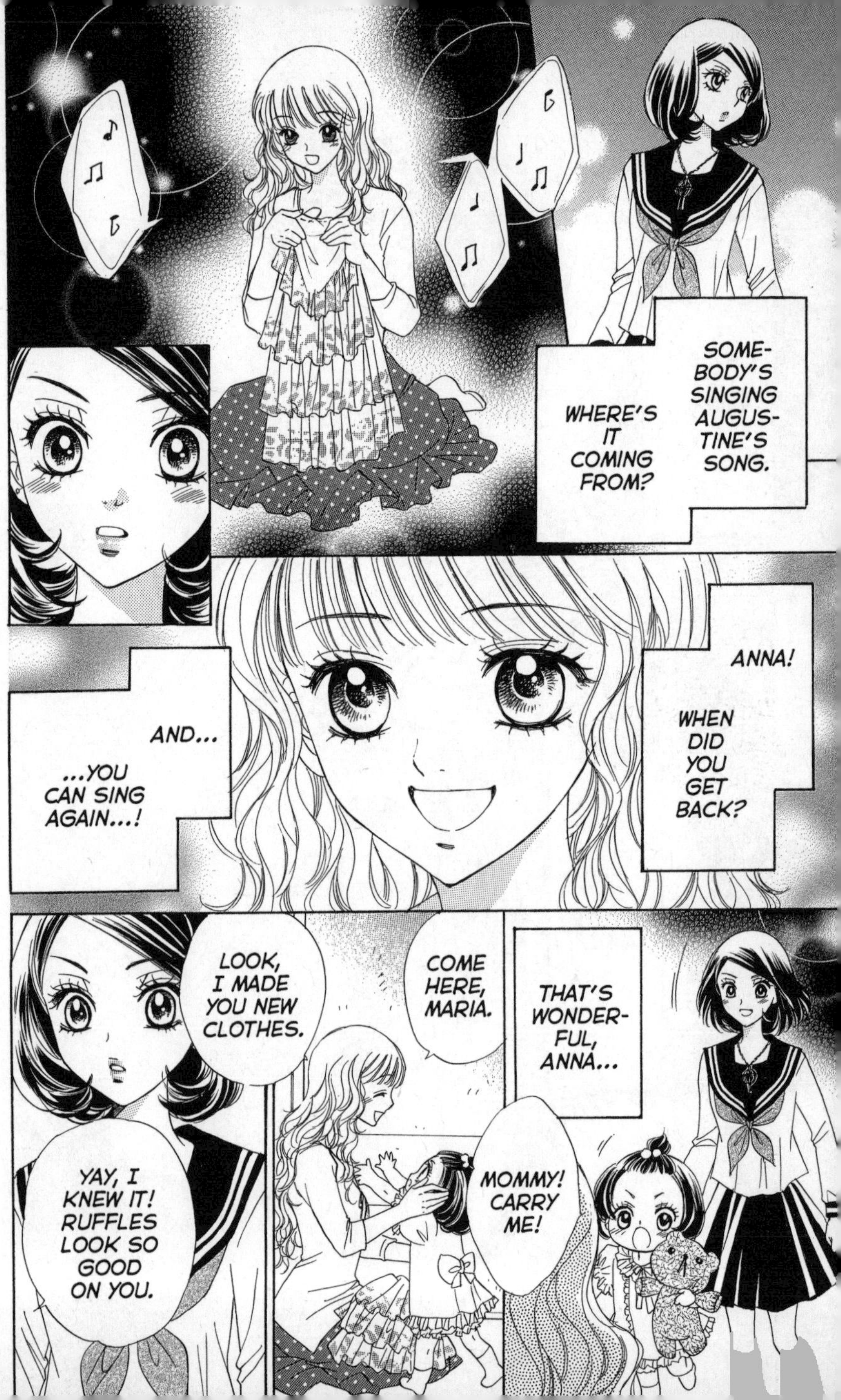
SOMEBODY'S SINGING AUGUSTINE'S SONG.
WHERE'S IT COMING FROM?
ANNA!
WHEN DID YOU GET BACK?
AND...
...YOU CAN SING AGAIN...!
THAT'S WONDERFUL, ANNA...
MOMMY! CARRY ME!
COME HERE, MARIA.
LOOK, I MADE YOU NEW CLOTHES.
YAY, I KNEW IT! RUFFLES LOOK SO GOOD ON YOU.

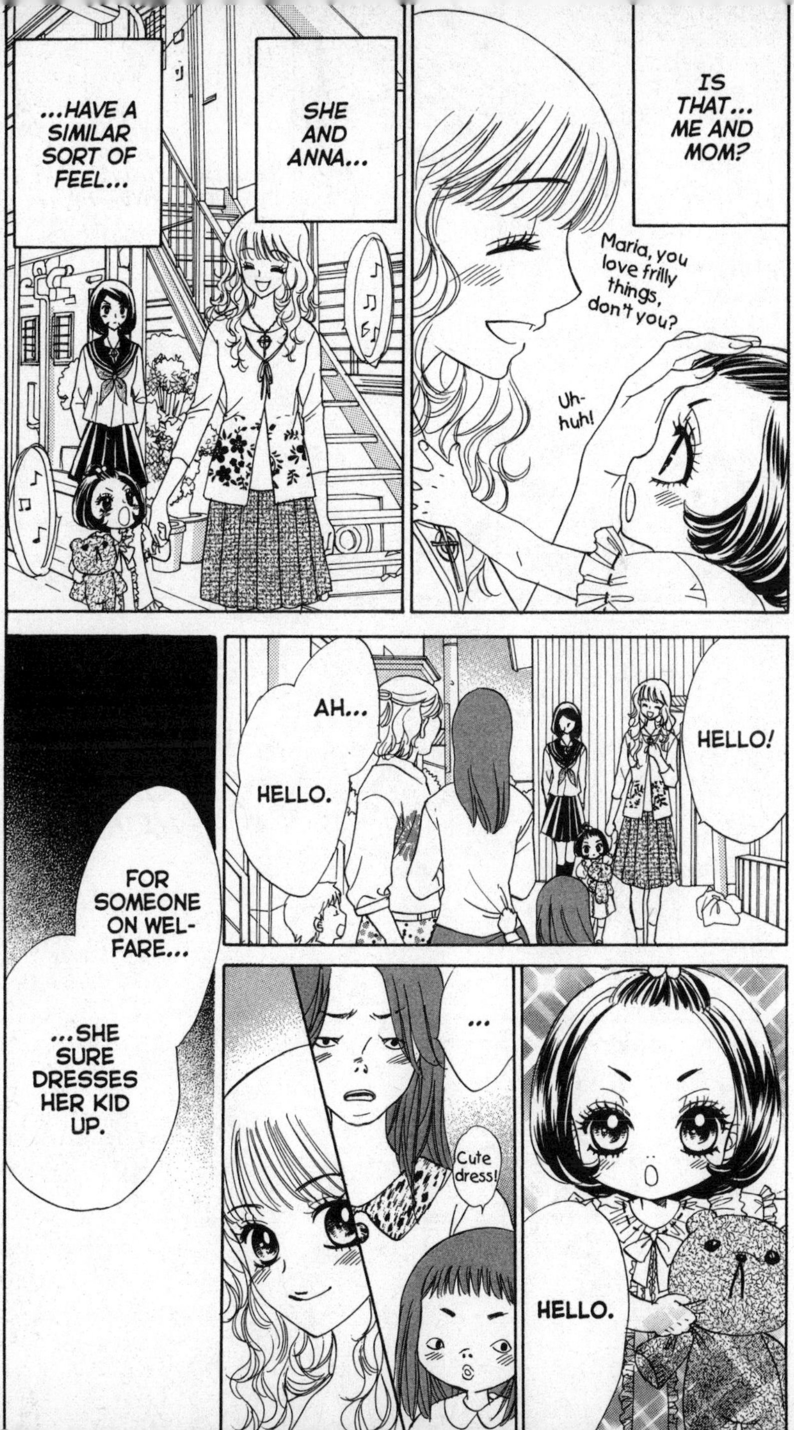
IS THAT... ME AND MOM?
Maria, you love frilly things, don't you?
Uh-huh!
SHE AND ANNA...
...HAVE A SIMILAR SORT OF FEEL...
HELLO!
AH...
HELLO.
HELLO.
...
Cute dress!
FOR SOMEONE ON WEL-FARE...
...SHE SURE DRESSES HER KID UP.

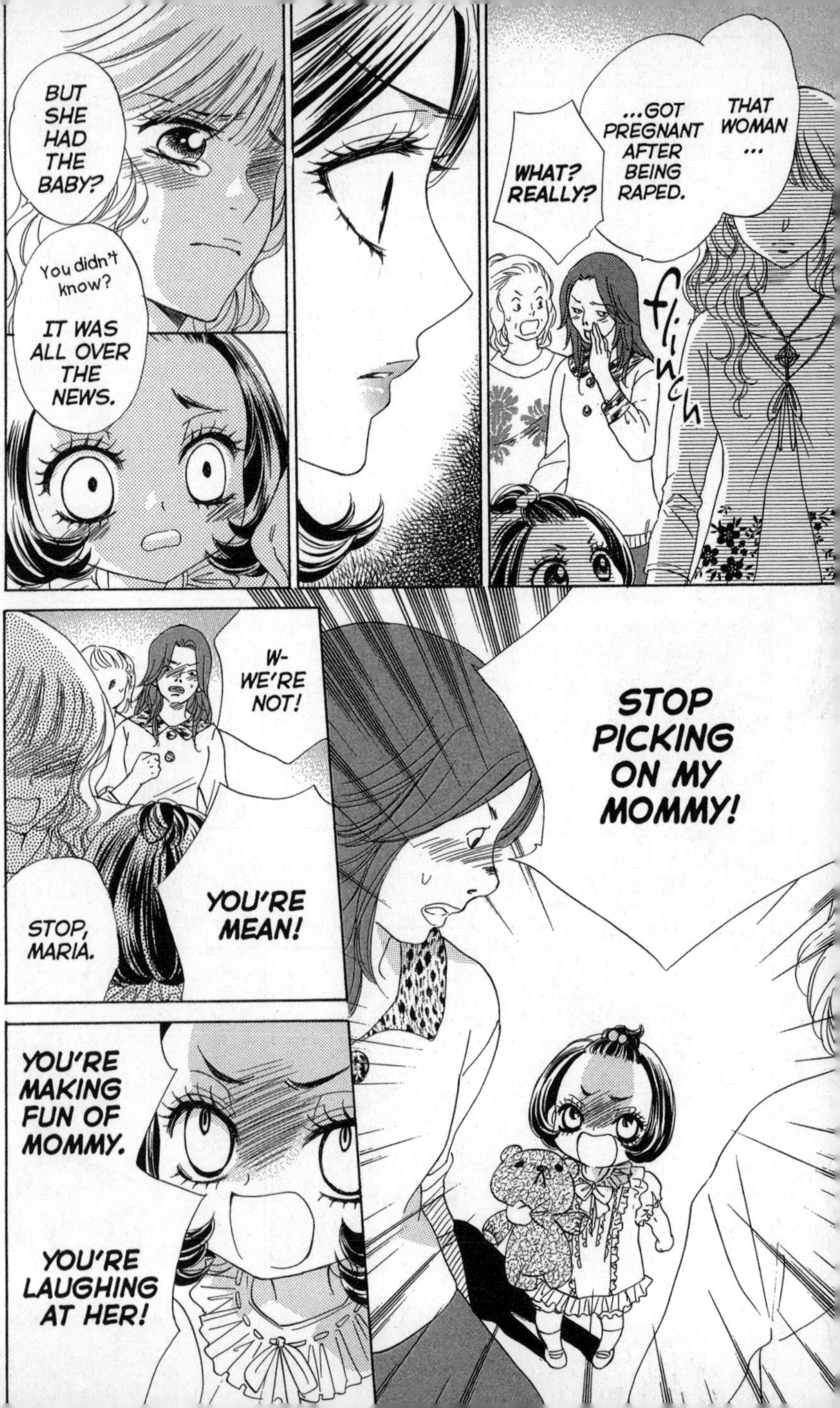
THAT WOMAN ...
...GOT PREGNANT AFTER BEING RAPED.
WHAT? REALLY?
flinch
BUT SHE HAD THE BABY?
You didn't know?
IT WAS ALL OVER THE NEWS.
STOP PICKING ON MY MOMMY!
W- WE'RE NOT!
YOU'RE MEAN!
STOP, MARIA.
YOU'RE MAKING FUN OF MOMMY.
YOU'RE LAUGHING AT HER!

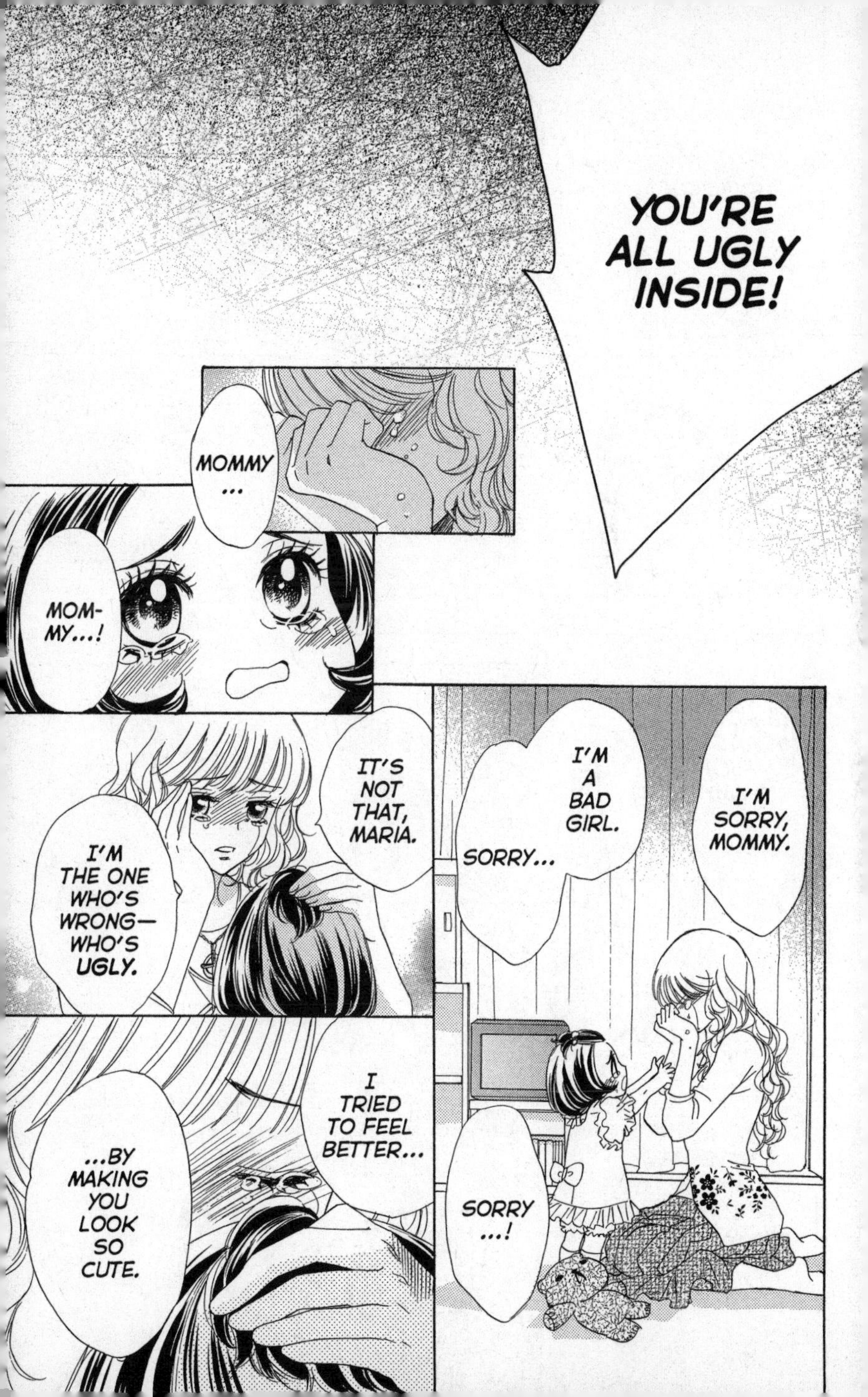
YOU'RE ALL UGLY INSIDE!
MOMMY...
MOMMY...!
I'M SORRY, MOMMY.
I'M A BAD GIRL.
SORRY...
SORRY...!
IT'S NOT THAT, MARIA.
I'M THE ONE WHO'S WRONG—WHO'S UGLY.
I TRIED TO FEEL BETTER...
...BY MAKING YOU LOOK SO CUTE.

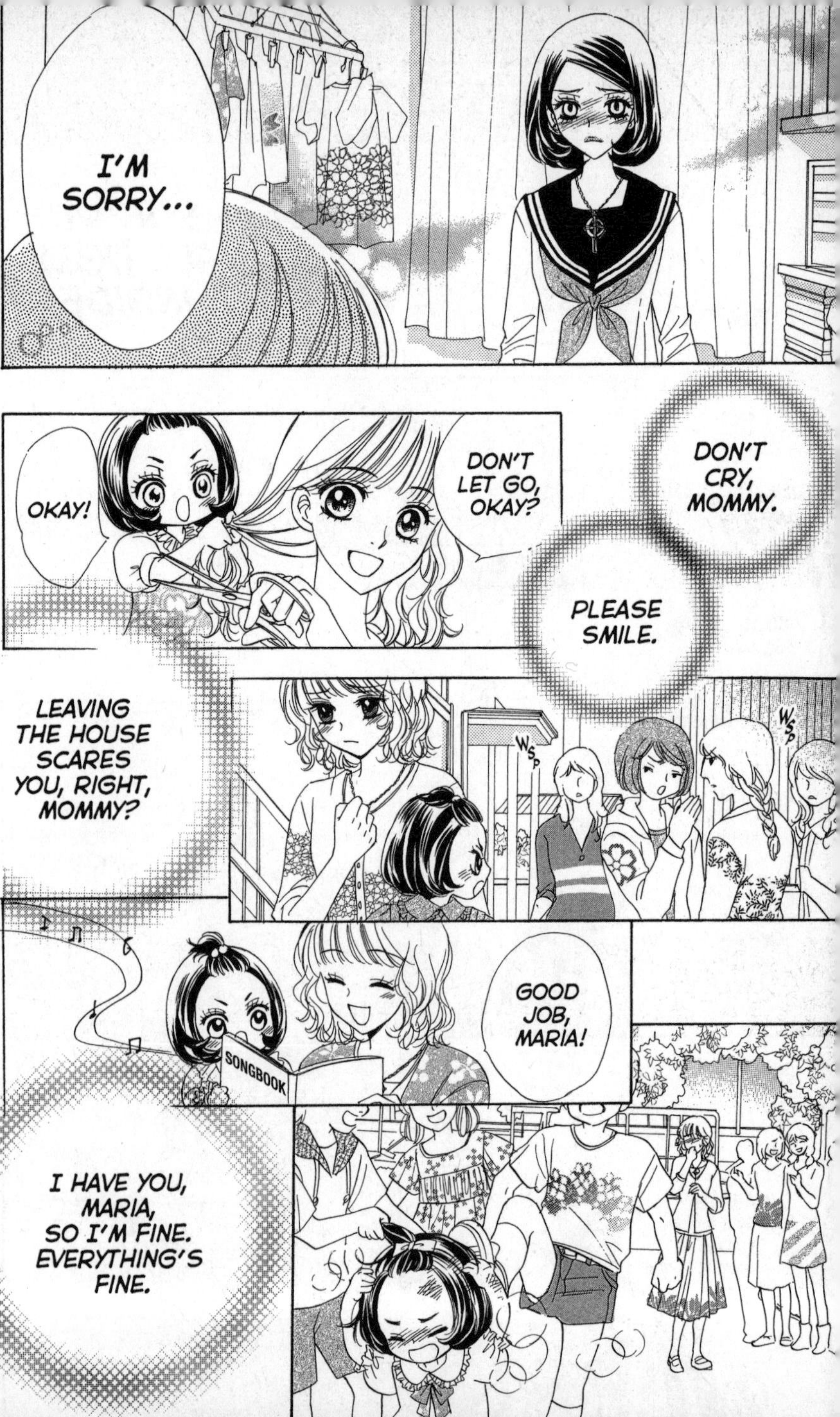
I'M SORRY...
DON'T CRY, MOMMY.
PLEASE SMILE.
DON'T LET GO, OKAY?
OKAY!
WSP
WSP
LEAVING THE HOUSE SCARES YOU, RIGHT, MOMMY?
GOOD JOB, MARIA!
SONGBOOK
I HAVE YOU, MARIA, SO I'M FINE. EVERYTHING'S FINE.

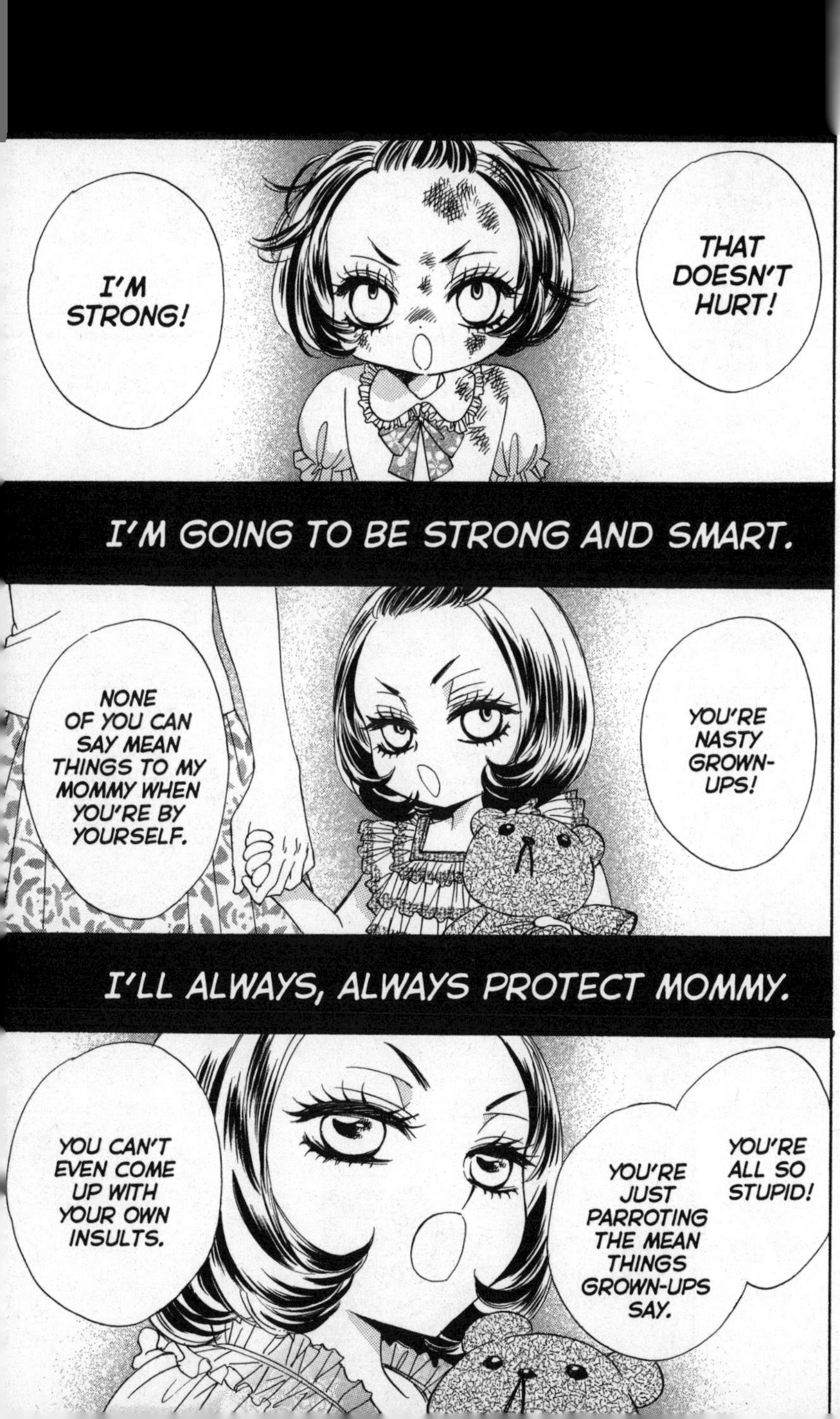
THAT DOESN'T HURT!
I'M STRONG!
I'M GOING TO BE STRONG AND SMART.
YOU'RE NASTY GROWN-UPS!
NONE OF YOU CAN SAY MEAN THINGS TO MY MOMMY WHEN YOU'RE BY YOURSELF.
I'LL ALWAYS, ALWAYS PROTECT MOMMY.
YOU'RE ALL SO STUPID!
YOU'RE JUST PARROTING THE MEAN THINGS GROWN-UPS SAY.
YOU CAN'T EVEN COME UP WITH YOUR OWN INSULTS.

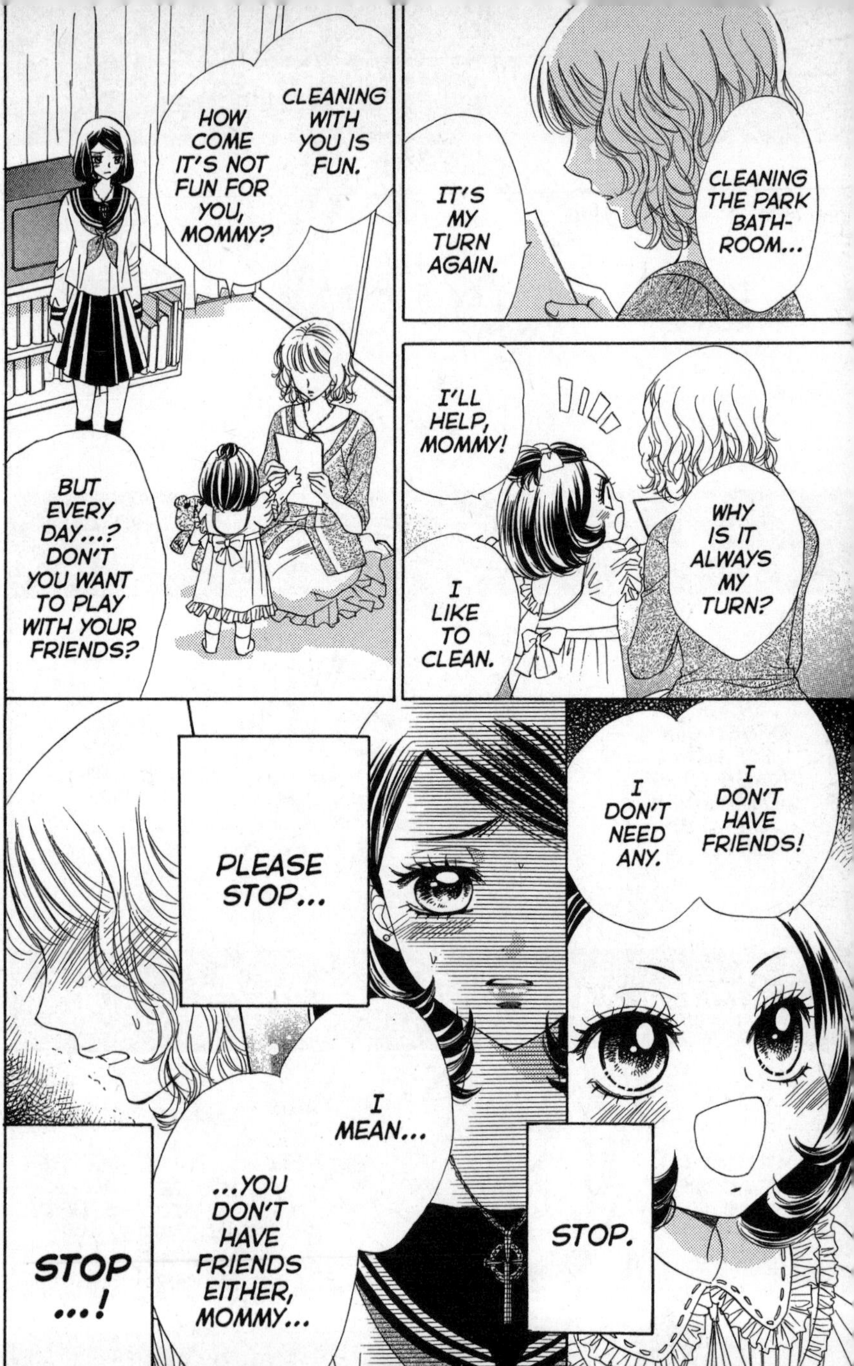
CLEANING THE PARK BATHROOM...
IT'S MY TURN AGAIN.
WHY IS IT ALWAYS MY TURN?
I'LL HELP, MOMMY!
I LIKE TO CLEAN.
CLEANING WITH YOU IS FUN.
HOW COME IT'S NOT FUN FOR YOU, MOMMY?
BUT EVERY DAY...? DON'T YOU WANT TO PLAY WITH YOUR FRIENDS?
I DON'T HAVE FRIENDS!
I DON'T NEED ANY.
STOP.
PLEASE STOP...
I MEAN...
...YOU DON'T HAVE FRIENDS EITHER, MOMMY...
STOP ...!

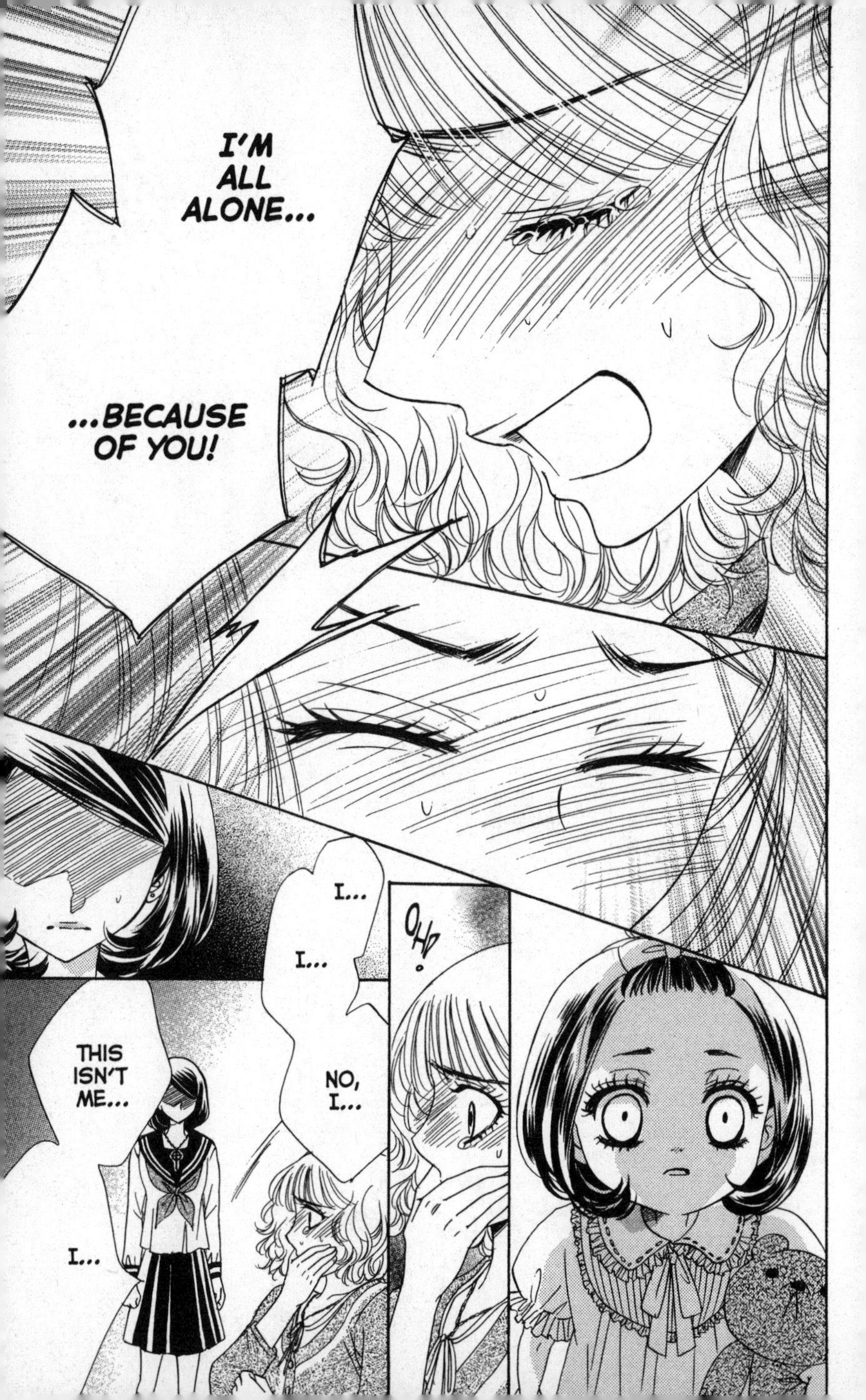
I'M ALL ALONE...
...BECAUSE OF YOU!
OH!?
I...
I...
NO, I...
THIS ISN'T ME...
I...

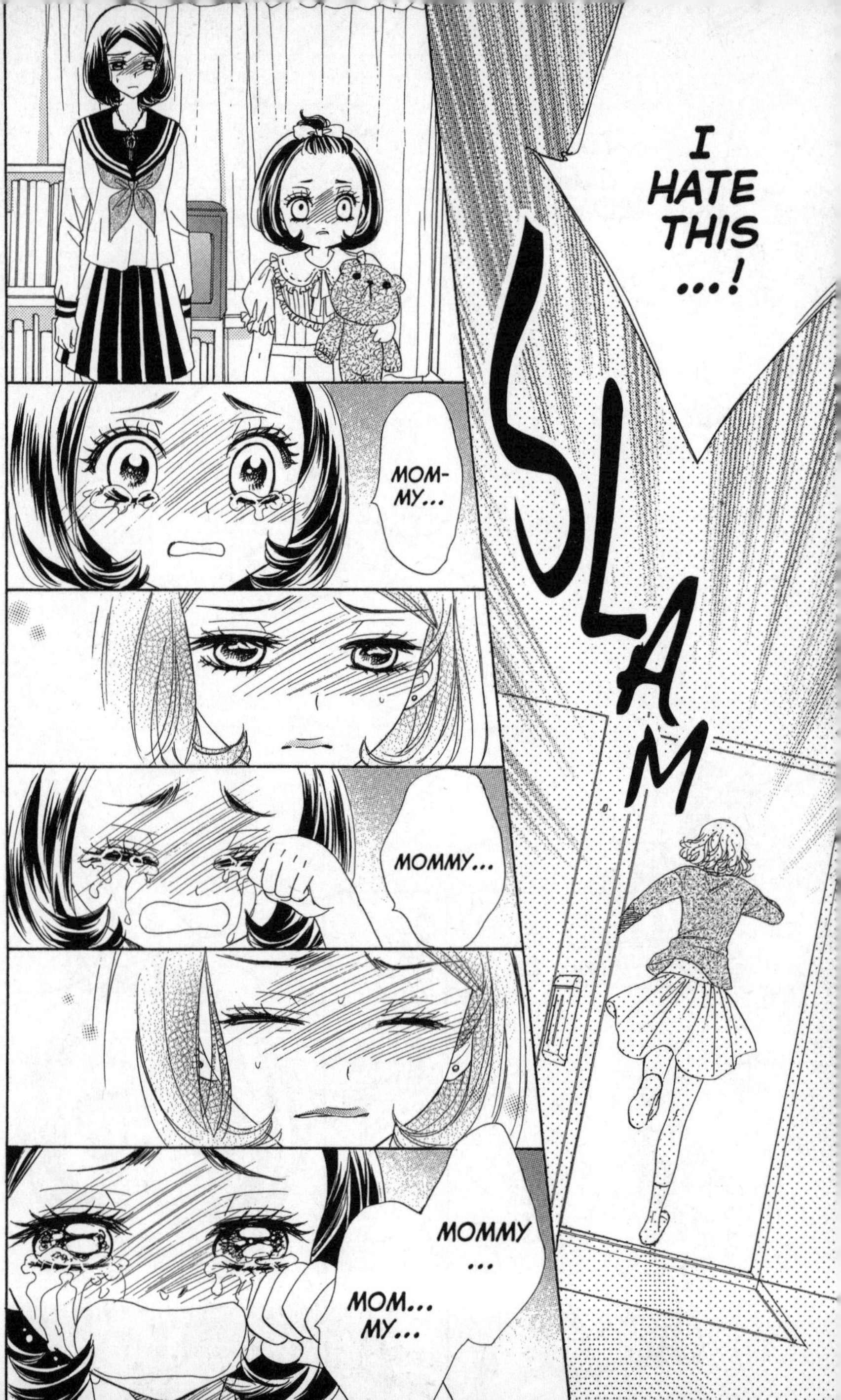
I HATE THIS ...!
SLAM
MOM-MY...
MOMMY...
MOMMY ...
MOM... MY...

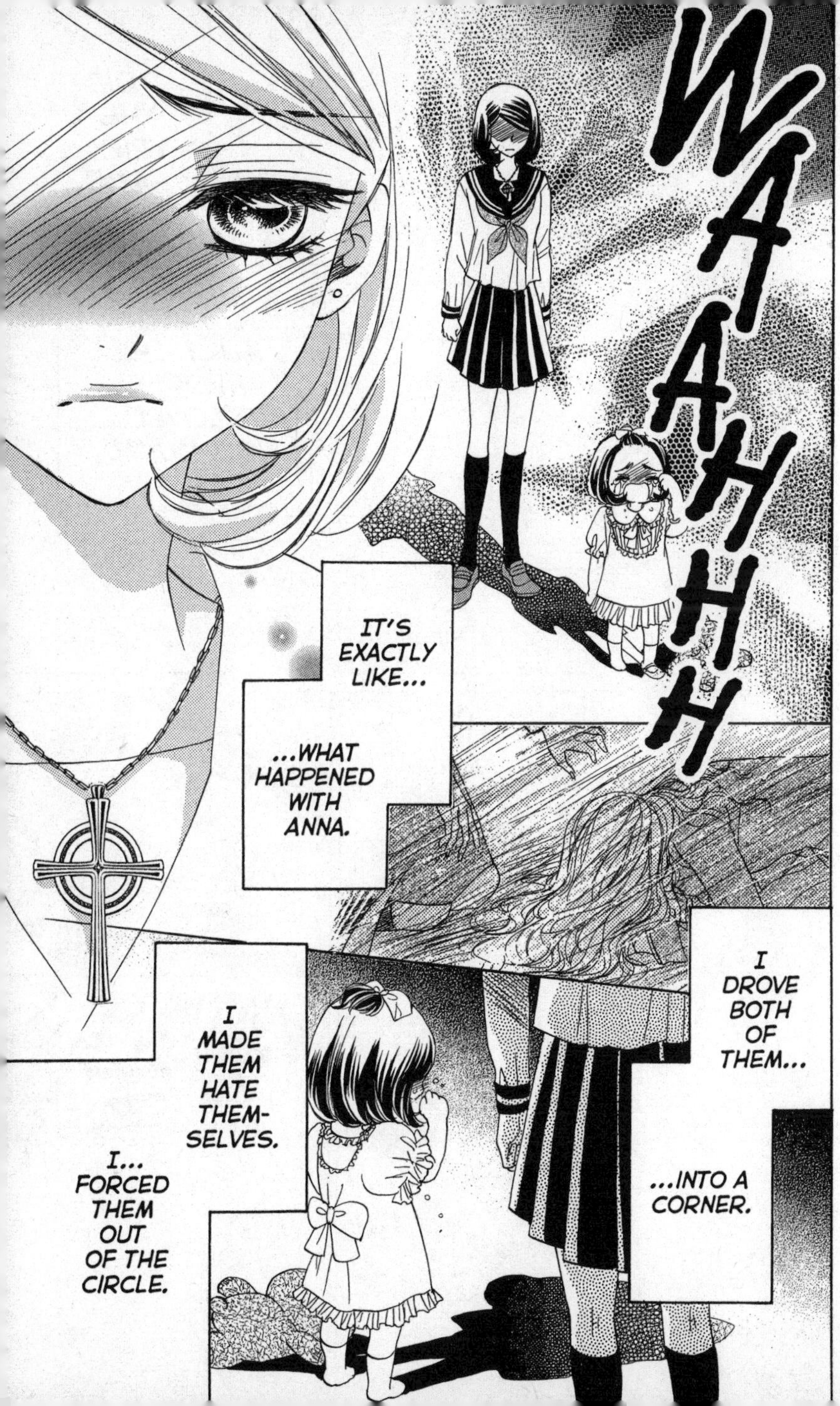
WAAHHH
IT'S EXACTLY LIKE...
...WHAT HAPPENED WITH ANNA.
I DROVE BOTH OF THEM...
...INTO A CORNER.
I MADE THEM HATE THEM-SELVES.
I... FORCED THEM OUT OF THE CIRCLE.

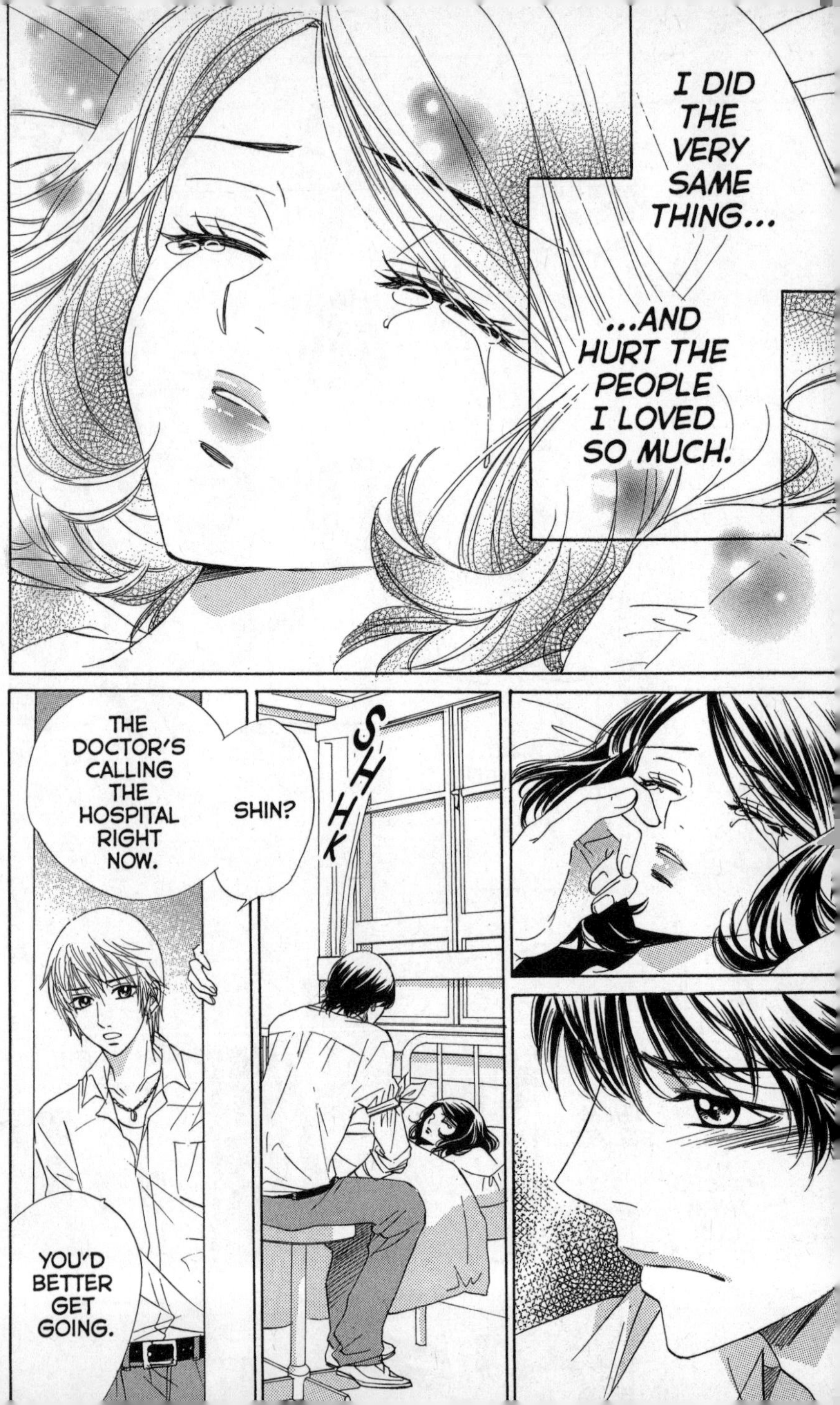
I DID THE VERY SAME THING...
...AND HURT THE PEOPLE I LOVED SO MUCH.
SHHK
SHIN?
THE DOCTOR'S CALLING THE HOSPITAL RIGHT NOW.
YOU'D BETTER GET GOING.

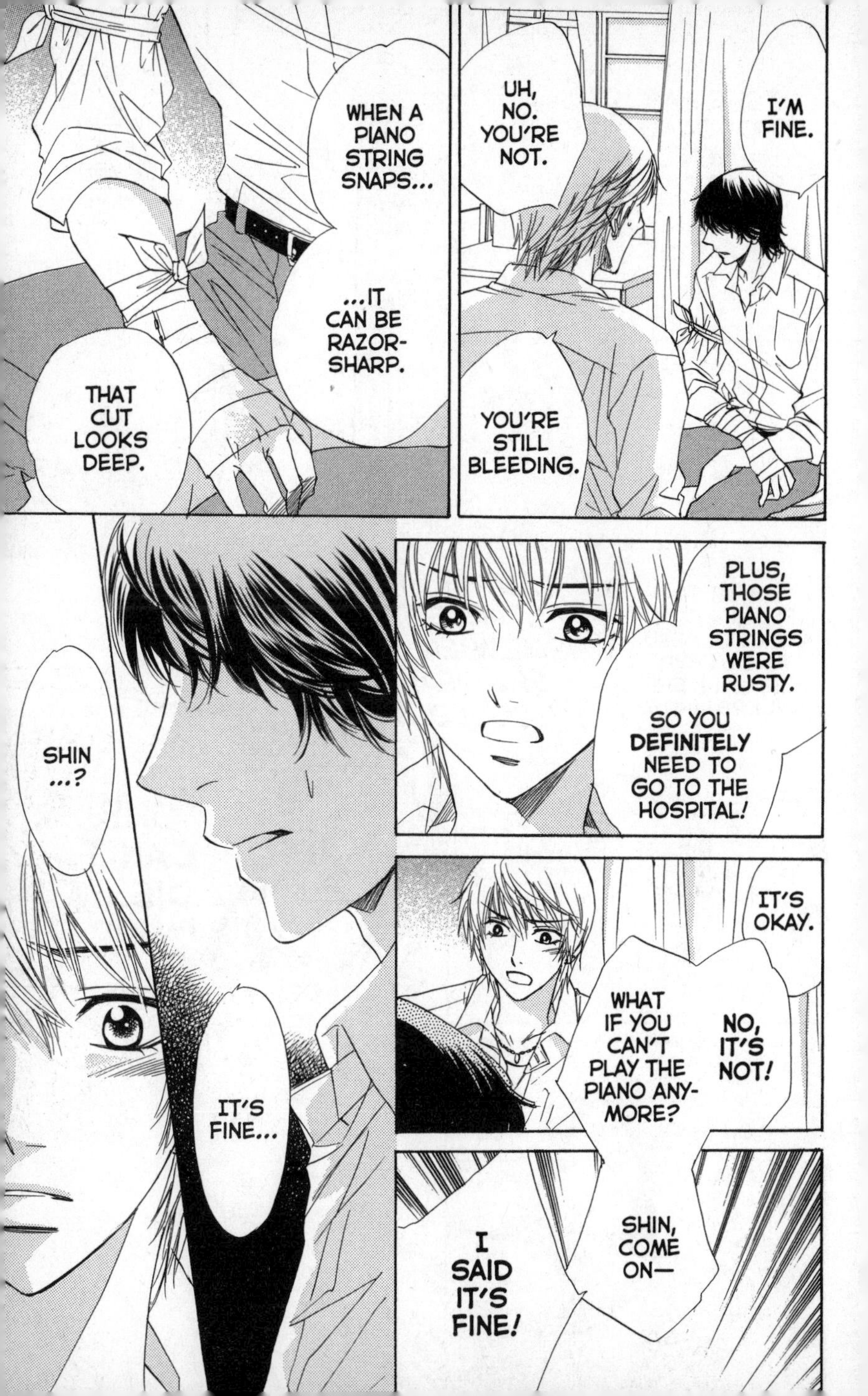

I'M FINE.
UH, NO. YOU'RE NOT.
YOU'RE STILL BLEEDING.
WHEN A PIANO STRING SNAPS...
...IT CAN BE RAZOR-SHARP.
THAT CUT LOOKS DEEP.
PLUS, THOSE PIANO STRINGS WERE RUSTY.
SO YOU **DEFINITELY** NEED TO GO TO THE HOSPITAL!
IT'S OKAY.
NO, IT'S NOT!
WHAT IF YOU CAN'T PLAY THE PIANO ANY-MORE?
SHIN, COME ON—
I SAID IT'S FINE!
IT'S FINE...
SHIN ...?

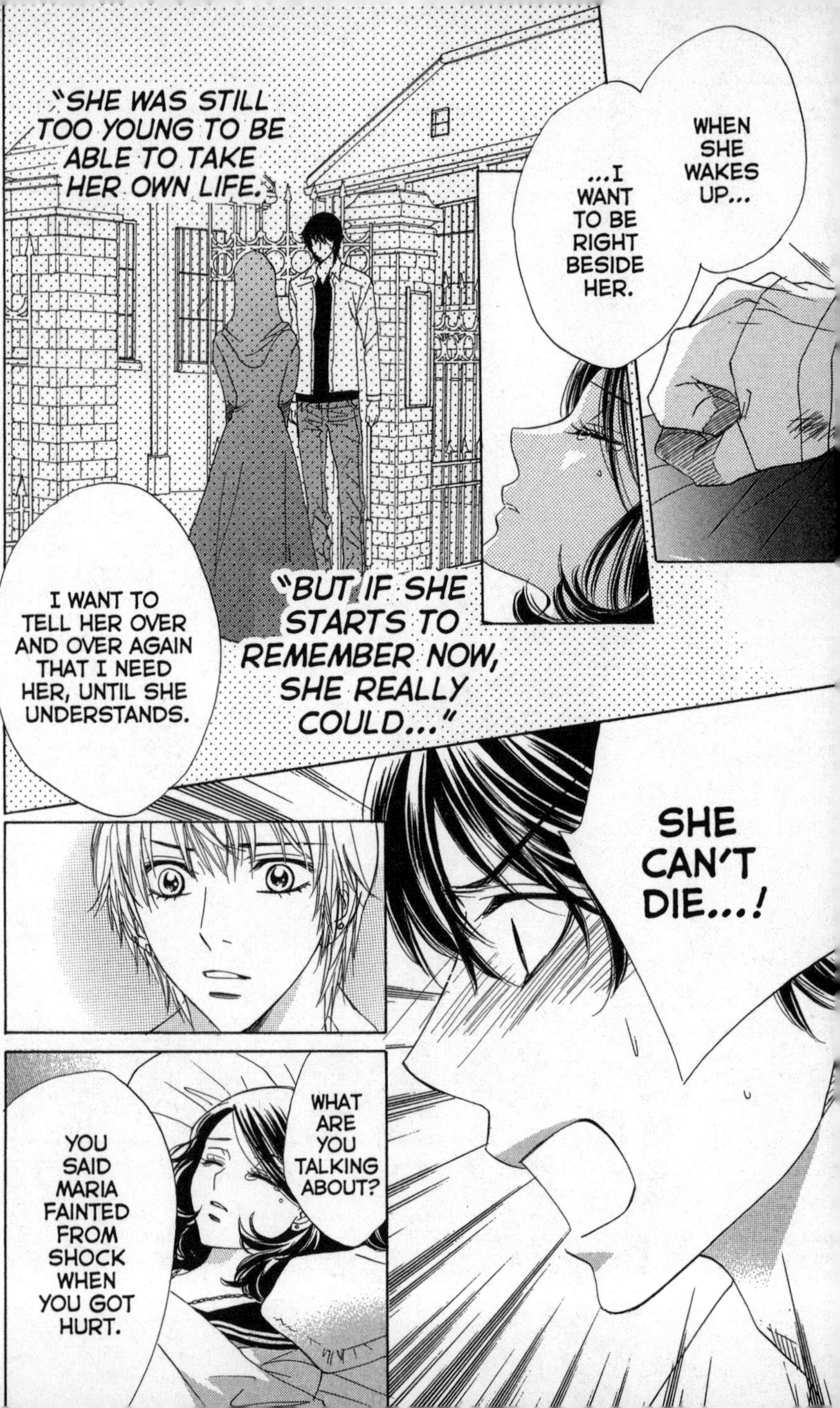
WHEN SHE WAKES UP...
...I WANT TO BE RIGHT BESIDE HER.
"SHE WAS STILL TOO YOUNG TO BE ABLE TO TAKE HER OWN LIFE.
I WANT TO TELL HER OVER AND OVER AGAIN THAT I NEED HER, UNTIL SHE UNDERSTANDS.
"BUT IF SHE STARTS TO REMEMBER NOW, SHE REALLY COULD..."
SHE CAN'T DIE...!
WHAT ARE YOU TALKING ABOUT?
YOU SAID MARIA FAINTED FROM SHOCK WHEN YOU GOT HURT.

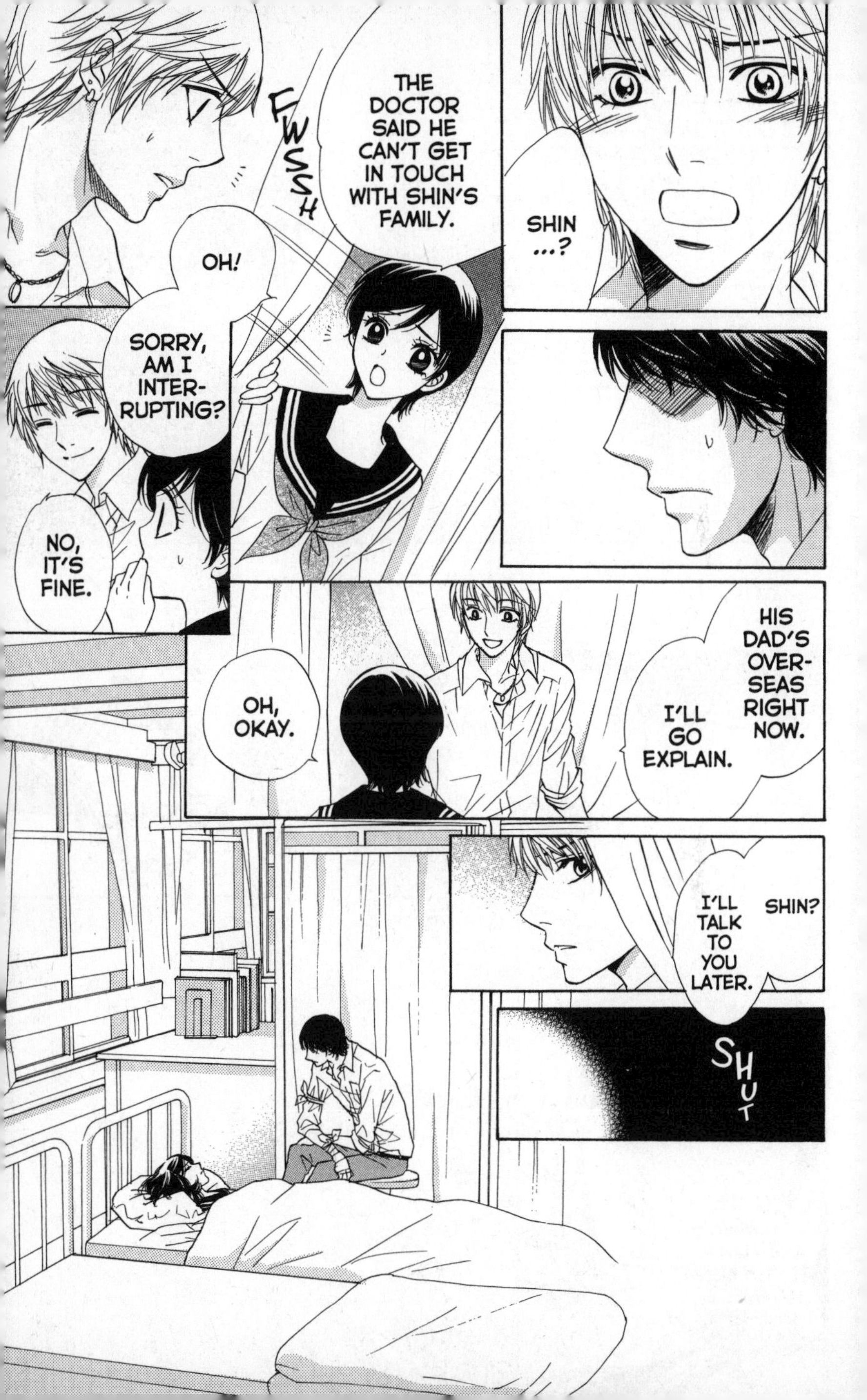
SHIN ...?
FWSSH
OH!
SORRY, AM I INTER-RUPTING?
NO, IT'S FINE.
THE DOCTOR SAID HE CAN'T GET IN TOUCH WITH SHIN'S FAMILY.
HIS DAD'S OVER-SEAS RIGHT NOW.
I'LL GO EXPLAIN.
OH, OKAY.
SHIN?
I'LL TALK TO YOU LATER.
SHUT

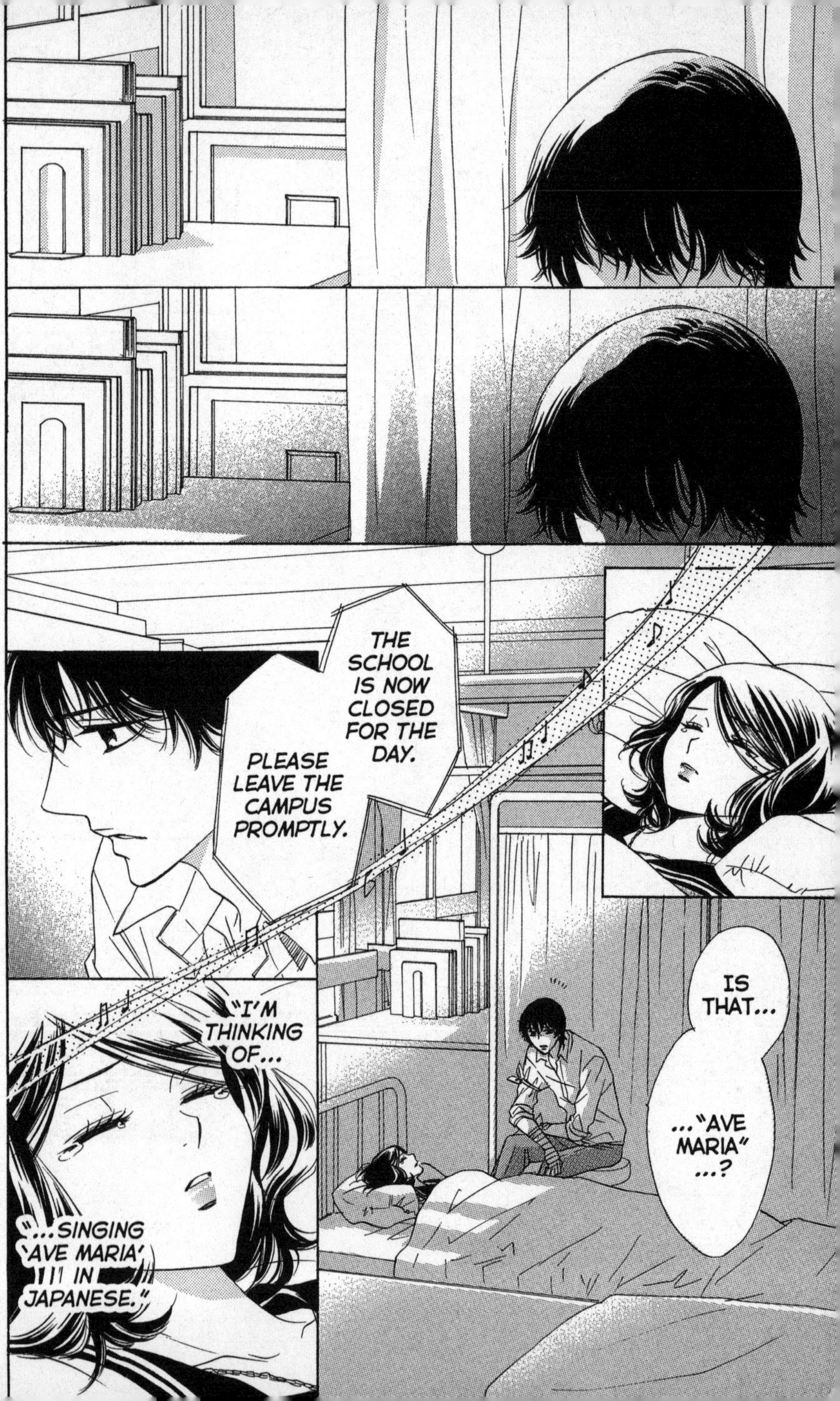
THE SCHOOL IS NOW CLOSED FOR THE DAY.
PLEASE LEAVE THE CAMPUS PROMPTLY.
IS THAT...
..."AVE MARIA" ...?
"I'M THINKING OF...
"...SINGING 'AVE MARIA' IN JAPANESE."

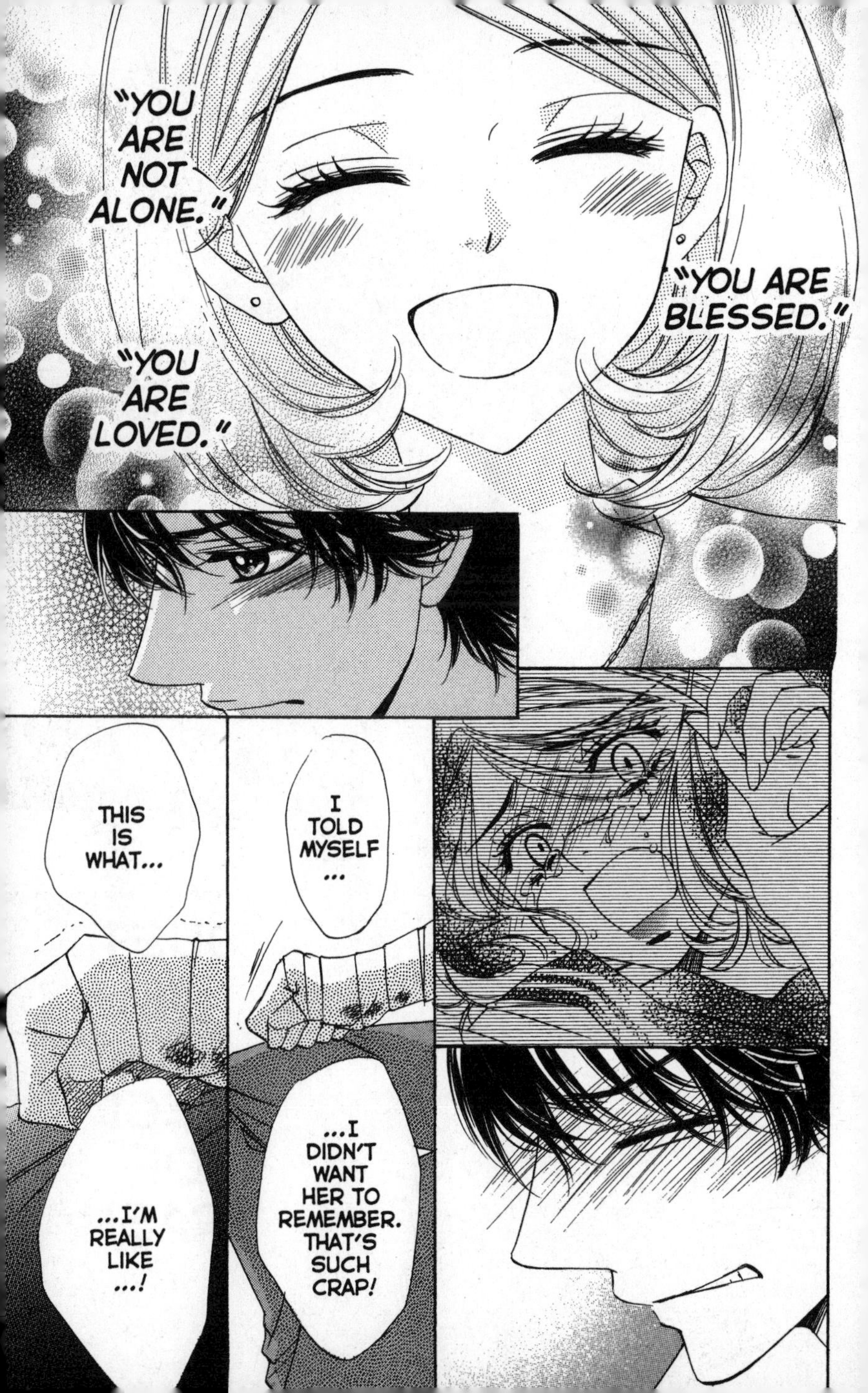
"YOU ARE BLESSED."
"YOU ARE NOT ALONE."
"YOU ARE LOVED."
I TOLD MYSELF ...
...I DIDN'T WANT HER TO REMEMBER. THAT'S SUCH CRAP!
THIS IS WHAT...
...I'M REALLY LIKE ...!

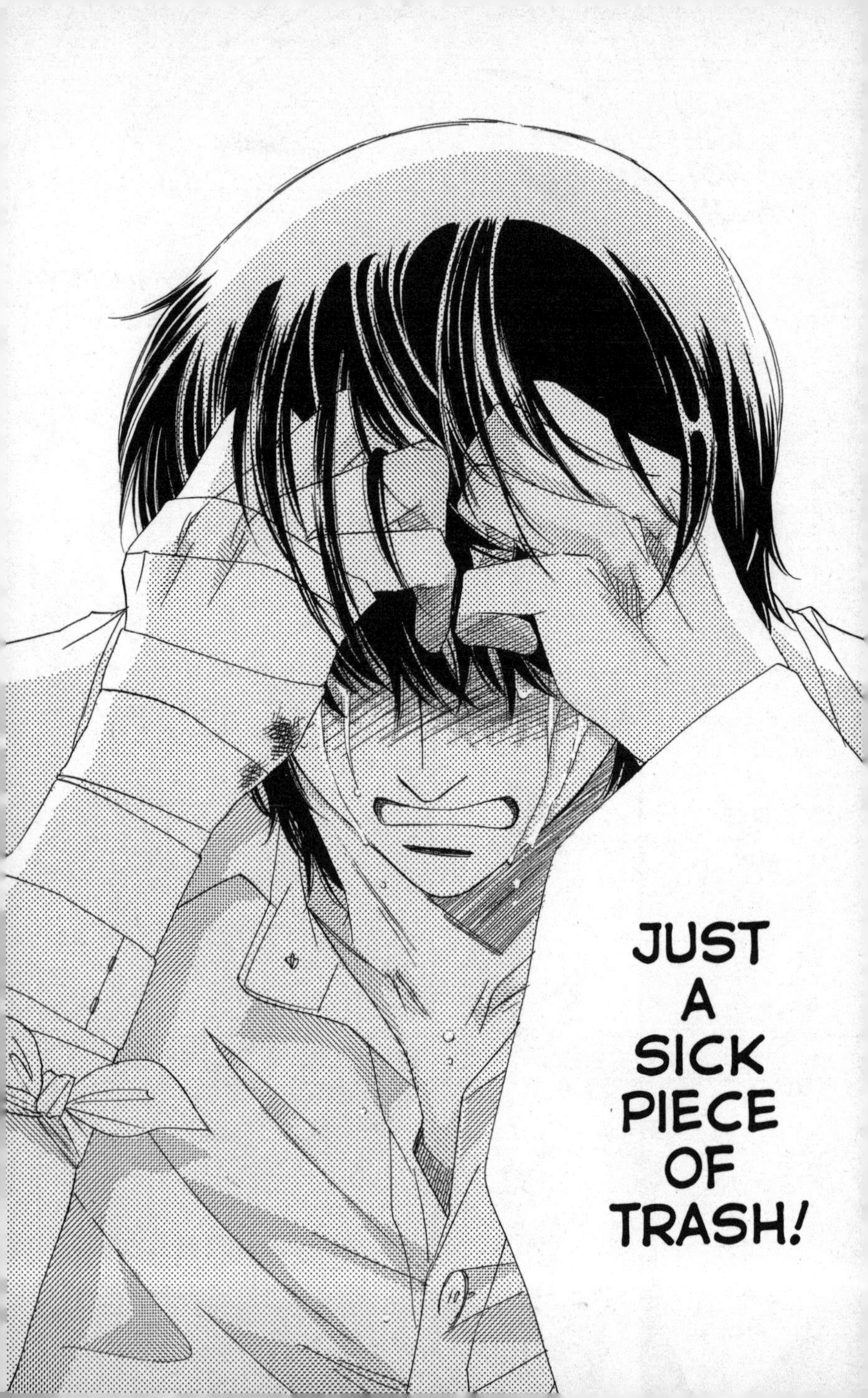
JUST A SICK PIECE OF TRASH!

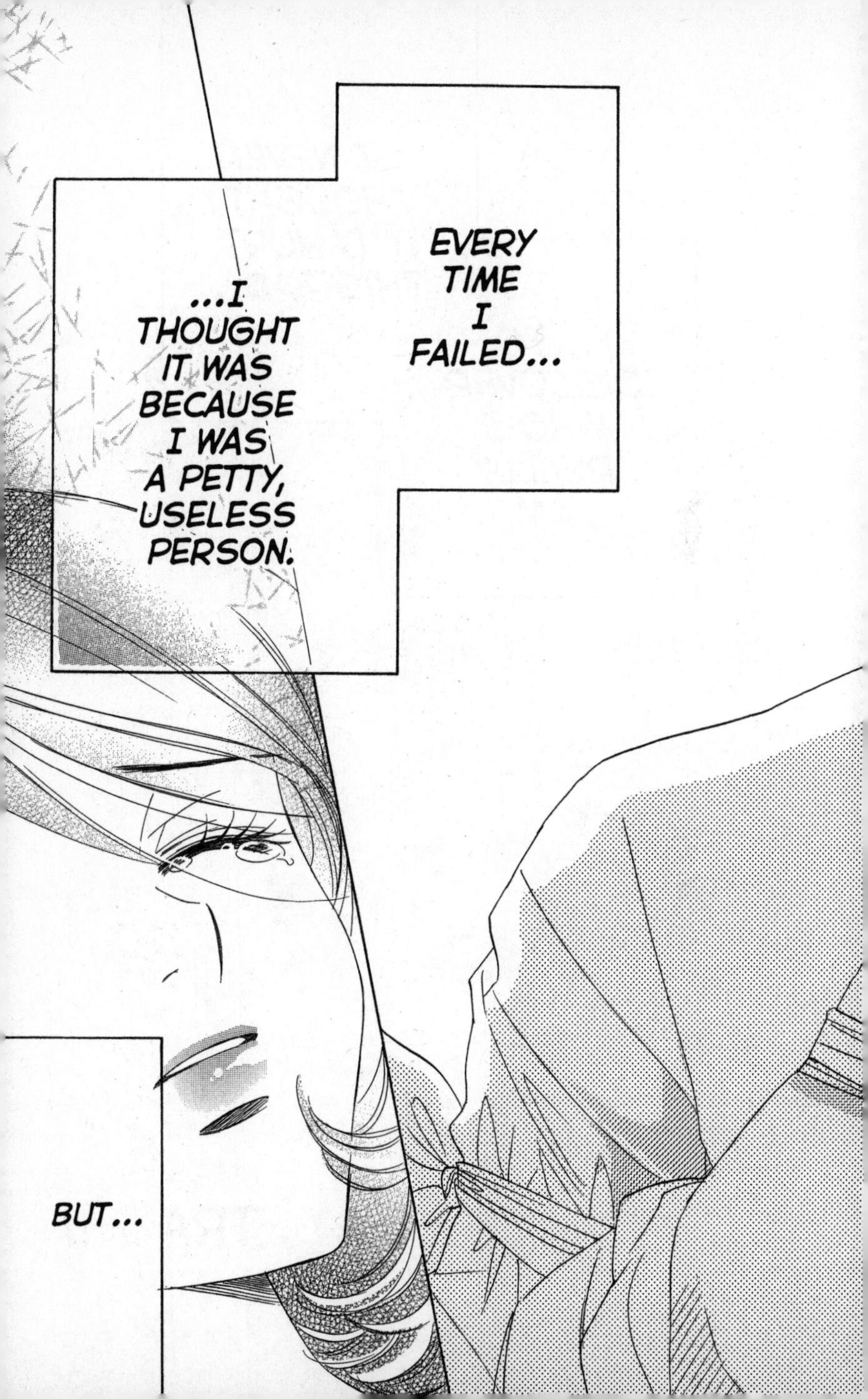
EVERY TIME I FAILED...
...I THOUGHT IT WAS BECAUSE I WAS A PETTY, USELESS PERSON.
BUT...

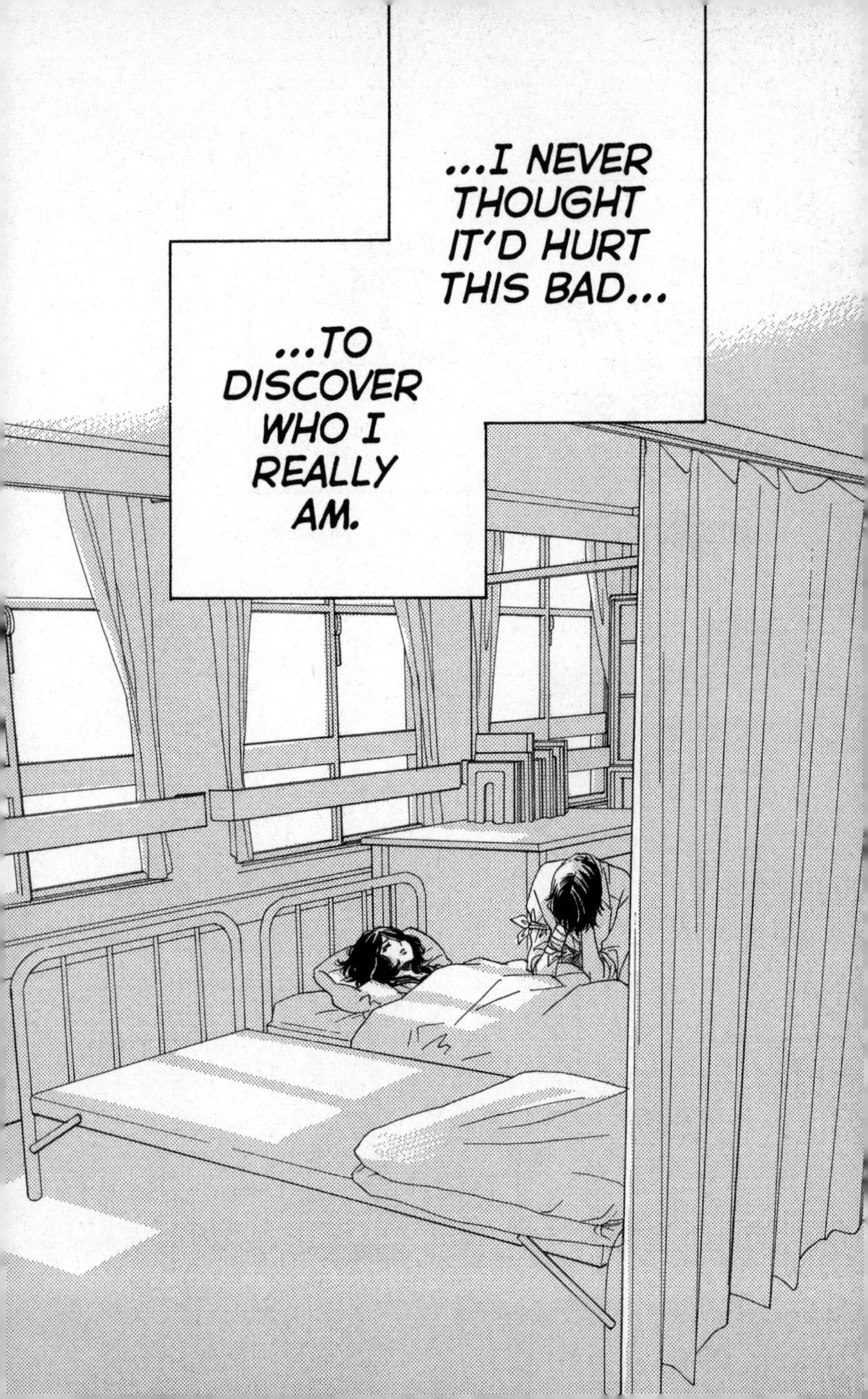
...I NEVER THOUGHT IT'D HURT THIS BAD...
...TO DISCOVER WHO I REALLY AM.

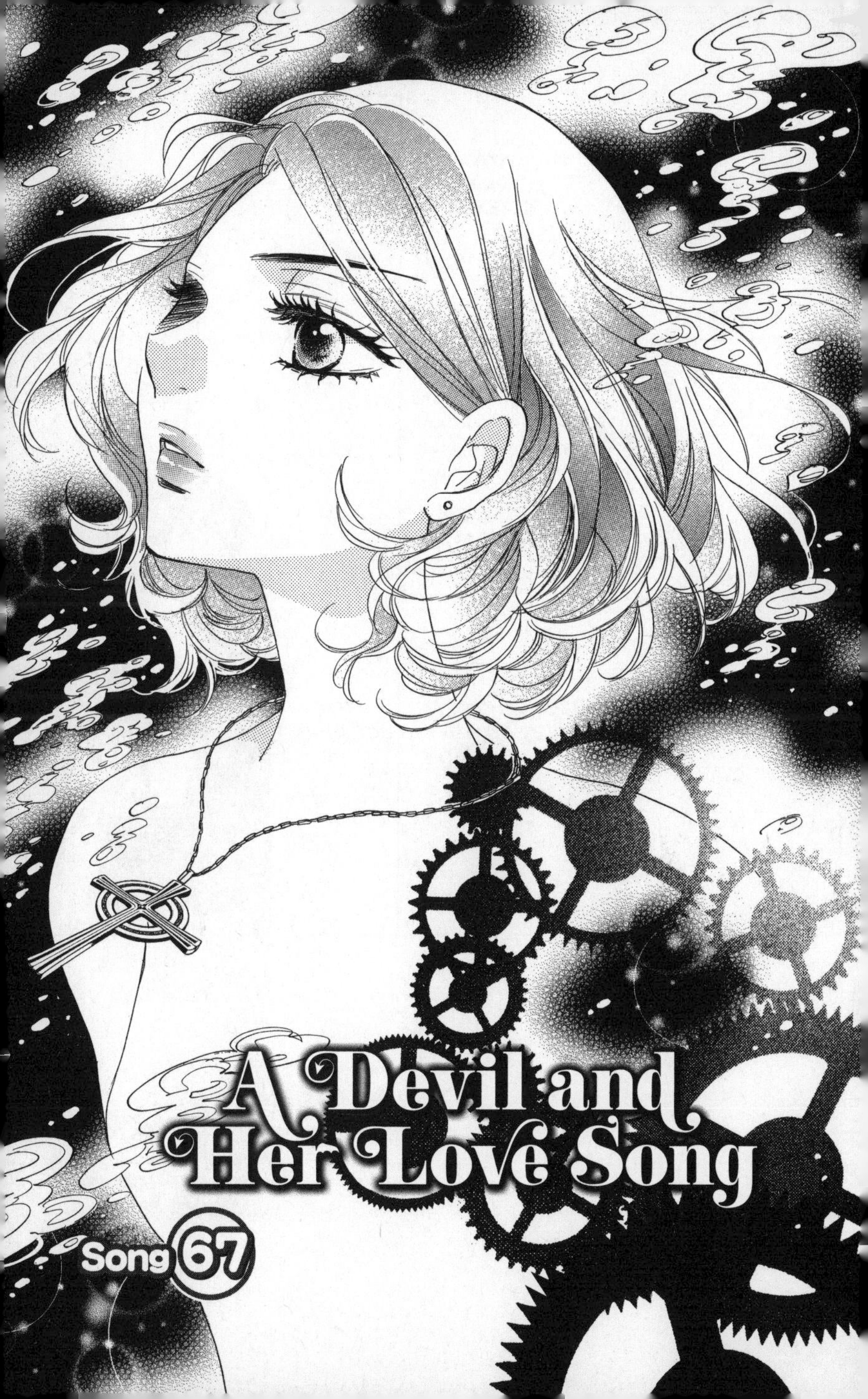
A Devil and Her Love Song
Song 67

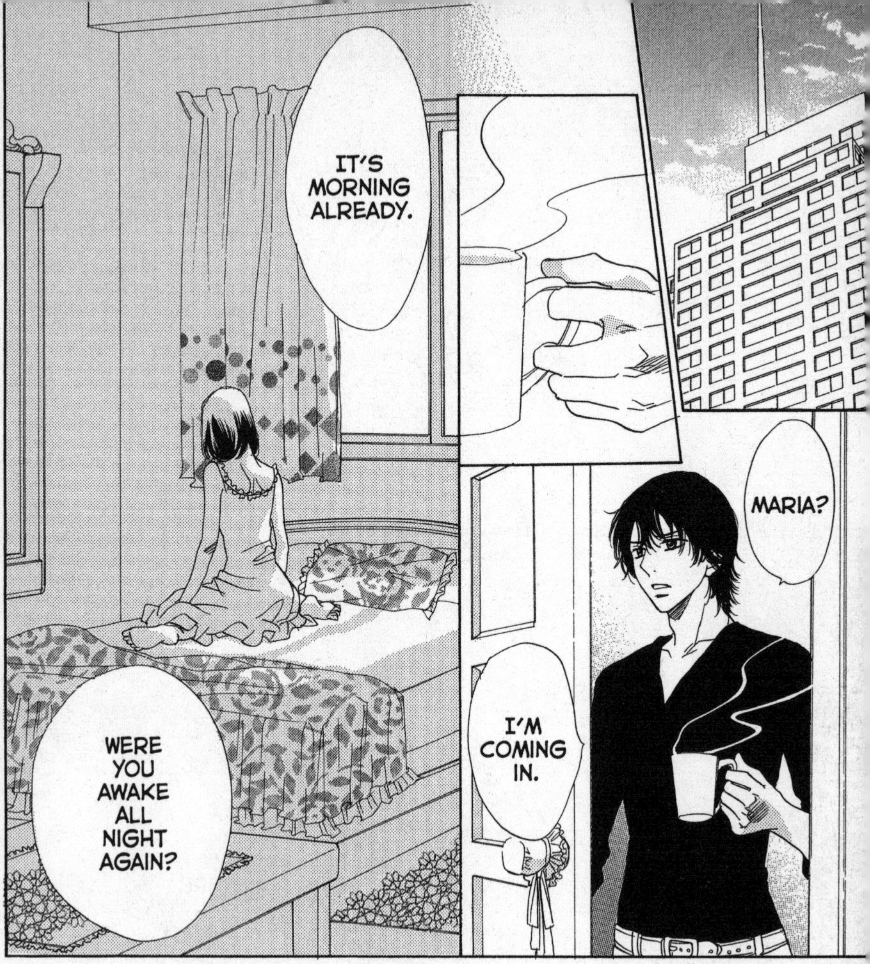
MARIA?
I'M COMING IN.
IT'S MORNING ALREADY.
WERE YOU AWAKE ALL NIGHT AGAIN?

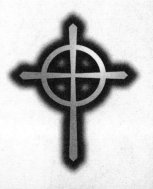

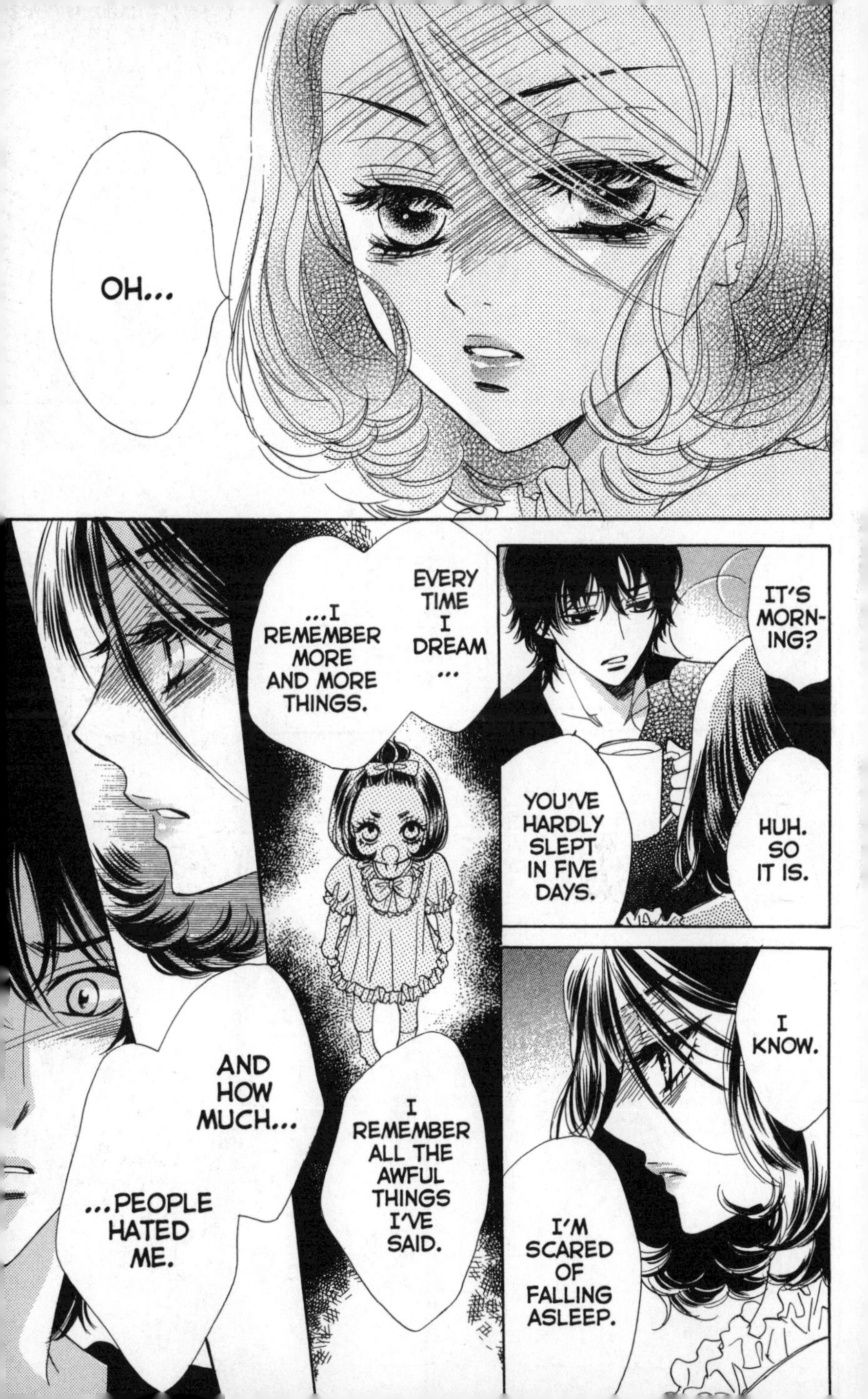
OH...
IT'S MORNING?
HUH. SO IT IS.
YOU'VE HARDLY SLEPT IN FIVE DAYS.
I KNOW.
I'M SCARED OF FALLING ASLEEP.
EVERY TIME I DREAM...
...I REMEMBER MORE AND MORE THINGS.
I REMEMBER ALL THE AWFUL THINGS I'VE SAID.
AND HOW MUCH...
...PEOPLE HATED ME.

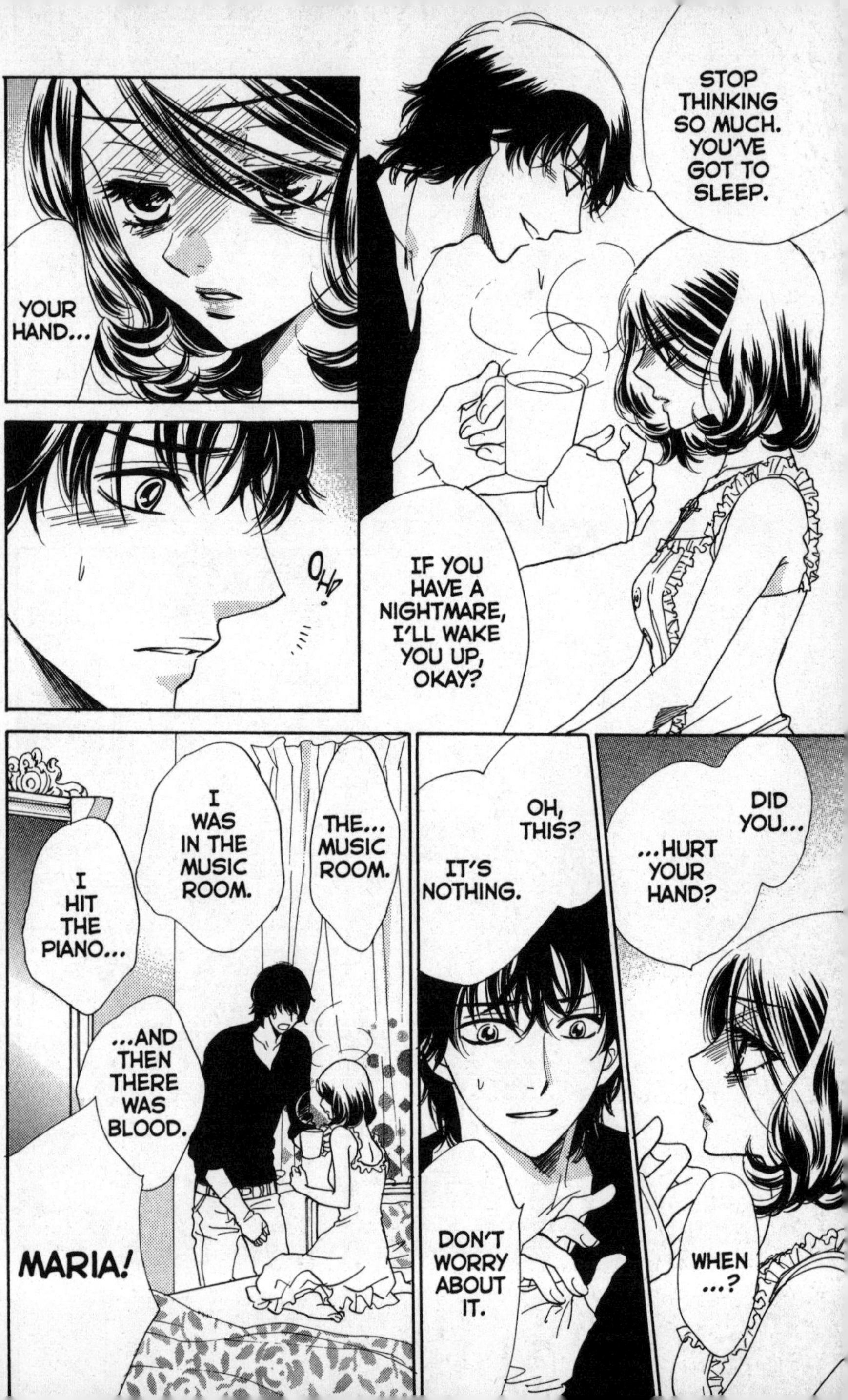
STOP THINKING SO MUCH. YOU'VE GOT TO SLEEP.
IF YOU HAVE A NIGHTMARE, I'LL WAKE YOU UP, OKAY?
YOUR HAND...
OH!
DID YOU...
...HURT YOUR HAND?
WHEN ...?
OH, THIS?
IT'S NOTHING.
DON'T WORRY ABOUT IT.
THE... MUSIC ROOM.
I WAS IN THE MUSIC ROOM.
I HIT THE PIANO...
...AND THEN THERE WAS BLOOD.
MARIA!

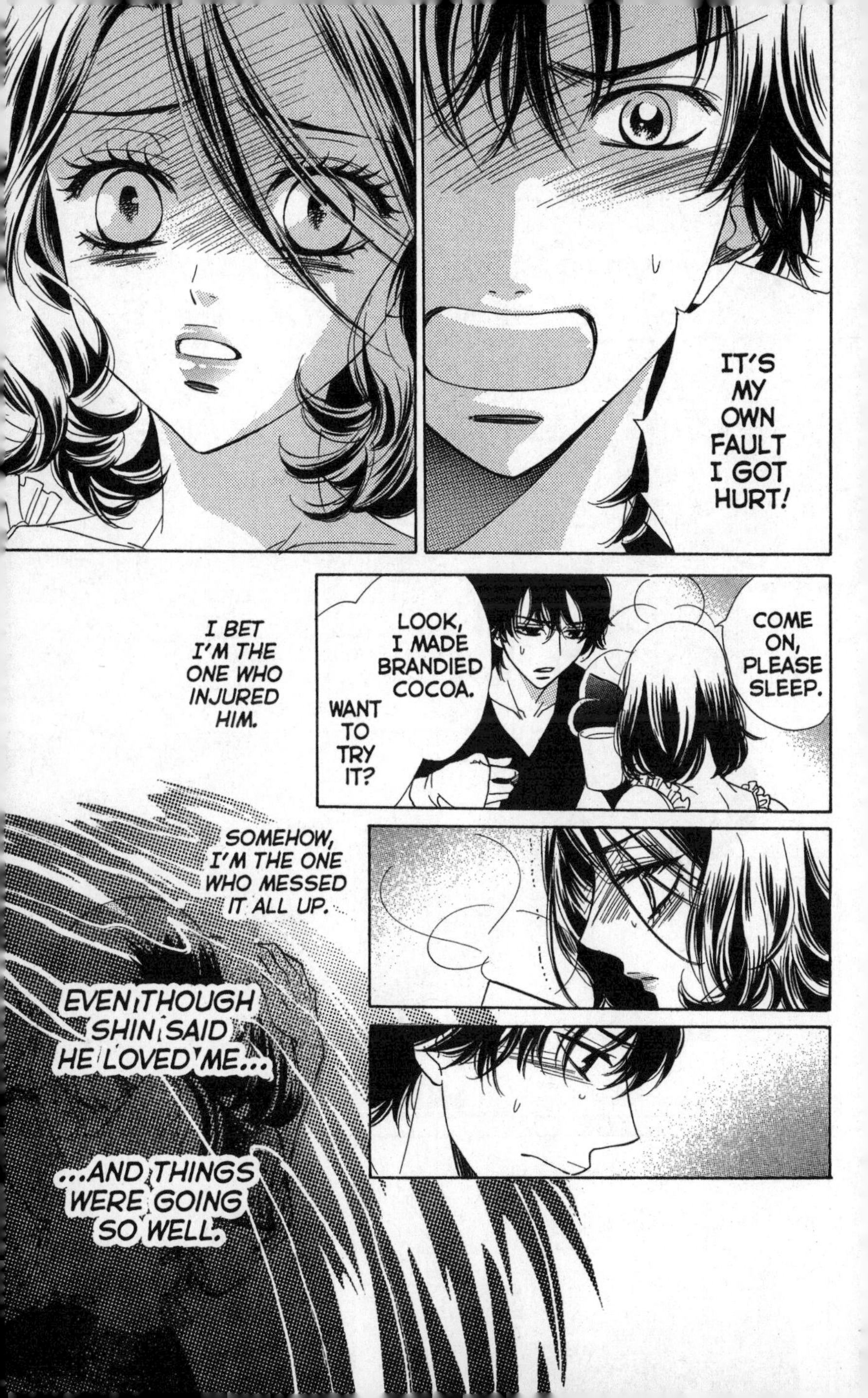
IT'S MY OWN FAULT I GOT HURT!
COME ON, PLEASE SLEEP.
LOOK, I MADE BRANDIED COCOA.
WANT TO TRY IT?
I BET I'M THE ONE WHO INJURED HIM.
SOMEHOW, I'M THE ONE WHO MESSED IT ALL UP...
EVEN THOUGH SHIN SAID HE LOVED ME...
...AND THINGS WERE GOING SO WELL.

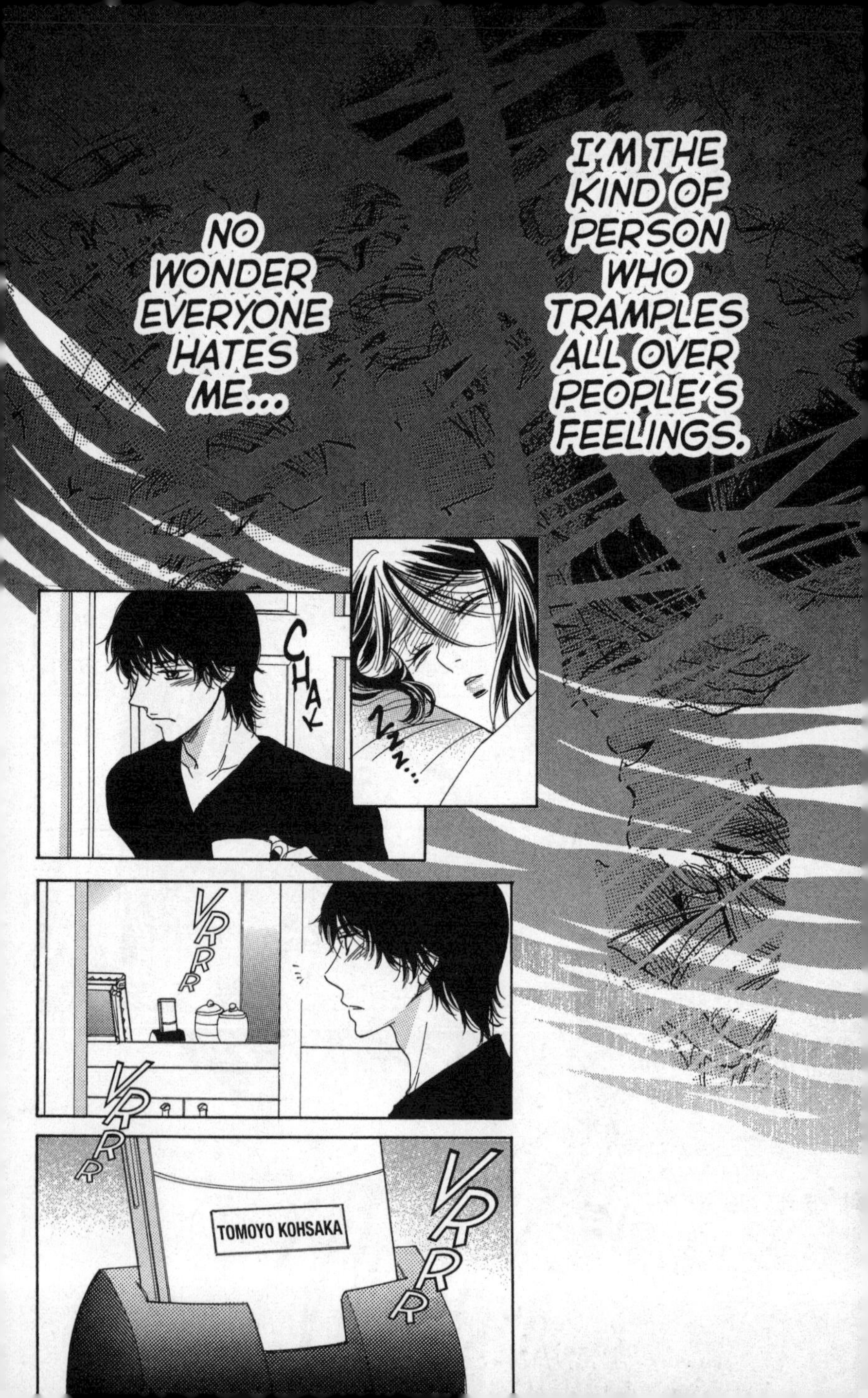
I'M THE KIND OF PERSON WHO TRAMPLES ALL OVER PEOPLE'S FEELINGS.
NO WONDER EVERYONE HATES ME...
ZZZ...
CHAK
VRRRR
VRRR
VRRR
TOMOYO KOHSAKA

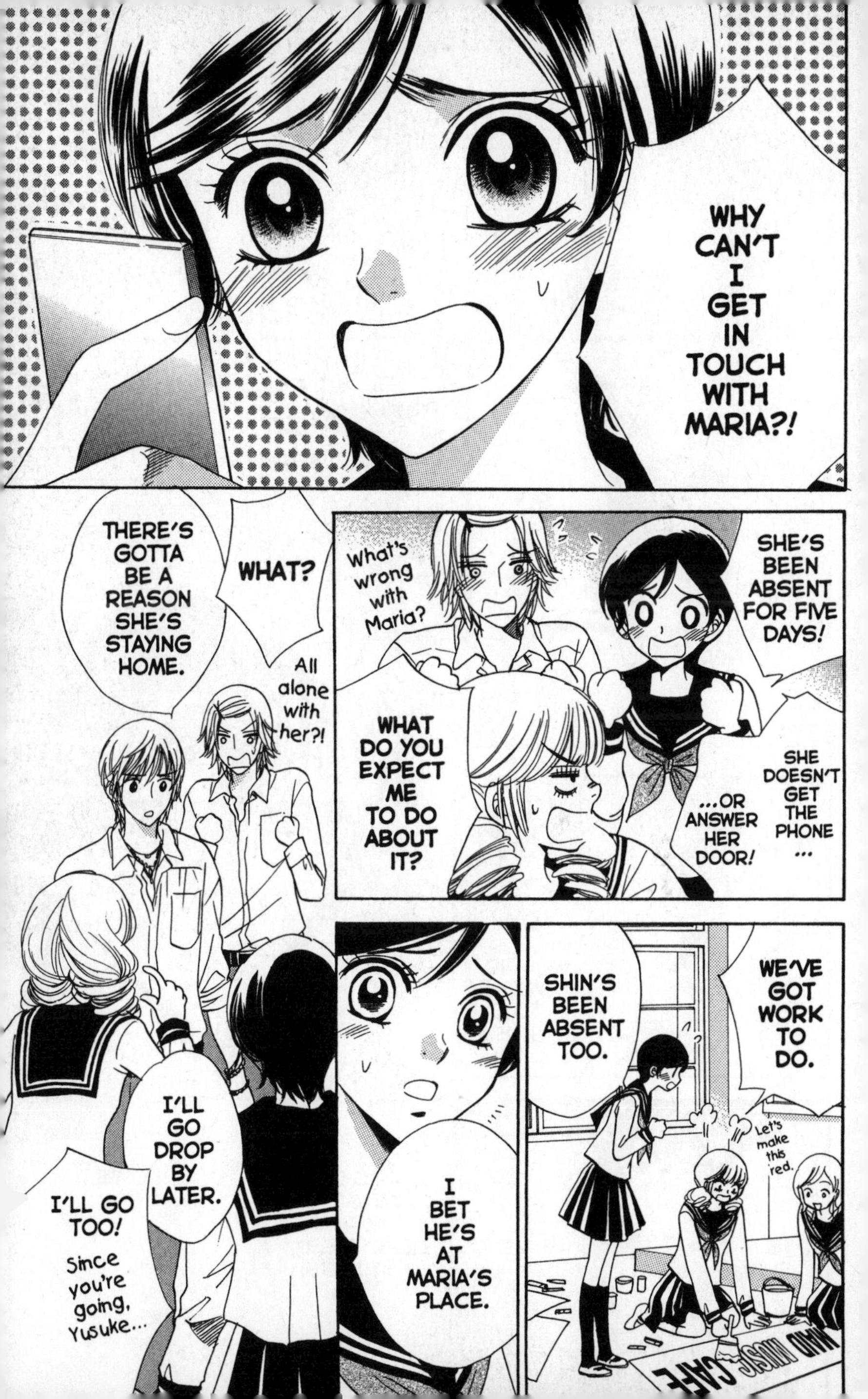
WHY CAN'T I GET IN TOUCH WITH MARIA?!
SHE'S BEEN ABSENT FOR FIVE DAYS!
What's wrong with Maria?
SHE DOESN'T GET THE PHONE ...
...OR ANSWER HER DOOR!
WHAT DO YOU EXPECT ME TO DO ABOUT IT?
WE'VE GOT WORK TO DO.
SHIN'S BEEN ABSENT TOO.
Let's make this red.
I BET HE'S AT MARIA'S PLACE.
WHAT?
THERE'S GOTTA BE A REASON SHE'S STAYING HOME.
All alone with her?!
I'LL GO DROP BY LATER.
I'LL GO TOO!
Since you're going, Yusuke...

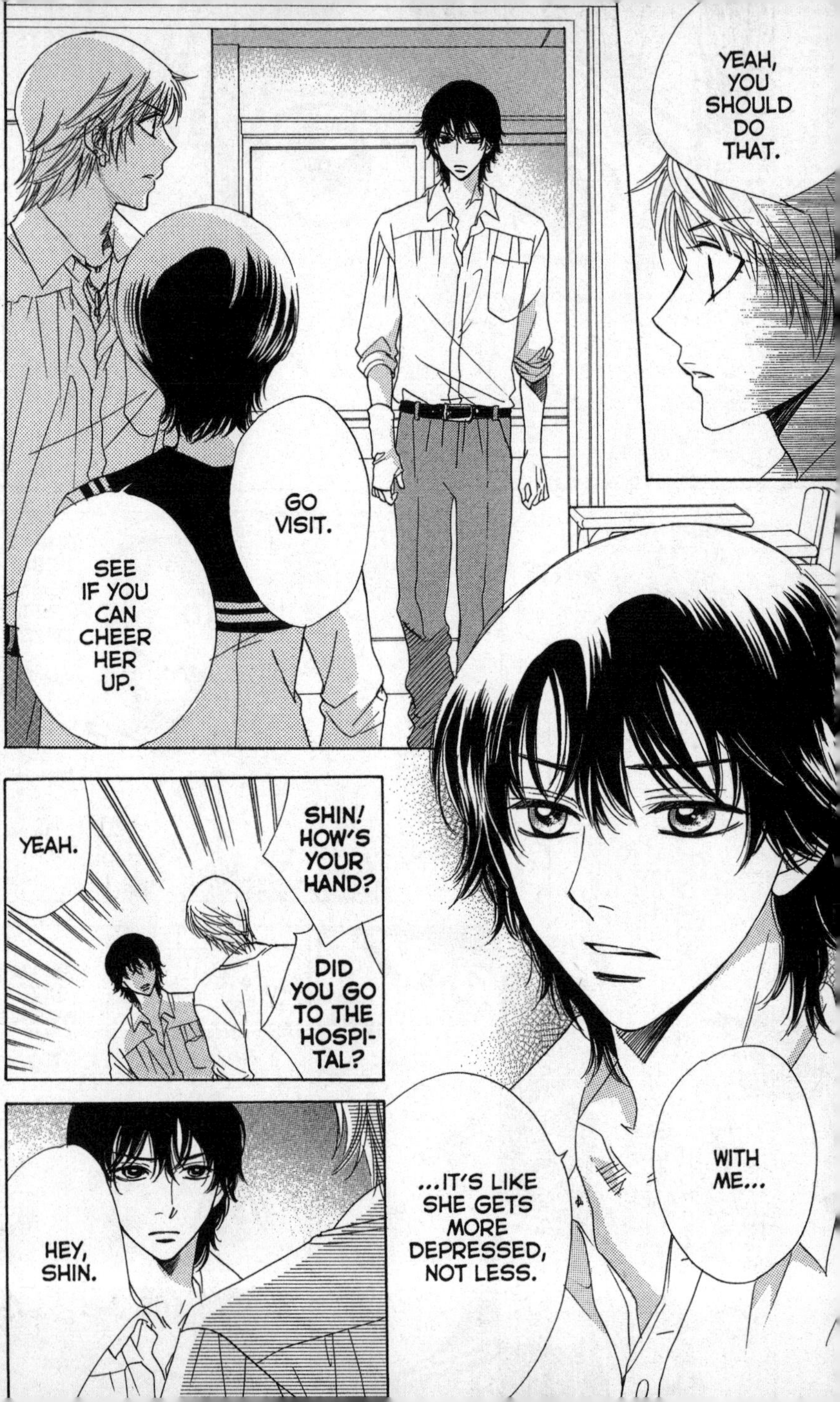
YEAH, YOU SHOULD DO THAT.
GO VISIT.
SEE IF YOU CAN CHEER HER UP.
SHIN! HOW'S YOUR HAND?
DID YOU GO TO THE HOSPITAL?
YEAH.
HEY, SHIN.
WITH ME...
...IT'S LIKE SHE GETS MORE DEPRESSED, NOT LESS.

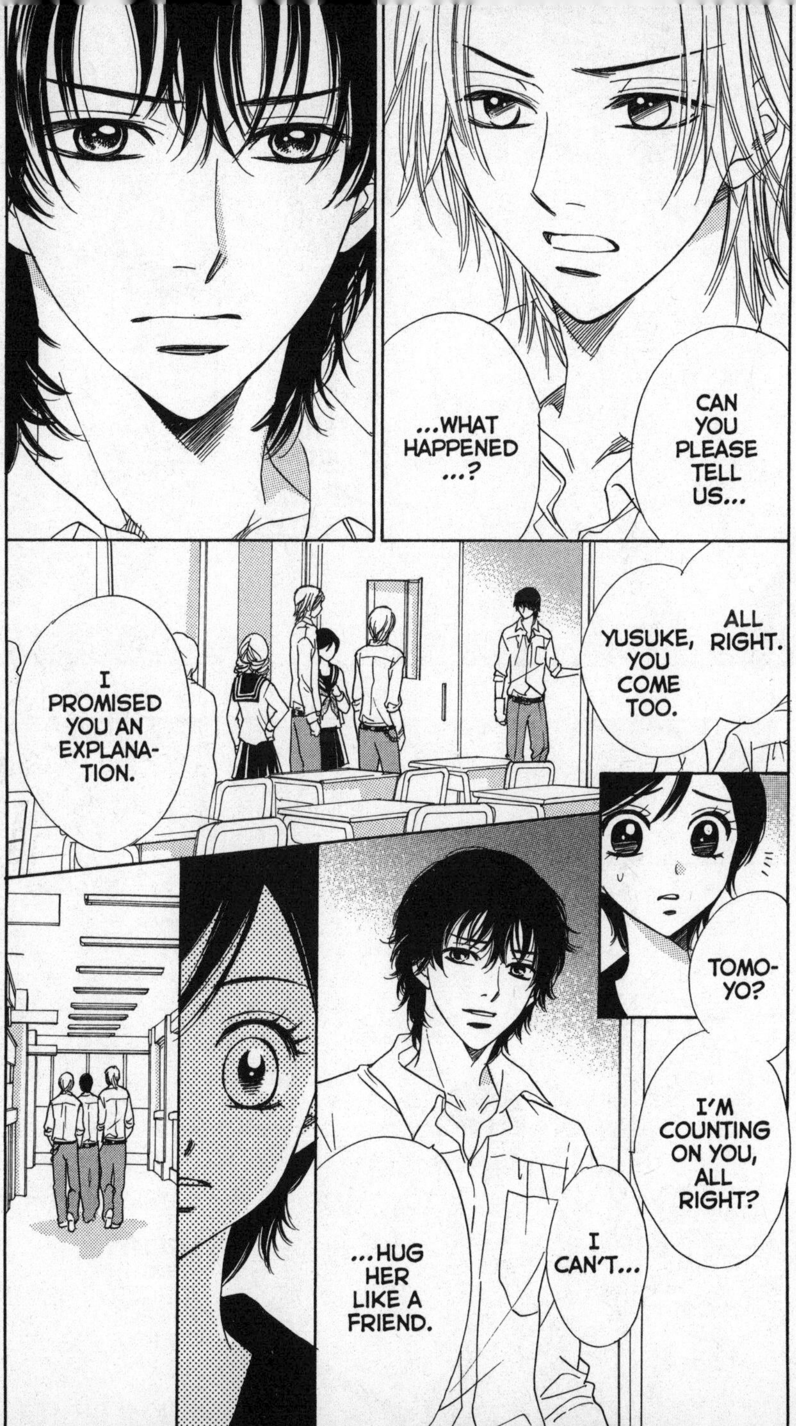
CAN YOU PLEASE TELL US...
...WHAT HAPPENED ...?
ALL RIGHT.
YUSUKE, YOU COME TOO.
I PROMISED YOU AN EXPLANA-TION.
TOMO-YO?
I'M COUNTING ON YOU, ALL RIGHT?
I CAN'T...
...HUG HER LIKE A FRIEND.

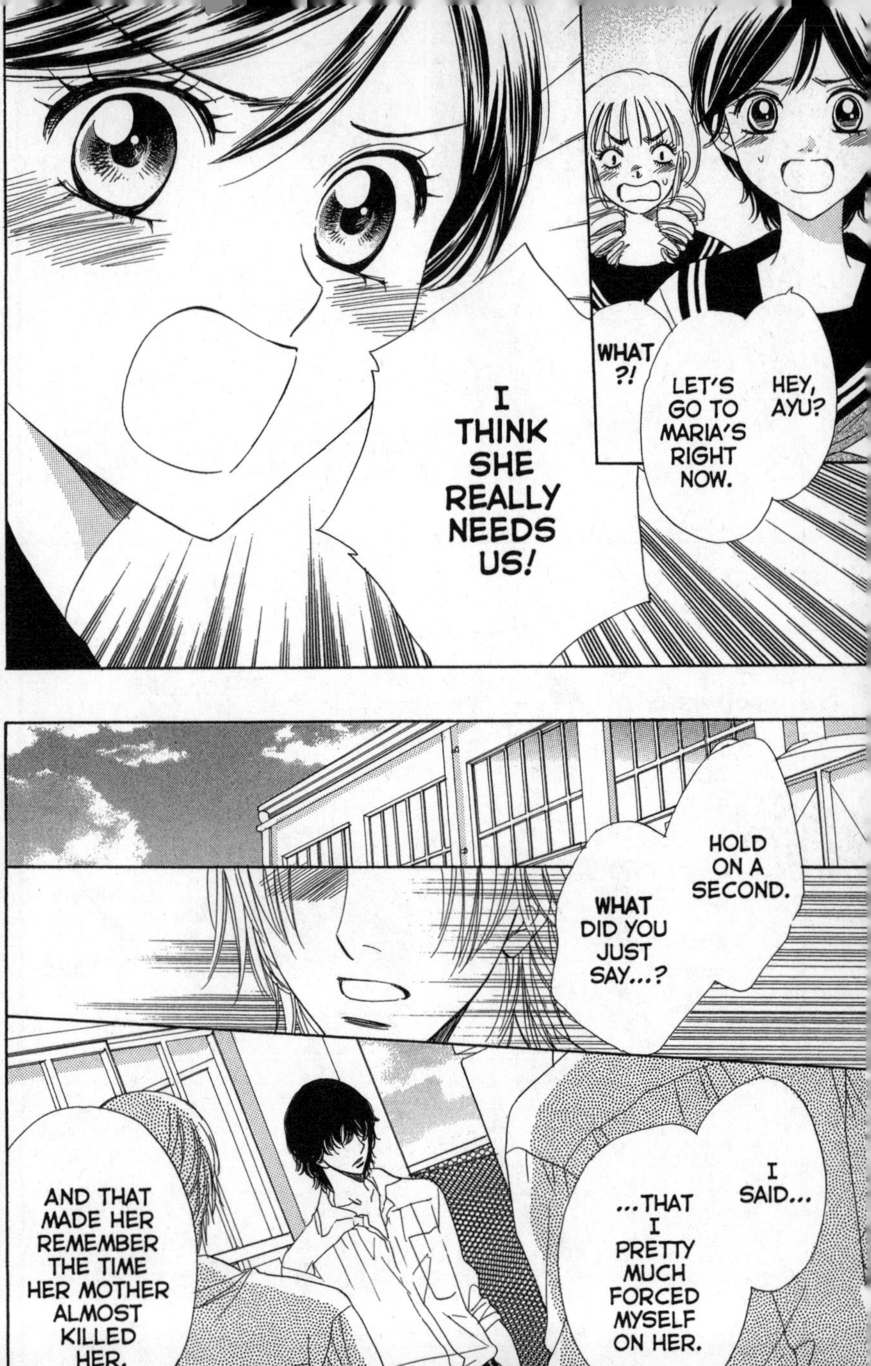
HEY, AYU?
LET'S GO TO MARIA'S RIGHT NOW.
WHAT?!
I THINK SHE REALLY NEEDS US!
HOLD ON A SECOND.
WHAT DID YOU JUST SAY...?
I SAID...
...THAT I PRETTY MUCH FORCED MYSELF ON HER.
AND THAT MADE HER REMEMBER THE TIME HER MOTHER ALMOST KILLED HER.

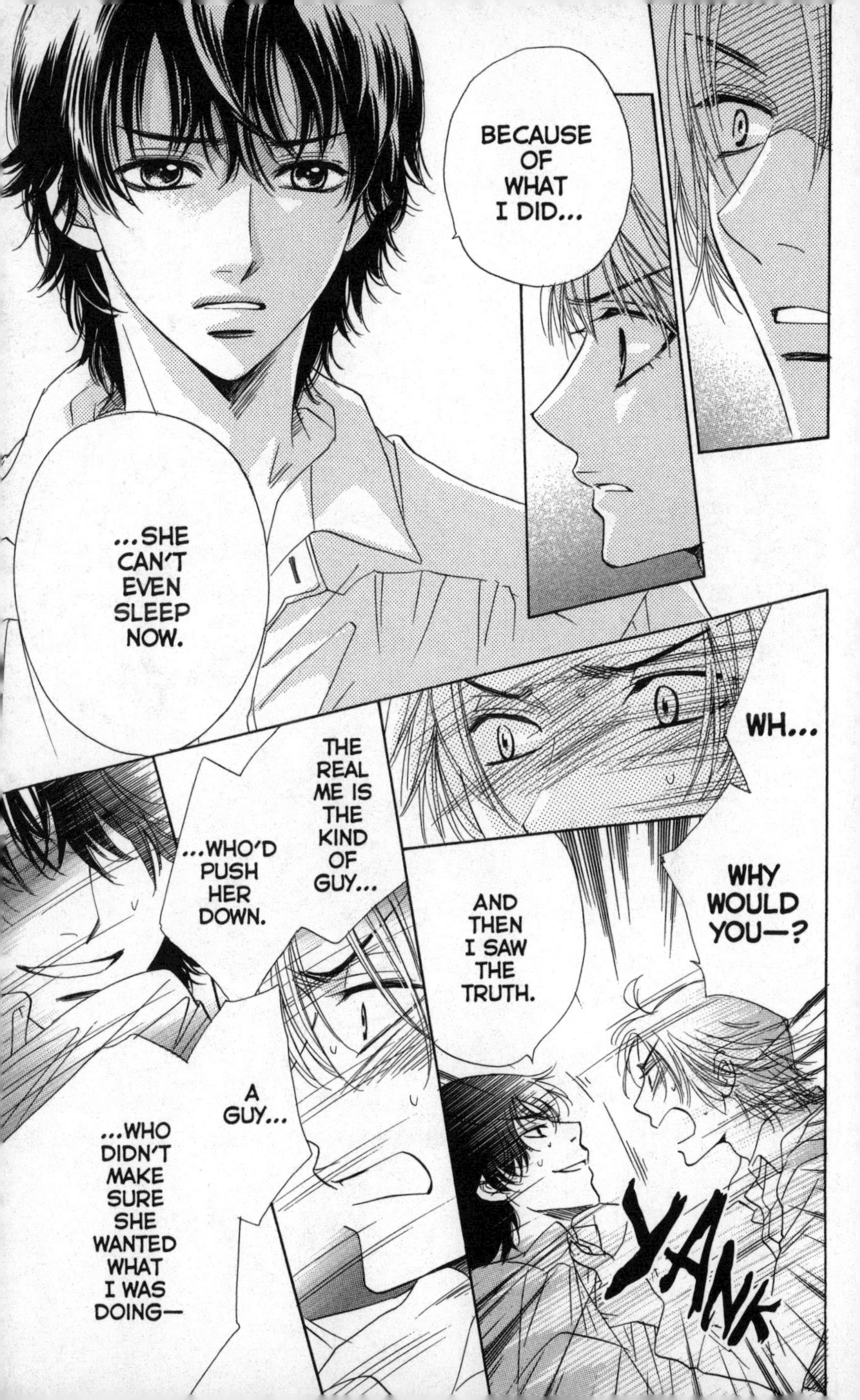
BECAUSE OF WHAT I DID...
...SHE CAN'T EVEN SLEEP NOW.
WH...
THE REAL ME IS THE KIND OF GUY...
...WHO'D PUSH HER DOWN.
WHY WOULD YOU—?
AND THEN I SAW THE TRUTH.
YANK
A GUY...
...WHO DIDN'T MAKE SURE SHE WANTED WHAT I WAS DOING—

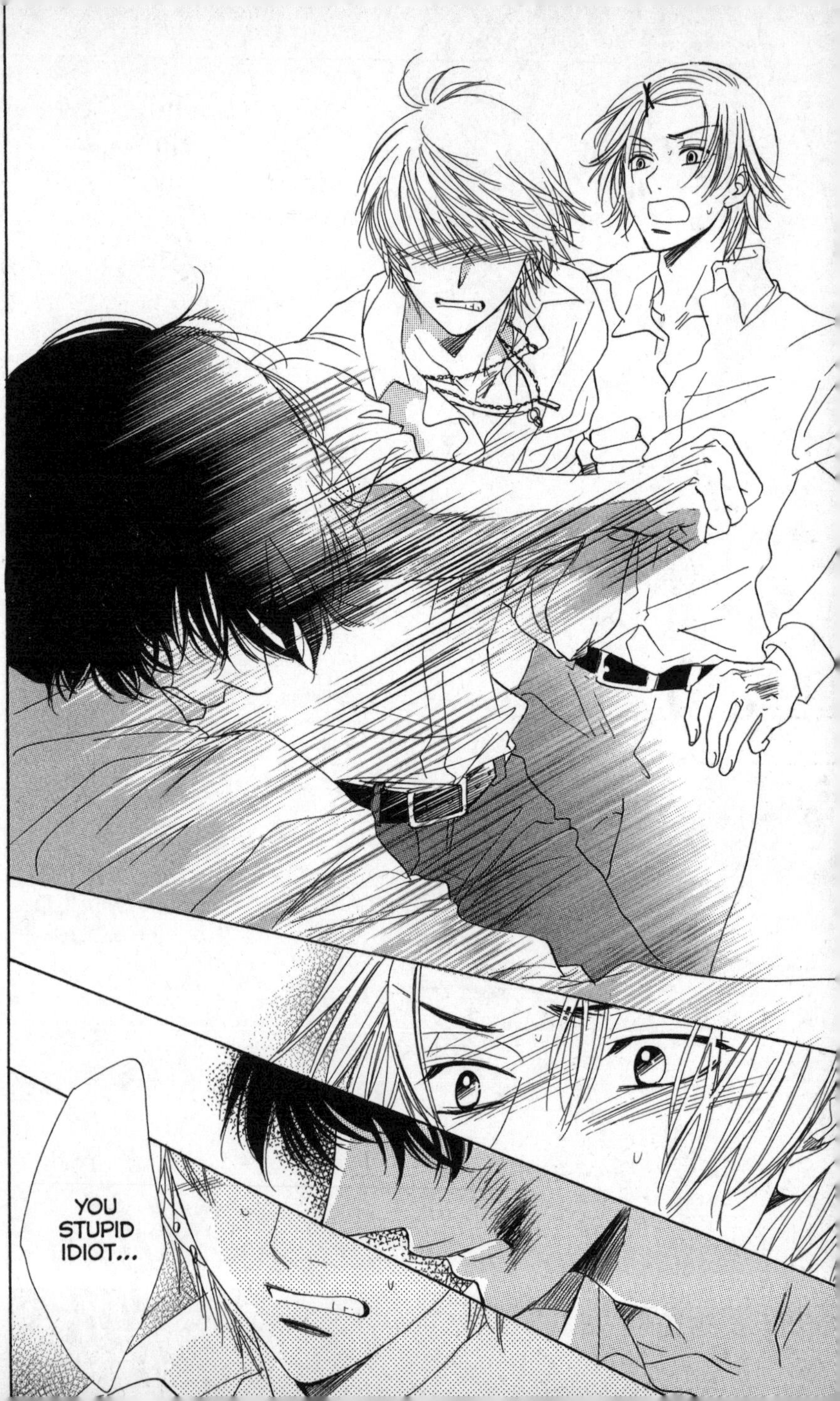
YOU STUPID IDIOT...

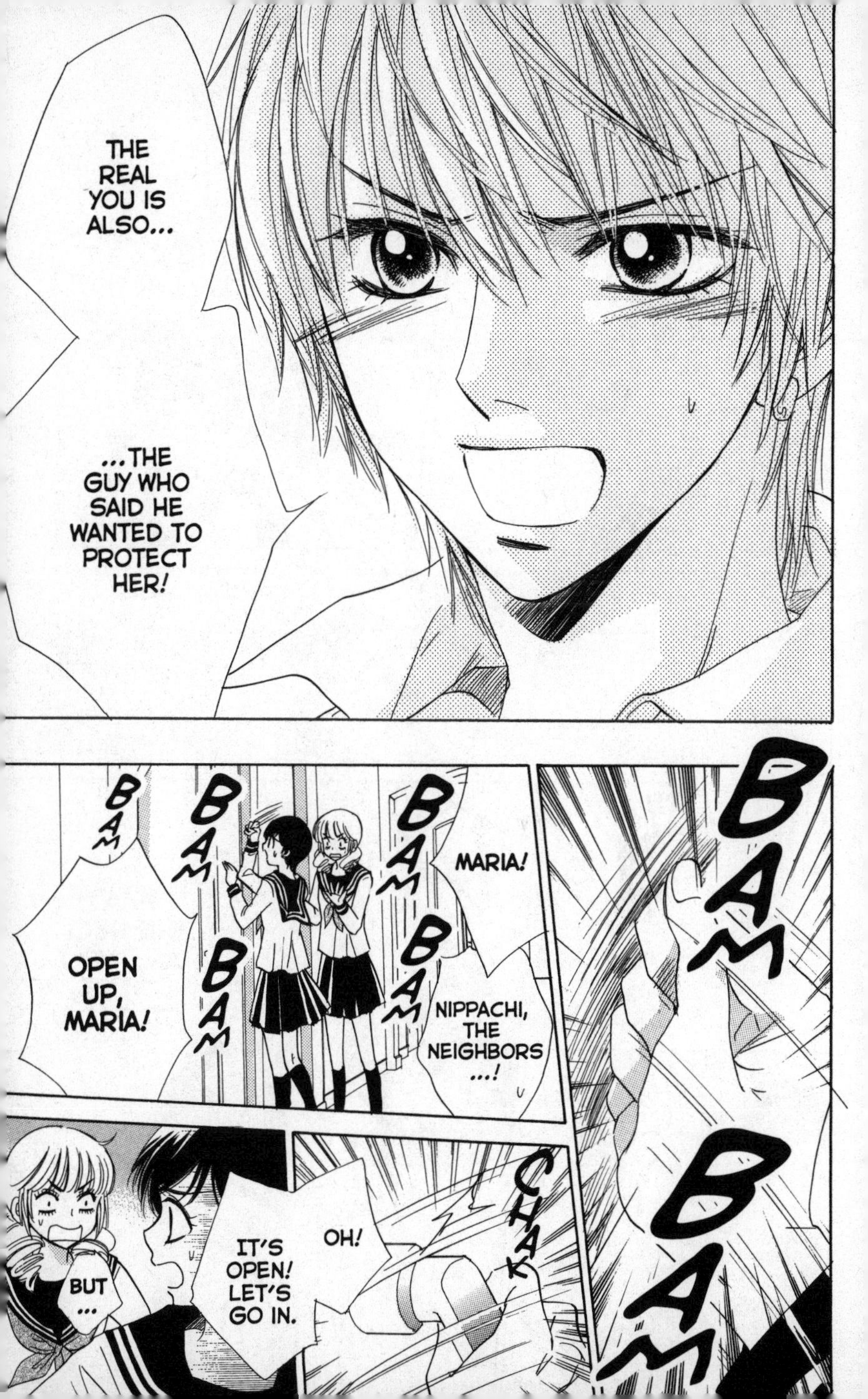
THE REAL YOU IS ALSO...
...THE GUY WHO SAID HE WANTED TO PROTECT HER!
BAM BAM
BAM BAM BAM
MARIA!
NIPPACHI, THE NEIGHBORS ...!
BAM BAM
BAM
OPEN UP, MARIA!
CHAK
OH!
IT'S OPEN! LET'S GO IN.
BUT ...

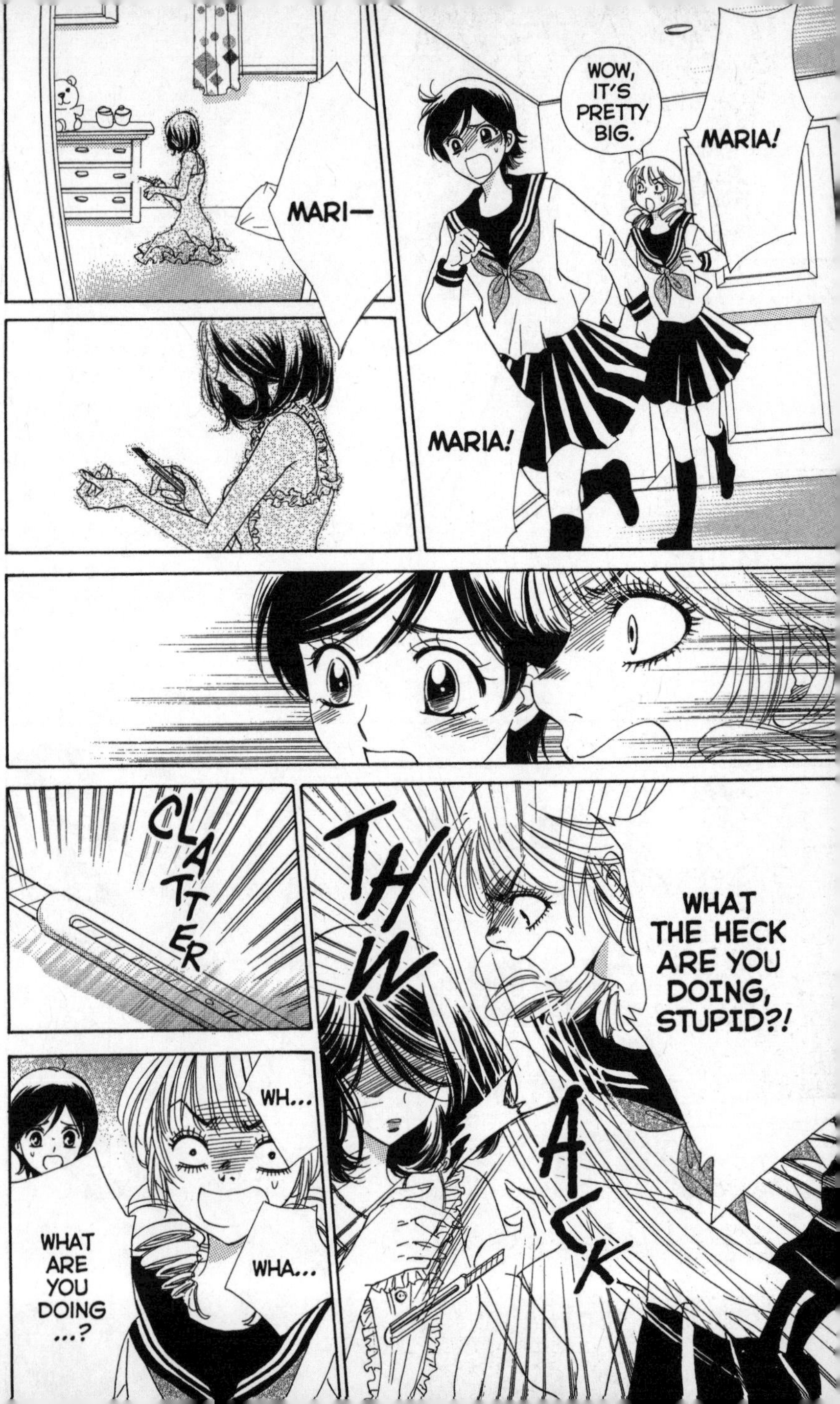
MARIA!
WOW, IT'S PRETTY BIG.
MARIA!
MARI—
WHAT THE HECK ARE YOU DOING, STUPID?!
THWACK
CLATTER
WH...
WHA...
WHAT ARE YOU DOING...?

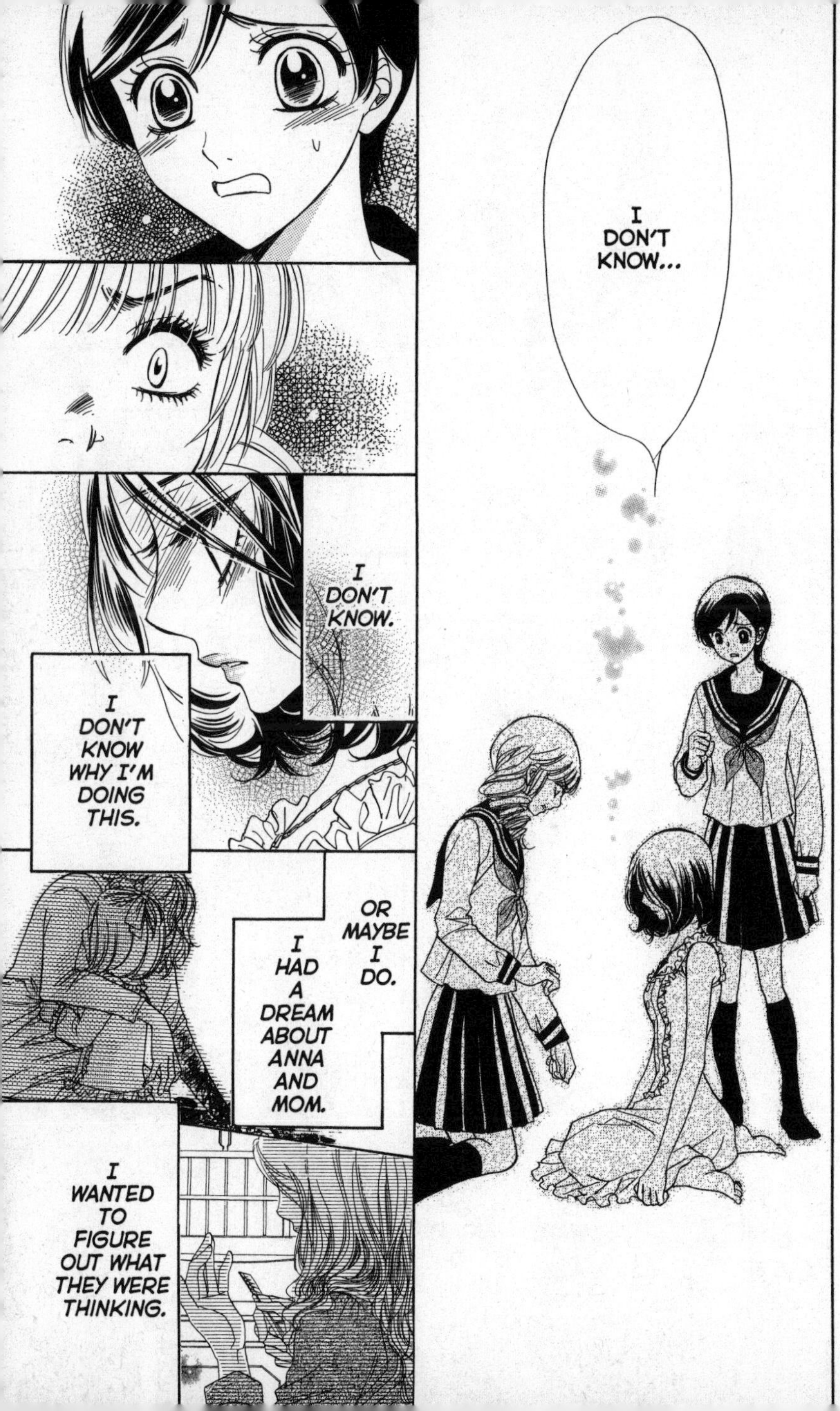
I DON'T KNOW...
I DON'T KNOW.
I DON'T KNOW WHY I'M DOING THIS.
OR MAYBE I DO.
I HAD A DREAM ABOUT ANNA AND MOM.
I WANTED TO FIGURE OUT WHAT THEY WERE THINKING.

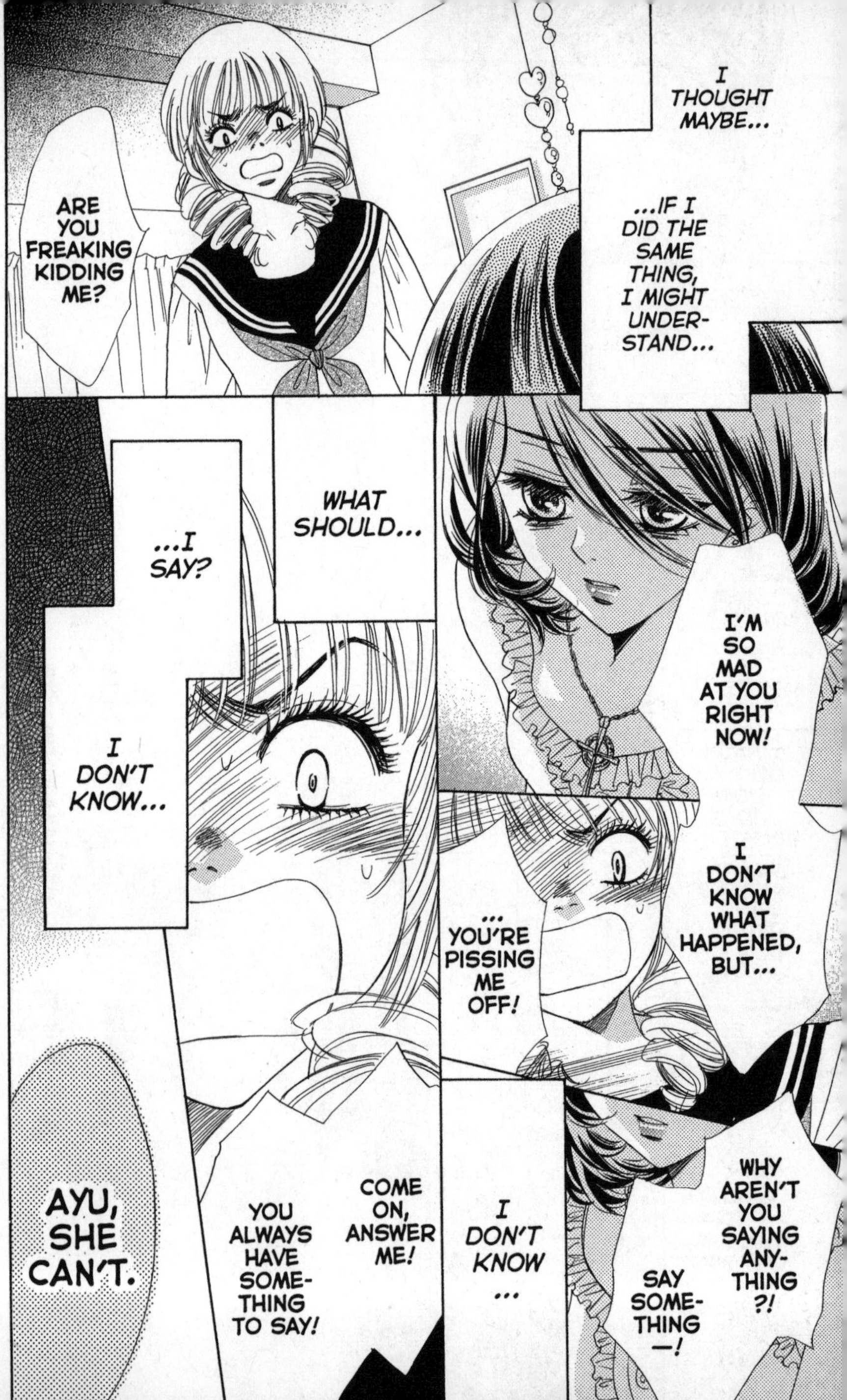
I THOUGHT MAYBE...
...IF I DID THE SAME THING, I MIGHT UNDERSTAND...
ARE YOU FREAKING KIDDING ME?
I'M SO MAD AT YOU RIGHT NOW!
I DON'T KNOW WHAT HAPPENED, BUT...
...YOU'RE PISSING ME OFF!
WHAT SHOULD...
...I SAY?
I DON'T KNOW...
WHY AREN'T YOU SAYING ANYTHING?!
SAY SOMETHING—!
I DON'T KNOW...
COME ON, ANSWER ME!
YOU ALWAYS HAVE SOMETHING TO SAY!
AYU, SHE CAN'T.

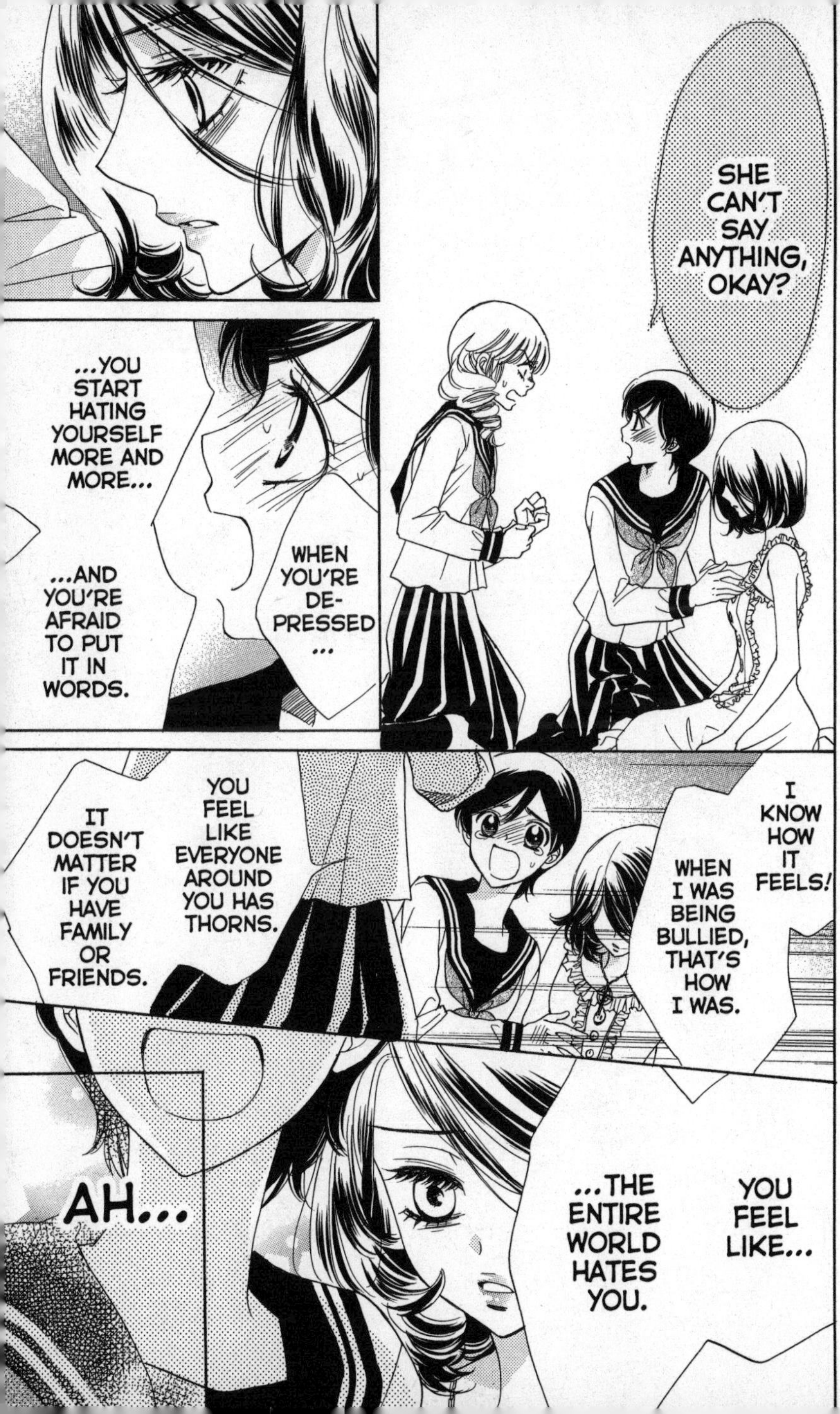
SHE CAN'T SAY ANYTHING, OKAY?
WHEN YOU'RE DE-PRESSED...
...YOU START HATING YOURSELF MORE AND MORE...
...AND YOU'RE AFRAID TO PUT IT IN WORDS.
I KNOW HOW IT FEELS!
WHEN I WAS BEING BULLIED, THAT'S HOW I WAS.
YOU FEEL LIKE EVERYONE AROUND YOU HAS THORNS.
IT DOESN'T MATTER IF YOU HAVE FAMILY OR FRIENDS.
YOU FEEL LIKE...
...THE ENTIRE WORLD HATES YOU.
AH...

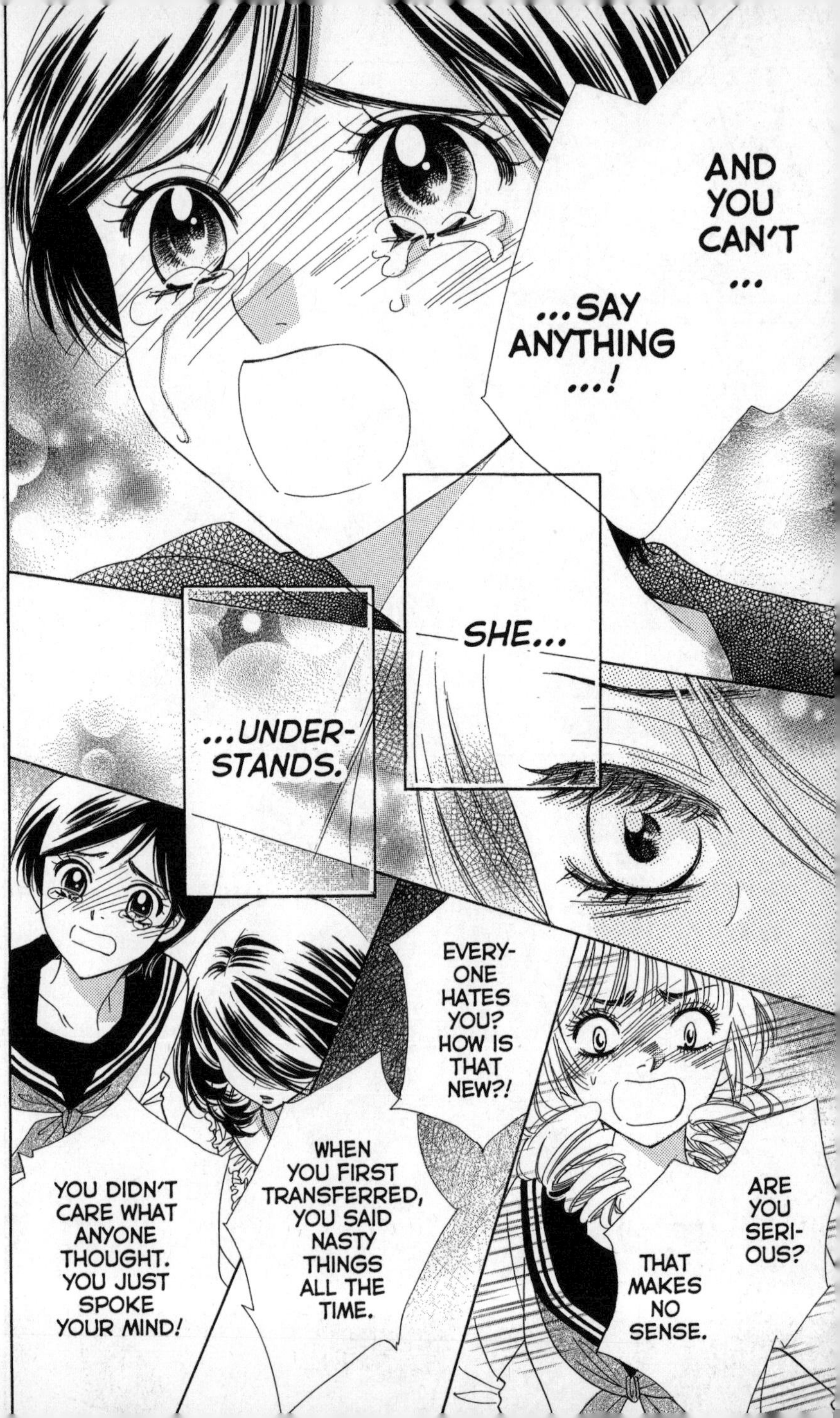
AND YOU CAN'T ...
...SAY ANYTHING ...!
SHE...
...UNDER-STANDS.
ARE YOU SERI-OUS?
THAT MAKES NO SENSE.
EVERY-ONE HATES YOU? HOW IS THAT NEW?!
WHEN YOU FIRST TRANSFERRED, YOU SAID NASTY THINGS ALL THE TIME.
YOU DIDN'T CARE WHAT ANYONE THOUGHT. YOU JUST SPOKE YOUR MIND!

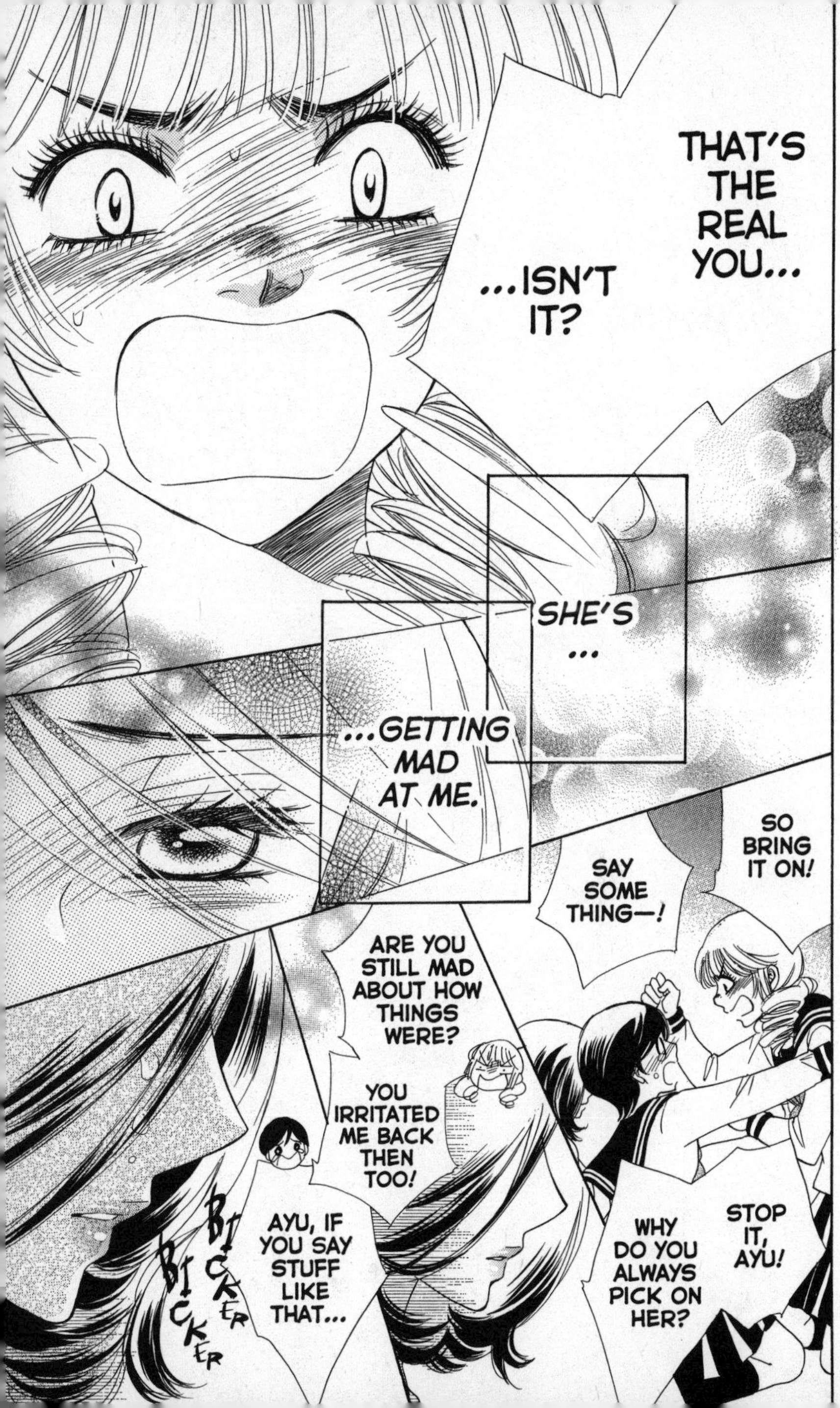
THAT'S THE REAL YOU...
...ISN'T IT?
SHE'S ...
...GETTING MAD AT ME.
SO BRING IT ON!
SAY SOME THING—!
ARE YOU STILL MAD ABOUT HOW THINGS WERE?
YOU IRRITATED ME BACK THEN TOO!
STOP IT, AYU!
WHY DO YOU ALWAYS PICK ON HER?
AYU, IF YOU SAY STUFF LIKE THAT...
BICKER BICKER

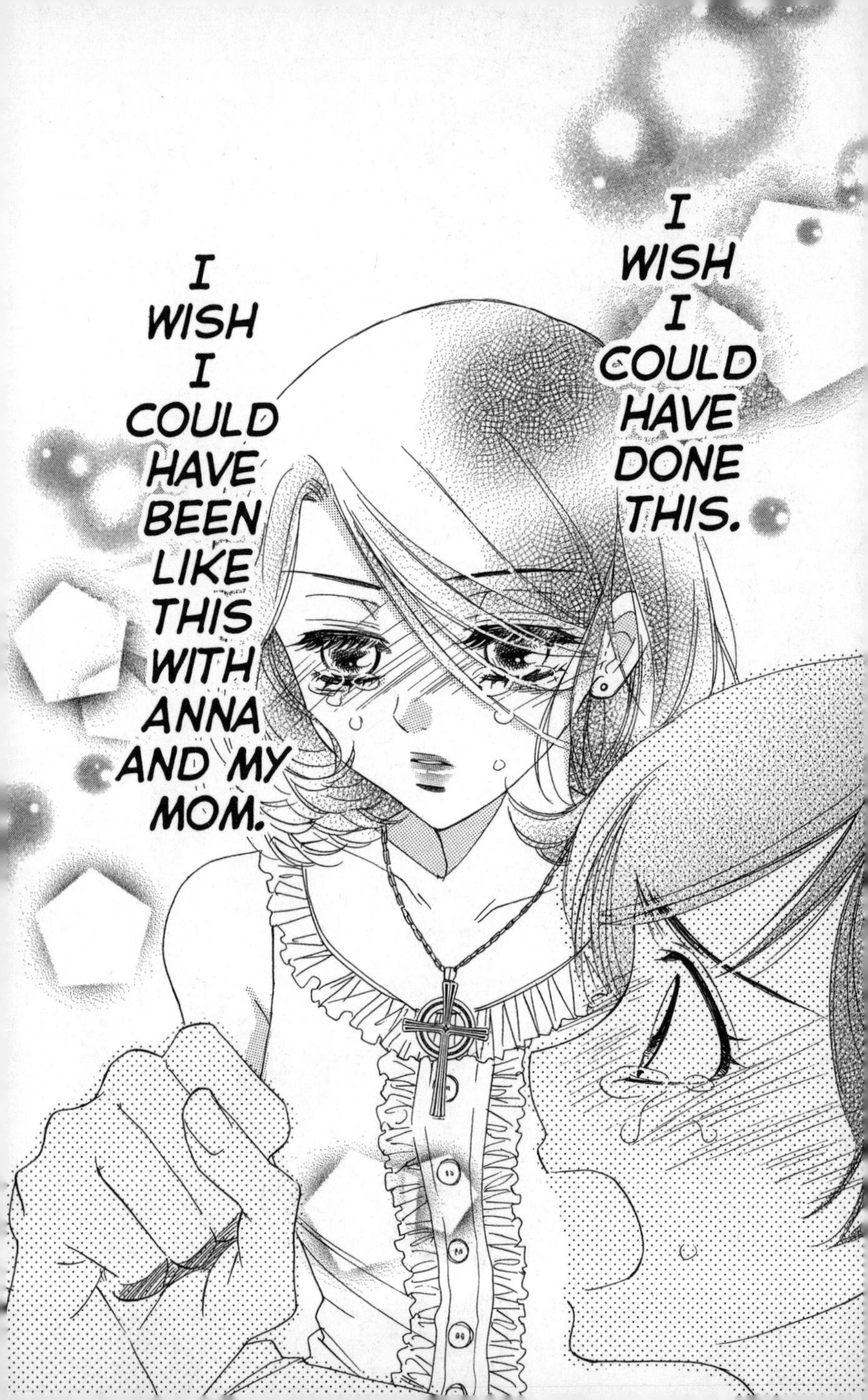
I WISH I COULD HAVE DONE THIS.
I WISH I COULD HAVE BEEN LIKE THIS WITH ANNA AND MY MOM.

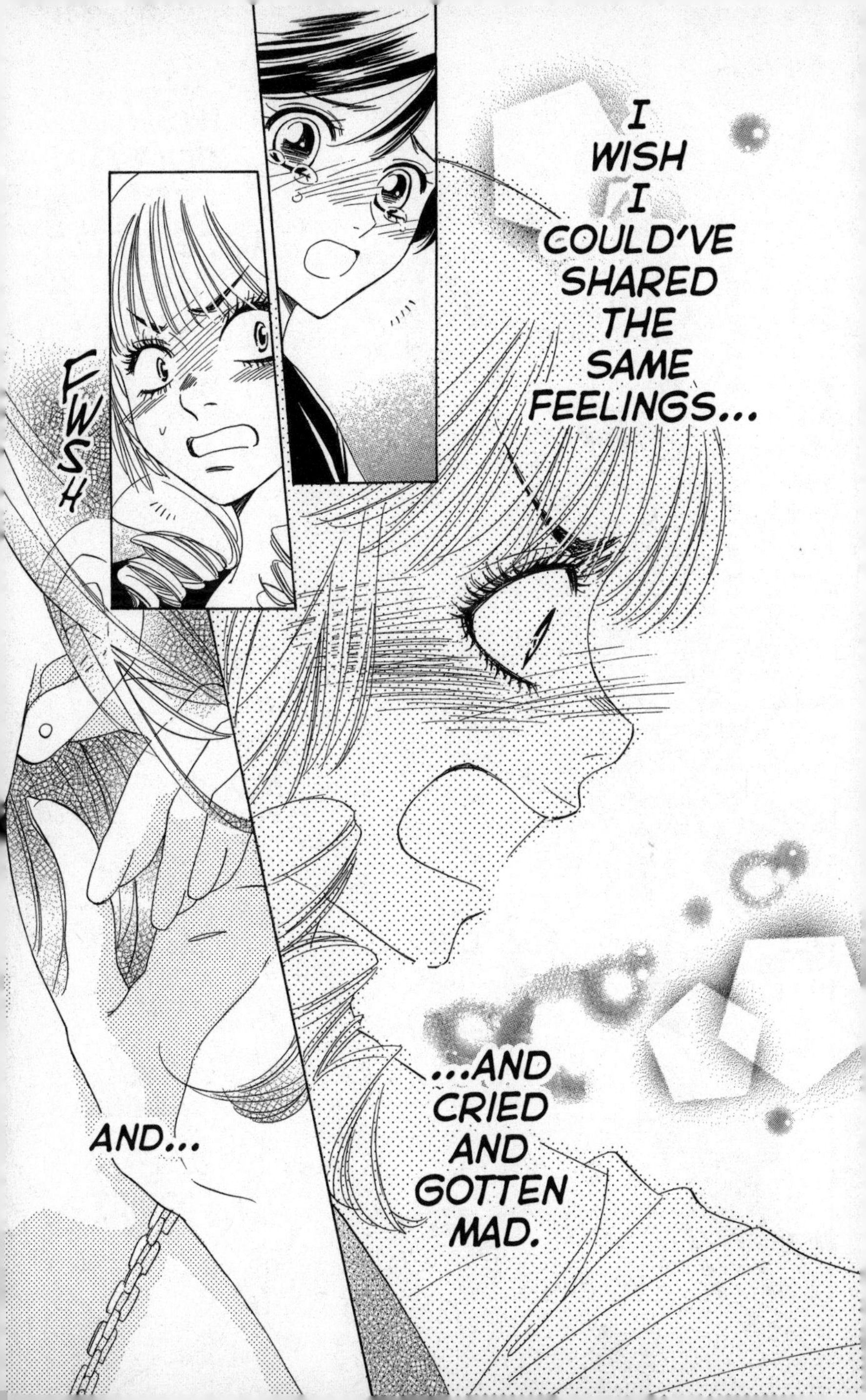
I WISH I COULD'VE SHARED THE SAME FEELINGS...
FWSH
...AND CRIED AND GOTTEN MAD.
AND...

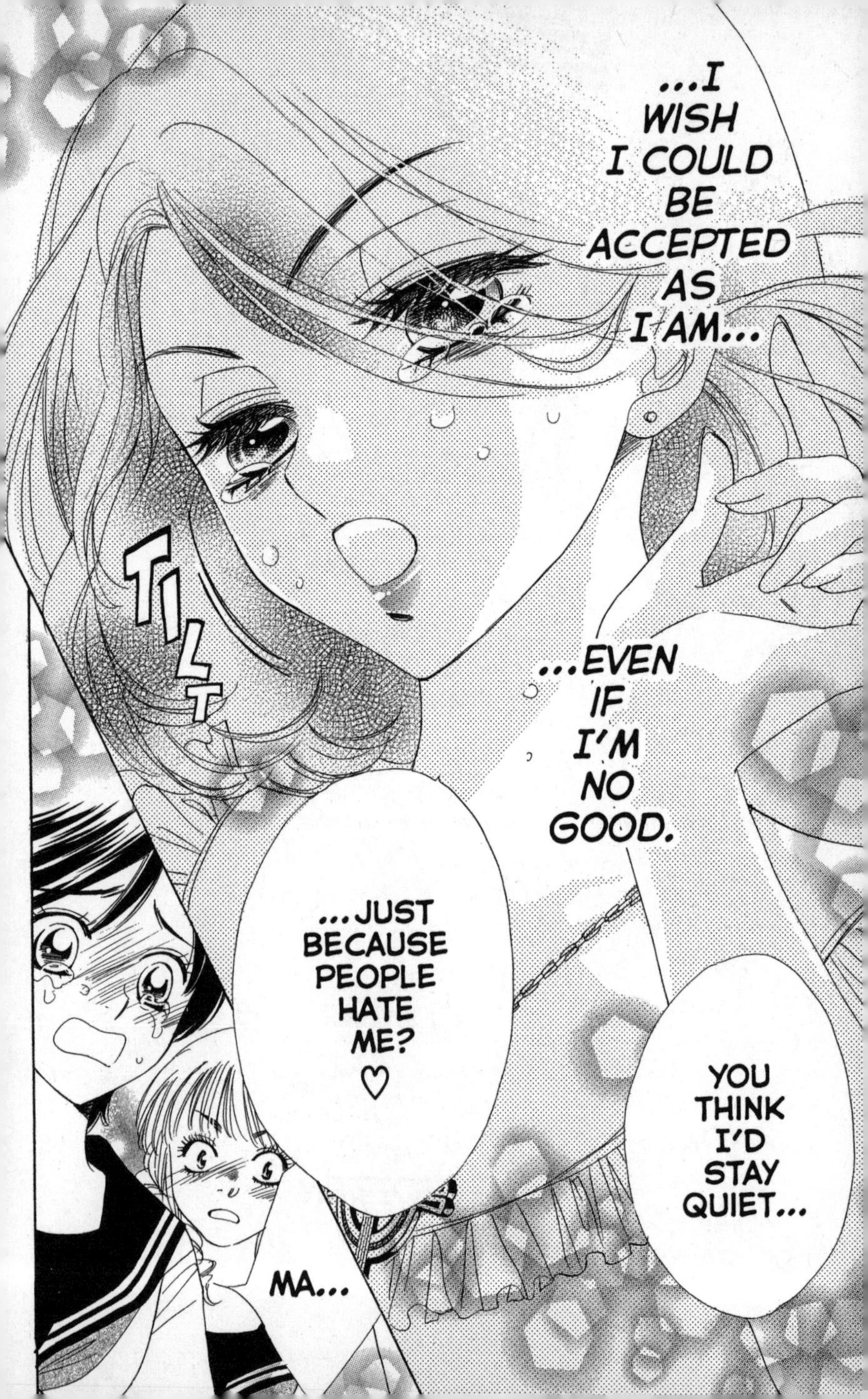
...I WISH I COULD BE ACCEPTED AS I AM...
...EVEN IF I'M NO GOOD.
TILT
YOU THINK I'D STAY QUIET...
...JUST BECAUSE PEOPLE HATE ME? ♡
MA...

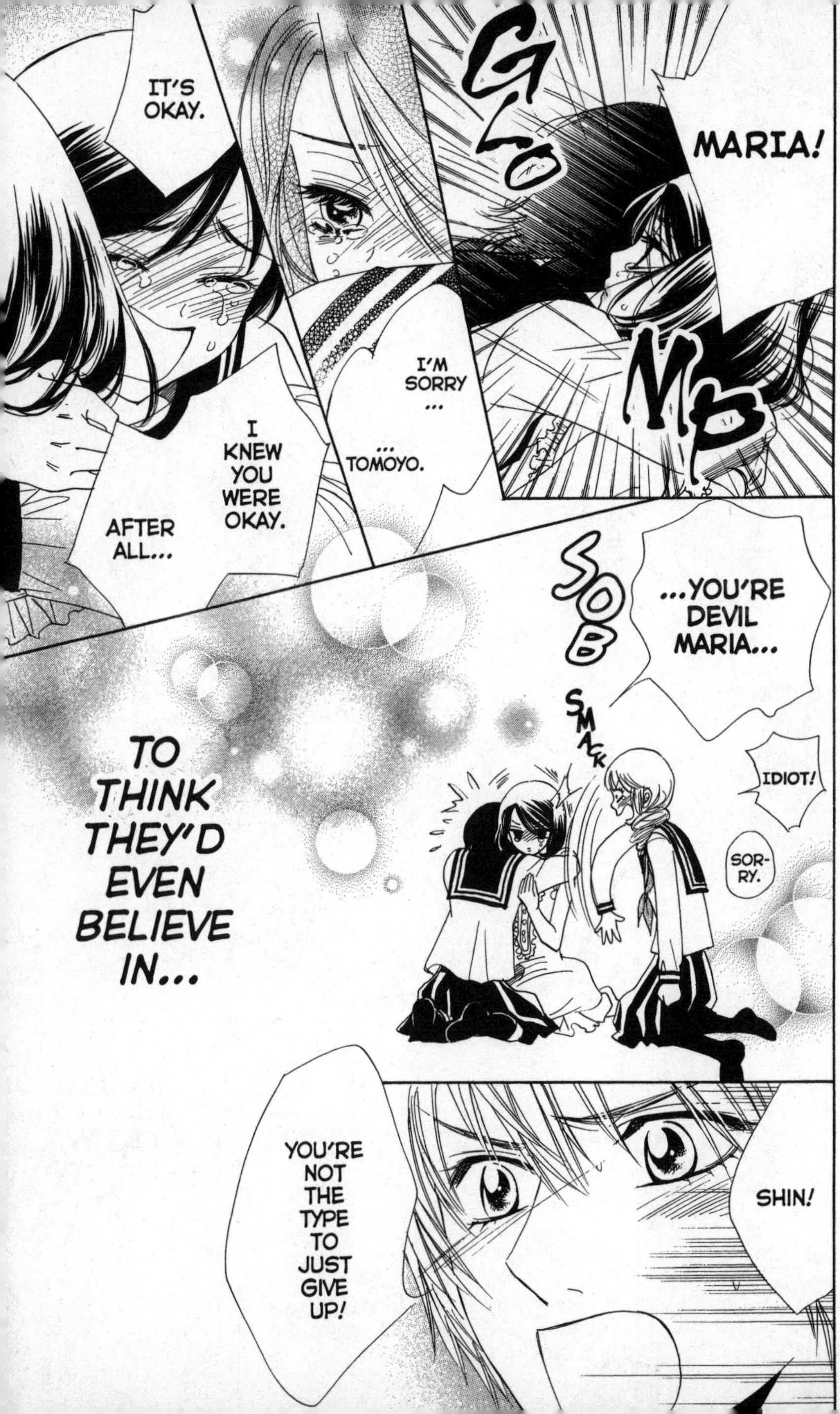
MARIA!
I'M SORRY ...
... TOMOYO.
IT'S OKAY.
I KNEW YOU WERE OKAY.
AFTER ALL...
SOB
...YOU'RE DEVIL MARIA...
SMACK
IDIOT!
SORRY.
TO THINK THEY'D EVEN BELIEVE IN...
SHIN!
YOU'RE NOT THE TYPE TO JUST GIVE UP!

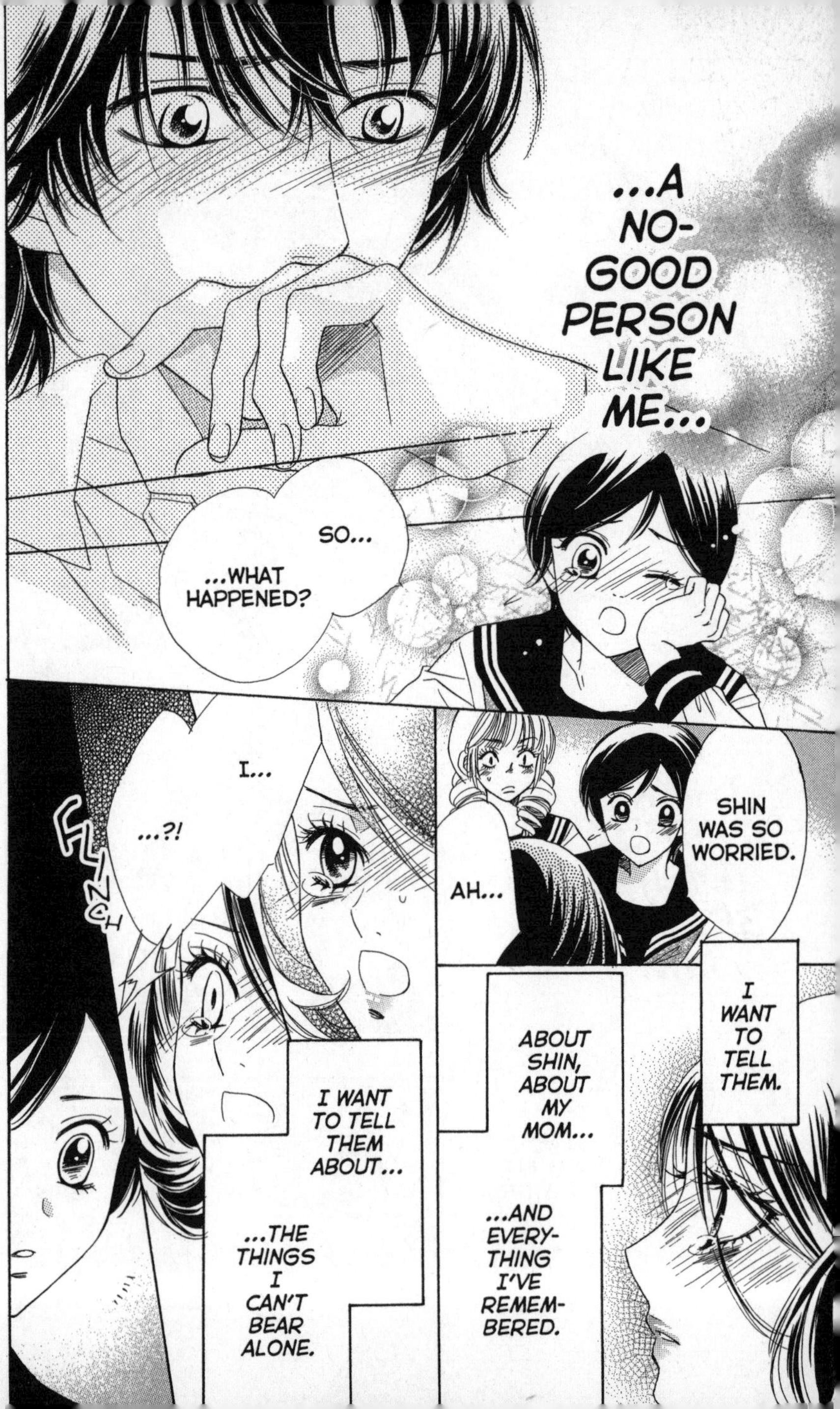
...A NO-GOOD PERSON LIKE ME...
SO...
...WHAT HAPPENED?
SHIN WAS SO WORRIED.
AH...
I WANT TO TELL THEM.
ABOUT SHIN, ABOUT MY MOM...
...AND EVERYTHING I'VE REMEMBERED.
I...
...?!
FLINCH
I WANT TO TELL THEM ABOUT...
...THE THINGS I CAN'T BEAR ALONE.

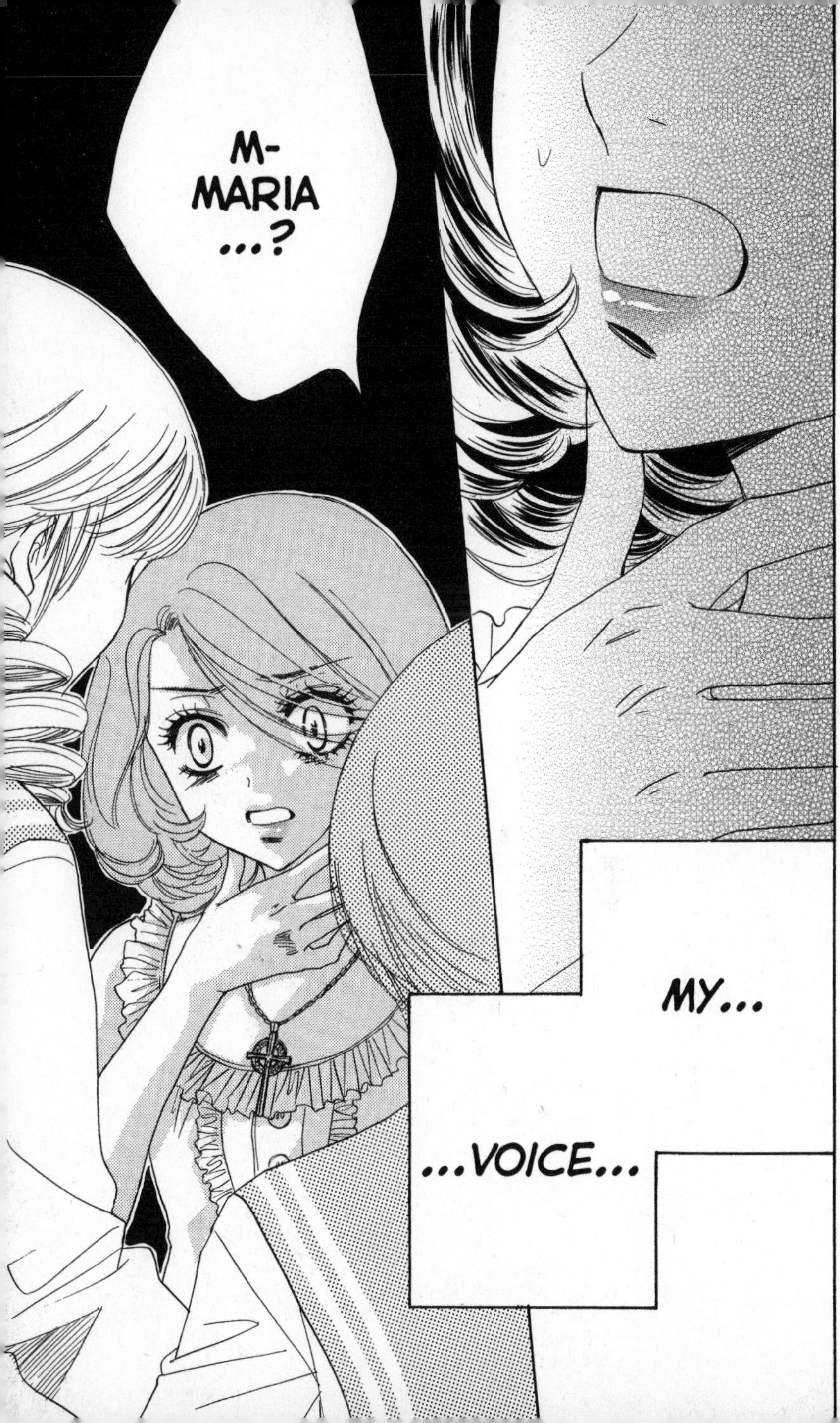
M-MARIA...?
MY...
...VOICE...

A Devil and
Her Love Song

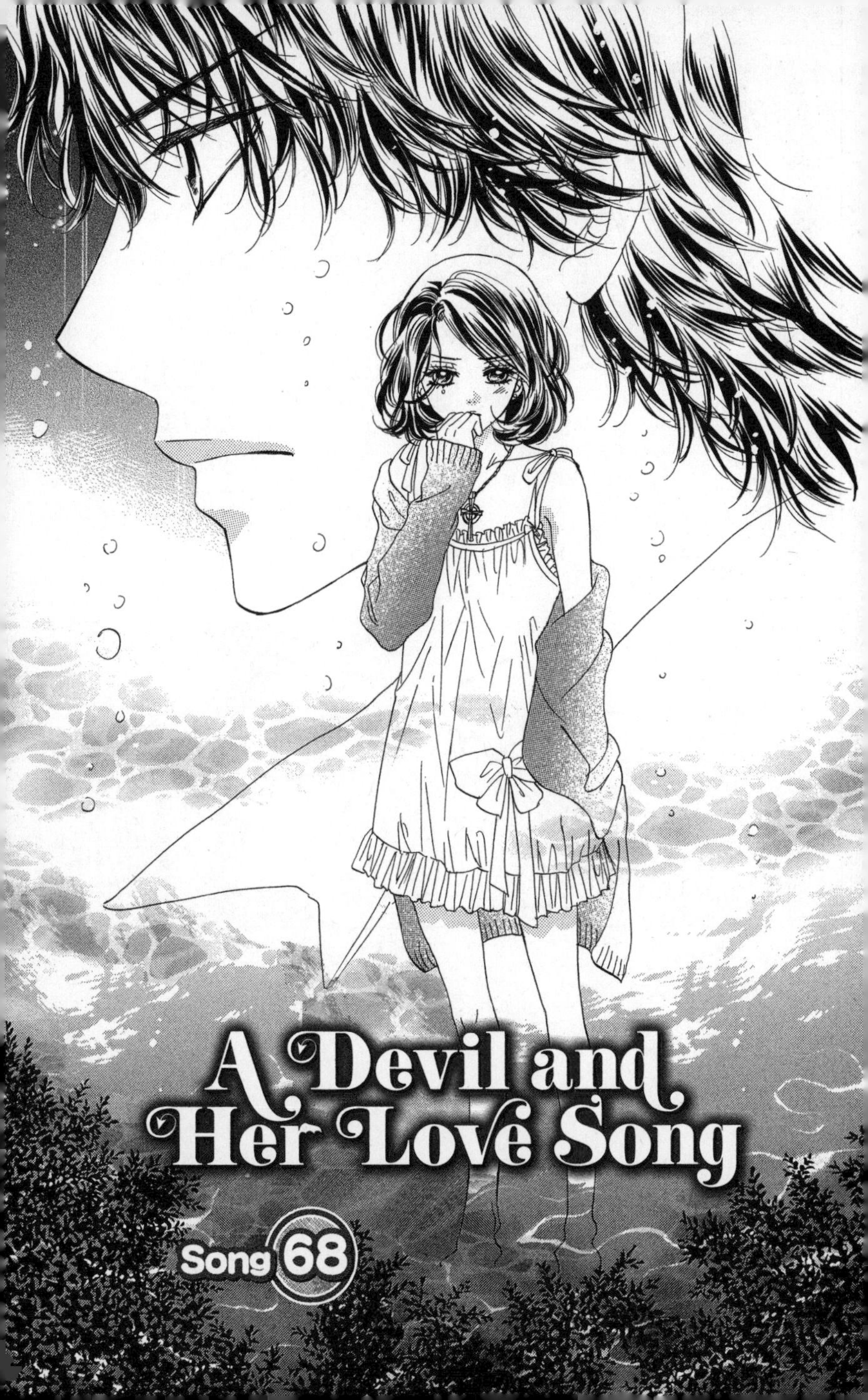
A Devil and Her Love Song
Song 68

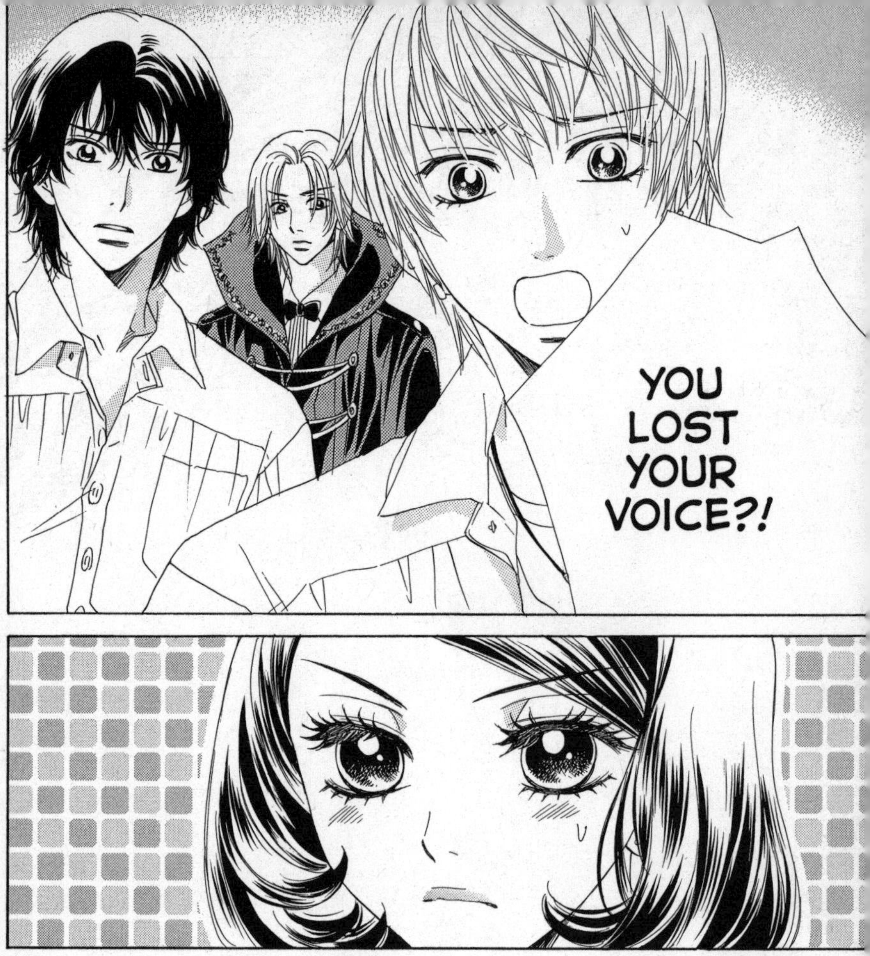
YOU LOST YOUR VOICE?!

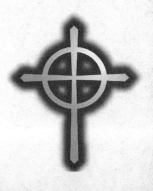

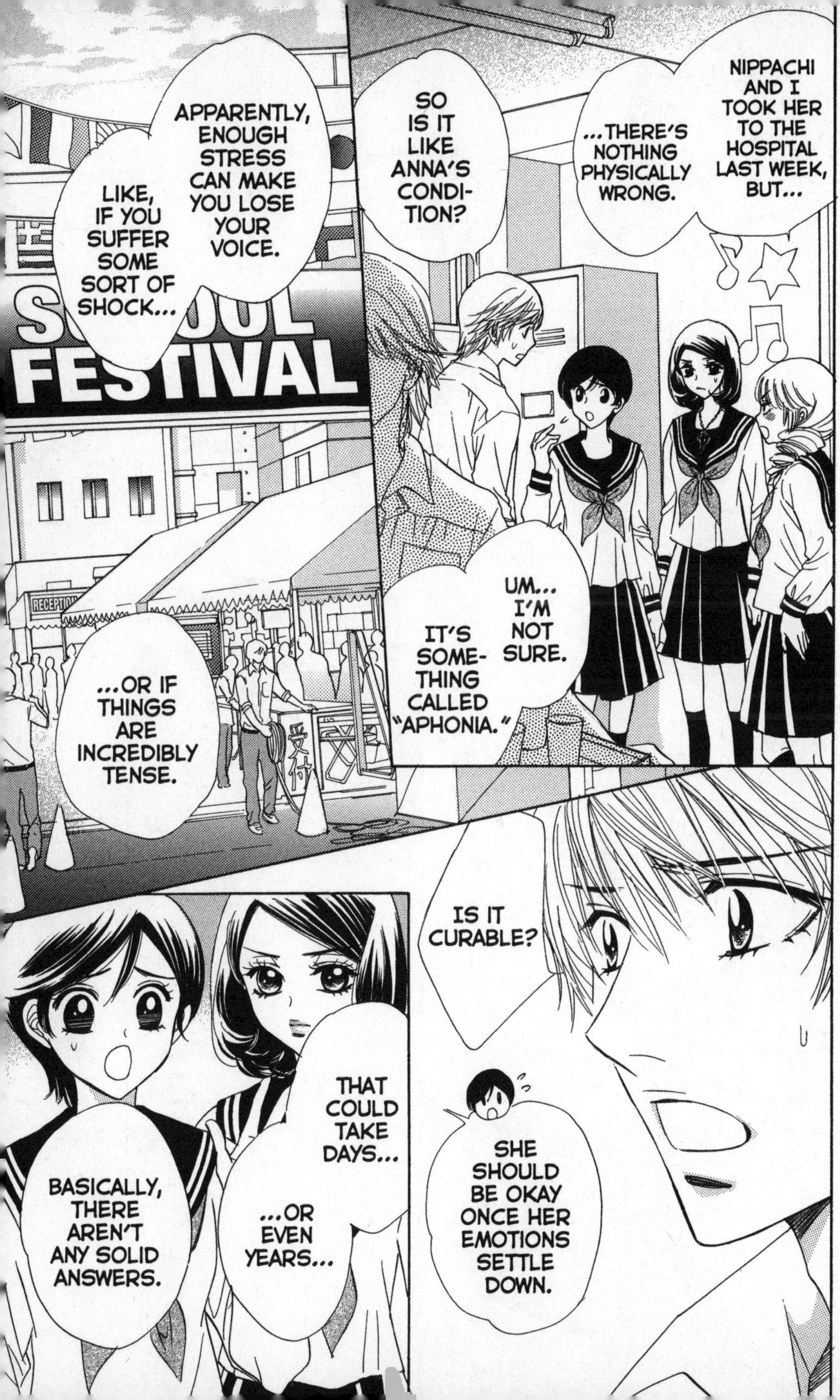
NIPPACHI AND I TOOK HER TO THE HOSPITAL LAST WEEK, BUT...
...THERE'S NOTHING PHYSICALLY WRONG.
SO IS IT LIKE ANNA'S CONDITION?
UM... I'M NOT SURE.
IT'S SOMETHING CALLED "APHONIA."
APPARENTLY, ENOUGH STRESS CAN MAKE YOU LOSE YOUR VOICE.
LIKE, IF YOU SUFFER SOME SORT OF SHOCK...
FESTIVAL
RECEPTION
...OR IF THINGS ARE INCREDIBLY TENSE.
IS IT CURABLE?
SHE SHOULD BE OKAY ONCE HER EMOTIONS SETTLE DOWN.
THAT COULD TAKE DAYS...
...OR EVEN YEARS...
BASICALLY, THERE AREN'T ANY SOLID ANSWERS.

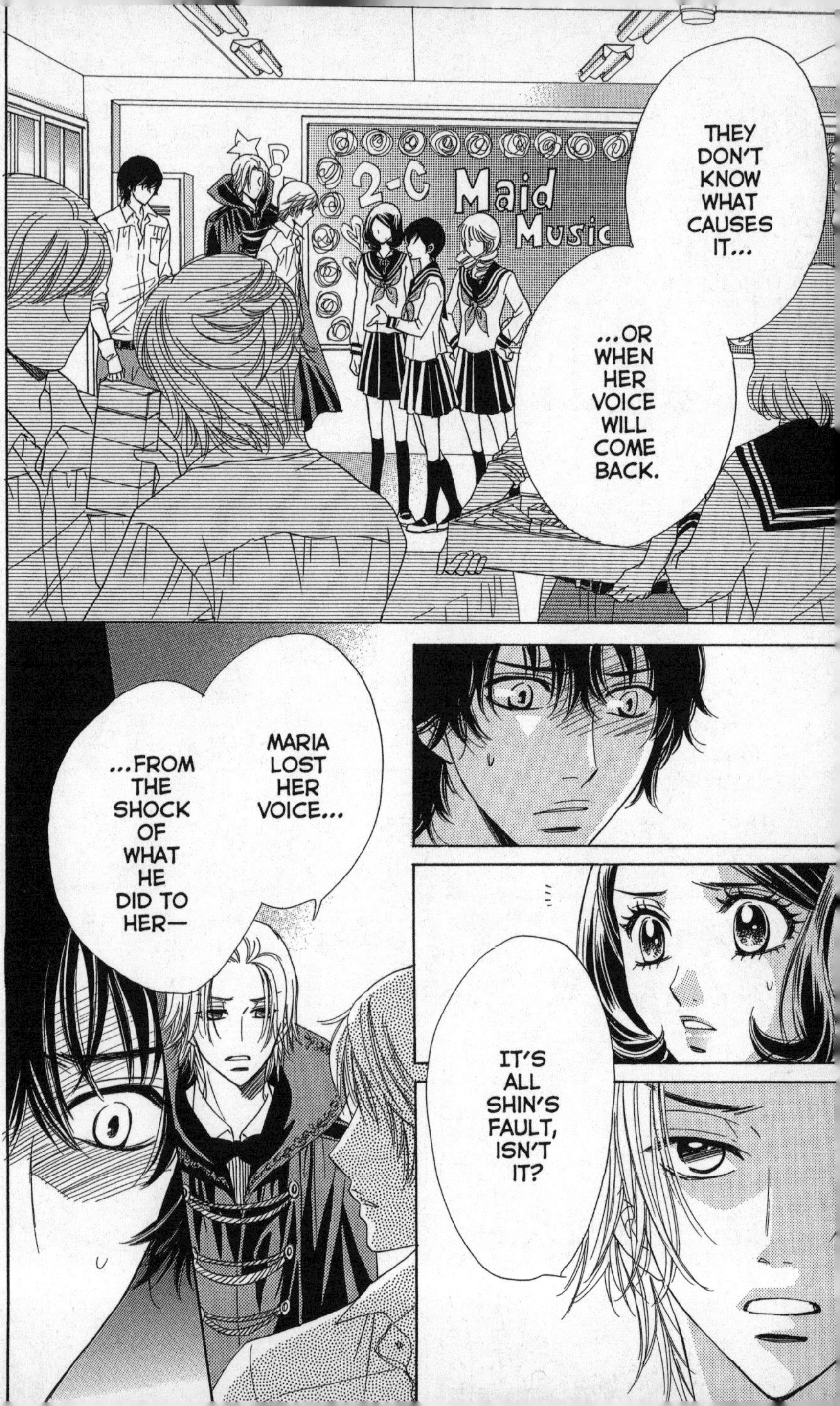
THEY DON'T KNOW WHAT CAUSES IT...
...OR WHEN HER VOICE WILL COME BACK.
2-C Maid Music
IT'S ALL SHIN'S FAULT, ISN'T IT?
MARIA LOST HER VOICE...
...FROM THE SHOCK OF WHAT HE DID TO HER—

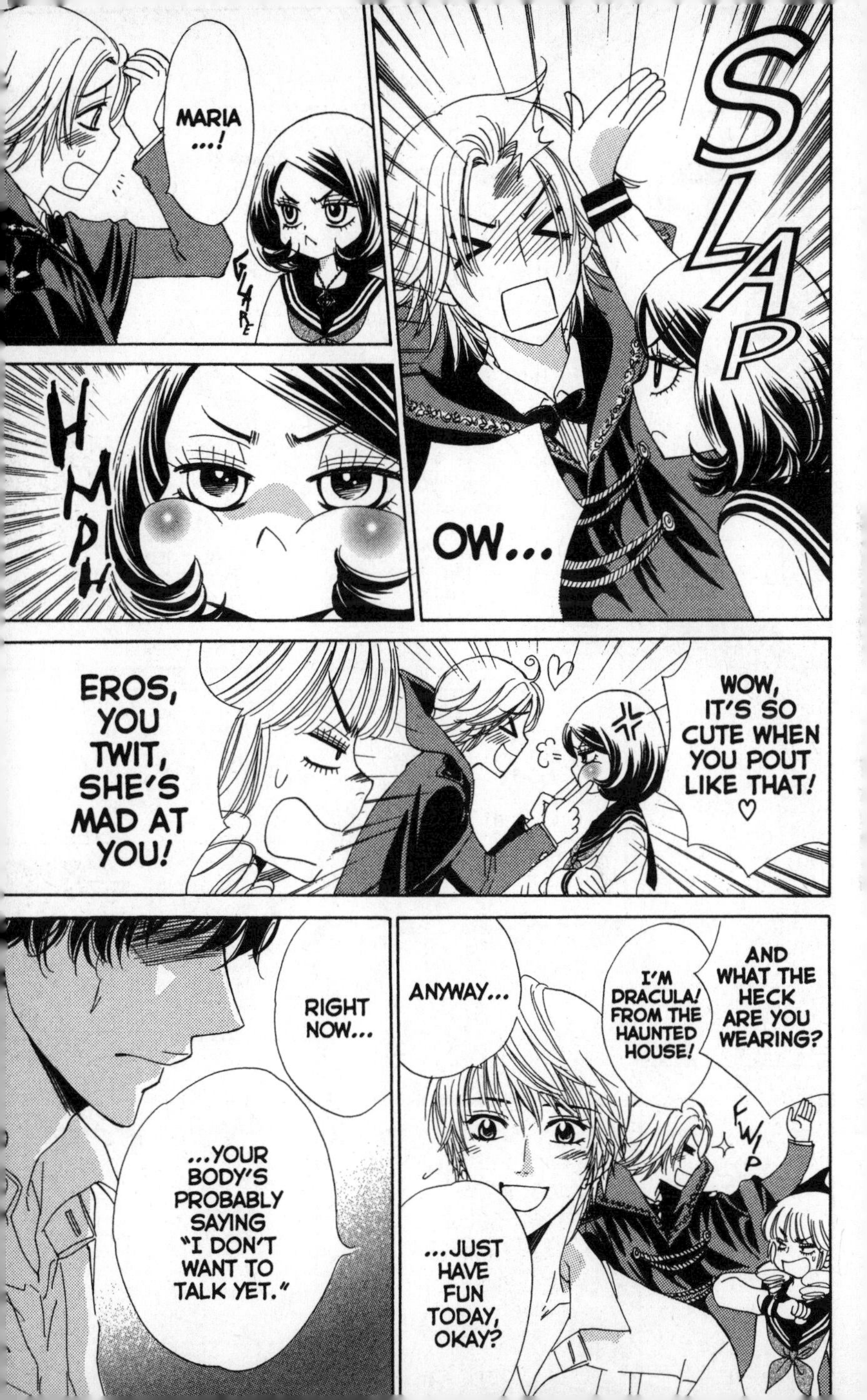
SLAP
OW...
MARIA ...!
GLARE
HMPH
WOW, IT'S SO CUTE WHEN YOU POUT LIKE THAT! ♡
EROS, YOU TWIT, SHE'S MAD AT YOU!
AND WHAT THE HECK ARE YOU WEARING?
I'M DRACULA! FROM THE HAUNTED HOUSE!
FWIP
ANYWAY...
...JUST HAVE FUN TODAY, OKAY?
RIGHT NOW...
...YOUR BODY'S PROBABLY SAYING "I DON'T WANT TO TALK YET."

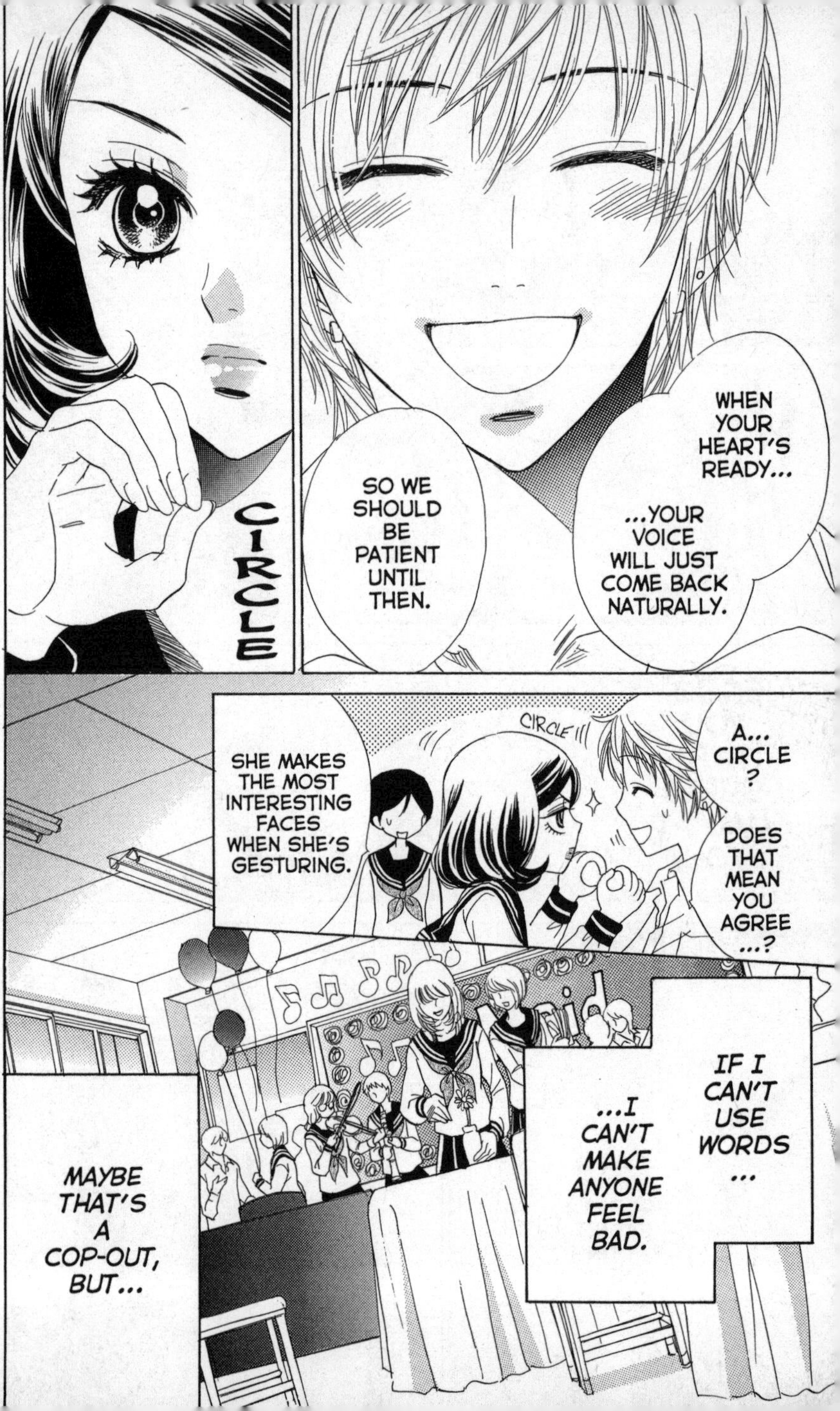
WHEN YOUR HEART'S READY...
...YOUR VOICE WILL JUST COME BACK NATURALLY.
SO WE SHOULD BE PATIENT UNTIL THEN.
CIRCLE
A... CIRCLE?
DOES THAT MEAN YOU AGREE...?
CIRCLE
SHE MAKES THE MOST INTERESTING FACES WHEN SHE'S GESTURING.
IF I CAN'T USE WORDS...
...I CAN'T MAKE ANYONE FEEL BAD.
MAYBE THAT'S A COP-OUT, BUT...

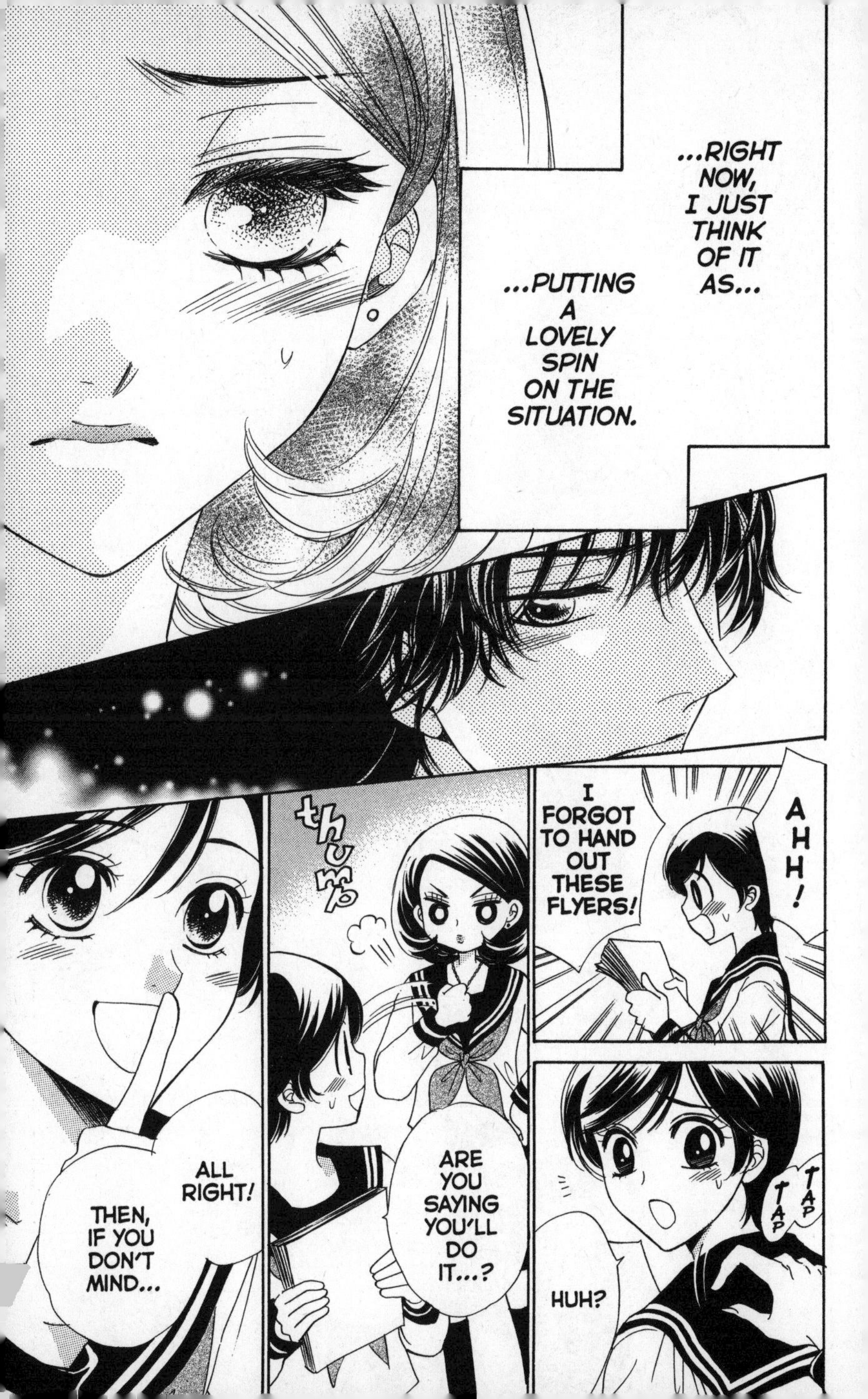
...RIGHT NOW, I JUST THINK OF IT AS...
...PUTTING A LOVELY SPIN ON THE SITUATION.
AHH!
I FORGOT TO HAND OUT THESE FLYERS!
TAP TAP
HUH?
thump
ARE YOU SAYING YOU'LL DO IT...?
ALL RIGHT!
THEN, IF YOU DON'T MIND...

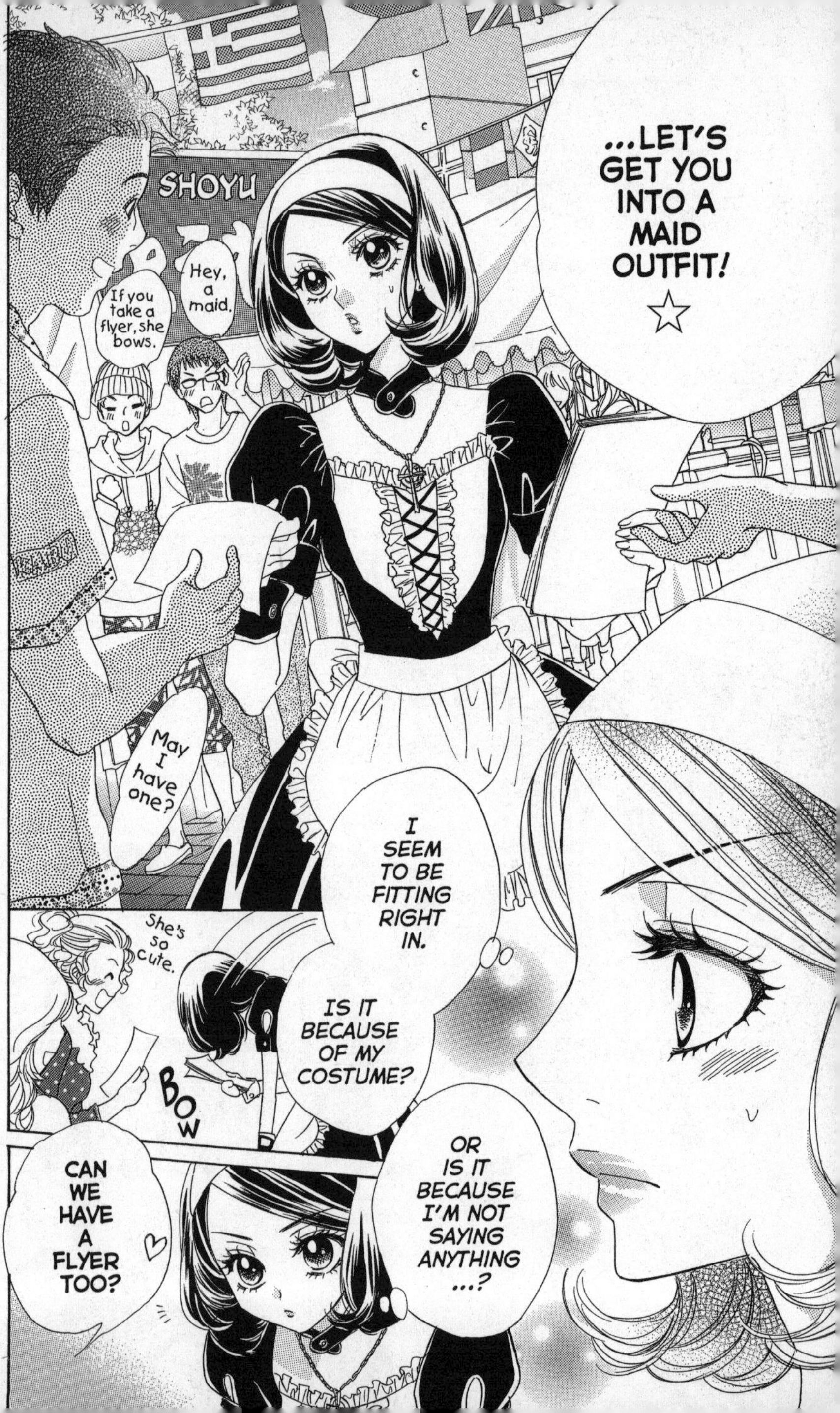
...LET'S GET YOU INTO A MAID OUTFIT! ☆
SHOYU
Hey, a maid.
If you take a flyer, she bows.
May I have one?
I SEEM TO BE FITTING RIGHT IN.
IS IT BECAUSE OF MY COSTUME?
OR IS IT BECAUSE I'M NOT SAYING ANYTHING ...?
She's so cute.
BOW
CAN WE HAVE A FLYER TOO? ♡

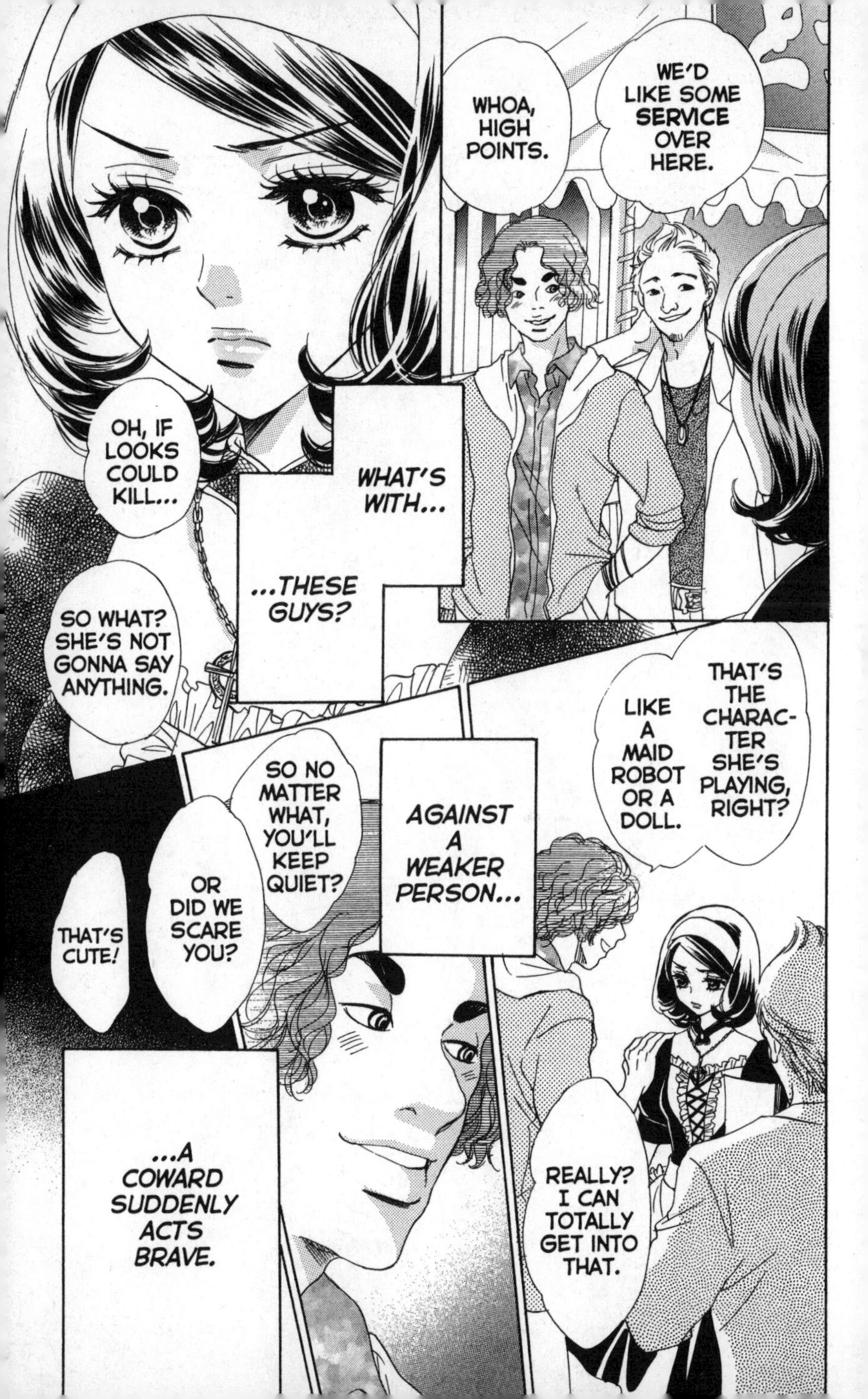
WE'D LIKE SOME SERVICE OVER HERE.
WHOA, HIGH POINTS.
WHAT'S WITH...
...THESE GUYS?
OH, IF LOOKS COULD KILL...
SO WHAT? SHE'S NOT GONNA SAY ANYTHING.
THAT'S THE CHARAC-TER SHE'S PLAYING, RIGHT?
LIKE A MAID ROBOT OR A DOLL.
REALLY? I CAN TOTALLY GET INTO THAT.
AGAINST A WEAKER PERSON...
SO NO MATTER WHAT, YOU'LL KEEP QUIET?
OR DID WE SCARE YOU?
THAT'S CUTE!
...A COWARD SUDDENLY ACTS BRAVE.

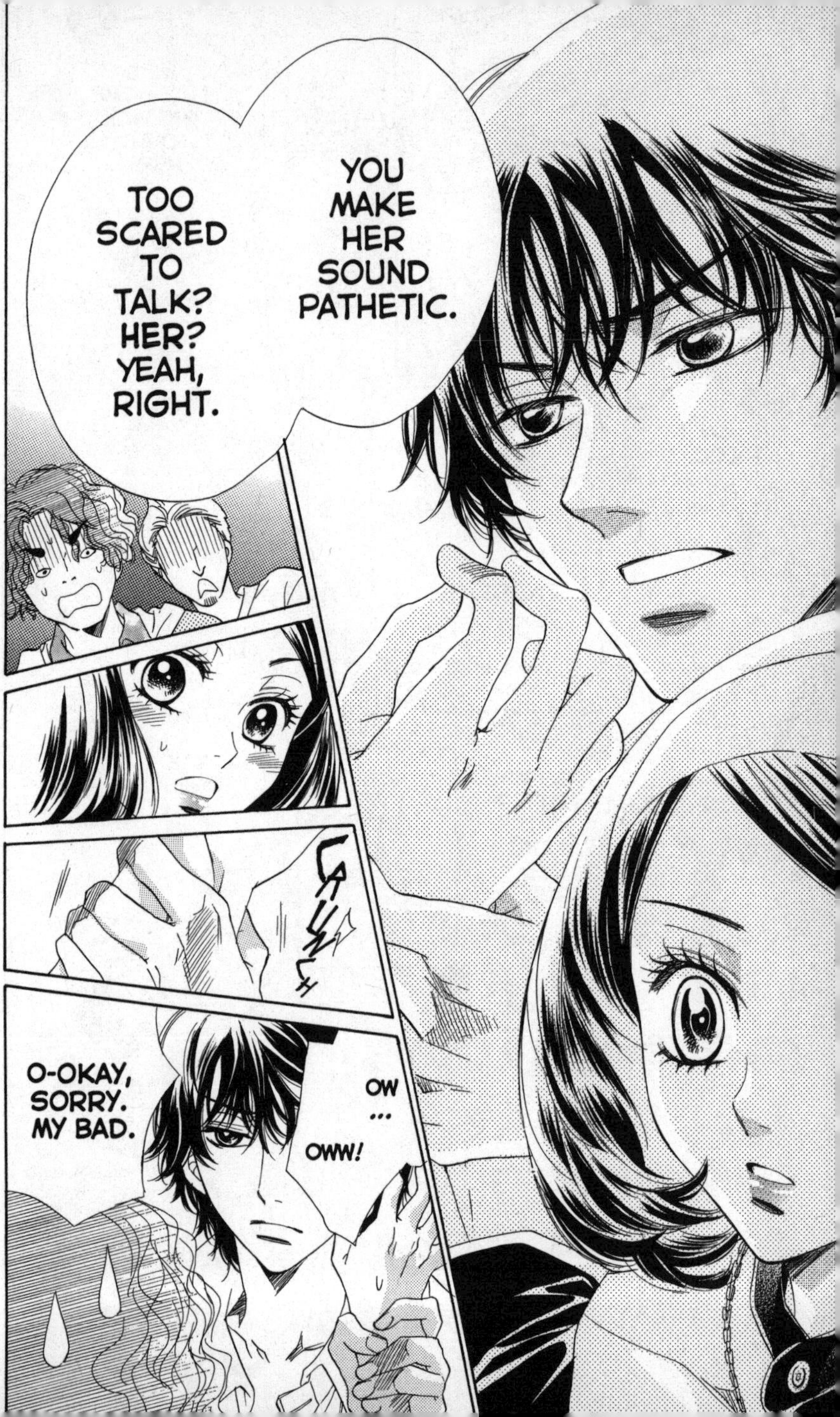
YOU MAKE HER SOUND PATHETIC.
TOO SCARED TO TALK? HER? YEAH, RIGHT.
CRUNCH
OW ... OWW!
O-OKAY, SORRY. MY BAD.

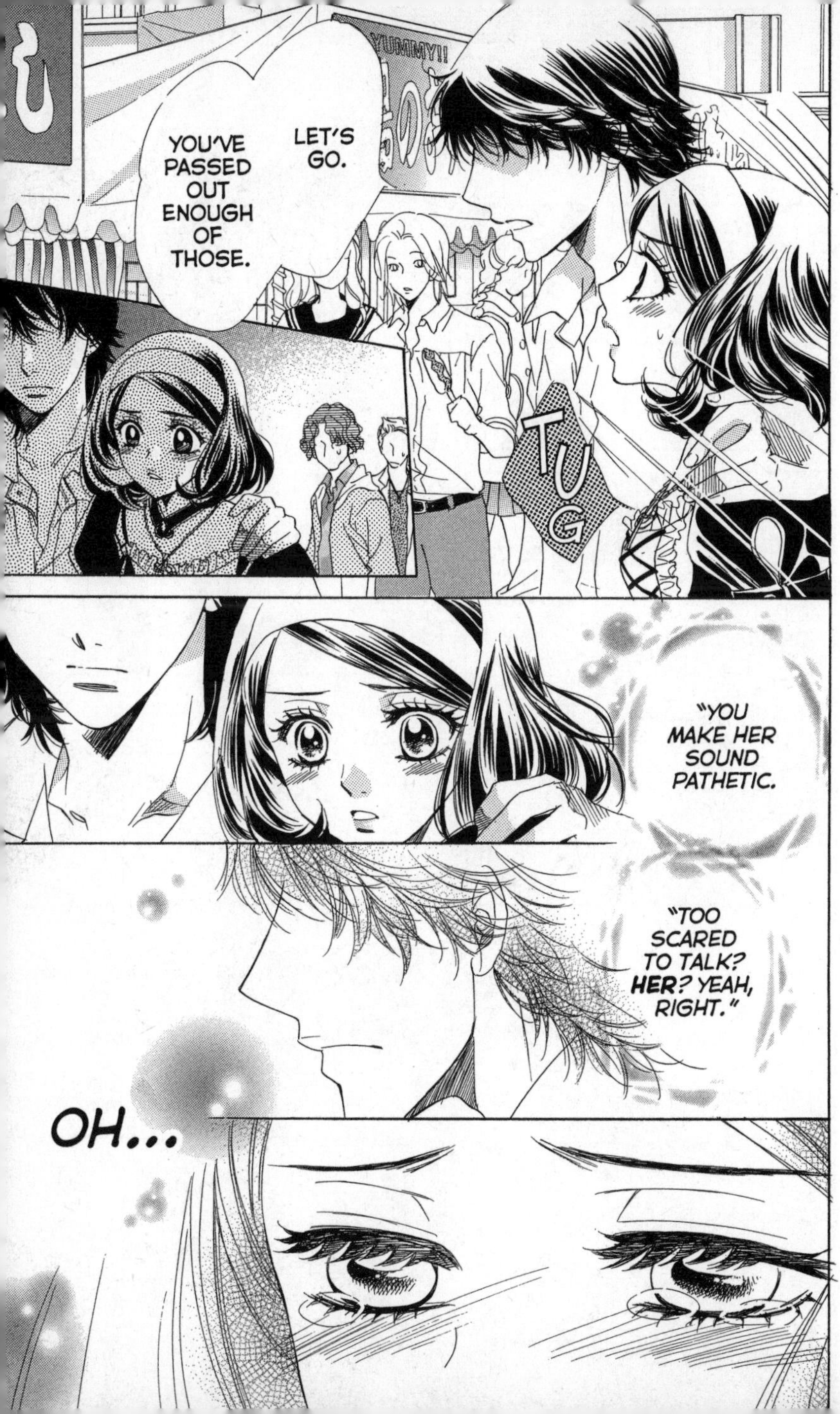
YUMMY!!
LET'S GO.
YOU'VE PASSED OUT ENOUGH OF THOSE.
TUG
"YOU MAKE HER SOUND PATHETIC.
"TOO SCARED TO TALK? HER? YEAH, RIGHT."
OH...

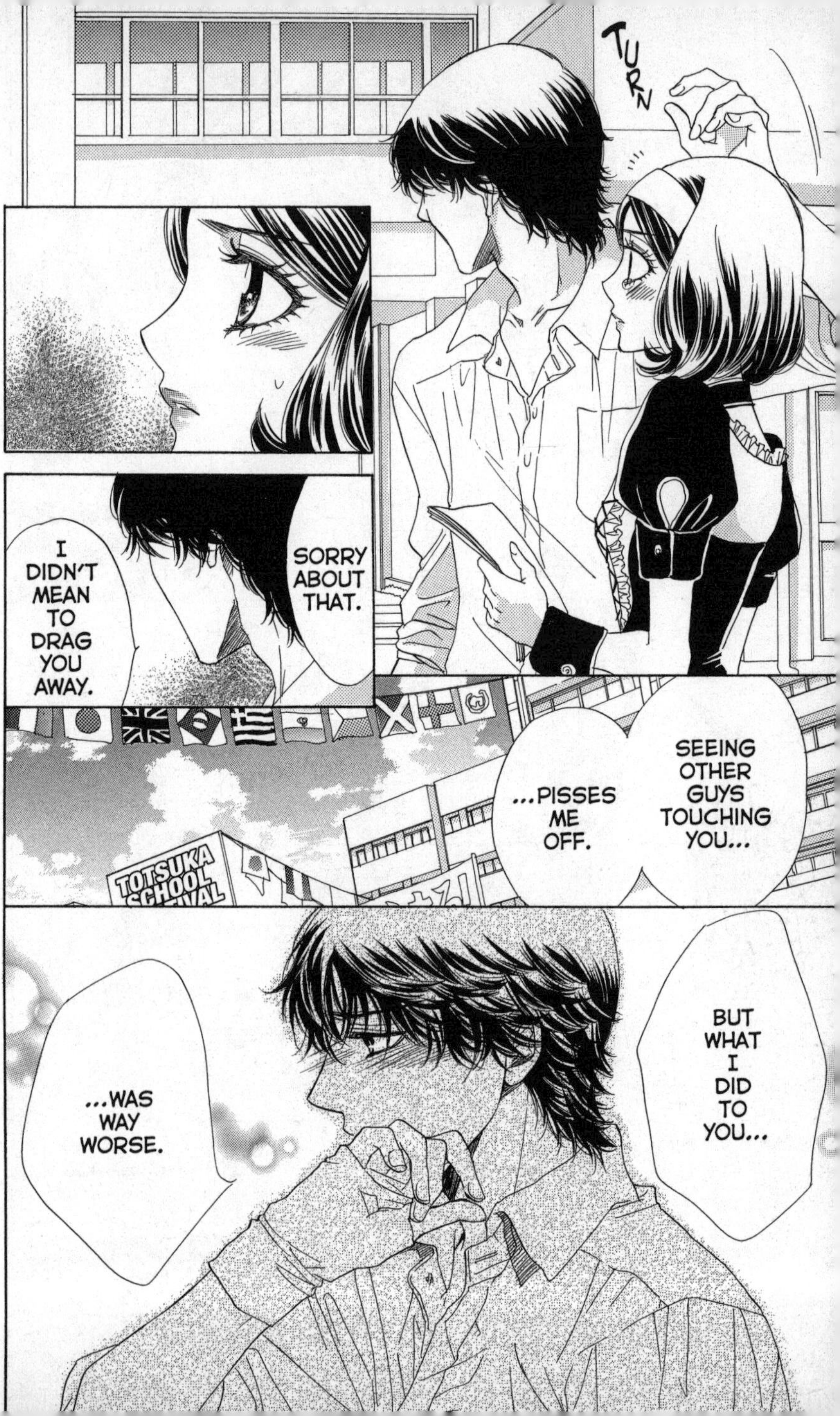
TURN
SORRY ABOUT THAT.
I DIDN'T MEAN TO DRAG YOU AWAY.
SEEING OTHER GUYS TOUCHING YOU...
...PISSES ME OFF.
TOTSUKA SCHOOL
BUT WHAT I DID TO YOU...
...WAS WAY WORSE.

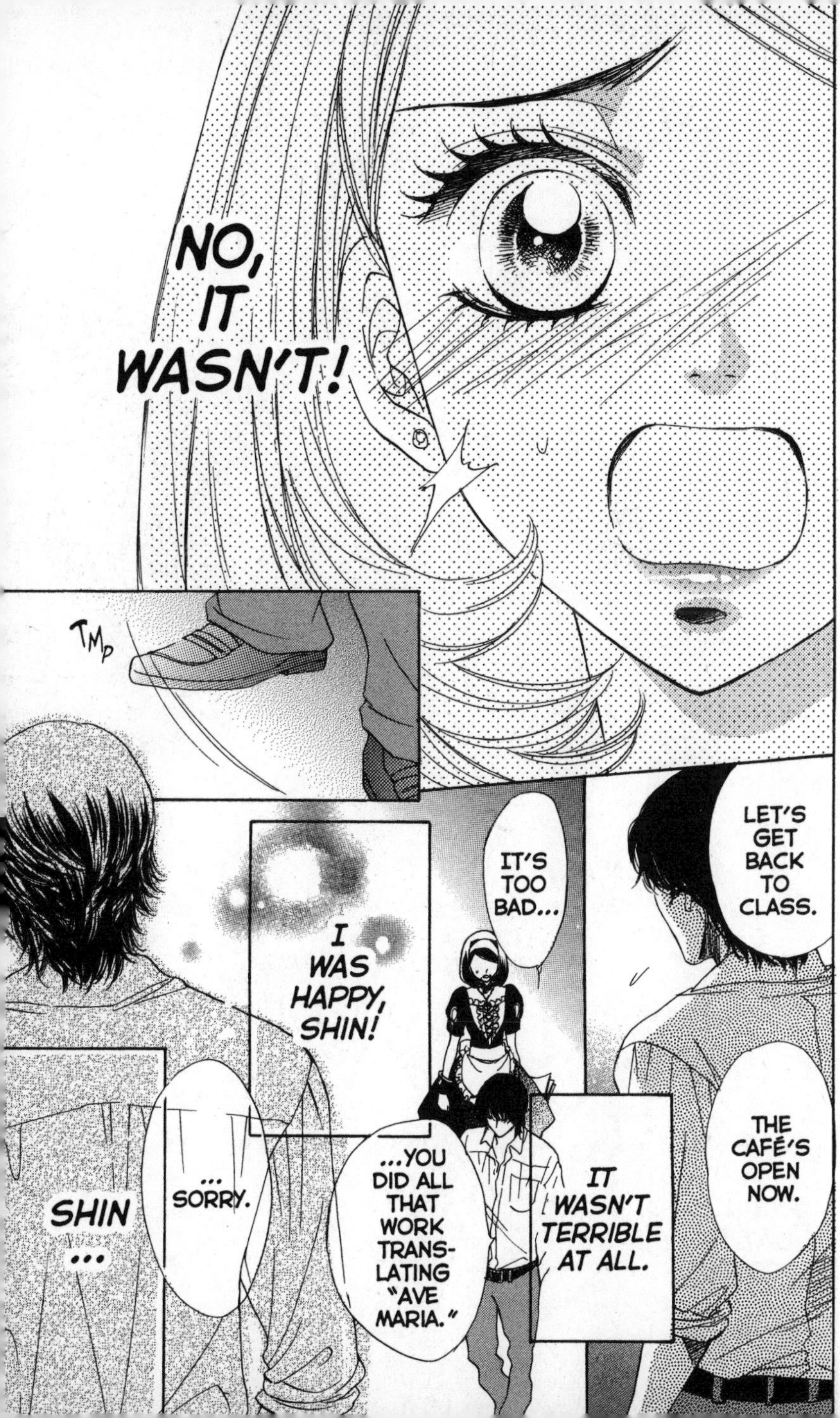
NO, IT WASN'T!
TMP
LET'S GET BACK TO CLASS.
THE CAFÉ'S OPEN NOW.
IT WASN'T TERRIBLE AT ALL.
IT'S TOO BAD...
...YOU DID ALL THAT WORK TRANS-LATING "AVE MARIA."
I WAS HAPPY, SHIN!
... SORRY.
SHIN ...

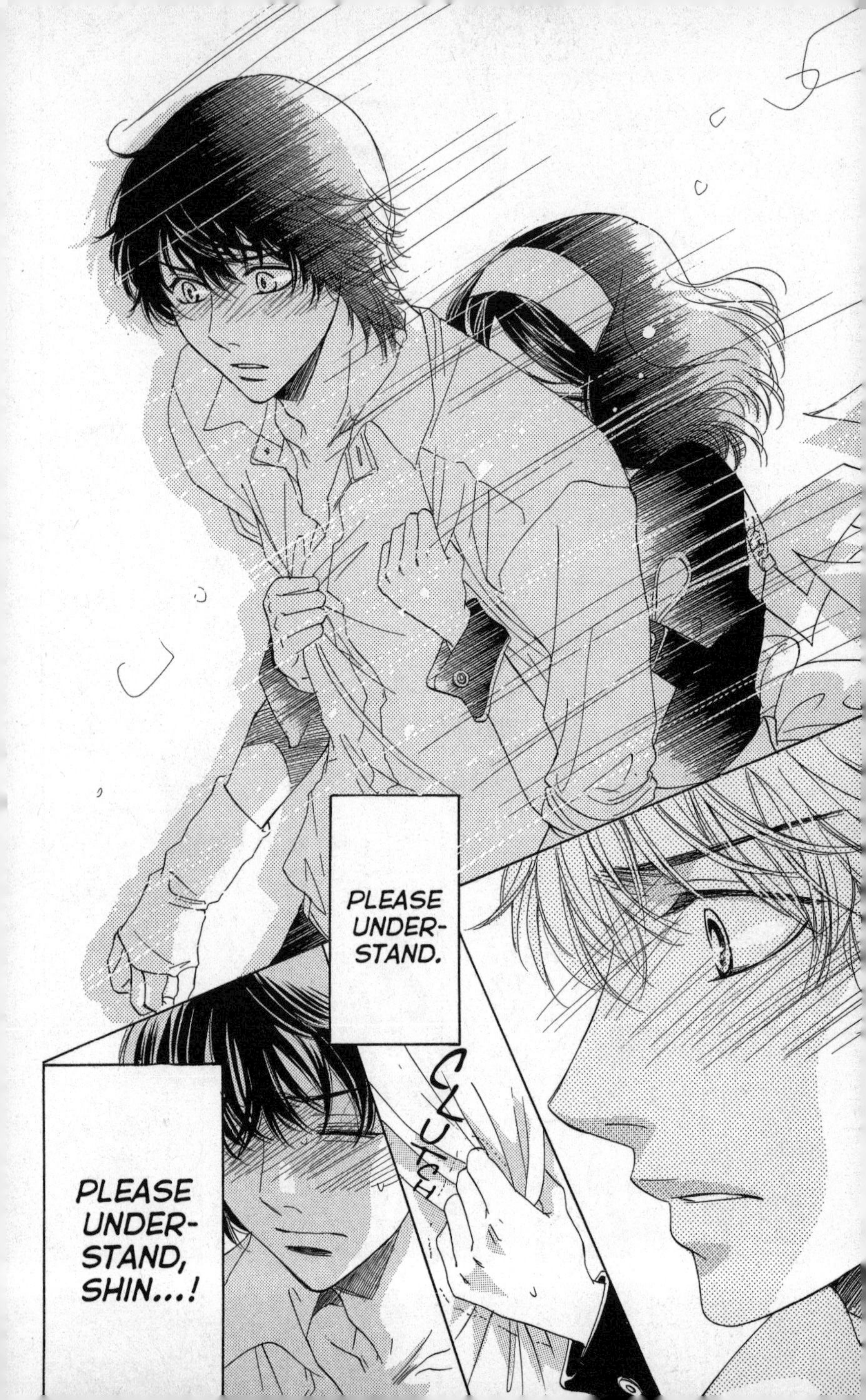
PLEASE UNDER-STAND.
CLUTCH
PLEASE UNDER-STAND, SHIN...!

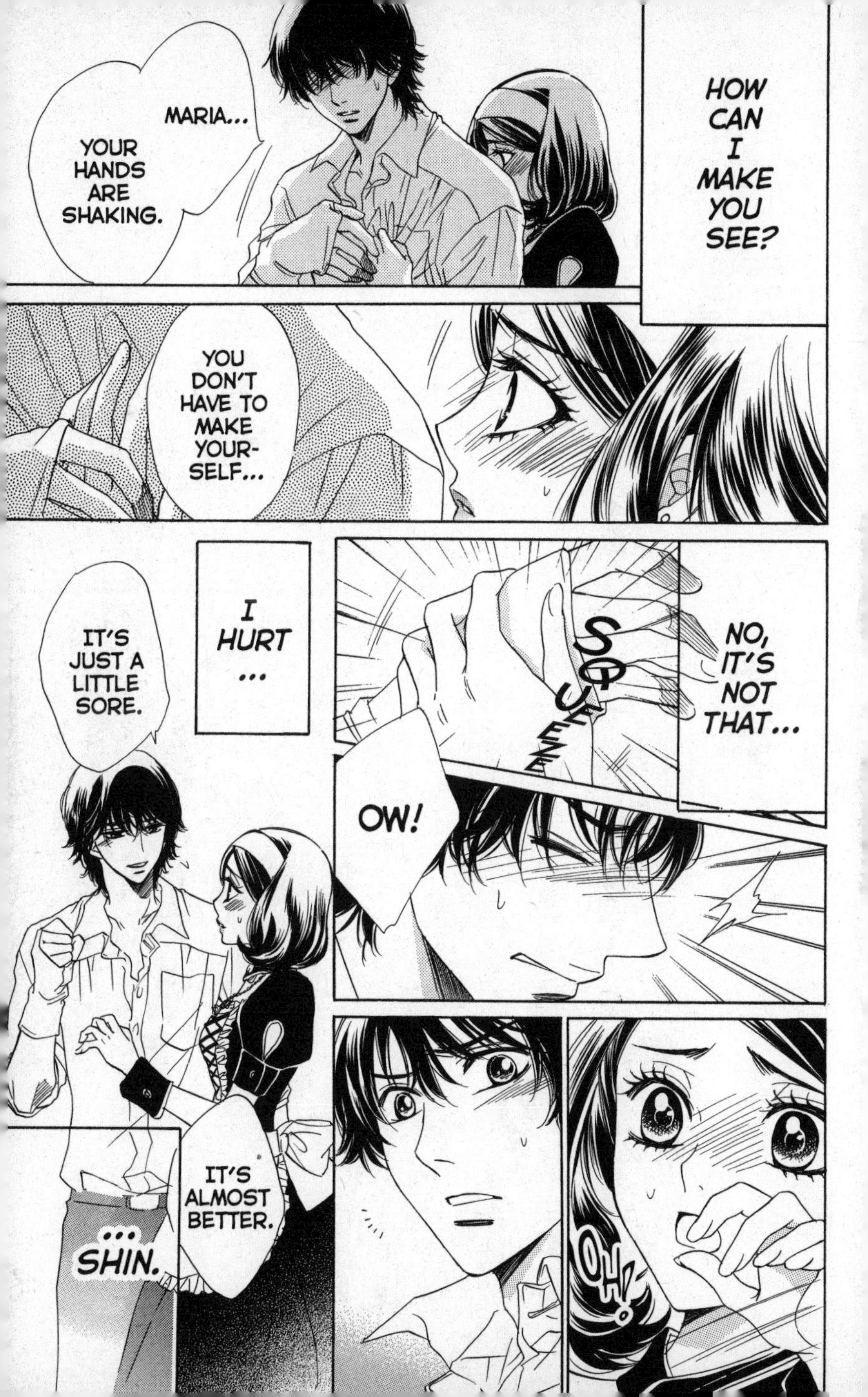
HOW CAN I MAKE YOU SEE?
MARIA...
YOUR HANDS ARE SHAKING.
YOU DON'T HAVE TO MAKE YOURSELF...
NO, IT'S NOT THAT...
SQUEEZE
OW!
I HURT...
IT'S JUST A LITTLE SORE.
OH!
IT'S ALMOST BETTER.
...SHIN.

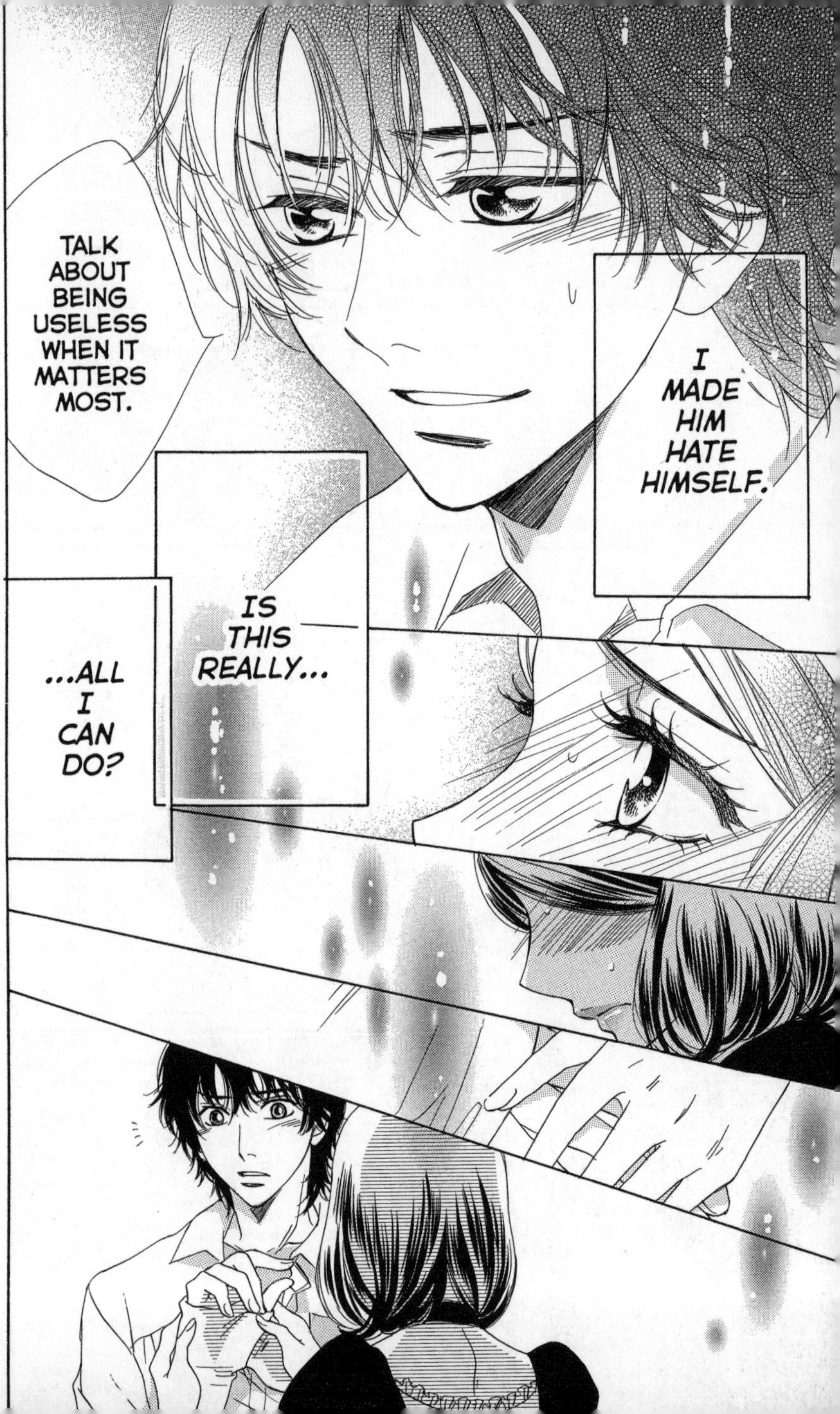
I MADE HIM HATE HIMSELF.
TALK ABOUT BEING USELESS WHEN IT MATTERS MOST.
IS THIS REALLY...
...ALL I CAN DO?

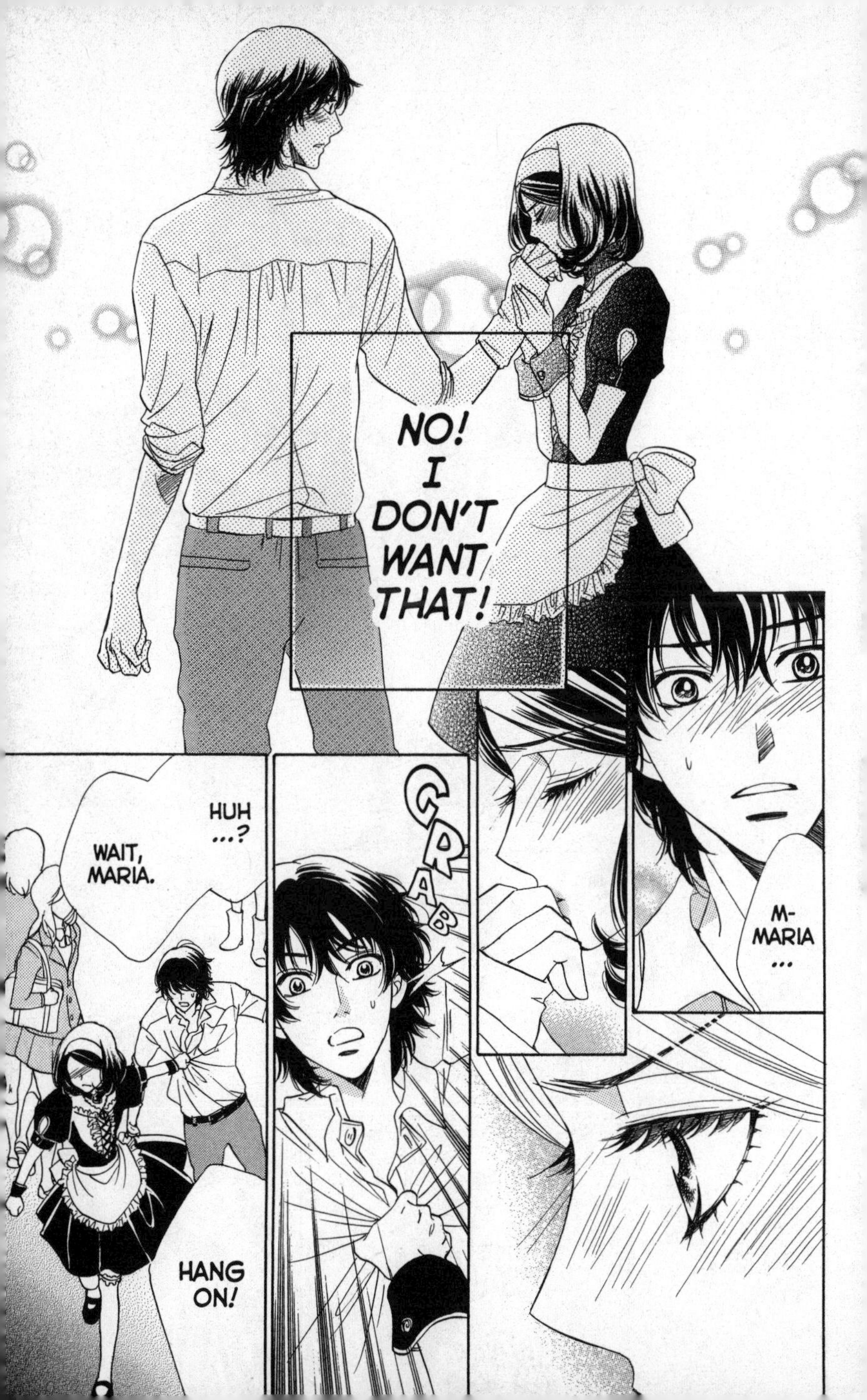
NO! I DON'T WANT THAT!
M-MARIA...
GRAB
HUH...?
WAIT, MARIA.
HANG ON!

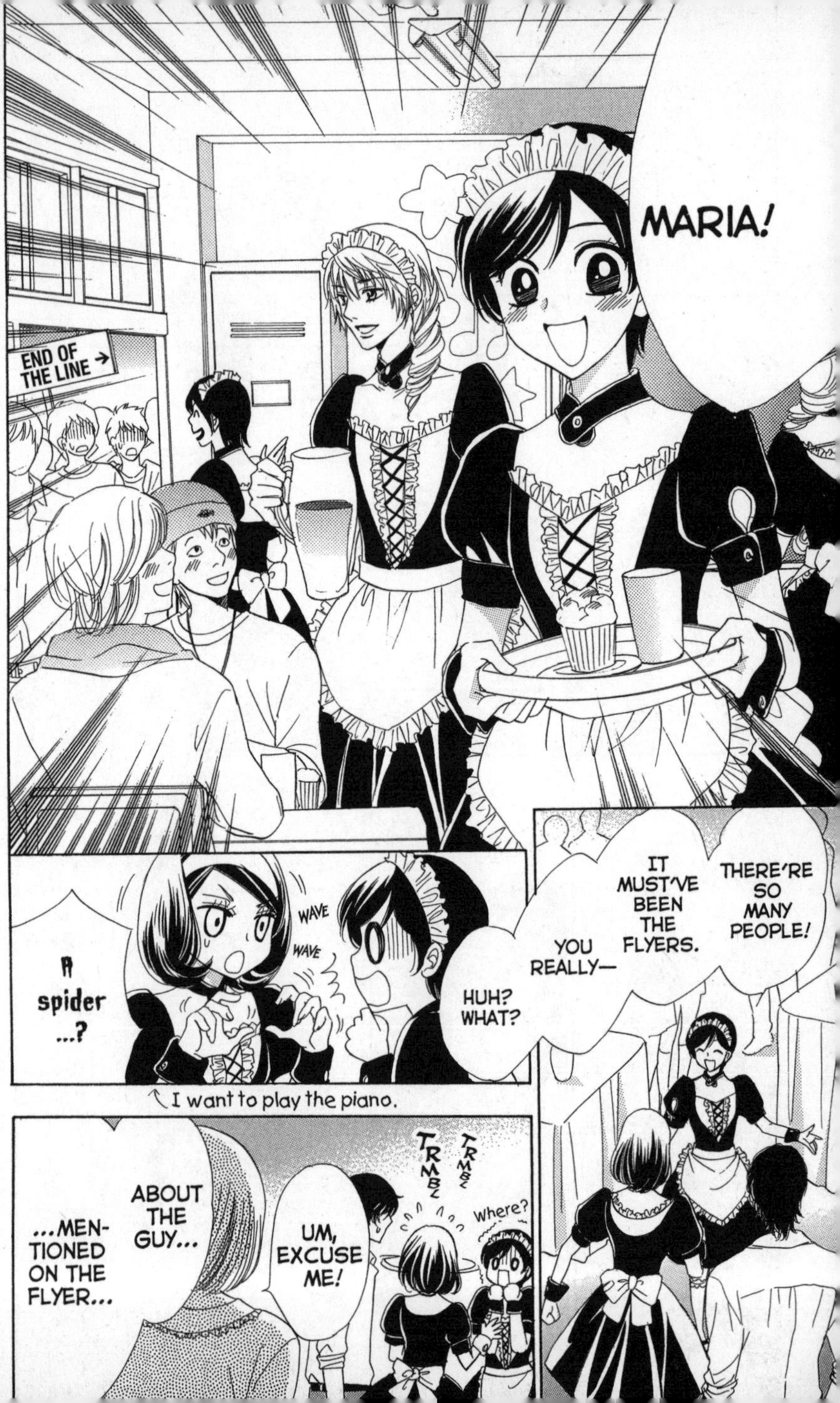
MARIA!
END OF THE LINE →
THERE'RE SO MANY PEOPLE!
IT MUST'VE BEEN THE FLYERS.
YOU REALLY—
HUH? WHAT?
WAVE
WAVE
A spider ...?
↑ I want to play the piano.
TRMBZ
TRMBZ
Where?
UM, EXCUSE ME!
ABOUT THE GUY...
...MEN-TIONED ON THE FLYER...

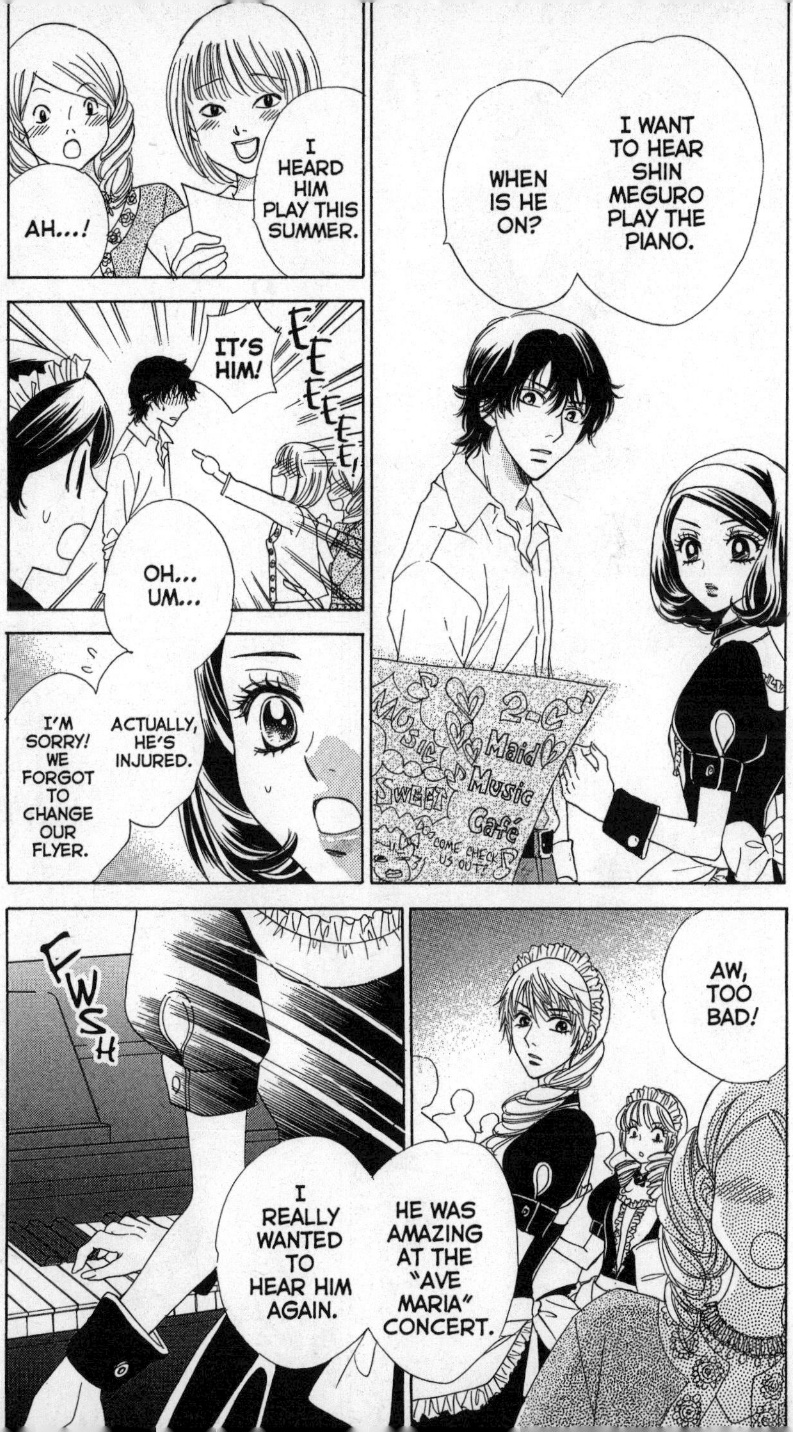
I WANT TO HEAR SHIN MEGURO PLAY THE PIANO.
WHEN IS HE ON?
2-C Maid Music Café
MUSIC
SWEET
COME CHECK US OUT!
I HEARD HIM PLAY THIS SUMMER.
AH...!
EEEEEE!
IT'S HIM!
OH... UM...
ACTUALLY, HE'S INJURED.
I'M SORRY! WE FORGOT TO CHANGE OUR FLYER.
AW, TOO BAD!
HE WAS AMAZING AT THE "AVE MARIA" CONCERT.
I REALLY WANTED TO HEAR HIM AGAIN.
FWSH

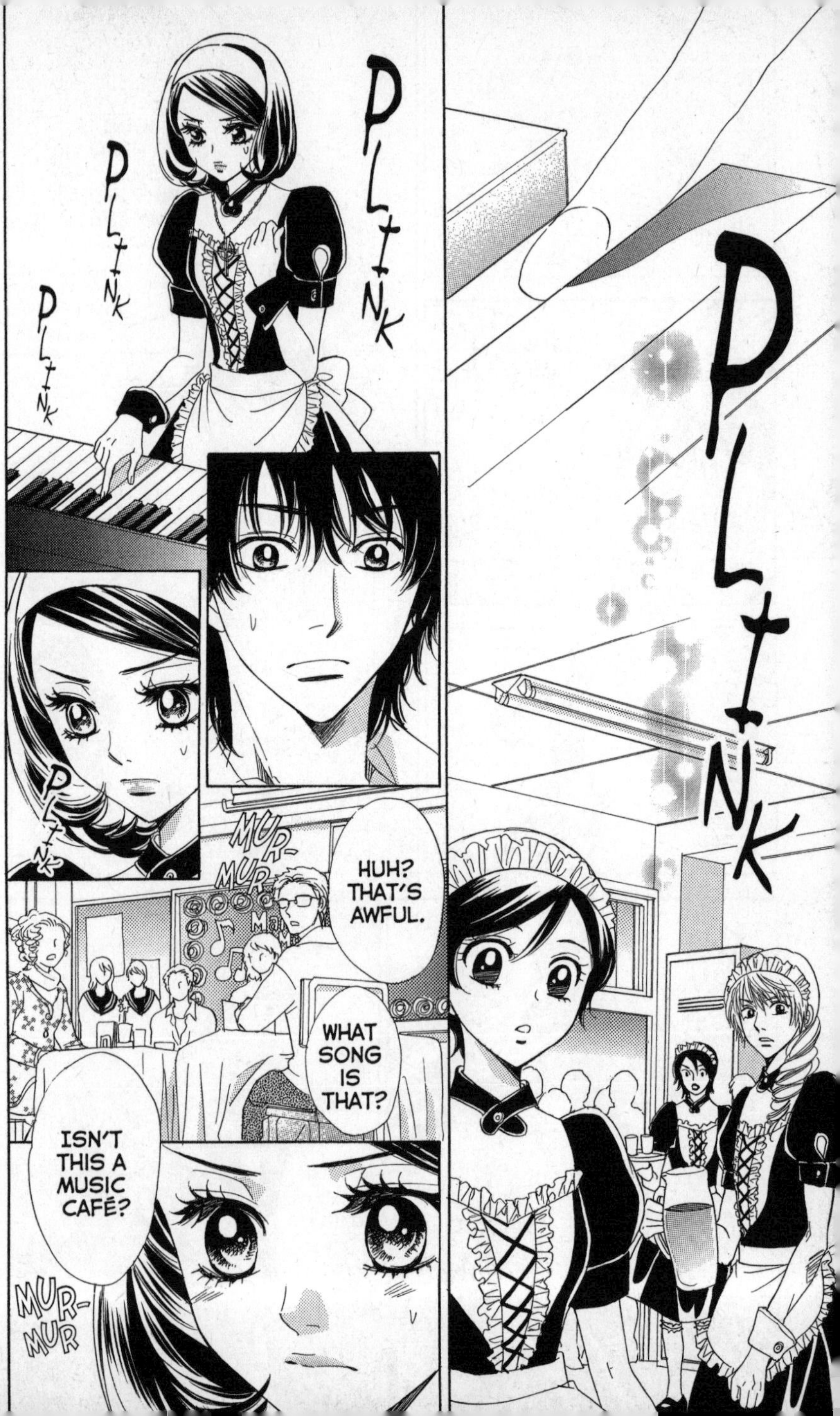
PLINK
PLINK
PLINK
PLINK
PLINK
MUR-MUR
HUH? THAT'S AWFUL.
WHAT SONG IS THAT?
ISN'T THIS A MUSIC CAFÉ?
MUR-MUR

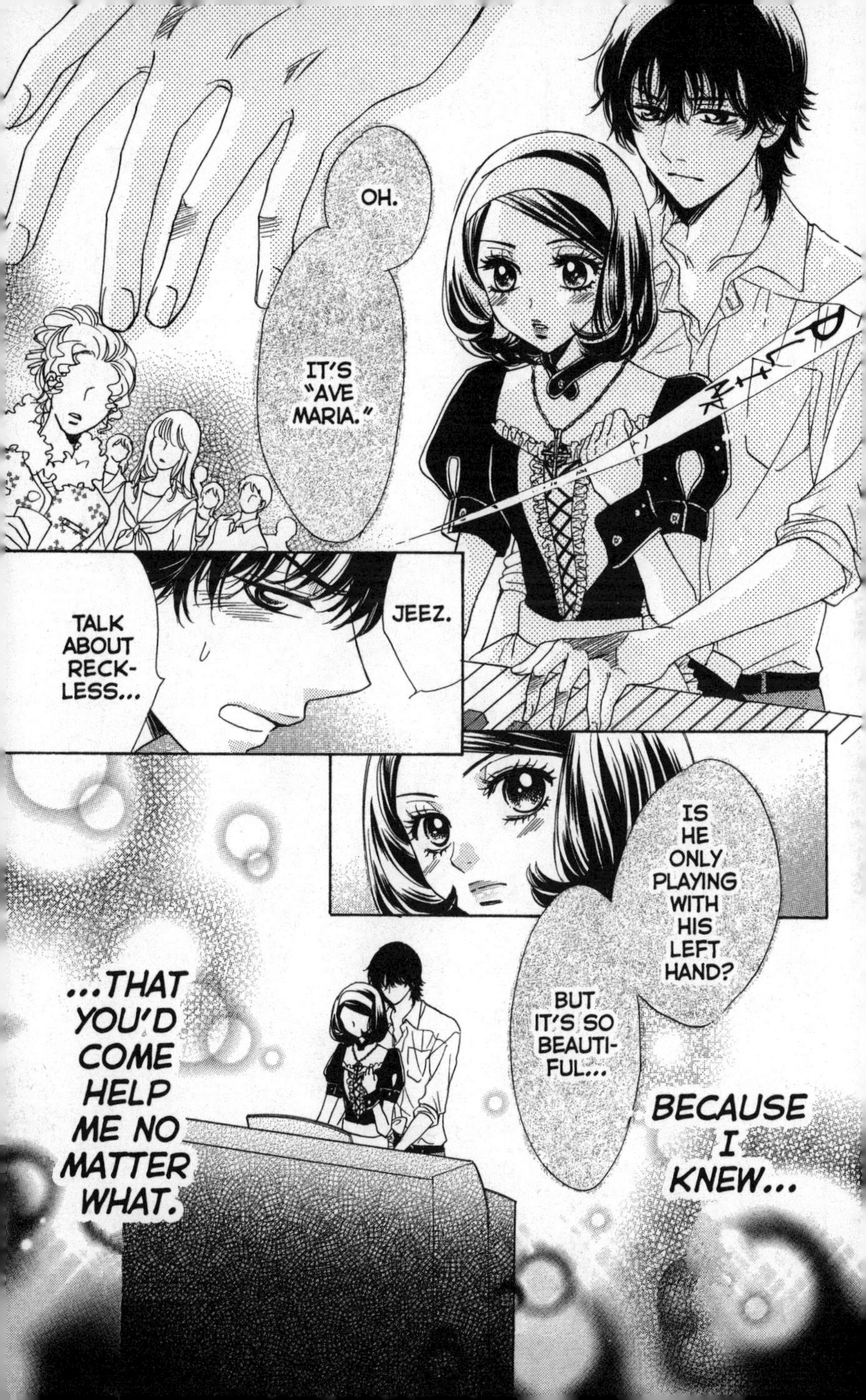
OH.
IT'S "AVE MARIA."
JEEZ.
TALK ABOUT RECK-LESS...
IS HE ONLY PLAYING WITH HIS LEFT HAND?
BUT IT'S SO BEAUTI-FUL...
BECAUSE I KNEW...
...THAT YOU'D COME HELP ME NO MATTER WHAT.

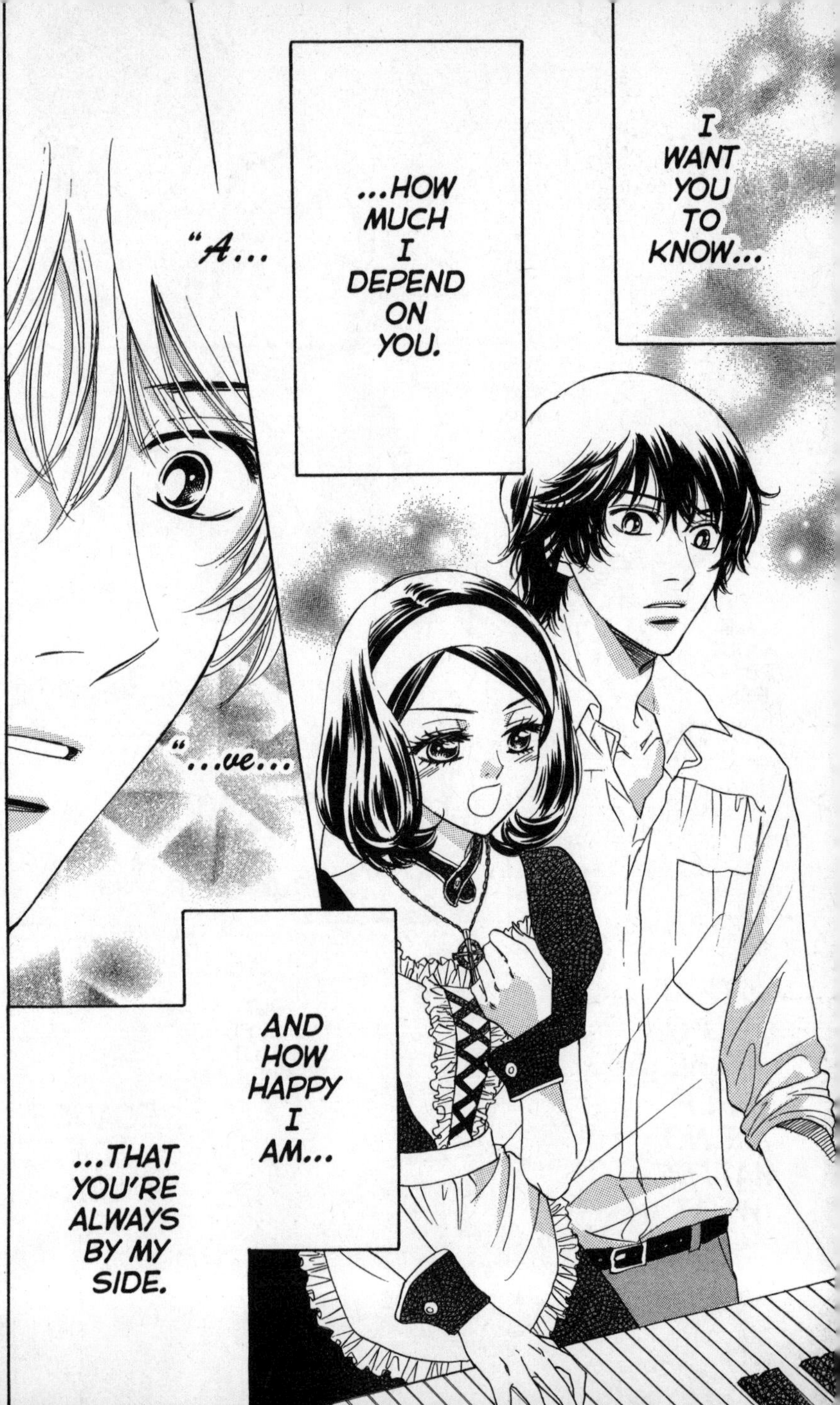
I WANT YOU TO KNOW...
...HOW MUCH I DEPEND ON YOU.
"A...
"...ve...
AND HOW HAPPY I AM...
...THAT YOU'RE ALWAYS BY MY SIDE.

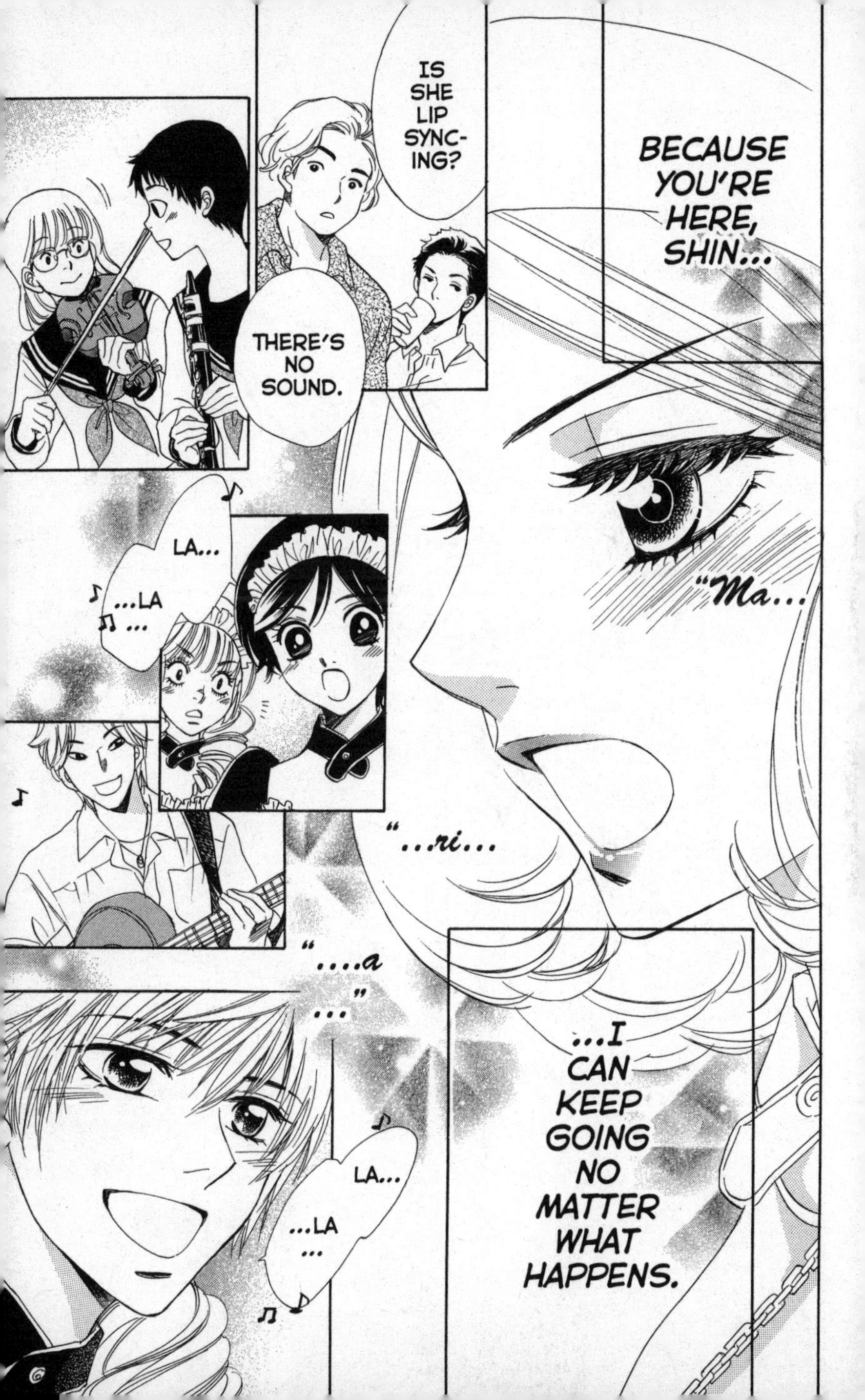
BECAUSE YOU'RE HERE, SHIN...
IS SHE LIP SYNC-ING?
THERE'S NO SOUND.
"Ma...
"...ri...
"....a
"...
LA... ...LA ...
...I CAN KEEP GOING NO MATTER WHAT HAPPENS.
LA... ...LA ...

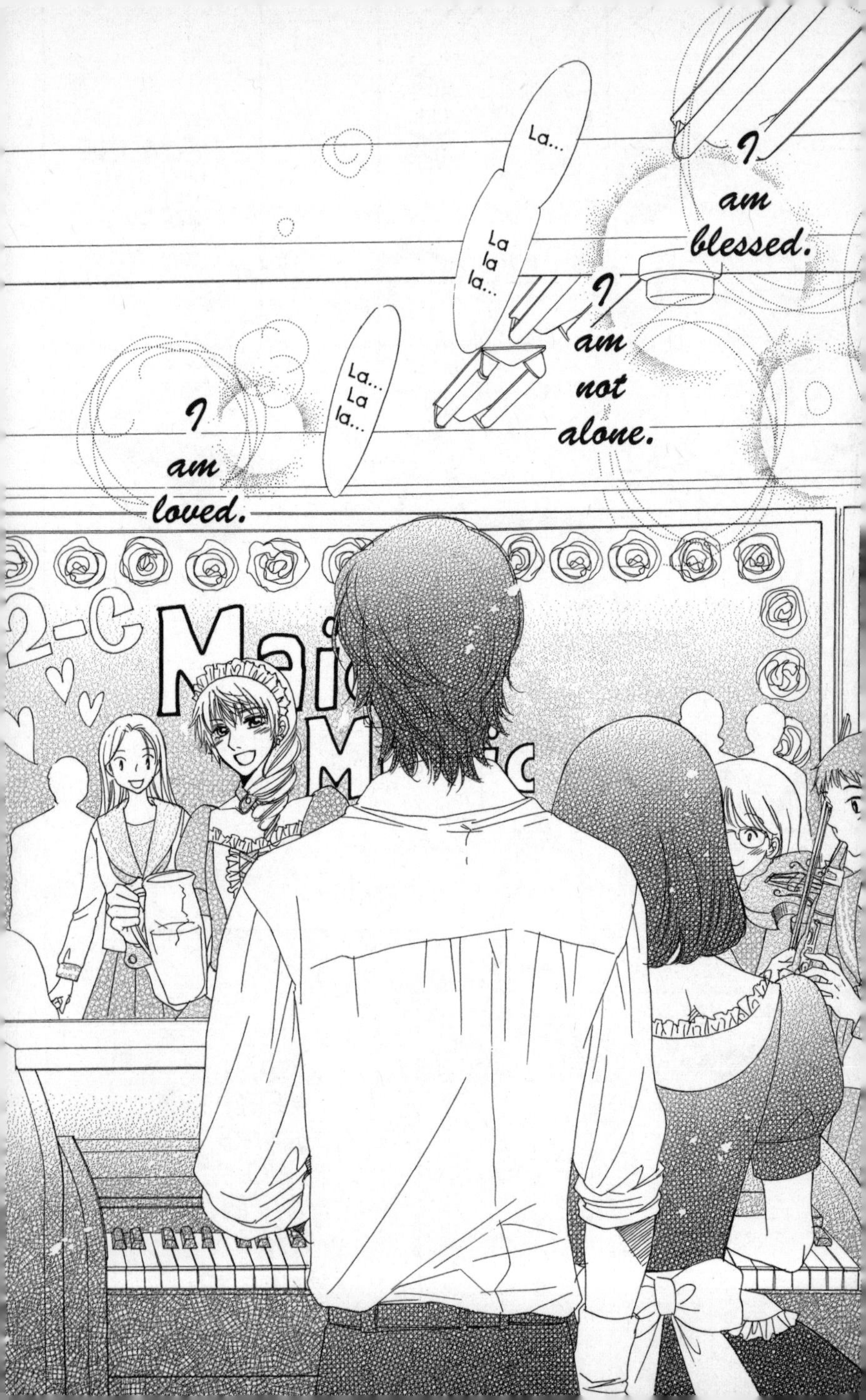
I am blessed.
La...
La la la...
I am not alone.
La... La la...
I am loved.
2-C

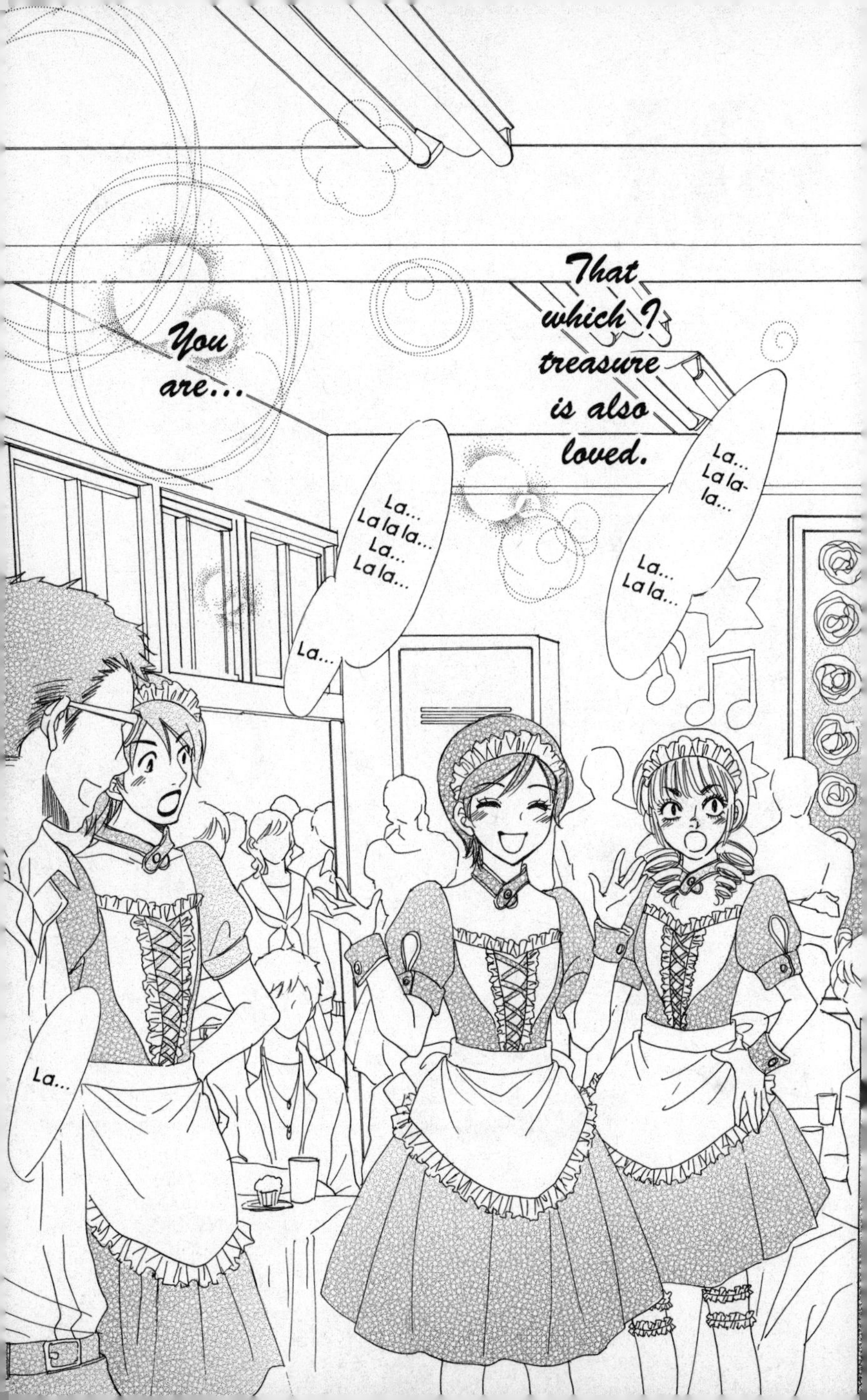
That which I treasure is also loved.
You are...
La... La la-la... La... La la...
La... La la la... La... La la... La...
La...

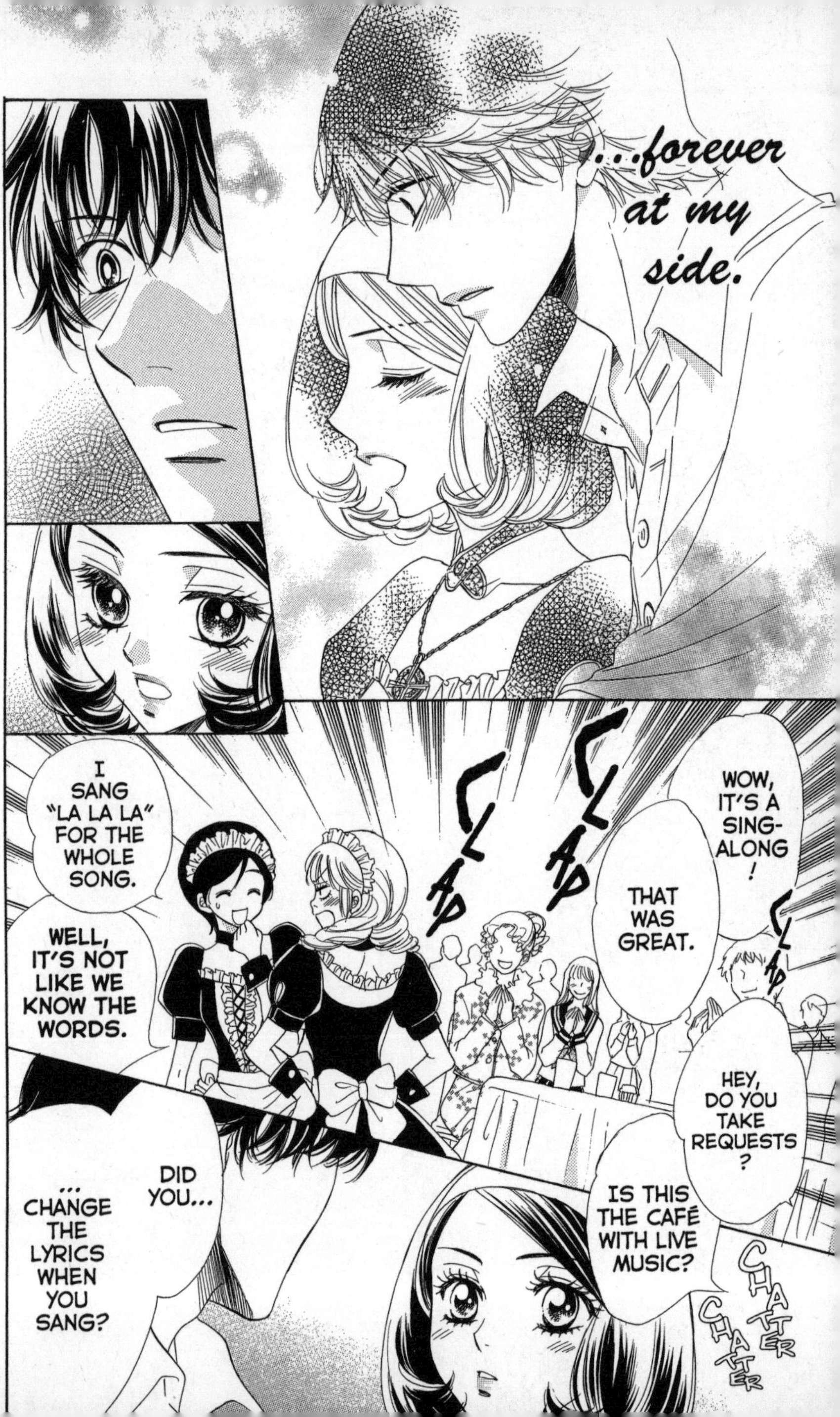
...forever at my side.
CLAP CLAP
WOW, IT'S A SING-ALONG!
THAT WAS GREAT.
CLAP
I SANG "LA LA LA" FOR THE WHOLE SONG.
WELL, IT'S NOT LIKE WE KNOW THE WORDS.
HEY, DO YOU TAKE REQUESTS?
IS THIS THE CAFÉ WITH LIVE MUSIC?
CHATTER CHATTER
DID YOU...
...CHANGE THE LYRICS WHEN YOU SANG?

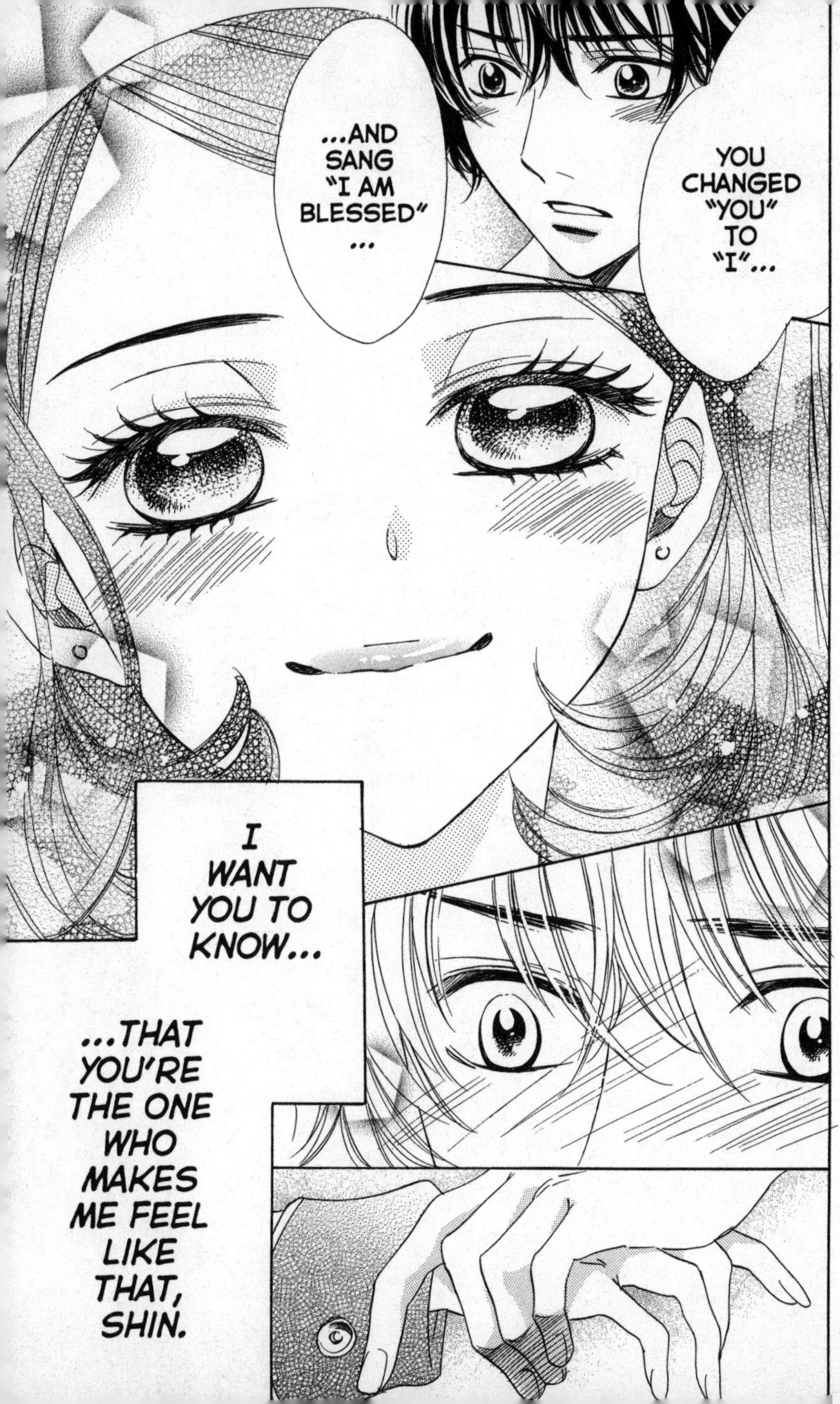
YOU CHANGED "YOU" TO "I"...
...AND SANG "I AM BLESSED"...
I WANT YOU TO KNOW...
...THAT YOU'RE THE ONE WHO MAKES ME FEEL LIKE THAT, SHIN.

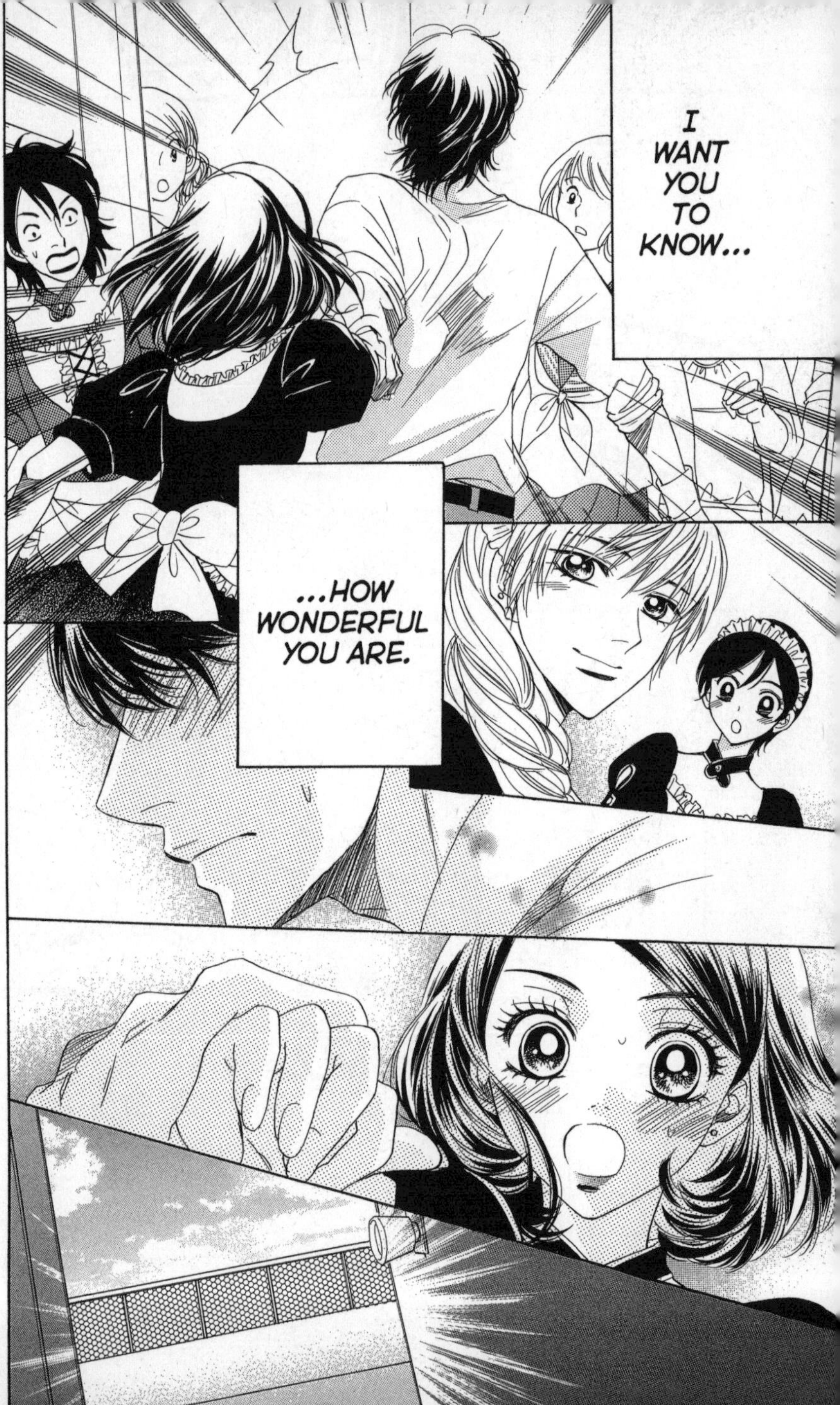
I WANT YOU TO KNOW...
...HOW WONDERFUL YOU ARE.

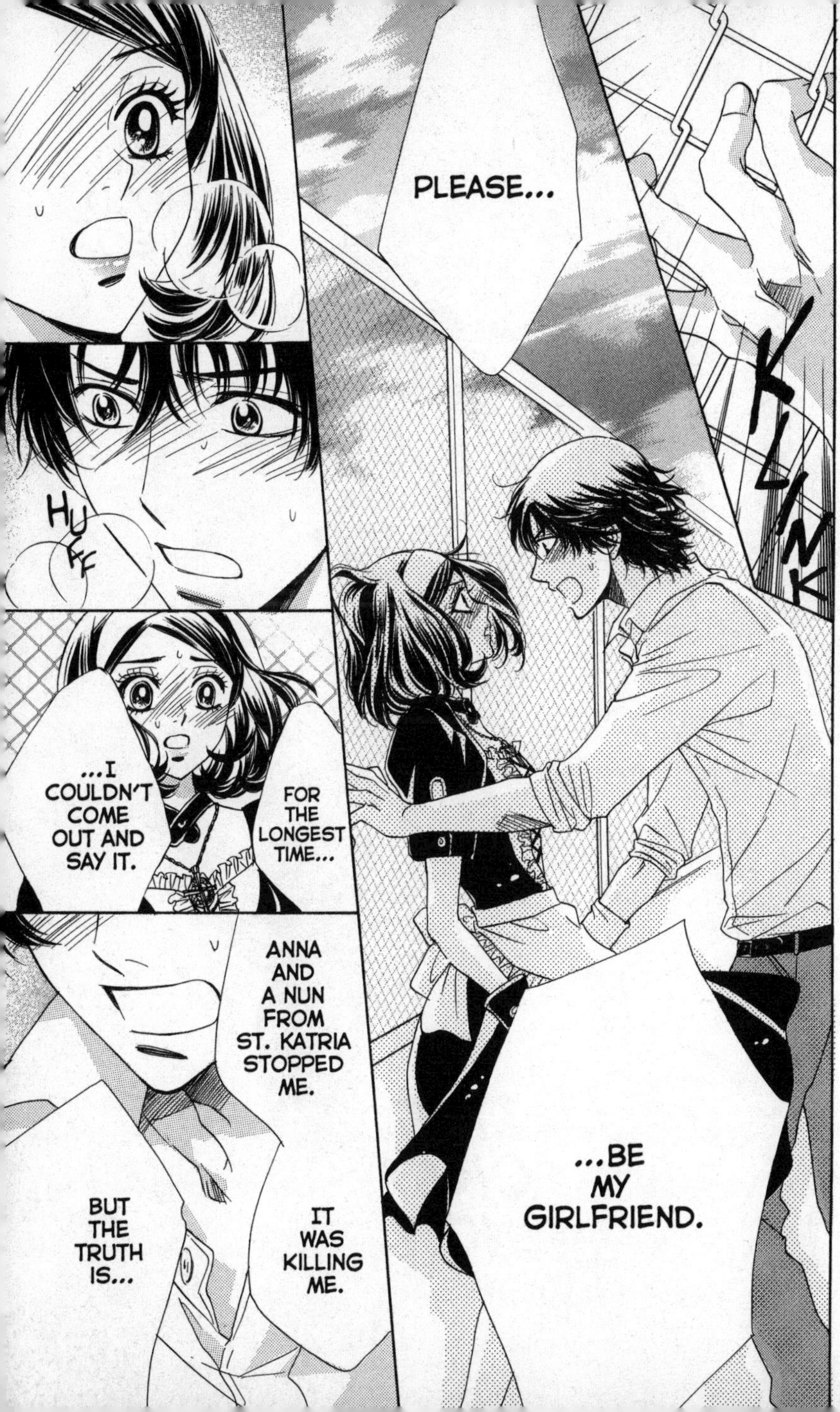
KLINK
PLEASE...
...BE MY GIRLFRIEND.
HUFF
FOR THE LONGEST TIME...
...I COULDN'T COME OUT AND SAY IT.
ANNA AND A NUN FROM ST. KATRIA STOPPED ME.
BUT THE TRUTH IS...
IT WAS KILLING ME.

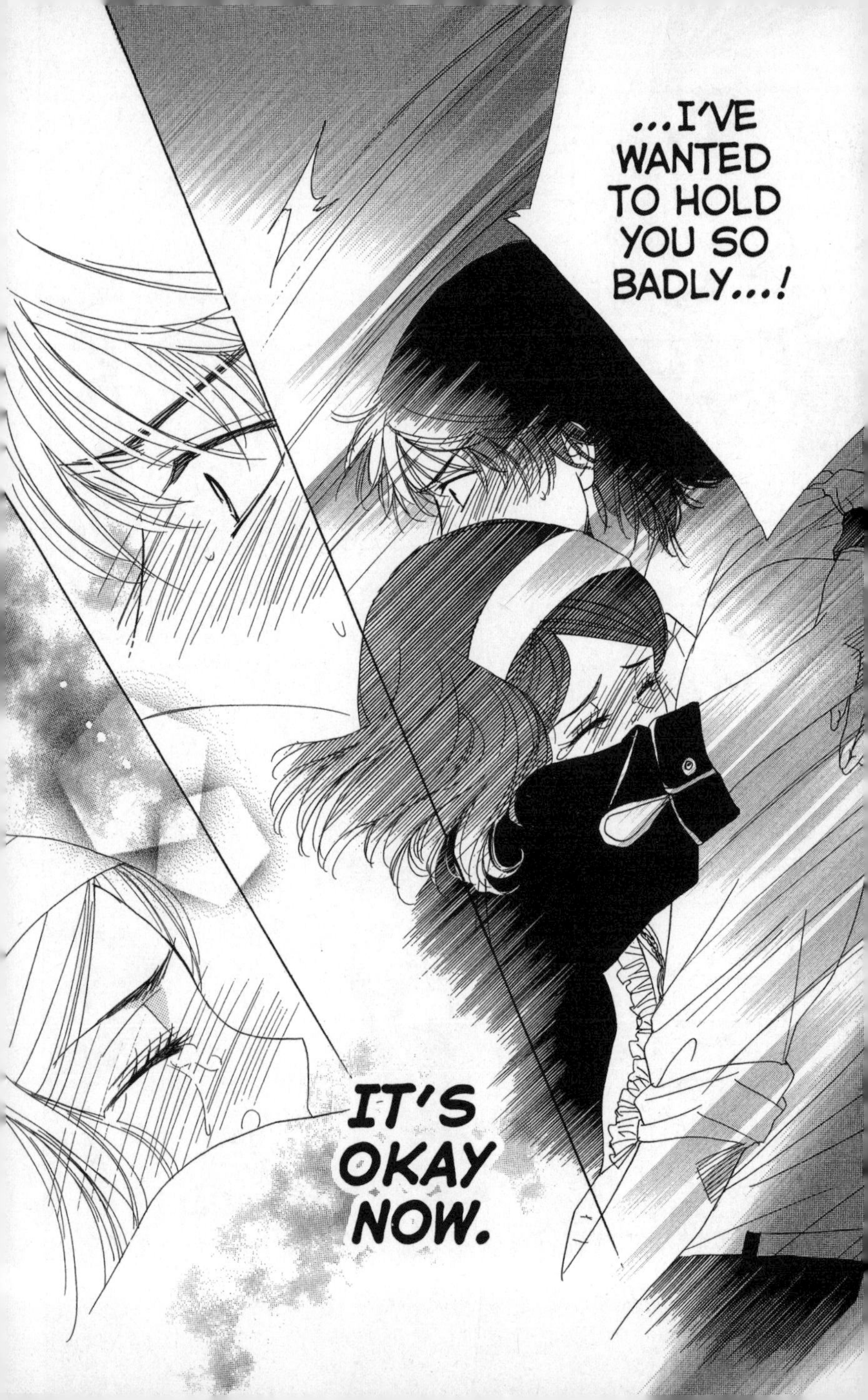
...I'VE WANTED TO HOLD YOU SO BADLY...!
IT'S OKAY NOW.

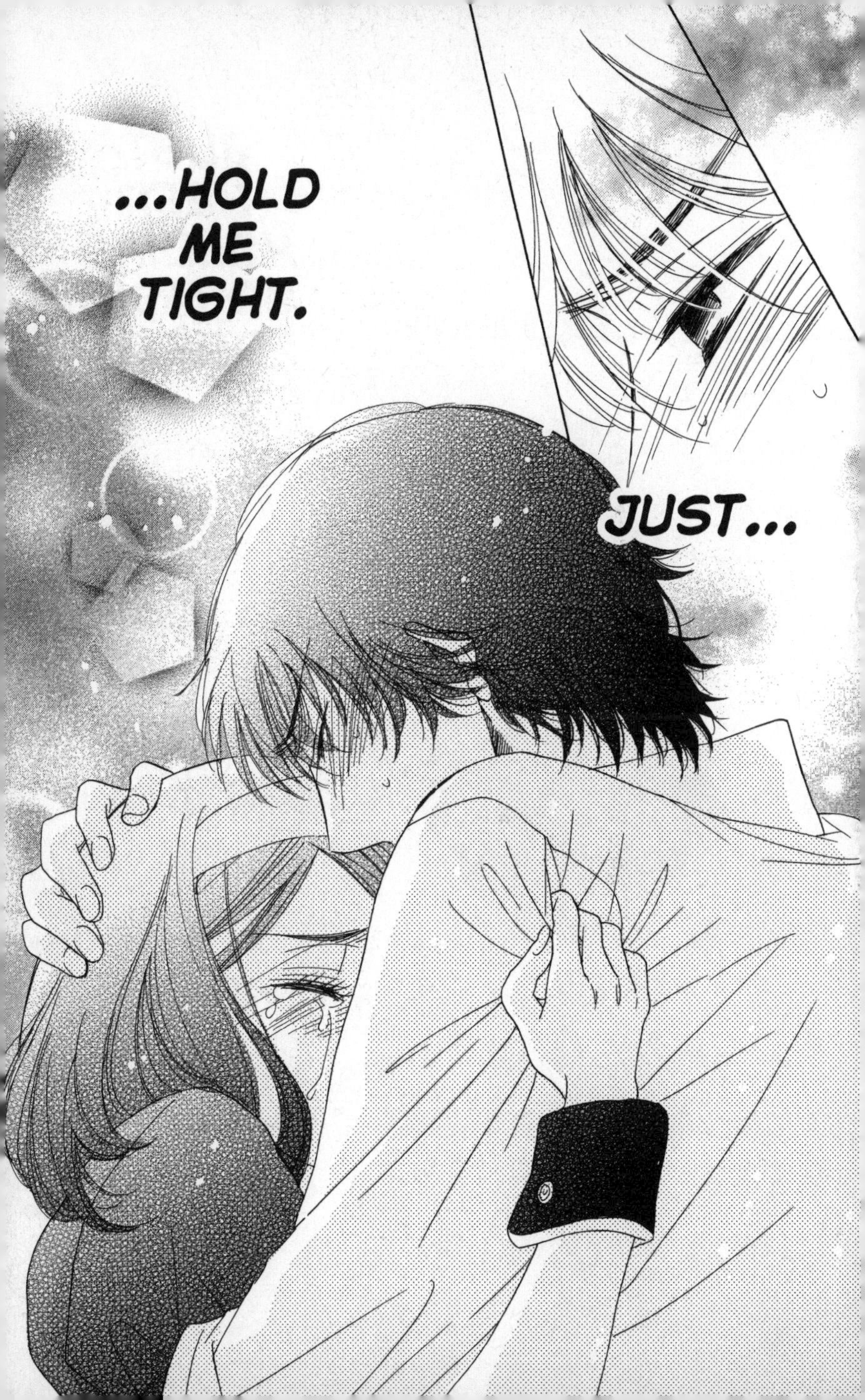
JUST...
...HOLD ME TIGHT.

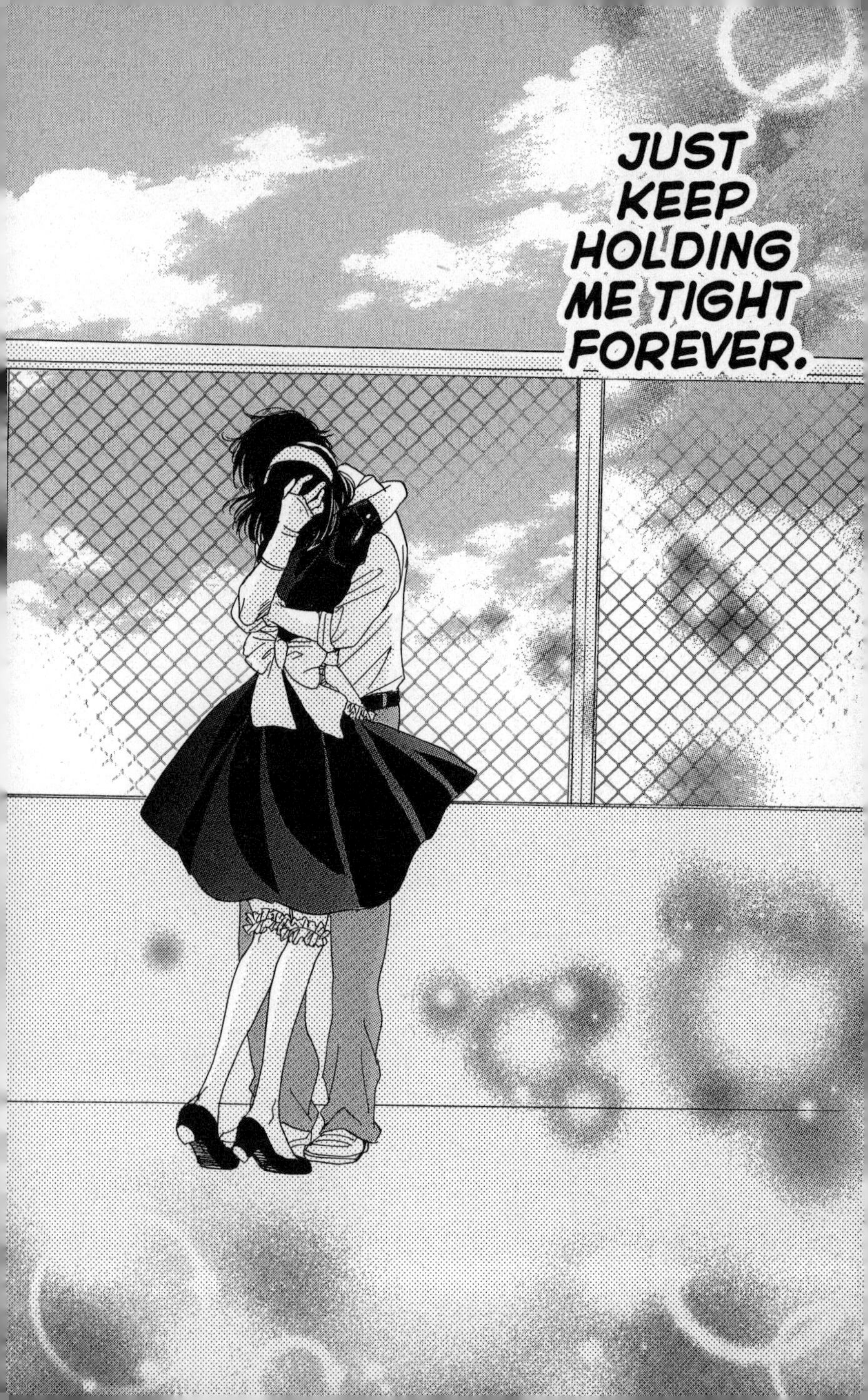
JUST KEEP HOLDING ME TIGHT FOREVER.

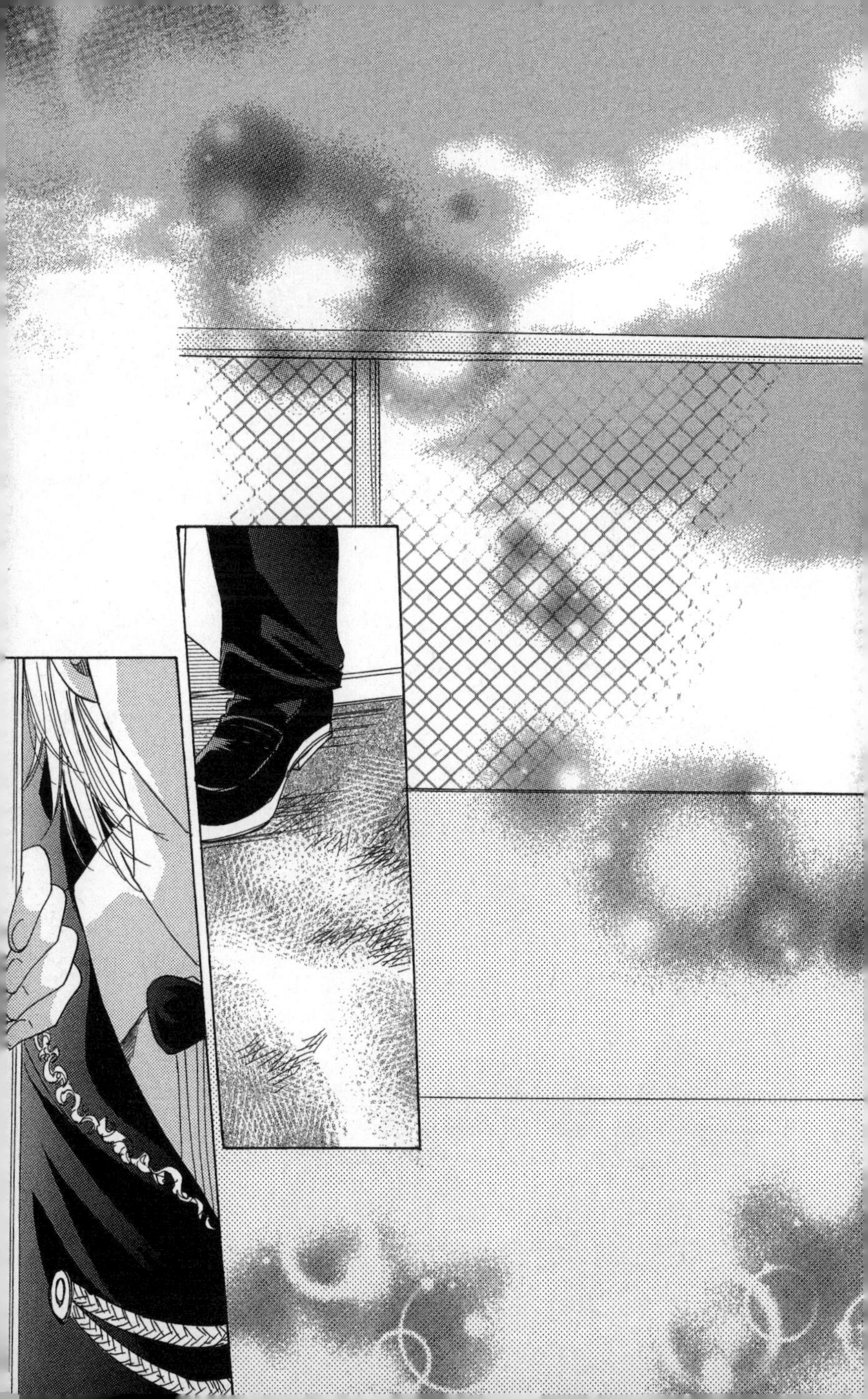

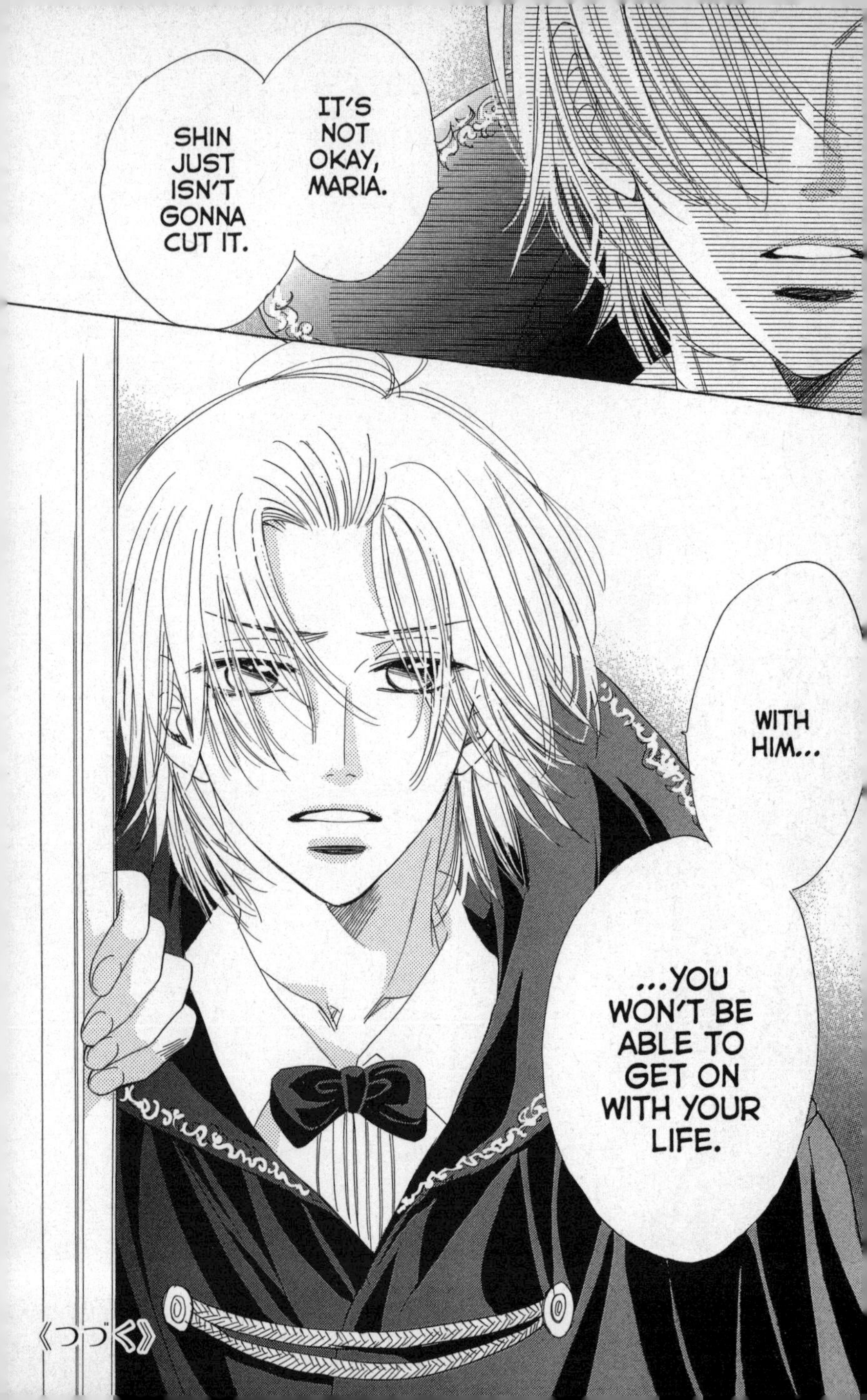
IT'S NOT OKAY, MARIA.
SHIN JUST ISN'T GONNA CUT IT.
WITH HIM...
...YOU WON'T BE ABLE TO GET ON WITH YOUR LIFE.
《つづく》

Continued
in
volume 11

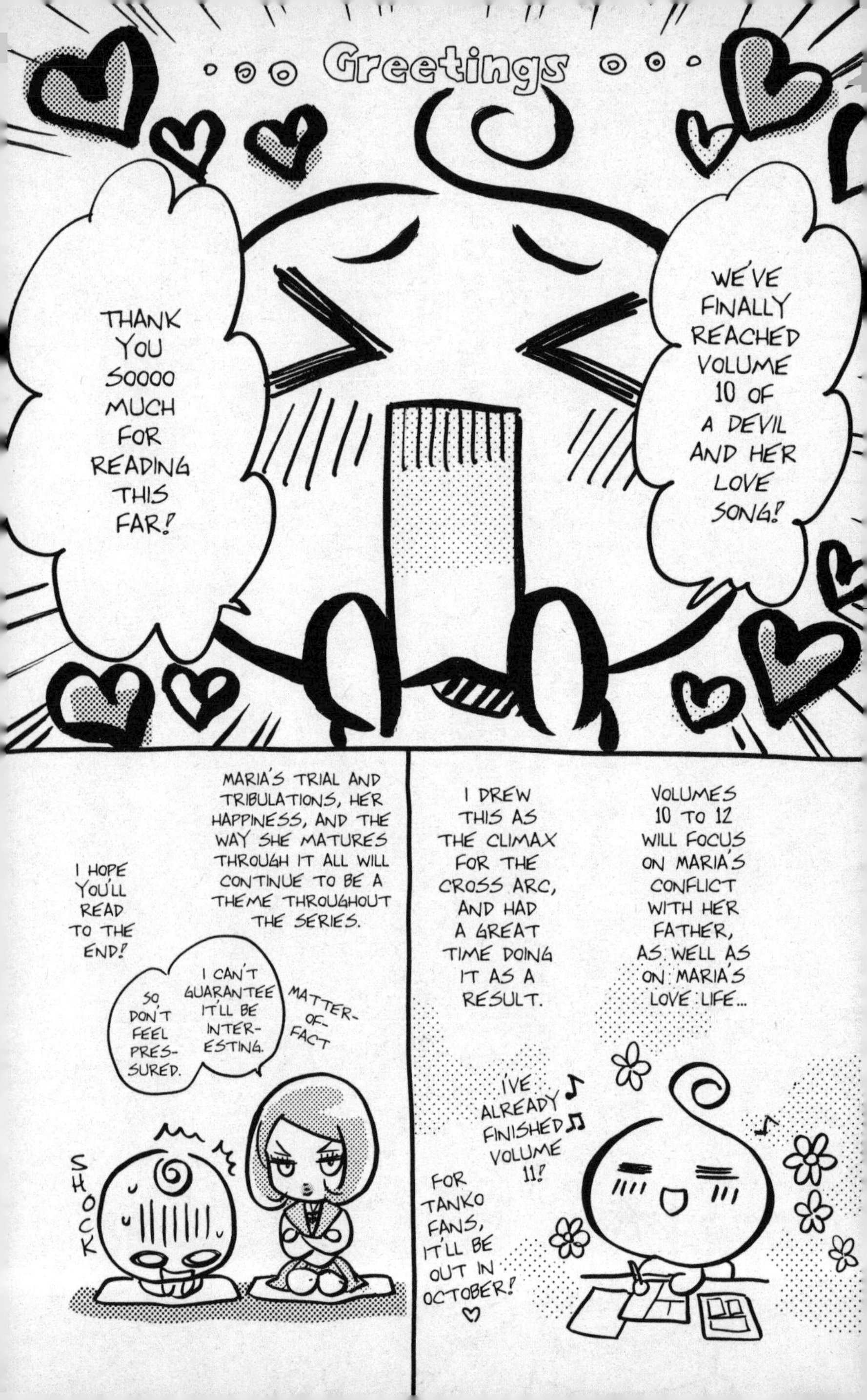
Greetings
WE'VE FINALLY REACHED VOLUME 10 OF A DEVIL AND HER LOVE SONG!
THANK YOU SOOOO MUCH FOR READING THIS FAR!
VOLUMES 10 TO 12 WILL FOCUS ON MARIA'S CONFLICT WITH HER FATHER, AS WELL AS ON MARIA'S LOVE LIFE...
I DREW THIS AS THE CLIMAX FOR THE CROSS ARC, AND HAD A GREAT TIME DOING IT AS A RESULT.
I'VE ALREADY FINISHED VOLUME 11!
FOR TANKO FANS, IT'LL BE OUT IN OCTOBER!
MARIA'S TRIAL AND TRIBULATIONS, HER HAPPINESS, AND THE WAY SHE MATURES THROUGH IT ALL WILL CONTINUE TO BE A THEME THROUGHOUT THE SERIES.
I HOPE YOU'LL READ TO THE END!
MATTER-OF-FACT
I CAN'T GUARANTEE IT'LL BE INTERESTING.
SO DON'T FEEL PRESSURED.
SHOCK

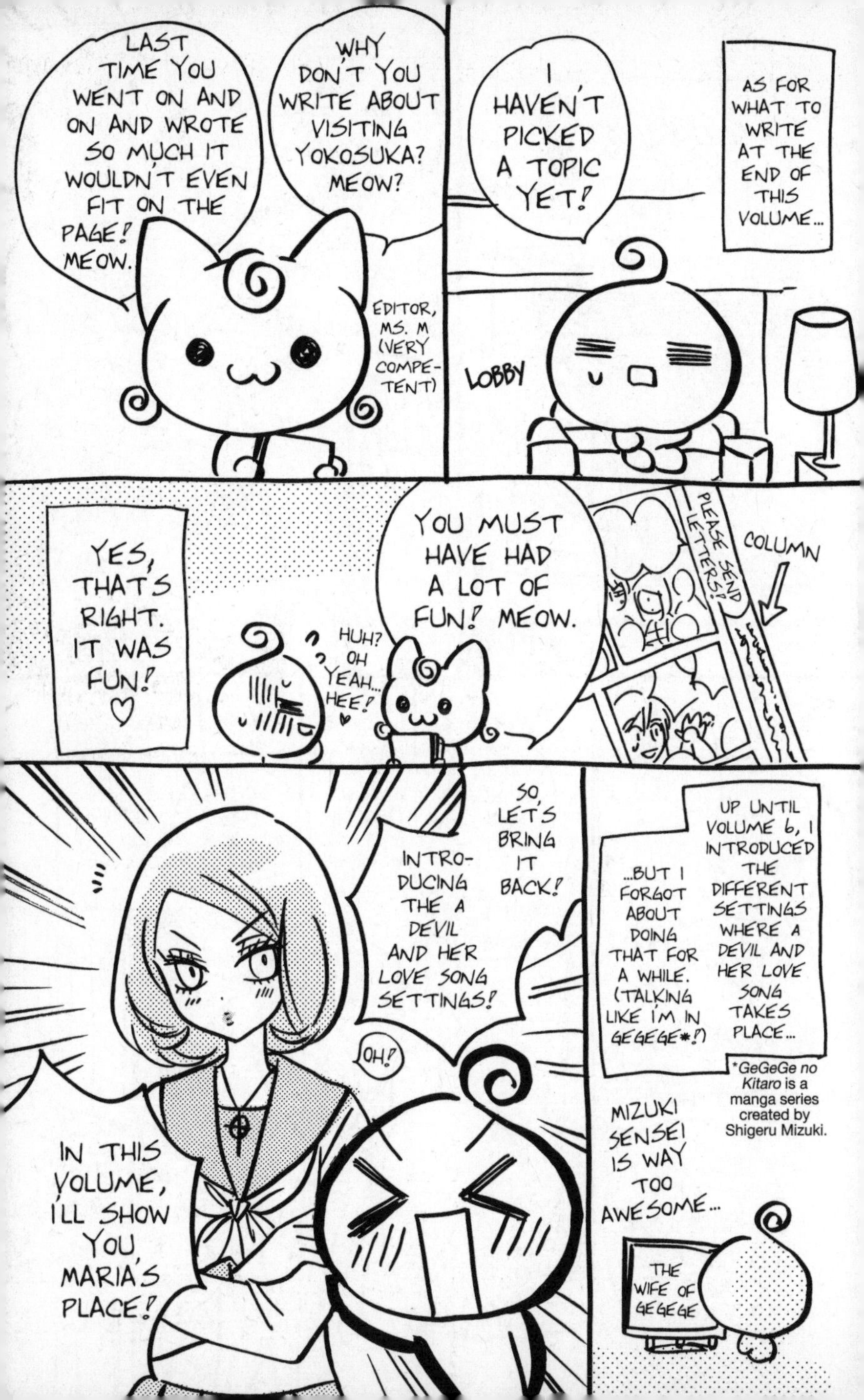
AS FOR WHAT TO WRITE AT THE END OF THIS VOLUME...
I HAVEN'T PICKED A TOPIC YET!
LOBBY
WHY DON'T YOU WRITE ABOUT VISITING YOKOSUKA? MEOW?
LAST TIME YOU WENT ON AND ON AND WROTE SO MUCH IT WOULDN'T EVEN FIT ON THE PAGE! MEOW.
EDITOR, MS. M (VERY COMPETENT)
COLUMN
PLEASE SEND LETTERS!
YOU MUST HAVE HAD A LOT OF FUN! MEOW.
HUH? OH YEAH... HEE! ♡
YES, THAT'S RIGHT. IT WAS FUN! ♡
UP UNTIL VOLUME 6, I INTRODUCED THE DIFFERENT SETTINGS WHERE A DEVIL AND HER LOVE SONG TAKES PLACE...
...BUT I FORGOT ABOUT DOING THAT FOR A WHILE. (TALKING LIKE I'M IN GEGEGE*!)
*GeGeGe no Kitaro is a manga series created by Shigeru Mizuki.
MIZUKI SENSEI IS WAY TOO AWESOME...
THE WIFE OF GEGEGE
SO, LET'S BRING IT BACK!
INTRODUCING THE A DEVIL AND HER LOVE SONG SETTINGS!
OH!
IN THIS VOLUME, I'LL SHOW YOU, MARIA'S PLACE!

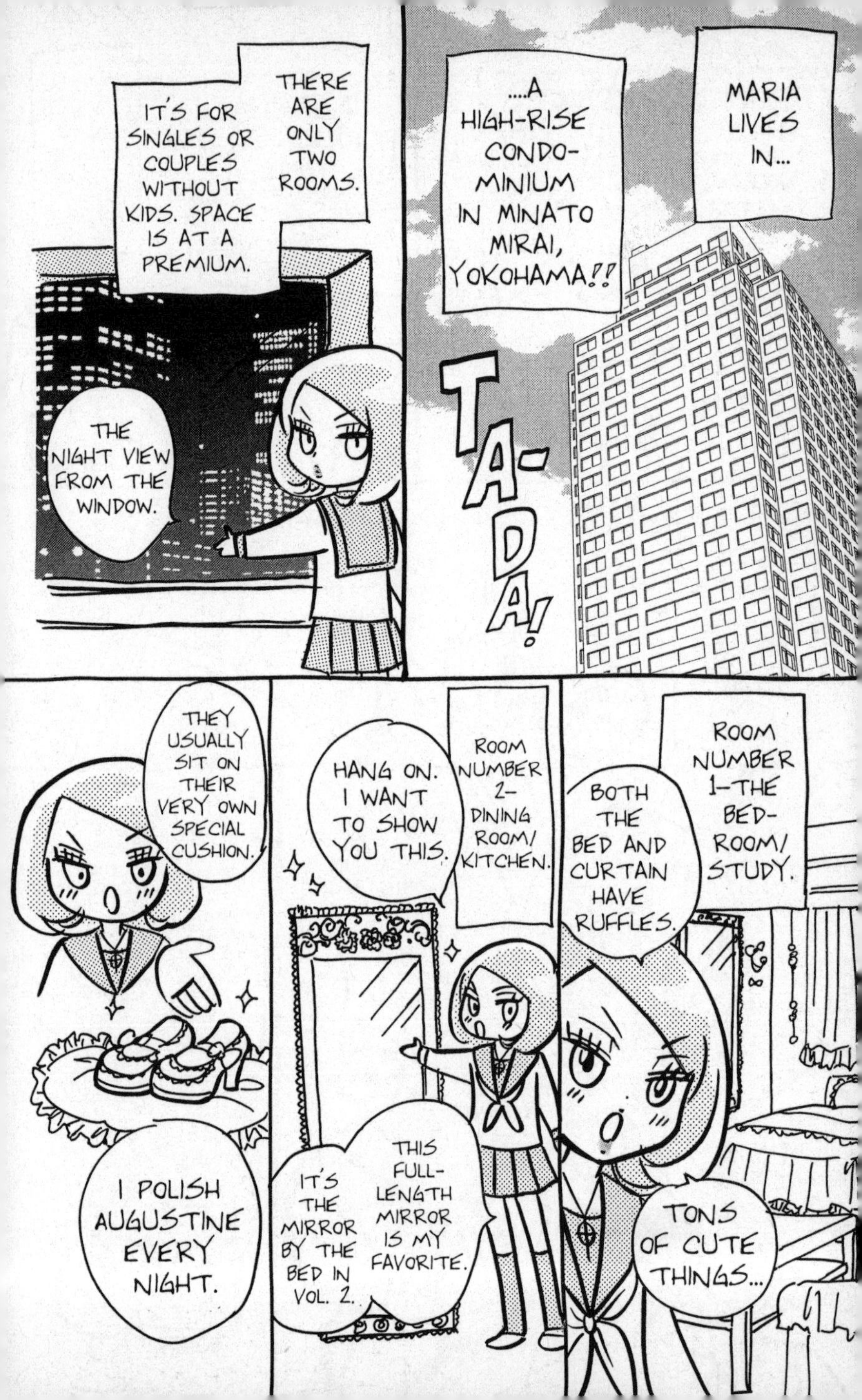
MARIA LIVES IN...
....A HIGH-RISE CONDO-MINIUM IN MINATO MIRAI, YOKOHAMA!?
TA-DA!
THERE ARE ONLY TWO ROOMS.
IT'S FOR SINGLES OR COUPLES WITHOUT KIDS. SPACE IS AT A PREMIUM.
THE NIGHT VIEW FROM THE WINDOW.
ROOM NUMBER 1—THE BED-ROOM/STUDY.
BOTH THE BED AND CURTAIN HAVE RUFFLES.
TONS OF CUTE THINGS...
ROOM NUMBER 2—DINING ROOM/KITCHEN.
HANG ON. I WANT TO SHOW YOU THIS.
THIS FULL-LENGTH MIRROR IS MY FAVORITE.
IT'S THE MIRROR BY THE BED IN VOL. 2.
THEY USUALLY SIT ON THEIR VERY OWN SPECIAL CUSHION.
I POLISH AUGUSTINE EVERY NIGHT.

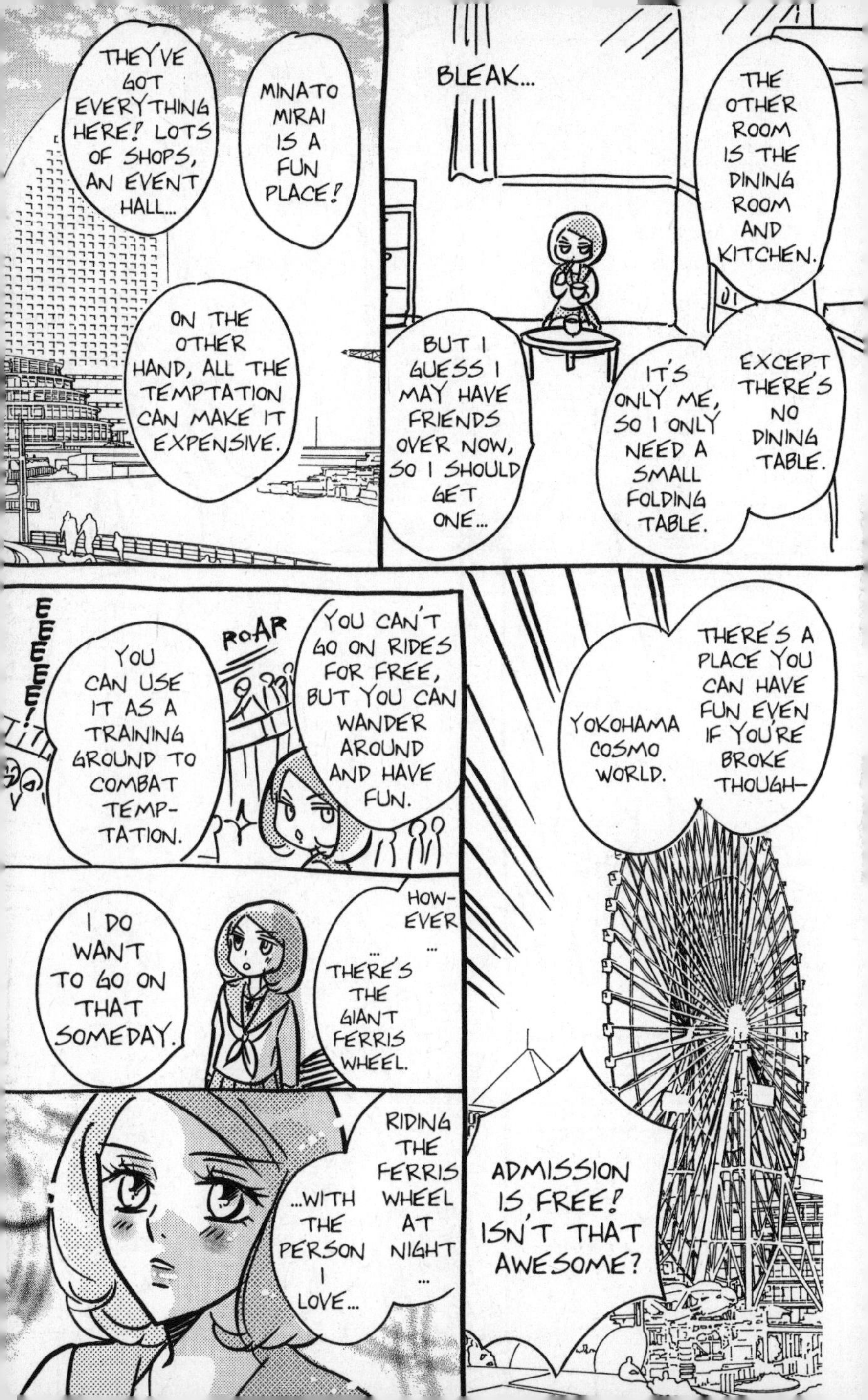
THE OTHER ROOM IS THE DINING ROOM AND KITCHEN.
BLEAK...
EXCEPT THERE'S NO DINING TABLE.
IT'S ONLY ME, SO I ONLY NEED A SMALL FOLDING TABLE.
BUT I GUESS I MAY HAVE FRIENDS OVER NOW, SO I SHOULD GET ONE...
MINATO MIRAI IS A FUN PLACE!
THEY'VE GOT EVERYTHING HERE! LOTS OF SHOPS, AN EVENT HALL...
ON THE OTHER HAND, ALL THE TEMPTATION CAN MAKE IT EXPENSIVE.
THERE'S A PLACE YOU CAN HAVE FUN EVEN IF YOU'RE BROKE THOUGH—
YOKOHAMA COSMO WORLD.
ADMISSION IS FREE! ISN'T THAT AWESOME?
YOU CAN'T GO ON RIDES FOR FREE, BUT YOU CAN WANDER AROUND AND HAVE FUN.
ROAR
YOU CAN USE IT AS A TRAINING GROUND TO COMBAT TEMPTATION.
EEEEEE!
HOW-EVER... ...THERE'S THE GIANT FERRIS WHEEL.
I DO WANT TO GO ON THAT SOMEDAY.
RIDING THE FERRIS WHEEL AT NIGHT...
...WITH THE PERSON I LOVE...

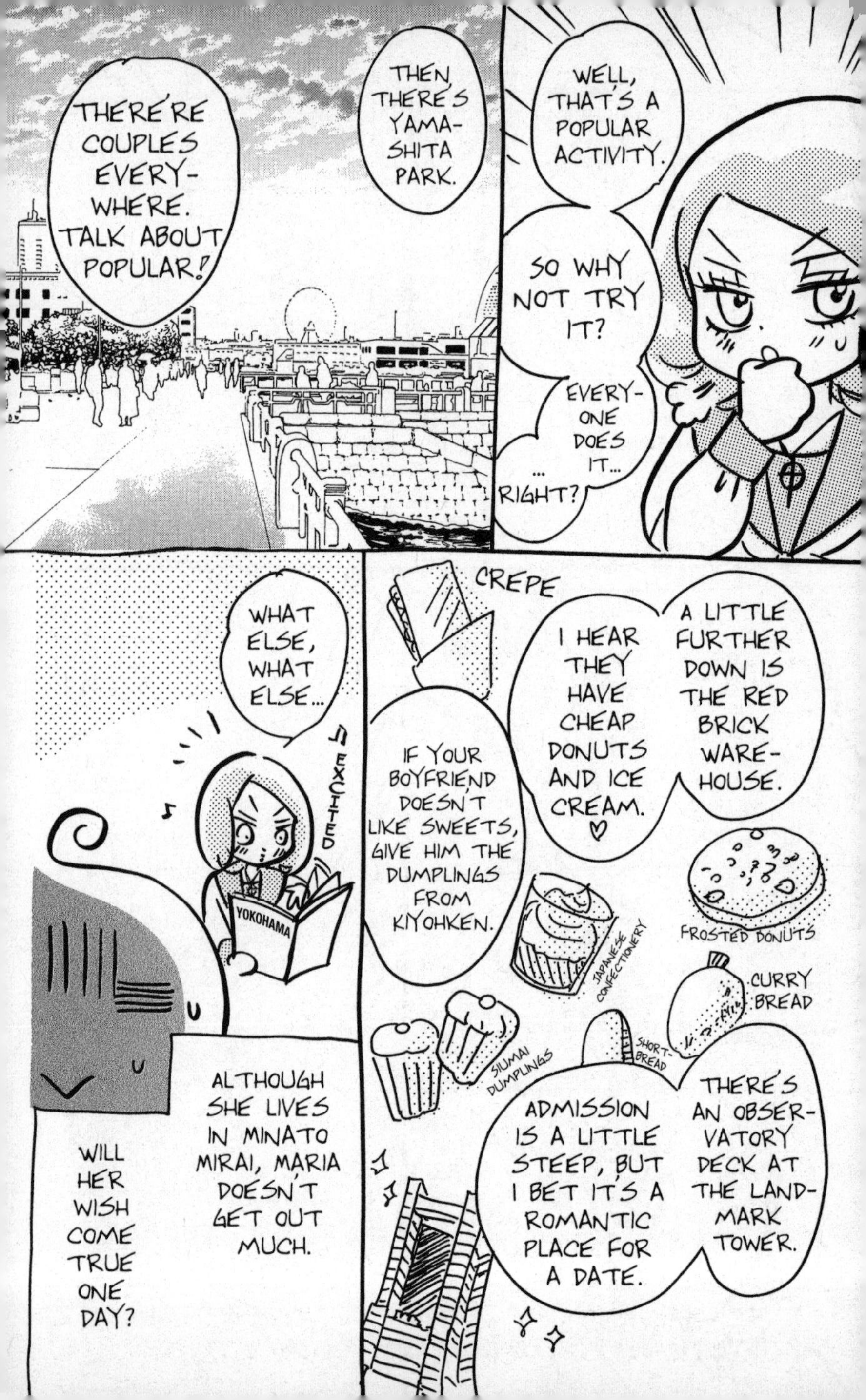
WELL, THAT'S A POPULAR ACTIVITY.
SO WHY NOT TRY IT?
EVERYONE DOES IT...
...RIGHT?
THEN, THERE'S YAMASHITA PARK.
THERE'RE COUPLES EVERYWHERE. TALK ABOUT POPULAR!
A LITTLE FURTHER DOWN IS THE RED BRICK WAREHOUSE.
I HEAR THEY HAVE CHEAP DONUTS AND ICE CREAM. ♡
CREPE
FROSTED DONUTS
IF YOUR BOYFRIEND DOESN'T LIKE SWEETS, GIVE HIM THE DUMPLINGS FROM KIYOHKEN.
JAPANESE CONFECTIONERY
CURRY BREAD
SHORTBREAD
SIUMAI DUMPLINGS
THERE'S AN OBSERVATORY DECK AT THE LANDMARK TOWER.
ADMISSION IS A LITTLE STEEP, BUT I BET IT'S A ROMANTIC PLACE FOR A DATE.
WHAT ELSE, WHAT ELSE...
EXCITED
YOKOHAMA
ALTHOUGH SHE LIVES IN MINATO MIRAI, MARIA DOESN'T GET OUT MUCH.
WILL HER WISH COME TRUE ONE DAY?

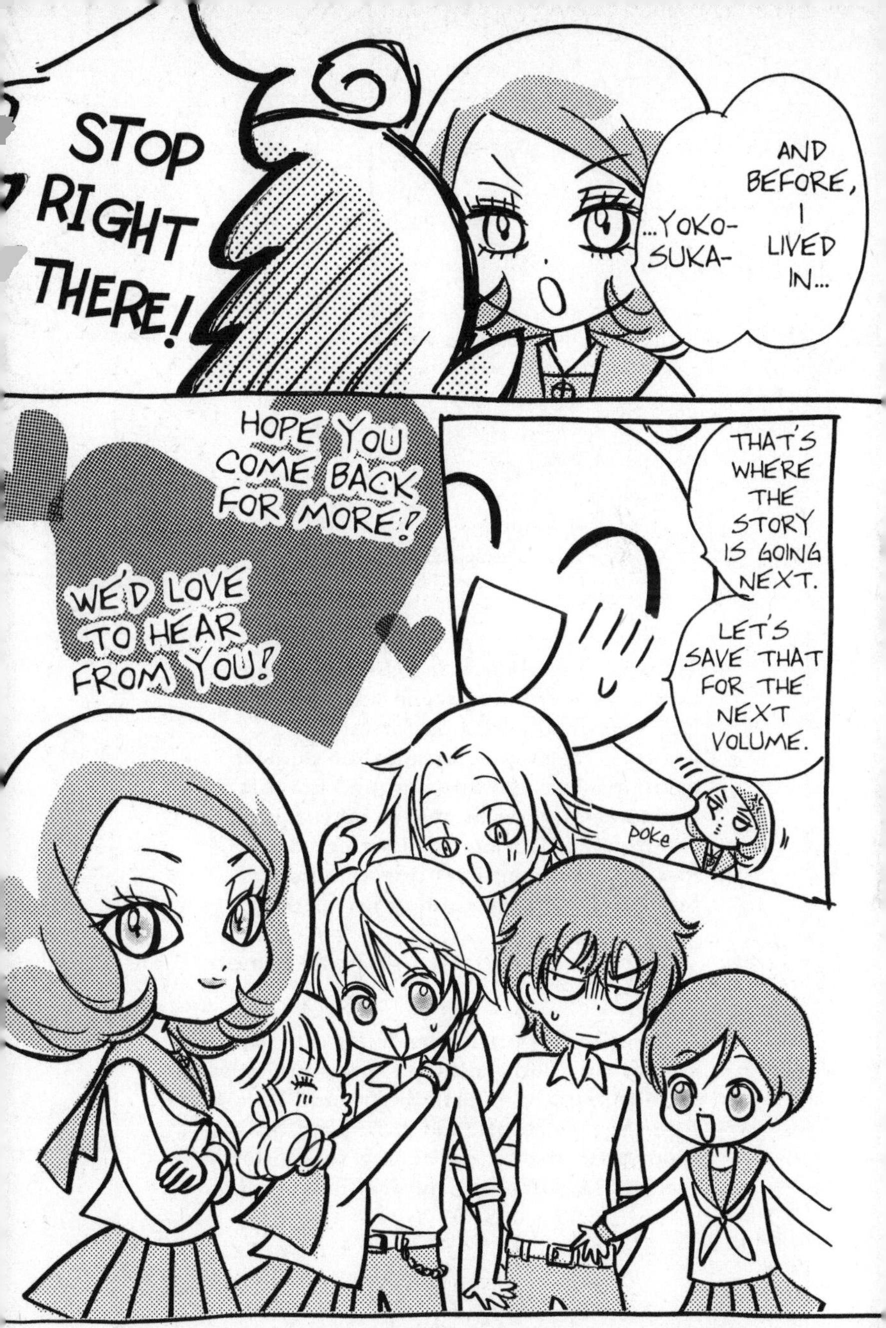
AND BEFORE, I LIVED IN...
...YOKO-SUKA-
STOP RIGHT THERE!
THAT'S WHERE THE STORY IS GOING NEXT.
LET'S SAVE THAT FOR THE NEXT VOLUME.
poke
HOPE YOU COME BACK FOR MORE!
WE'D LOVE TO HEAR FROM YOU!

Miyoshi Tomori c/o A Devil and Her Love Song Editor
Viz Media P.O. Box 77010 San Francisco, CA 94107

Volume 10 of *A Devil and Her Love Song* is here at last! The first scene was something that I was really looking forward to drawing. It's only because of the support of my readers and those around me that my untalented self is able to draw this way. I will reflect on my undeserved blessings and continue to work hard. I hope you will keep reading my work.

-Miyoshi Tomori

Miyoshi Tomori made her debut as a manga creator in 2001, and her previous titles include *Hatsukare* (First Boyfriend), *Tongari Root* (Square Root), and *Brass Love!!* In her spare time she likes listening to music in the bath and playing musical instruments.

A DEVIL AND HER LOVE SONG
Volume 10
Shojo Beat Edition

STORY AND ART BY
MIYOSHI TOMORI

English Adaptation/Ysabet MacFarlane
Translation/JN Productions
Touch-up Art & Lettering/Monalisa de Asis
Design/Courtney Utt
Editor/Amy Yu

AKUMA TO LOVE SONG © 2006 by Miyoshi Tomori
All rights reserved. First published in Japan in 2006
by SHUEISHA Inc., Tokyo.
English translation rights arranged
by SHUEISHA Inc.

Printed in the U.S.A.

Published by VIZ Media, LLC
P.O. Box 77010
San Francisco, CA 94107

10 9 8 7 6 5 4 3 2 1
First printing, August 2013

www.viz.com   www.shojobeat.com

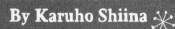
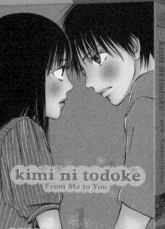

Surprise!

You may be reading the wrong way!

It's true: In keeping with the original Japanese comic format, this book reads from right to left—so action, sound effects, and word balloons are completely reversed. This preserves the orientation of the original artwork—plus, it's fun! Check out the diagram shown here to get the hang of things, and then turn to the other side of the book to get started!

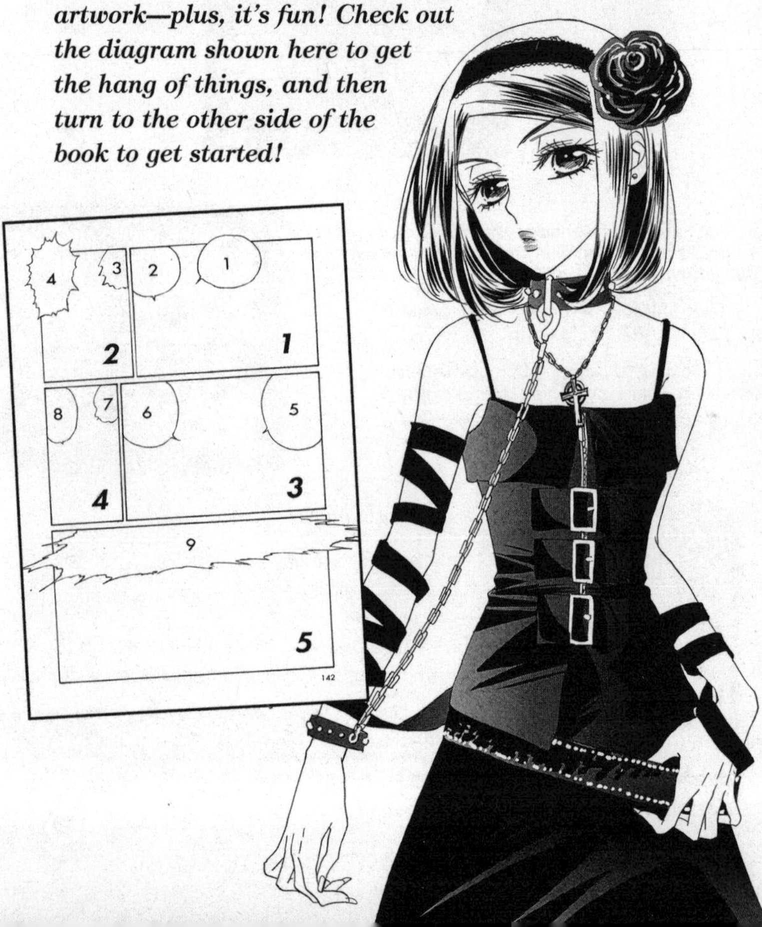
1
2
3
4
1
2
5
6
7
8
3
4
9
5
142